NATO AND INTERNATIONAL INSTITUTIONAL LAW

NATO AND INTERNATIONAL INSTITUTIONAL LAW

Anne Verhelst

INTERSENTIA

Intersentia
Lefebvre Sarrut Belgium SA
Rue Haute 139/6
1000 Bruxelles
Belgium
Email: contact@larcier-intersentia.com

Distribution for the UK, Ireland and
Rest of the World (excl. France, Belgium and Luxembourg)
Ingram Publisher Services UK
1 Deltic Avenue, Rooksley
Milton Keynes MK13 8LD
United Kingdom
Tel: +44 1752 202 301 | Fax: +44 1752 202 331
Email: ipsuk.customercare@ingramcontent.com

Distribution for France and Rest of the World (excl. Ireland and the UK)
Interforum Editis
92 avenue de France
75013 Paris
France

Distribution for Belgium and Luxembourg (exl. France, Ireland and the UK)
Larcier-Intersentia
Rue Haute, 139/6
1000 Bruxelles
Belgium

NATO and International Institutional Law

Cover design by Danny Juchtmans / www.dsigngraphics.be
Cover image: Surplace n° 2, 2002 – Raoul De Keyser / Museum Dhondt-Dhaenens © Family Raoul De Keyser / SABAM Belgium 2025

ISBN 978-1-83970-550-2
D/2025/06040/0027
NUR 828

British Library Cataloguing in Publication Data. A catalogue record for this book is available from the British Library.

To my grandmother

FOREWORD BY JAN WOUTERS

It is a great pleasure to introduce this book, the fruit of a highly productive PhD scholarship funded by FWO Flanders, and of which I had the privilege being the supervisor.

The book offers the first-ever comprehensive analysis of NATO's legal and institutional evolution. At a pivotal moment in NATO's history—against the backdrop of the war in Ukraine and renewed debates on defence spending—this work invites critical reflection on the legal principles underlying NATO's actions and decisions.

Through rigorous analysis, the book examines NATO's transformation in light of international law, exploring issues such as NATO's expanded powers and operations, including the legality of non-Article 5 operations, and scrutinises its evolving membership conditions.

The book provides invaluable insights into NATO's decision-making processes, which, notably, are not codified in any official text. Through meticulous analysis and historical case studies, such as Operation Allied Force in Kosovo and the 2003 deadlock over defensive aid to Turkey, it examines the organisation's consensus rule and the potential for adopting more efficient voting procedures, as experts have recently recommended. These discussions extend to the broader question of accountability of international organisations: can NATO or its Member States be held legally responsible in court for decisions that breach international law?

Beyond NATO, this book provides lessons for other international organisations, such as the United Nations and the European Union, offering a comparative perspective on institutional law. Its final chapter provides a basis for debate, as it outlines recommendations to bolster NATO's legal framework, ensuring its legitimacy and effectiveness as it operates for the security of over one billion people.

For legal scholars, policymakers, diplomats, and students of international law and the law of international organizations, this book is an indispensable resource. It combines a robust theoretical foundation with practical insights, shedding light on NATO's legal architecture and its implications for the future of international organisations and global security.

Prof. Dr. Jan Wouters
Full Professor of International Law and the Law
of International Organizations at KU Leuven, Belgium

FOREWORD BY ELENA LAZAROU

As a practitioner in the field of transatlantic security and defence, I highly recommend this book for its timely relevance and balanced legal analysis of NATO. At this crucial moment for the EU Common Security and Defence Policy, the book provides valuable insights into the decision-making processes and the allocation of responsibility in security operations, offering lessons for the EU in this domain. By drawing on national and international case law, it also offers arguments for lawyers handling cases involving international organisations. The book and its recommendations equip policymakers and practitioners with the analytical tools needed to assess the legal implications of proposed security and defence policies, negotiate agreements with and within the Alliance and uphold international legal norms.

Dr. Elena Lazarou
Head of the External Policies Unit at the
European Parliamentary Research Service (2020–2024)

FOREWORD BY NIELS BLOKKER

This book fills a vacuum and is timely. There are hardly any academic studies analysing NATO through an international organisations law lens, and this is precisely the merit of this book. At a time when NATO is playing a key role, following the invasion of Ukraine, it is essential to fully understand its foundations and transformation not only from a political but also from a legal perspective. In this book, Anne Verhelst discusses key institutional characteristics of NATO, demonstrating that it is not only a military and political alliance, but also an international organisation.

Prof. Dr. Niels Blokker
Professor of International Institutional Law at Leiden University,
The Netherlands

CONTENTS

LIST OF ABBREVIATIONS

ACCS	Air Command Control System
ACE	Allied Command Europe
ACT	Allied Command Transformation
ADREPS	Air Defence Representatives
AFCENT	Allied Forces Central Europe
AGS	Alliance Ground Surveillance
AMDC	Air and Missile Defence Committee
AMIS	African Union Mission in Sudan
AMISOM	African Union Mission in Somalia
ANP	Annual National Programme
APAG	Atlantic Policy Advisory Group
ARRC	Allied Command Europe Rapid Reaction Corps
ATA	Atlantic Treaty Association
AWACS	Airborne Warning and Control Systems
BMD	Ballistic Missile Defence
CAS	Close Air Support
CBC	Civil Budget Committee
CBRN	Chemical, Biological, Radiological and Nuclear
CEPC	Civil Emergency Planning Committee
CEPS	Central Europe Pipeline System
CFSP	Common Foreign and Security Policy (EU)
CICR	Committee on Information and Cultural Relations
CNAD	Conference of National Armaments Directors
COEC	Council Operations and Exercises Committee
COMEDS	Committee of the Chiefs of Military Medical Services in NATO
COMINFORM	Communist Information Bureau
CPG	Comprehensive Political Guidance
CSDP	Common Security and Defence Policy (EU)
DGIMS	Director of the NATO International Military Staff
DGP	Senior Defence Group on Proliferation
DPC	Defence Planning Committee
DPPC	Defence Policy and Planning Committee
DRC	Defence Review Committee
EADRCC	Euro-Atlantic Disaster Response Coordination Centre

EAPC	Euro-Atlantic Partnership Council
ECOWAS	Economic Community of West African States
ECHR	European Convention of Human Rights
ECtHR	European Court of Human Rights
EOL	Exchange of Letters
ESDA	European Security and Defence Assembly
ESDP	European Security and Defence Policy
EU	European Union
EULEX Kosovo	European Union Rule of Law Mission in Kosovo
EWG	Executive Working Group
FAO	Food and Agriculture Organization
HLTF	High Level Task Force on Conventional Arms Control
IAMD	Integrated Air and Missile Defence
ICI	Istanbul Cooperation Initiative
ICRC	International Committee of the Red Cross
ICTY	International Criminal Tribunal for the former Yugoslavia
IFOR	Implementation Force
IGC	Intergovernmental Conference
ILC	International Law Commission
ILO	International Labour Organization
IMF	International Monetay Fund
IMS	International Military Staff
INF	Intermediate-Range Nuclear Forces
INFOSEC	Information Security Branch
IPAPs	Individual Partnership Action Plans
IPU	Inter-Parliamentary Union
ISAF	International Security Assistance Force
JCP	Joint Committee on Proliferation
JFC	Joint Force Command(er)
KFOR	Kosovo Force
KVCC	Kosovo Verification Coordination Centre
KVM	Kosovo Verification Mission
MBC	Military Budget Committee
MBT	Modified Brussels Treaty
MC	Military Committee
MCMG	Military Committee Meteorological Group
MILOC Group	Military Oceanography Group
MNBGs	Multinational Battle Groups
MNF	US-led Multinational Force (in Iraq)
MSA	Maritime Situational Awareness
NAAG	NATO Army Armaments Group
NAC	North Atlantic Council
NACC	North Atlantic Cooperation Council

NADC	NATO Air Defence Committee
NADREPS	National Armaments Directors' Representatives
NAEWF	NATO Airborne Early Warning Force
NAFAG	NATO Air Force Armaments Group
NAPMA	NATO Airborne Early Warning and Control Programme Management Agency
NATMC	NATO Air Traffic Management Committee
NATO PA	NATO Parliamentary Assembly
NATO	North Atlantic Treaty Organisation
NBC	Nuclear, Biological, Chemical
NC3A	NATO Consultation, Command and Control Agency
NCISS	NATO Communications and Information Systems School
NCS	NATO Committee for Standardization
NCSREPs	Group of NCS Representatives
NFS	NATO Force Structure
NGC	NATO-Georgia Commission
NHMO	NATO HAWK Management Office
NIAG	NATO Industrial Advisory Group
NMI	NATO Mission Iraq
NNAG	NATO Navy Armaments Group
NPC	NATO Pipeline Committee
NPG	Nuclear Planning Group
NPG/HLG	Nuclear Planning Group High Level Group
NRC	NATO-Russia Council
NRF	NATO Response Force
NSC	NATO Security Committee
NSPA	NATO Support and Procurement Agency
NSPO	NATO Support and Procurement Organisation
NSSG	NATO Standardisation Staff Group
NTM-I	NATO Training Mission – Iraq
NUC	NATO-Ukraine Commission
OAE	Operation Active Endeavour
OCC	Operational Capabilities Concept
OECD	Organisation for Economic Co-operation and Development
OEF	(US-led) Operation Enduring Freedom
OHR	Office of the High Representative
OIC	Organisation of Islamic Cooperation
OMIK	OSCE Mission in Kosovo
OSCE	Organisation for Security and Cooperation in Europe
PADP	Panel on Air Defence Philosophy
PADREPS	Partner Air Defence Representatives
PADW	Panel on Air Defence Weapons

PC	Political Committee
PCC	Partnership Coordination Cell
PCG	Policy Coordination Group
PCSC	Partnership and Cooperative Security Committee
PfP	Partnership for Peace
PJC	Permanent Joint Council
PMSC/PfP	Political-Military Steering Committee on Partnership for Peace
RAP	Readiness Action Plan
RPPB	Resource Policy and Planning Board
RTA	Research and Technology Agency
SAC	Supreme Allied Commanders
SACEUR	Supreme Allied Commander Europe
SACLANT	Supreme Allied Commander Atlantic
SACT	Supreme Allied Commander Transformation
SCOM	Science Committee
SGP	Senior Politico-Military Group on Proliferation
SHAPE	Supreme Headquarters Allied Powers Europe
SNLC	Senior NATO Logisticians' Conference
SOFA	Status of Forces Agreements
SPS	Science for Peace and Security Committee
TEU	Treaty on the European Union
UN	United Nations
UNESCO	United Nations Educational, Scientific and Cultural Organization
UNAMID	United Nations/African Union Mission in Darfur
UNHCR	UN High Commissioner for Refugees
UNIPTF	UN International Police Task Force
UNMIK	UN Mission in Kosovo
UNPROFOR	United Nations Protection Force [former Yugoslavia]
USSR	Union of the Soviet Socialist Republics
VCC	Verification Coordinating Committee
VJTF	Very High Readiness Joint Task Force
WEAG	Western European Armaments Group
WEU	Western European Union
WHO	World Health Organization

CHAPTER 1
INTRODUCTION

1. INTRODUCTION

It is a core principle of the law of international organisations that the constituent treaty of the organisation defines the scope and limitations of its powers. Typically, the constitution (also called 'constituent treaty' or 'founding treaty') defines the powers of the organisation, sets out its institutional framework, and prescribes its decision-making procedures.[1] But the 1949 North Atlantic Treaty (1949 Treaty), in which the North Atlantic Treaty Organisation (NATO) finds its origin, does not refer or even allude to NATO as an organisation, the powers attributed to it, its organs, its decision-making principles or its membership conditionality. Despite this, NATO has, over a time span of 76 years, grown from 12 to 32 Member States and has conducted over 40 military operations. While its main aim, laid down in the North Atlantic Treaty, is collective self-defence, it has, over the years, increasingly shifted this aim in the direction of collective security, now taking action in domains like cybersecurity, terrorism, and conflict management. Importantly, this was done without ever amending the 1949 Treaty. Article 5 of the 1949 Treaty states that 'the Parties to the Agreement consider an armed attack against one as an armed attack against all.' Yet, anno 2025, NATO conducts non-Article 5 crisis management response operations (NA5CROs) all around the world, provides training to Iraqi soldiers, co-ordinates the supply of lethal weapons to Ukraine, supports UNSC peacekeeping operations with AWACS aircraft, provides firefighting aid to Greece and Bulgaria, and much more. These powers are not mentioned anywhere in the North Atlantic Treaty. It is a fundamental principle of international institutional law that an organisation only has those powers attributed to it by its Member States (principle of attributed powers or *compétence d'attribution*).[2] Its activities must always be

---

1 N. Blokker and H. Schermers, *International Institutional Law*, Leiden, Boston, Brill Nijhoff, 2018, § 206–917, 155–605.

2 This in contrast to States, which are free to act as long as this is in accordance with international law. See N. Blokker and H. Schermers, *op.cit.*, 165–167; C.F. Amerasinghe, *Principles of the Institutional Law of International Organizations*, Cambridge, Cambridge University Press, 2005, 100. See J. Klabbers, *An Introduction to International Institutional Law*, Cambridge, Cambridge University Press, 2020, 50 and 53; D. Sarooshi, *International organizations and their exercise of sovereign powers*, Oxford, Oxford University Press, 2007; P. Sands and P. Klein, *Bowett's Law of International Institutions*, London, Thomson, Sweet & Maxwell, 2001, 292; P.

based on some power given to it, usually by its constitution.[3] For this reason, an international organisation typically expands its activities by formally amending its constituent treaty.[4] But in contrast to other international organisations (e.g. EU, UN, IMF, WHO), NATO has never amended its treaty.[5] Its powers seem to have expanded organically and pragmatically, without the solid legal footing of treaty amendment. This would mean that the national parliaments of NATO Member States, and by extension their citizens, have had no say in NATO obtaining these new and far-reaching powers. Regarding NATO's institutional structure, the following questions arise. As recently as December 2021, the multinational fuel company Supreme brought proceedings against the Supreme Headquarters Allied Powers Europe (SHAPE), NATO's military headquarters, before the European Court of Justice (CJEU). This case was preceded by years of complicated legal proceedings, in which Supreme demanded that SHAPE pay billions of dollars in damages for breach of contract. The procedures were long and costly for SHAPE because NATO has no basic text that provides SHAPE with immunity from jurisdiction, which is a fundamental protection mechanism in public international law. The Supreme saga is but one instance of a broader issue: while the North Atlantic Treaty is very thin on institutional issues, NATO's institutional structure is currently very thick. The 1949 North Atlantic Treaty is exceptionally vague in establishing NATO's institutional framework. Most constituent treaties of international organisations are far more detailed in this regard.[6] Regarding NATO's decision-making, the following quiz was presented

---

Klein, 'Les compétences et pouvoirs de l'organisation international' in E. Lagrange and J.-M. Sorel (eds.), *Droit des organisations internationales*, Issy-les-Moulineaux, LGDJ, 2013, 714–734. See also PCIJ 1926, *Jurisdiction of the European Commission of the Danube between Galatz and Braila*, Advisory Opinion, *Publ. PCIJ* Series B, no 14, 64.

3 N. Blokker and H. Schermers, *op. cit.*, § 209, 166; D. Sarooshi, *op. cit.*, 19–27; C.F. Amerasinghe, *op. cit.*, 100 and H. Schermers, 'Internationaal institutioneel recht', *Internationale Spectator* 1963, 292.

4 N. Blokker and H. Schermers, *op. cit.*, § 209A, 169.

5 N. Blokker and H. Schermers, *op. cit.*, § 1641, 1057. Consider the amendments to the TEU and the TFEU and read the impressive list composed by Amerasinghe on the amendments to the UN Charter and the basic documents of the FAO, UNESCO, the WHO as well as the IMF. See C.F. Amerasinghe, *Principles of the Institutional Law of International Organizations*, Cambridge, Cambridge University Press, 2005, 447. See also L. Philips, 'Constitutional Revision in the Specialized Agencies', *American Journal of International Law* 1968, 657. For another list see A. Peters, 'L'acte constitutif de l'organisations internationale' in E. Lagrange and J.-M. Sorel (eds.), *op. cit.*, 223. See also R. Zacklin, *The Amendment of the Constitutive Instruments of the UN and Specialized Agencies*, Leiden, A. W. Sijthoff, 1968; A. Vîlcan, *An assessment of the successive European Union treaty amendments from a federalist perspective,* doctoral dissertation, Leuven, KU Leuven, Faculty of Social Sciences, 2011 and E. David, *Droit des organisations internationales*, Brussels, Université Libre de Bruxelles, 2000–2001, 95–99.

6 Compare this to the institutional provision of the WEU, which is an international organisation and military alliance like NATO, see Article XIII Modified Brussels Treaty. *Cf.* N. Blokker, 'Constituent Instruments' in J. Cogan, I. Hurd and I. Johnstone (eds.), *The Oxford Handbook of International Organizations*, 2016, 946 and F. Fabbrini, 'Do NATO Obligations Trump European Budgetary Constraints?', *Harvard National Security Journal* 2018, 131.

to 22 people in the expert audience during the author's second doctoral seminar on 4 October 2021:

Imagine today is 22 March 1999. The North Atlantic Council is meeting to decide on the launch of air operations in Kosovo. All NATO Member States are represented in the NAC. You are the Greek representative. Your government and the Greek public are opposed to these air operations. What can you, as the Greek representative in the NAC, do during this decision-making round? Can you:

A. vote against NATO's decision to intervene in Kosovo?
B. block the decision by raising objections?
C. join the consensus decision but opt out of taking part in the air operations?
D. convince fellow NATO Member States to undertake air operations outside the NATO context?[7]

The results of the poll were as follows: 52% voted for option A, 38% for B, 10% for C, and 0% for D.[8] But in truth, option D is correct and option A is incorrect. This suggests that NATO's decision-making procedures are poorly understood. In fact, remarkably little is known about them, because, unlike most international organisations (e.g. the EU, the UN and the OECD), the 1949 Treaty nor any other basic document sets out any decision-making procedures or voting rules for NATO's decision-making bodies.[9] There are no rules for the adoption of acts, nor is their legal and normative standing specified. This is remarkable, considering that decision-making is ultimately the most important activity of international organisations.[10] Another important topic is NATO membership, as it features in the media, in transatlantic politics, in debates about EU defence, and in the lives of citizens. Whereas the constituent instrument of an international organisation

7 Consisting of approximately 22 people, including Belgian and Dutch professors of international institutional law, current and former NATO and SHAPE legal advisers, one diplomat, and KU Leuven international law PhD researchers. *Cf.* doctoral seminar by Anne Verhelst, KU Leuven, online, 4 October 2021.

8 Doctoral seminar by Anne Verhelst, KU Leuven, online, 4 October 2021.

9 Almost all international organisations have official voting rules described in their constituent instrument. Consider (non-exhaustively) Article 16.3 TEU, Article 231 TFEU, Article 27 UN Charter, Article 6 OECD Convention, Article 59 OAS Charter, article 16.2 ILO Constitution, Article 9.2 ECOWAS Treaty, Article 20 Statute of the Council of Europe and Article IX.1 WTO Agreement. *Cf.* A. Payton, 'Consensus Procedures in International Organizations', *European University Institute Working Paper* 2010, 1; E. Posner and A. Sykes, 'Voting Rules in International Organizations', *University of Chicago Public Law and Legal Theory Working Paper* 2014, 2–27 and E. McIntyre, 'Weighted Voting in International Organizations', *International Organization* 1954, 484–497.

10 See E. Ustor, *Decision-making in the Council for Mutual Economic Assistance*, Leiden, Martinus Nijhoff Publishers, 1971, 174. See also I. Dekker and R. Wessel, 'Governance by International Organizations: Rethinking the Normative Force of International Decisions' in I. Dekker and W. Werner (eds.), *Governance and International Legal Theory*, Leiden, Nijhoff, 2004, 215; J. Klabbers, *op. cit.*, 154; P. Klein, 'International Organizations or Institutions: Decision-Making Process' in X. (ed.), *Max Planck Encyclopedia of Public International Law*, Oxford, Oxford University Press, 2019, § 1; J. D'Aspremont and D. Ventura, 'La composition des organes et le processus décisionnel' in E. Lagrange and J.-M. Sorel (eds.), *op. cit.*, § 796, 404.

typically sets forth the conditions for membership and the procedure for the accession of new members, the legal aspects of admission to NATO are obscure. Article 10 of the 1949 Treaty does not contain detailed legal conditions for NATO membership, providing only a brief description of what is expected of candidates.[11] But in practice, NATO does use specific criteria to evaluate candidate Member States. Candidates are explicitly expected to adhere to the principles of democracy, individual liberty, and the rule of law. They must demonstrate a commitment to promoting stability and well-being through economic liberty, social justice, and environmental responsibility, to settle ethnic disputes, among other requirements.[12] Strikingly, Article 10 has never been amended to this end. As NATO has only grown over the past 76 years, and has never dwindled, an important question arises: in the absence of a treaty provision, is there any legal basis for the suspension or expulsion of a NATO Member State? To reiterate the four domains mentioned (NATO powers, institutional framework, decision-making and membership), the problem statement öf this book is that NATO, as an international organisation, appears to have grown away from the North Atlantic Treaty in an organic and pragmatic way, without the solid legal footing of constitutional amendment. This leads one to ask to what extent the Alliance has respected or departed from the fundamental principles of the law of international organisations. In light of these legal gaps, the question arises whether the creative ways in which NATO has transformed itself over time are lawful and legitimate. In the words of Prof. Dr. Jan Klabbers, 'When an organisation adapts itself by bypassing formal amendment procedures and instead uses quasi-legislation or has a practice develop, this may contribute to a loss of legitimacy of the organisation, which in turn affects its viability.'[13] For over seven decades, research on NATO has mainly been conducted by political scientists, historians and international relations experts. Rarely has it been analysed in terms of law.[14] The existing literature on NATO can be divided into three categories:

---

11 A. Duxbury, *The Participation of States in International Organizations: The Role of Human Rights and Democracy*, Cambridge, Cambridge University Press, 2011, 129 and as inspired by N. Minogue, 'The North Atlantic Treaty at 70: Article 10', *Emory International Law Review* 2019, 171–72.

12 See Articles 4, 6, 70, 72 of the 1995 Study on NATO Enlargement. See § 5 and § 6 of the 1994 Ministerial Communiqué, available online at www.nato.int/docu/comm/comm94.htm (last accessed January 2025). See also Article I.1 of the 1999 Membership Action Plan, approved by NATO Heads of State and Government participating in the Washington Summit, Washington D.C., 24 April 1999 (MAP 1999), available online at www.nato.int/cps/en/natohq/official_texts_27444.htm#:~:text=The%20Membership%20Action%20Plan%20(MAP, preparations%20for%20possible%20future%20membership. (last accessed January 2025).

13 J. Klabbers, *op.cit.*, 91.

14 Notably E. Stein and D. Carreau, 'Law and Peaceful Change in a Subsystem: Withdrawal of France from the North Atlantic Treaty Organization', *The American Journal of International Law* 1986, 577–640; L. Schaus, 'Le Conseil de l'Atlantique Nord, son fondement et ses structures, ses compétences et ses missions', *Chronique De Politique Etrangère* 1974, 337–386 and S. Trifunovska, *The North Atlantic Treaty Organization: International Encyclopedia of Laws*, Alpen-aan-den-Rhijn, Wolters Kluwer, 2012.

- A first strand of literature discusses key episodes in NATO history. Much of this research is dedicated to the reinvention of NATO after the end of the Cold War[15] and its stance after 9/11.[16] The Alliance's operations in the Balkans,[17] Iraq,[18] and Afghanistan are also thoroughly discussed.[19]
- A second strand of literature concerns specific topics, like NATO's rounds of enlargement,[20] its different partnerships programs,[21] and the issues of disarmament and cyber defence. These have been subject to much academic scrutiny.[22]
- A third strand concerns the Member States and their relationship to each other. Topics that have been analysed in depth include the alleged dominance of the US within the organisation,[23] the withdrawal of France from NATO's integrated military structure,[24] and UK policy, due to its close association with the US.[25] Surprisingly, there has been very little research on the legal aspects of accession to NATO.

---

15 M. Brenner, *NATO and Collective Security*, London, Palgrave MacMillan, 1998; R. McCalla, 'NATO's persistence after the Cold War', *International Organization* 1996, 445–475 and D. Yost, *NATO Transformed: the Alliance's New Roles in International Security*, Washington D.C., United States Institute of Peace Press, 1998.

16 E. Hallams, *NATO Beyond 9/11*, London, Palgrave MacMillan, 2013 and R. Moore, *NATO's new mission: projecting stability in a post-Cold War world*, London, Praeger Security International, 2007.

17 J. Seroka, 'Security Considerations in the Western Balkans: NATO's evolution and expansion', *East European Quarterly* 2007, 25–38 and S. Kay, *NATO and the Future of European Security*, Oxford, Rowman & Littlefield, 1998.

18 S. Carney, *Allied Participation in Operation Iraqi Freedom*, Washington D.C., Center of Military History, 2011.

19 V. Morelli, *NATO in Afghanistan: A Test of the Transatlantic Alliance*, Philadelphia, Diane Publishing, 2009 and S. Hartin and A. Hoehn, *Risking NATO: testing the limits of the Alliance in Afghanistan*, Santa Monica, Rand Publishing, 2010.

20 J. Gaddis, 'History, grand strategy and NATO enlargement', *Global Politics and Strategy* 1998, 145–151; M. Fierke and A. Wiener, 'Constructing Institutional Interests: EU and NATO enlargement', *Journal of European Public Policy* 1999, 721–742 and R. Menotti, 'US Policy and NATO enlargement: Clinton's unspoken agenda', *International Politics* 1999, 235–271.

21 T. Flockhart, *Cooperative Security: NATO's Partnership Policy in a Changing World*, Copenhagen, DIIS Report, 2014 and D. Yost, *NATO's Balancing Act*, Washington D.C., US Institute of Peace, 2014.

22 M. Taddeo and L. Glorioso, *Ethics and Policies for Cyber Operations: a NATO Cooperative Cyber Defence Centre of Excellence Initiative*, Berlin, Springer, 2017 and J. Burton, 'NATO's cyber defence: strategic challenges and institutional adaptation', *Defence Studies* 2015, 1–22.

23 D. Andrews, *The Atlantic Alliance under Stress: US-European Relations after Iraq*, Cambridge, Cambridge University Press, 2005; E. Hallams, *The US and NATO since 9/11: the transatlantic alliance renewed*, London, Taylor & Francis, 2013 and S. Sloan, *Permanent Alliance? NATO and the Transatlantic Bargain from Truman to Obama*, London, Continuum, 2010.

24 E. Stein and D. Carreau, 'Law and Peaceful Change in a Subsystem: Withdrawal of France from the North Atlantic Treaty Organization', 577–640 and G. Martin, 'The 1967 withdrawal from NATO – a cornerstone of de Gaulle's grand strategy?', *Journal of Transatlantic Studies* 2011, 232–243.

25 D. Auerswald and P. Saideman, *NATO in Afghanistan: Fighting Together, Fighting Alone*, New Jersey, Princeton University Press, 2014.

While the work done in these three strands is important and should be acknowledged as such, one cannot but conclude that there are considerable knowledge gaps with regard to the institutional and legal foundations and the evolution of the North Atlantic Treaty. The Treaty stands in contrast to the fully-fledged constituent treaties of other international organisations (e.g. EU, UN, WTO, OECD), which have been the subject of ample research. Within the field of the law of international organisations, scholarship almost exclusively concerns the UN and the EU (and to a lesser extent the WTO),[26] leaving the North Atlantic Treaty in dire need of academic scrutiny. This book aims to provide the first-ever in-depth analysis of the North Atlantic Treaty as NATO's constituent instrument, and of its transformation. The present research will focus on the North Atlantic Treaty's four most important legal areas: NATO's powers (Article 4 and 5), institutional structure (Article 9), decision-making (Article 9), and membership (Article 10). These are the core legal provisions of the 1949 Treaty. In contrast, Articles 1 and 2 state the principles of dispute settlement and peaceful relations between Parties to the Treaty. Article 3 prescribes that the Parties maintain their defence capacities. Article 6 defines the geographical scope of article 5. Article 7 defines NATO's relationship with the UN and article 8 prohibits the Parties from entering into engagements that are in conflict with the 1949 Treaty. Articles 11 to 14 are administrative in nature. Another reason why the four core legal areas were chosen is that they have evolved away the furthest from the text of the Treaty.

2. RESEARCH OBJECTIVES

Did the transformation of NATO's activities, institutional framework, decision-making, and membership take place within the confines of international institutional law or beyond them? This book aims to fill the knowledge gap that exists in relation to this question. Additionally, this book aims to provide a deeper critical understanding of the position NATO takes up within the law of international organisations. Gaining an understanding of the position of a particular international organisation *vis-à-vis* all international organisations is one of the core objectives of the legal scholarship in the area of the law of international organisations.[27] The development of the North Atlantic Treaty will be assessed in light of the following principles of international institutional law:

- the principle of attributed powers or *compétence d'attribution*. Organisations have only those powers attributed to them by the Member States. Their

[26] *Cf.* N. Blokker and H. Schermers, *op. cit.*, 2018; C.F. Amersinghe, *op. cit.*, 2005 and J. Klabbers, *op. cit.*, 2020.

[27] N. Blokker and H. Schermers, *op. cit.*, § 6–13, 4–9.

activities must be based on some power given to them, usually by their constitutions (chapter 2)[28];
- the principles of the lawful establishment of subsidiary bodies and the lawful delegation of powers to them (chapter 3)[29];
- generally, states cannot be held liable for the acts of organisations by virtue of their membership of those organisations alone (chapter 3 and 4)[30];
- public international organisations are established by an international agreement, have at least one organ with a will of its own, and are established under international law (chapter 3)[31];
- to allow them to carry out their mission, international organisations and their staff enjoy immunity from the jurisdiction of national courts (chapter 3)[32];
- international organisations must make their decisions in accordance with established procedures and within the confines of the constituent instrument (chapter 4)[33];
- international organisations cannot make binding operational decisions unless their constitutions expressly allow this power (chapter 4)[34];

---

28 N. Blokker and H. Schermers, *op. cit.*, § 209, 165–167; C.F. Amerasinghe, *op. cit.*, 100. See J. Klabbers, *op. cit.*, 50 and 53; P. Sands and P. Klein, *op. cit.*, 292; H. Schermers, 'Internationaal institutioneel recht', *Internationale Spectator* 1963, 292; P. Klein, 'Les compétences et pouvoirs de l'organisation international', in E. Lagrange and J.-M. Sorel (eds.), *op. cit.*, 714–734. See also PCIJ 1926, *Jurisdiction of the European Commission of the Danube between Galatz and Braila*, Advisory Opinion, *Publ. PCIJ* Series B, no. 14, 64.

29 D. Sarooshi, 'Delegation to UN Subsidiary Organs' in D. Sarooshi (ed.), *The United Nations and the Development of Collective Security*, Oxford, Oxford University Press, 1999, 89, 119, 128–129; N. Blokker and H. Schermers, *op. cit.*, § 205, 163 and § 1201, 787; UN, *United Nations Juridical Yearbook*, 2000, 354–358; S. Torres Bernárdez, 'Subsidiary Organs' in R. Dupuy (ed.), *Manuel sur les organisations internationales*, Leiden, Brill Nijhoff, 1998, 148–149 and C. Colliard, *Institutions des relations internationales*, Paris, Dalloz, 1978, 656–57. See also R. Higgins, P. Webb et al., *Oppenheim's International Law: United Nations*, Oxford, Oxford University Press, 2017, § 6.06, 155. *Cf.* ICJ 1954, *Effect of Awards*, Advisory Opinion, ICJ Rep 1954, 47.

30 ILC, Article 62, Commentary no. 2, *Report of the Law Commission on the Work of its Sixty-Third Session*, UN Doc. A/CN.4/L.77, UN GAOR 66th Sess (2009) and C. Ryngaert, 'The European Court of Human Rights' Approach to the Responsibility of Member States in connection with Acts of International Organizations', *International & Comparative Law Quarterly* 2001, 997.

31 N. Blokker and H. Schermers, *op. cit.*, § 34, 41; J. Crawford, *Brownlie's Principles of Public International Law*, Oxford, Oxford University Press, 2012, 170; I. Seidl-Hohenveldern and G. Loibl, *Das Recht der Internationalen Organisationen, einschließlich der Supranationalen Gemeinschaften*, Keulen, Heymann, 2000, 8; ILC 2003, *Draft report of the International Law Commission on the work of its fifty-fifth session: chapter IV (Responsibility of international organizations)*, UN Doc. A/CN.4/L.636/Add.1, 7–8.

32 N. Blokker and N. Schrijver, *Immunity of International Organizations*, Leiden, Brill Nijhoff, 2015, 1–17.

33 N. Blokker and H. Schermers, *op. cit.*, § 917–18, 632.

34 N. Blokker and S. Schermers, *op. cit.*, § 1320, 857; P. Sands and P. Klein, *op. cit.*, 280; K. Skubiszewski, 'The Elaboration of general multilateral conventions and of non-contractual instruments having a normative function or objective – Resolutions of the General Assembly of the United Nations', *Annuaire de l'Institut de droit international* 1985, 35; G. Ulfstein, 'Les

- the expansion of membership conditions cannot be incompatible with the object and purpose of the constituent instrument (chapter 5)[35];
- in the absence of a treaty provision to that end, the suspension or expulsion of a Member State is only possible if there is a lawful basis for it (chapter 5).

The specific research objectives of this book are the following:

The first specific objective is to determine how and to what extent NATO dealt with the fundamental principles of the law of international organisations, both at the time of its inception and during the (seemingly organic) evolution of its organs and powers. To this end, legislation, *travaux préparatoires*, policy documents, international and national (constitutional) case law, political arrangements, and legal scholarship will be analysed. This topic will be addressed in chapters 2 and 3.

The second specific objective is to determine to what extent NATO's decision-making processes have been legally formalised and constrained—if at all. To this end, legislation, *travaux préparatoires*, policy documents, international and national (constitutional) case law, political arrangements, legal scholarship, and semi-structured expert interviews with official NATO staff (mostly members of the International Staff and the Office of Legal Affairs) will be analysed (see below). This topic will be addressed in chapter 4.

The third specific research objective is to critically assess the way NATO's membership conditionality has drifted away from article 10 North Atlantic Treaty over time, as well as the legal permissibility of suspension and expulsion of Member States in view of international (institutional) law. This assessment will be based on an analysis of international practices, *travaux préparatoires*, legal scholarship, diplomatic correspondence, NATO policy documents, and political arrangements, and supplemented with empirical data obtained through semi-structured interviews. This topic will be addressed in chapter 5.

This book proposes two hypotheses:

1. In the absence of a solid legal footing in the never-amended North Atlantic Treaty, NATO's powers, institutional framework, decision-making process, and membership conditions have, over time, transformed in a way that is inconsistent with the fundamental principles of the law of international organisations.
2. The North Atlantic Treaty cannot be regarded as a fully-fledged constituent treaty of an international organisation.

activités normatives de l'organisation internationale' in E. Lagrange and J.-M. Sorel (eds.), *op. cit.*, § 1466, 747.

35 Article 5 and 31 VCLT and A. Duxbury, *The Participation of States in International Organizations: The Role of Human Rights and Democracy*, Cambridge, Cambridge University Press, 2011, 137; Vienna Convention on the Law of Treaties, signed on 23 May 1969, entered into force on 27 January 1980, UNTS 1155, 331.

3. RESEARCH QUESTIONS

This book aims to answer two overarching research questions, which correspond to the three specific research objectives above:

1. To what extent has NATO departed from the fundamental principles of the law of international organisations in transforming itself since 1949?
2. What should one consider the North Atlantic Treaty to be if it cannot be regarded as a fully-fledged constituent treaty?

This translates into the following specific research questions:

- Does the expansion of NATO's powers to include non-Article 5 crisis response operations violate the principle of attributed powers? (chapter 2)
- Was NATO's institutional framework created and transformed in accordance with the principle of the lawful establishment of subsidiary bodies and the principle of the lawful delegation of powers to them? (chapter 3)
- Is the NATO Parliamentary Assembly a public international organisation? (chapter 3)
- What is the legal basis of NATO's immunity from jurisdiction? (chapter 3)
- To what extent are NATO decisions made within the confines of the constituent instrument and established practice? (chapter 4)
- What is the legal effect of NATO's decisions in light of the principle that international organisations cannot make binding operational decisions unless their constitutions expressly permit this? (chapter 4)
- As NATO's accession conditions were expanded, they have drifted increasingly further away from the text of Article 10 North Atlantic Treaty. Can this be considered a tolerable interpretation of the 1949 Treaty or does it constitute an imposition of new conditions that goes beyond the International Court of Justice's *Admissions* Opinion? (chapter 5)
- In the absence of a provision in the North Atlantic Treaty, is there a basis in international law for the suspension or expulsion of a NATO Member State? (chapter 5)

CHAPTER 2
THE EVOLUTION OF THE NORTH ATLANTIC TREATY POWERS: WITHIN OR BEYOND THE LAW?

1. INTRODUCTION

On 4 April 1949 the North Atlantic Treaty was signed and adopted by 12 States. The 1949 Treaty forms the basis of the North Atlantic Treaty Organisation (NATO), a political and military alliance and international organisation. NATO's primary task, as laid down in Article 5 of the 1949 Treaty, is collective self-defence: Allies commit themselves to defending any other Ally if an armed attack in the sense of Article 51 UN Charter takes place on Allied territory.[36] Throughout the Cold War period Article 5 was never invoked. In fact, it has only been invoked once, in the wake of the 9/11 attacks. Despite collective self-defence being the only power mentioned in the North Atlantic Treaty, NATO anno 2025 conducts non-Article 5 crisis management response operations all around the world: it provides military training to Iraqi soldiers, supports UNSC peacekeeping operations with AWACS aircraft, provides firefighting aid in the North Atlantic Area, and much more. The North Atlantic Treaty does not mention any of these powers. It is a fundamental principle of international institutional law that an organisation has only those powers attributed to it by its Member States (principle of attributed powers or *compétence d'attribution*).[37]

---

[36] Article 5 North Atlantic Treaty: 'The Parties agree that an armed attack against one or more of them in Europe or North America shall be considered an attack against them all and consequently they agree that, if such an armed attack occurs, each of them, in exercise of the right of individual or collective self-defence recognised by Article 51 of the Charter of the United Nations, will assist the Party or Parties so attacked by taking forthwith, individually and in concert with the other Parties, such action as it deems necessary, including the use of armed force, to restore and maintain the security of the North Atlantic area. Any such armed attack and all measures taken as a result thereof shall immediately be reported to the Security Council. Such measures shall be terminated when the Security Council has taken the measures necessary to restore and maintain international peace and security.'

[37] This in contrast to States, which are free to act as long as this is in accordance with international law. See N. Blokker and H. Schermers, *op. cit.*, § 209, 165–167; C.F. Amerasinghe, *op. cit.*, 100. See J. Klabbers, *op. cit.*, 50 and 53; D. Sarooshi, *op. cit.*, 2007; P. Sands and

The activities of international organisations must always be based on some power given to them, usually by the constitution.[38] For this reason, an international organisation typically expands its activities by formally amending its constituent treaty.'[39] Most international organisations have amended their constituent instruments at least once.[40] After all, circumstances change and the world is a dynamic place. To this end, most constituent instruments contain a specific clause for the formal revision or amendment of the text.[41] The 1949 Treaty contains such a clause. Article 12 of the North Atlantic Treaty states:

> After the Treaty has been in force for ten years, or at any time thereafter, the Parties shall, if any of them so requests, consult together for the purpose of reviewing the Treaty, having regard for the factors then affecting peace and security in the North Atlantic area, including the development of universal as well as regional arrangements under the Charter of the United Nations for the maintenance of international peace and security.

Strikingly, Article 12 has never been invoked. One should not confuse the textual adaptation of Article 6 by the 1951 Accession Protocol of Turkey and Greece with an amendment. The Article was adapted to expressly include the words 'the territory of Turkey'. Every time a new Member State joins NATO the geographical area mentioned in Article 6 is expanded to include that new Member's territory. So, strictly speaking, this adaptation of Article 6 was not necessary.[42] Aside from this, article 6 was informally modified in 1963 when the North Atlantic Council noted France's declaration on the independence of Algeria. The phrase 'Algerian Departments' in Article 6 became legally inapplicable because, on this point, the performance of the 1949 Treaty had become impossible in accordance with Article 61 of the Vienna Convention on

P. Klein, *op. cit.*, 292; P. Klein, 'Les compétences et pouvoirs de l'organisation international', in E. Lagrange and J.-M. Sorel (eds.), *op. cit.*, 714–734. See also PCIJ 1926, *Jurisdiction of the European Commission of the Danube between Galatz and Braila*, Advisory Opinion, *Publ. PCIJ* Series B, no. 14, 64.

38 N. Blokker and H. Schermers, *op. cit.*, § 209, 166; D. Sarooshi, *op. cit.*, at 19–27 and C.F. Amerasinghe, *op. cit.*, 100; H. Schermers, 'Internationaal institutioneel recht', 292.

39 N. Blokker and H. Schermers, *op. cit.*, § 209A, 169.

40 Read the impressive list composed by Amerasinghe on the amendments to the UN Charter, the FAO, UNESCO, the WHO, and the IMF, see C.F. Amerasinghe, *op. cit.*, 447. See also L. Philips, 'Constitutional Revision in the Specialized Agencies', 657; for another list see A. Peters, 'L'acte constitutif de l'organisations internationale' in E. Lagrange and J.-M. Sorel (eds.), *op. cit.*, 223; E. David, *op. cit.*, 2000–2001, 95–99.

41 P. Sands and P. Klein, *op. cit.*, 451; L. Philips, 'Constitutional Revision in the Specialized Agencies', 654; R. Zacklin, *op. cit.*, 7 and H. Schermers, 'Les bases juridiques de l'action des organisations internationales' in R. Dupuy (ed.), *op. cit.*, 408–409.

42 A. Peters, 'L'acte constitutif de l'organisation internationale' in E. Lagrange and J.-M. Sorel (eds.), *op. cit.*, 224 and I. Novotny and A. Boeva, 'Scope and Historical Developments of Article 6', *Emory International Law Review* 2019, 125.

the Law of Treaties (VCLT). Thus, *prima facie* it seems that the Treaty has never been formally amended. This is remarkable, not least considering the broad expansion of powers that NATO has enjoyed.

2. NATO STRATEGIC CONCEPTS

In the 76 years it has existed, NATO has never enjoyed the luxury of stability. Few would dispute that NATO has been in a constant state of institutional and political transformation,[43] a process that was accelerated by the fall of the Berlin Wall and the demise of the Soviet Union. The political and security situation had changed so drastically that NATO was said to have lost its main *raison d'être*, i.e. collectively defending the North Atlantic Area against an armed attack in the sense of Article 51 UN Charter.[44] In response to this changed security environment, NATO has expanded its powers, tasks and activities over the last four decades. As discussed, this was not done through treaty amendment. The most important means through which NATO has expanded its mandate is through its Strategic Concepts. These are official documents that outline NATO's purpose and nature and its fundamental security tasks.[45] This chapter will examine the four post-Cold War Strategic Concepts: Strategic Concept 1991, Strategic Concept 1999, Strategic Concept 2010, and Strategic Concept 2022. They constitute the most important changes to NATO's tasks in comparison to the 1949 Treaty—in particular Strategic Concept 1999. For the most part, the Strategic Concepts reflect the Foreign Affairs Ministerial Communiqués[46] and Summit Declarations (endorsed by the NATO Heads of State and Heads of Government) that were adopted in the period prior to the promulgation of those Strategic Concepts. While the four post-Cold War Strategic Concepts were drafted by political authorities, the four Cold War Strategic Concepts were

---

43 M. Webber and A. Hyde-Price, *Theorising NATO: new perspectives on the Atlantic Alliance*, Abingdon, Routledge, 2016; D. Yost, *NATO transformed: the alliance's new roles in international security*, Washington D.C., United States Institute of Peace Press, 1998; E. Hallams, L. Ratti and B. Zyla, *NATO beyond 9/11: the transformation of the Atlantic alliance*, Basingstoke, Palgrave Macmillan, 2013; A. Rotfeld, 'The Future of NATO', *Polish Quarterly of International Affairs* 2006, 5–20; B. Heuser, 'The Atlantic alliance at 50: the origins and transformation of NATO', *Contemporary British History* 1999, 180–188 and K. Ifantis, 'NATO's Strategic Direction after Riga: NATO's Post-Cold War Adaption', *International Law Journal* 2007, 577–588.

44 E. Lübkemeier, 'NATO's Identity Crisis', *Bulletin of the Atomic Scientists* 1990, no. 8 and J. Shea, 'NATO at full stretch', *International Politics Reviews* 2016, 36.

45 *Cf. NATO Encyclopedia* 2019, 654. The NATO Encyclopedia is a compilation of information on the Alliance, published more or less annually, until 2019, by the NATO Public Diplomacy division, available online.

46 Confined to the Communiqués adopted by Ministers of Foreign Affairs.

drafted by the military. They were also classified at the time.[47] Between the signing of the North Atlantic Treaty in 1949 and the fall of the Berlin Wall, the Alliance was characterised by Cold War thinking. NATO's first four Strategic Concepts were formulated in this period, with a potential clash between the Alliance and the Warsaw Pact in mind.[48] It comes as no surprise that the terms 'nuclear deterrence', 'flexible reaction', and 'forward defence' were key notions in the first four Strategic Concepts. This makes the four Cold War Strategic Concepts less relevant to the present inquiry.

2.1. STRATEGIC CONCEPT 1991

Following the radically changed political and security situation after the end of the Cold War, NATO issued its first unclassified Strategic Concept in 1991. NATO's fundamental tasks are listed in § 20:

1. to provide one of the indispensable foundations for a stable security environment in Europe;
2. to serve, as provided for in Article 4 of the North Atlantic Treaty, as a transatlantic forum for Allied consultations;
3. to deter and defend against any threat of aggression against the territory of any NATO Member State;
4. to preserve the strategic balance within Europe.[49]

---

47 See *NATO Encyclopedia* 2018, 146, 658- 659, 660–662; A. Verhelst and J. Wouters, 'Zeventig jaar NAVO: juridische kanttekeningen bij een bijzondere internationale organisatie', in VRG (ed.), *Recht in Beweging*, Leuven, Gompel&Svacina, 2019, 239; G. Pedlow, *NATO Strategy Documents 1949–1969*, Mons, NATO International Staff Central Archives, 1997, 1–27; L. Kaplan, *The Long Entanglement: NATO's First Fifty Years*, Santa Barbara, Praeger Security International, 1999, 4–19 and T. Sayle, 'Canada, NATO, and the Berlin Crisis, 1961–1962: "Slow-boil" or "pressure cooker?"', *International Journal* 2013, 255–268.

48 Article 4 of the Warsaw Pact stipulated that an attack on one of the members equaled an attack on all. The Warsaw Pact was disbanded at the meeting of Foreign and Defence Ministers of the Warsaw Treaty Organization in Budapest on 25 February 1991. Text partially inspired by A. Verhelst and S. Trifunovska, *NATO: The North Atlantic Treaty Organization*, Alpen-aan-den-Rhijn, Wolters Kluwer, 2022, 24.

49 The full text of § 20 reads: 'to achieve its essential purpose, the Alliance performs the following fundamental security tasks: To provide one of the indispensable foundations for a stable security environment in Europe, based on the growth of democratic institutions and commitment to the peaceful resolution of disputes, in which no country would be able to intimidate or coerce any European nation or to impose hegemony through the threat or use of force. To serve, as provided for in Article 4 of the North Atlantic Treaty, as a transatlantic forum for Allied consultations on any issues that affect their vital interests, including possible developments posing risks for members' security, and for appropriate co-ordination of their efforts in fields of common concern. To deter and defend against any threat of aggression against the territory of any NATO member state. To preserve the strategic balance within Europe.'

This formulation is very much in line with how NATO's activities and purposes were conceived at its inception. § 32 reads that a coherent approach to crisis management 'is still to be determined.'[50] The Concept reaffirms the defensive nature of the Alliance (see § 30, § 35, and § 57). It also reconfirms NATO's initial objectives: § 15 posits that 'the essential purpose of the Alliance is to safeguard the freedom and security of its Member States by political and military means in accordance with the principles of the UN Charter and that this Alliance objective remains unchanged.' § 22 reads that 'the scope of the Alliance as well as their [Member States'] rights and obligations as provided for in the Washington Treaty remain unchanged.' Notwithstanding, in this document a military strategy made way for a grand strategy.[51] The 1991 Strategic Concept accentuates the broader dimensions of security, including its political, economic, social, and environmental aspects (§ 9, § 24, and § 29).[52] While this first publicly available Strategic Concept does express the political will of the Allies, it does not formulate a concrete plan to transform the Alliance in the future, as Bölingen puts it.[53]

2.2. STRATEGIC CONCEPT 1999

The 1999 Strategic Concept marks the most decisive moment in the transformation of NATO's powers.[54] In addition to the fundamental security tasks of consultation, security, deterrence, and defence, mentioned in the 1991 Strategic Concept,[55] the 1999 Concept lists two more tasks: crisis management

50 Para. 32: 'in these new circumstances there are increased opportunities for the successful resolution of crises at an early stage. The success of Alliance policy will require a coherent approach determined by the Alliance's political authorities choosing and co-ordinating appropriate crisis management measures as required from a range of political and other measures, including those in the military field [...].'

51 V. Rühe, 'Shaping Euro-Atlantic Policies: A Grand Strategy for a New Era', *Survival* 1993, 130.

52 See F. Carr and K. Ifantis, *NATO in the New European Order*, London, Palgrave MacMillan, 1996, 75.

53 S. Bölingen, *Die Transformation der NATO im Spiegel der Vertragsentwicklung*, Saarbrücken, Akademiker Verlag, 2012, 57.

54 M. Zapolskis, '1999 and 2010 NATO Strategic Concepts: A Comparative Analysis', *Lithuanian Annual Strategic Review* 2012, 35–56; P. Cornish, 'A Strategic Concept for the Twenty-first Century', *Defense Analysis* 1999, 241–260; S. Bölingen, *op. cit.*, 64–71; D. Yost, 'NATO's evolving purposes and the next Strategic Concept', *International Affairs* 2010, 495; J. Ringsmose and S. Rynning, *Come Home NATO: the Atlantic Alliance's New Strategic Concept*, Danish Institute for International Relations, Report, 2009, 10–15 and K. Kamp, 'Das neue Strategische Konzept der NATO. Entwicklung und Perspektiven', *Aus Politik und Zeitgeschichte* 1999, 19–25.

55 Allies deleted the 1991 Strategic Concept wording of 'maintaining the strategic balance within Europe', which Moscow found 'offensively reminiscent of the Cold War', see P. Necas, P. Terem and M. Keleman, 'From Washington to Lisbon: A new NATO strategic concept', *Obrana a strategie* [Defence & Strategy] 2009, 49.

and partnership.[56] The addition of these tasks constitutes the most significant departure from the 1991 text.[57] It represents a 'discontinuity' with the Alliance's purposes as formulated at its inception. As Yost puts it: 'In the 1991 Strategic Concept, Allied leaders declared that none of its weapons will ever be used except in self-defence.'[58] According to this author, Allies simply did not anticipate that in the following year they would begin engaging in demanding non-Article 5 operations in the Balkans. This transformation, which took place between 1991 and 1999, prompted by the Balkan Wars, can be seen in the Ministerial Communiqués of 1992. In December 1992 NATO Foreign Ministers made an explicit commitment to support peacekeeping and other operations under the authority of the UNSC, on a case-by-case basis and in accordance with its own procedures.[59] In the Ministerial Session earlier that year the North Atlantic Council made a similar commitment to what is now the OSCE.[60] The 1999 Strategic Concept goes further than the 1991 Concept because it allows NATO to undertake new activities. Most importantly (and controversially),[61] the 1999 Strategic Concept extends NATO's tasks to include crisis management. It does so by giving NATO the competence to conduct 'non-Article 5 crisis response operations' (NA5CROs). § 31 of the 1999 Strategic Concept states:

> In pursuit of its policy of preserving peace, preventing war, and enhancing security and stability and as set out in the fundamental security tasks, NATO will seek, in cooperation with other organisations, to prevent conflict, or, should a crisis arise, to contribute to its effective management, consistent with international law, including through the possibility of conducting non-Article 5 crisis response operations. The

---

56 Para. 10 Strategic Concept 1999, available online at www.nato.int/cps/en/natohq/official_texts_27433.htm (last accessed January 2025).

57 This addition of fundamental security tasks represents a discontinuity with the Alliance's purposes from its inception, during the Cold War and up until the 1991 Strategic Concept according to Yost: 'in the 1991 Strategic Concept, Allied leaders declared that "none of its weapons will ever be used except in self-defence".' According to Yost, the Allies simply did not anticipate that in the following year they would begin to engage in a wide range of demanding non-Article 5 operations in the Balkans. See D. Yost, 'NATO's evolving purposes and the next Strategic Concept', 491. Note how the 1999 text no longer explicitly states that the scope of the Alliance as laid down in the North Atlantic Treaty and Members' rights and obligations under the North Atlantic Treaty remain unchanged, *cf.* § 5 and § 22 of Strategic Concept 1991.

58 Yost, 'NATO's evolving purposes and the next Strategic Concept', 491.

59 NATO, Final Communiqué of the Ministerial meeting of the North Atlantic Council, Brussels, 17 December 1992, § 4.

60 NATO, Final Communiqué of the Ministerial Meeting of the North Atlantic Council, Oslo, 4 June 1992, § 11.

61 J. Roper, 'NATO's new role in crisis management', *The International Spectator* 1999, 51–61 and D. Yost, 'NATO's evolving purposes and the next Strategic Concept', 495: '[This] has been widely canvassed. To what extent is there a conflict or tension between the Alliance's original and enduring purpose of collective defence and its newer crisis management functions?'

> Alliance's preparedness to carry out such operations supports the broader objective of reinforcing and extending stability and often involves the participation of NATO's Partners. NATO recalls its offer, made in Brussels in 1994, to support on a case-by-case basis in accordance with its own procedures, peacekeeping and other operations under the authority of the UN Security Council or the responsibility of the OSCE, including by making available Alliance resources and expertise. In this context NATO recalls its subsequent decisions with respect to crisis response operations in the Balkans. Taking into account the necessity for Alliance solidarity and cohesion, participation in any such operation or mission will remain subject to decisions of member states in accordance with national constitutions.[62]

The Allied Joint Doctrine for NA5CROs provides a negative catch-all definition of such operations: 'NATO activities falling outside the scope of Article 5'.[63] The Doctrine further clarifies that NA5CROs include 'multifunctional operations, falling outside the scope of Article 5, which contribute to conflict prevention and resolution or serve humanitarian purposes, and crisis management in the pursuit of declared Alliance objectives' (Article 0104.b(1)). NA5CROs range from

> support operations primarily associated with civil agencies through operations in support of peace, countering irregular threat activities, to combat. In the framework of a NATO-led operation, this could include, but is not limited to, extraction operations, tasks in support of disaster relief and humanitarian operations, search and rescue or support to non-combatant evacuation operations, freedom of navigation and overflight enforcement, sanction and embargo enforcement, support to stabilization and reconstruction activities, peace enforcement, and counterinsurgency. (Article 0104.b(2))

Further on:

> NA5CRO may be limited in objective, means, area, and time depending on the desired end state; however, NA5CRO may include offense, defence, stability, and enabling activities. Depending on the situation, NA5CRO may be as demanding and intense as Article 5 operations, in particular during enforcement operations. (Article 0104.b(3))

It is remarkable how broad this notion is. By defining NA5CROs in a negative way, i.e. all operations which are not covered by Article 5, NATO opens the door to an almost unlimited array of missions and operations it could carry out. NA5CROs can include evacuation operations, overflight enforcement missions, peace enforcement, disaster relief, and much more. Most strikingly, these

---

62 Para. 31 of the 1999 Strategic Concept.

63 The agreement of nations to use the publication *Allied Joint Doctrine for Non-Article 5 Crisis Response Operations*, a NATO/PfP Unclassified Document (AJP-3.4(A) is recorded in STANAG 2180 (2010).

NA5CROs can be just as offensive as Article 5 operations. A non-exhaustive list of NATO's NA5CROs: NATO's training mission in Iraq (NTM-I, 2004–2011) and its ongoing NATO Mission Iraq (2014–present), its involvement and combat actions in the Balkans (i.e. Bosnia and Herzegovina, including IFOR and SFOR in the early 1990s, and FYROM (2001–2002)), its Resolute Support Training Mission in Afghanistan, from which it famously withdrew in August 2021, its controversial actions in Libya, and its support to firefighting efforts in Greece.[64] The controversy stirred by NATO's intervention in Libya was partly due to it being a NA5CRO and not a Treaty-based operation.[65] In contrast, there has been only one Article 5 operation in NATO's history, carried out in the wake of 9/11, even though the competence mentioned in Article 5 is the only competence mentioned in the constituent instrument. The expansion of NATO's competences to include NA5CROs was immediately controversial, as evidenced by remarks made by the US Deputy Secretary of State Talbott during the negotiations over the 1999 Strategic Concept:

> Future European challenges may involve non-article 5 missions; some commentators contend that such adaptations require a revision of the North Atlantic Treaty, or believe we are proposing one. This is untrue.[66]

The legal accuracy of this statement will be scrutinised further on in this chapter.

2.3. STRATEGIC CONCEPT 2010

The second most recent NATO Strategic Concept was adopted during the Lisbon Summit in 2010. Importantly, it outlines what are now known as NATO's 'three essential core tasks':

1. collective defence;
2. crisis management;
3. cooperative security.

---

64 NATO, *NATO Legal Deskbook* 2010, 242. Note that the content of the Legal Deskbook represents research by its authors (i.e. NATO legal advisers, academics, etc.) and is not an official statement of NATO. *NATO Handbook* 2006, 44–45. The NATO Handbook is published by the NATO's Public Diplomacy Division under the authority of the Secretary General as a reference book. It is not a formally agreed NATO document and does not represent NATO's official positions, available online at www.nato.int/docu/handbook/2006/hb-en-2006.pdf (last accessed January 2025).

65 G. Ulfstein and H. Christiansen, 'The Legality of the NATO bombing in Libya', *International & Comparative Law Quarterly* 2013, 159–171 and Y. Nahlawi, 'The legality of NATO's pursuit in regime change in Libya', *Journal on the Use of Force and International Law* 2018, 295–323.

66 Quote taken from B. Simma, 'NATO, the UN and the Use of Force: Legal Aspects', *European Journal of Law* 1999, 14–15.

In 1949 only one of these three tasks was mentioned.[67] This new formulation marked another step away from the four fundamental tasks. Compared to the 1999 document, the 2010 Strategic Concept puts more emphasis on NATO's role in the field of crisis management. § 21, for example, reads that 'the Alliance will engage actively before, during and after crises.' § 23 states that 'NATO has unique conflict management capacities.' The document also promulgates a few intended measures to make NATO's crisis management more effective.[68] But apart from refining the formulation of NATO's (now three) fundamental tasks and broadening the concept of security (building upon the 1991 notion), the 2010 Strategic Concept does not result in any major shift in NATO's powers, tasks, and activities. This conclusion is supported by research in the political sciences, which generally found the 2010 Strategic Concept to be an 'evolutionary' document rather than a 'revolutionary' one.[69]

2.4. STRATEGIC CONCEPT 2022

Set in motion in 2021 and accelerated by the Russian invasion of Ukraine in February 2022, the most recent Strategic Concept was adopted in June 2022. Here, the core tasks of the Alliance are still threefold. They are similar but not identical to those promulgated in 2010:

1. deterrence and defence (rather than 'collective defence');
2. crisis management and prevention ('prevention' being a new term);
3. cooperative security.

The security landscape changed after the invasion of Ukraine. The 2022 Concept emphasises that the Alliance's key purpose is collective defence as laid down in Article 5.[70] So, while the 2022 Strategic Concept reiterates NATO's three core tasks, it also restores the emphasis on NATO's one and only Treaty-based task: that of deterrence and defence. In essence, the 2022 Strategic Concept attests

---

67 See U. Fastenrath, 'Inhaltsänderung völkerrechtlicher Verträge ohne Beteiligung des Gesetzgebers – Verfassungsrechtliche Zulässigkeit und innerstaatliche Wirkung' in R. Geiger (ed.), *Völkerrechtlicher Vertrag und staatliches Recht vor dem Hintergrund zunehmender Verdichtung der internationalen Beziehungen*, Leipzig, Nomos, 2000, 112.

68 Para. 21 and 23 Strategic Concept 2010, available online at www.nato.int/docu/handbook/2006/hb-en-2006.pdf (last accessed January 2025).

69 M. Zapolskis, '1999 and 2010 NATO Strategic Concepts: A Comparative Analysis', 52 and 56.

70 Para. 1 and para. 6 Strategic Concept 2022 and S. Clapp, 'Outcome of the Madrid NATO Summit', *European Parliament Research Service Briefing* 2022, 1 and W. Alberque, 'the new NATO Strategic Concept and the end of arms control', *IISS Analysis* 2022, 1, available online at www.iiss.org/online-analysis/online-analysis//2022/06/the-new-nato-strategic-concept-and-the-end-of-arms-control?_cldee=ilznOqPtloUz8hwG (last accessed January 2025).

to the fact that the Alliance is now operating in a fundamentally new threat environment, but it does not bestow new tasks or powers on the Alliance.[71]

2.5. NEGOTIATING, DRAFTING, AND ADOPTING A STRATEGIC CONCEPT

Two procedural facts will be kept in mind throughout the following analysis. Firstly, the North Atlantic Council (NAC) is NATO's highest decision-making body. It can meet at three levels: Permanent Representatives,[72] Foreign or Defence Ministers, and Heads of State and Government ('NATO Summits'). The NAC has the same powers, regardless of the level at which it meets.[73] Secondly, decisions within NATO are made by consensus and common accord.[74] There is no voting. Decision-making by consensus is the procedure at all levels of the organisation: the committee level, the NAC in permanent session, the NAC at the level of the Ministers, the NAC at the level of the Heads of State and Government etc. All post-Cold War Strategic Concepts were adopted by consensus by the NATO Heads of State and Government.

2.5.1. 1991

At the NATO London Summit of 1990, it was understood that the changed geopolitical and security situation after the fall of the Berlin Wall would require a new strategy.[75] The London Declaration of that same year expressed the intention to strengthen the Alliance's political pillar, with Article 2 of the 1949 Treaty as the legal basis.[76] Those who drafted the Concept understood very early on that the new military strategy would have to reflect the Alliance's

---

71 S. Clapp, 'Outcome of the Madrid NATO Summit', 2 and E. Herold, O. Schmitt and S. Sloan, 'NATO's Strategic Concept: responding to Russia and China', *Defence Studies* 2022, 560.

72 Each Member State is represented in the NAC by one Permanent Representative. The NAC in Permanent Session is chaired by the NATO Secretary General or by his or her deputy and meets at NATO HQ at least once a week, and more often when needed. See A. Verhelst and S. Trifunosvka, *op. cit.*, 62.

73 See *NATO Encyclopedia* 2018, 394–395.

74 Commentary 17 to Article 2 ARIO, ILC 2011, *Articles on the responsibility of international organizations with Commentaries*, text adopted by the International Law Commission at its sixty-third session, in 2011, and submitted to the General Assembly as a part of the Commission's report covering the work of that session (UN Doc. A/66/10). The report, which also contains commentaries to the articles (para. 88), appears in *Yearbook of the International Law Commission*, 2011, vol. II, Part Two. See also ILC 2011, *Comments and observations received from international organizations on the Responsibility of International Organizations*, UN Doc. A/CN.4/637 and Add.1, 168 (under the section entitled 'Draft article 63 ... North Atlantic Treaty Organization'). See also chapter 4.

75 M. Legge, 'The Making of NATO's New Strategy', *NATO Review* 1991, 9–14 and H. Wegener, 'The Transformed Alliance', *NATO Review* 1990, 1–9.

76 Para. 2 London Declaration 1990 and M. Legge, 'The Making of NATO's New Strategy', 10.

political approach to the changed security situation, as explained by Legge.[77] The drafting of this first unclassified Strategic Concept was entrusted to an internal group composed mostly of NATO staff members with a military background. After about 16 months and 12 drafts,[78] the document was ultimately approved by consensus by the Permanent Representatives in the NAC, before being endorsed by the NATO Heads of State and Government during the 1991 Rome Summit.[79] It became NATO's first publicly available Strategic Concept.

2.5.2. 1999

In July 1997 the NATO Heads of State and Government met in Madrid. They agreed that the 1991 Strategic Concept had to be updated in response to Europe's new security situation, largely prompted by the Balkan Wars.[80] The Heads of State and Government tasked the NAC with initiating the negotiations and drafting.[81] The process was completed in two stages. In the first stage, the Allies organised debates on which main issues the new Strategic Concept should and should not cover.[82] This process took about six months.[83] In the second stage, a detailed draft of the text was prepared. This process was supported by the NATO International Staff. The government representatives debated the draft text in NATO committees.[84] After these negotiations the text moved from the committee level to the NAC in permanent session, where it was eventually approved by consensus. It officially became NATO's 1999 Strategic Concept when it was adopted by the Heads of State and Government at the 1999 Washington Summit.[85]

2.5.3. 2010

In 1991 and 1999 the Strategic Concepts had been negotiated mainly by the Ambassadors in the NAC, supported by their deputies and staff in NATO committees and by the civil servants of the NATO International Staff. In 2010,

---

77 M. Legge, 'The Making of NATO's New Strategy', 10.

78 M. Legge, 'The Making of NATO's New Strategy', 13.

79 Para. 4 NATO, Rome Declaration on Peace and Cooperation, issued by the Heads of State and Government participating in the meeting of the North Atlantic Council, Rome, 8 November 1991.

80 Para. 19 NATO, Madrid Declaration on Euro-Atlantic security and co-operation, issued by the Heads of State and Government participating in the meeting of the North Atlantic Council, Madrid, 8 July 1997.

81 Para. 19 Madrid Declaration on Euro-Atlantic security and co-operation.

82 P. Cornish, 'A Strategic Concept for the Twenty-first Century', 248.

83 As described by A. Cragg, 'A New Strategic Concept for a new era', *NATO Review* 1999, 19.

84 P. Cornish, 'A Strategic Concept for the Twenty-first Century', 248.

85 Para. 4 NATO, Washington Summit Communiqué, issued by the Heads of State and Government participating in the meeting of the North Atlantic Council, Washington D.C., 24 April 1999.

however, the NATO Secretary General took up a more prominent role in the negotiating and drafting process.[86]

Despite the new challenges that had emerged since the 1999 Strategic Concept, there was little sense of political urgency and it proved difficult to bring the Allies together to draft a new Strategic Concept.[87] An intermediate solution was found: during the 2004 Istanbul Summit the Heads of State and Government tasked the NAC (in permanent session) with advancing a new document, which would be called the 'Comprehensive Political Guidance' (CPG).[88] In the end, the CPG turned out to be mainly a military document, which the Allies realised soon afterwards would be insufficient. A fully fledged Strategic Concept was needed. And so, the Final Communiqué of the 2008 Bucharest Summit asked the Council in permanent session to prepare the Declaration on Alliance Security for adoption at the Summit.[89] On the basis of this mandate, the NAC began negotiations and drafting. The Declaration was then issued at the Strasbourg and Kehl Summit in April 2009. In the last paragraph, the NATO Heads of State and Government tasked the NATO Secretary General with developing a new Strategic Concept:

> [We] task the Secretary General to convene and lead a broad-based group of qualified experts, who in close consultation with all Allies will lay the ground for the Secretary General to develop a new Strategic Concept and submit proposals for its implementation for approval at our next summit. The Secretary General will keep the Council in permanent session involved throughout the process.[90]

The NATO Secretary General at the time, Jaap de Hoop Scheffer, began the works, which were to be completed in three phases, as explained by Ramirez.[91] The first phase was one of *reflection*, made up of seminars attended by relevant stakeholders, including non-specialists. Each seminar dealt with a specific aspect of the Strategic Concept.[92] De Hoop Scheffer's successor, Secretary General Anders Fogh Rasmussen, then appointed a group of 12 experts operating under the leadership

---

86 P. Necas, P. Terem and M. Keleman, 'From Washington to Lisbon: A new NATO strategic concept', 60. In the past, 'Secretary Generals had merely assisted Allied governments who took the direct control of negotiations – with the permanent representations at NATO Headquarters drafting the document and national officials flying in for NAC meetings to solve sticky issues, of which there were always, predictably, many', in J. Ringsmose and S. Rynning, *op. cit.*, 13.

87 J. Ringsmose and S. Rynning, *op. cit.*, 9.

88 NATO, Istanbul Summit Communiqué issued by the Heads of State and Government participating in the meeting of the North Atlantic Council, Istanbul, 28 June 2004, § 21.

89 Para. 3 NATO, Bucharest Summit Declaration, issued by the Heads of State and Government participating in the meeting of the North Atlantic Council, Bucharest, 3 April 2008.

90 Last para. NATO, Declaration on Alliance Security Issued by the Heads of State and Government participating in the meeting of the North Atlantic Council, Strasbourg/Kehl, 4 April 2009.

91 E. Ramirez, 'The New NATO Strategic Concept: A Vision from Spain', 163.

92 NATO, A Roadmap for the New Strategic Concept.

of Dr. Madeleine Albright.[93] The Allies, their partners, the EU, the UN, NGOs, and other interested actors were consulted in the process. The Group of Experts met periodically with the Secretary General and submitted a progress report to the Foreign Ministers in December 2009.[94] The second phase was one of *consultation*. The Group of Experts travelled to each NATO Member State to present its results, asking the national governments for feedback.[95] During this phase the Group was still meeting periodically with the Secretary General, the NAC, and other stakeholders at NATO Headquarters. On 17 May 2010 the Group of Experts presented its recommendations to the Secretary General.[96] On the basis of this work, the Secretary General presented his own report to Allies. Thus began the third and final *drafting and negotiation* phase. Allies, notably in the NAC, asked their national governments for political guidance. Specific topics were discussed and negotiated in various NATO committees.[97] Afterwards, the Secretary General prepared the first draft of the new Strategic Concept for negotiation in the NAC. After the text had been approved by the NAC at the level of the Permanent Representatives, the document was adopted by the Heads of State and Government during their 2010 NAC meeting in Lisbon, where it officially became NATO's 2010 Strategic Concept. Cleary, the creation process of the 2010 Strategic Concept was more transparent and inclusive than that of the 1991 and 1999 Concepts.[98]

2.5.4. 2022

With the long-term trends of disruptive technologies and a rising China in mind, the February 2022 invasion of Ukraine prompted the adoption of a new Strategic Concept. The creation process was led by Secretary General Jens Stoltenberg, who strove for greater transparency than in 2010. He did so by organising internal consultations and external engagements. The latter included events with partner States, civil society, and youth organisations.[99] After this phase of consultation the Allied representatives negotiated the Strategic Concept

93 See E. Ramirez, 'The New NATO Strategic Concept: A Vision from Spain', 163; D. Yost, 'NATO's evolving purposes and the next Strategic Concept', 507.

94 NATO, A Roadmap for the New Strategic Concept.

95 NATO, A Roadmap for the New Strategic Concept.

96 Norway Country Study Guide, *Strategic Information and Developments*, Washington D.C., International Business Publications, 2012, 119; NATO, News item 63644, 'Experts group presents report on new Strategic Concept for NATO', 17 May 2010, available online at www.nato.int/cps/en/natohq/news_63644.htm? (last accessed January 2025).

97 See NATO, A Roadmap for the New Strategic Concept.

98 See S. Babst, 'Startschuss für die Diskussion über das neue Strategische Konzept. Ein Bericht über die Konferenz NATO's New Strategic Concept: Launching the Process', *Zeitschrift für Aussen- und Sicherheitspolitik* 2009, 501–504.

99 NATO 2030, Analysis and Recommendations of the Reflection Group Appointed by the NATO Secretary General, 25 November 2020, available online at www.nato.int/nato_static_fl2014/assets/pdf/2020/12/pdf/201201-reflection-group-final-report-uni.pdf (last accessed January 2025).

in NATO HQ committees and the NAC. The final draft was adopted at the 2022 Madrid Summit.

2.6. INTERIM CONCLUSION

Since the 2010 Strategic Concept, NATO's three core tasks are collective defence, crisis management, and cooperative security. In the 1949 Treaty two of these three tasks were not mentioned. This expansion of NATO's tasks and activities to include crisis management in the 1999 Strategic Concept marks the most significant shift to date of NATO's powers away from its Treaty-based competences. As this work's analysis has revealed, NA5CROs are not attributed powers that can be traced back to the Treaty. But this does not necessarily mean that the international institutional law principle of attributed powers has been violated. After all, the doctrine of implied powers is supplementary to the principle of attributed powers. The implied powers of an international organisation, unlike its attributed powers, are not explicitly stated in the constituent document. The next section will closely examine whether the power of NATO to carry out NA5CROs is a lawful implied power according to the principles of international treaty law, case law, and legal doctrine. In addition, both the wording and the adoption process of each of the four post-Cold War Strategic Concepts support the *prima facie* conclusion that these are declaratory, political, non-legal documents. For this reason, they do not constitute a legal amendment to the Treaty in the strict sense. This *prima facie* conclusion does require closer scrutiny, because at this point in this inquiry it cannot be ruled out that the Treaty was informally amended by the Strategic Concepts. This would mean that the expansion of NATO's powers beyond the Treaty was lawful after all, a claim which has been contested before the German Constitutional Court for over two decades (see below).

3. THE EXPANSION OF NATO'S POWERS: LAWFULLY IMPLIED?

This section examines whether the expansion of NATO's powers to include NA5CROs is lawful. This will be investigated in light of the principles of international institutional law, international treaty law, case law, and legal scholarship. In international institutional law, treaty interpretation and the powers of an international organisation are inherently linked. The reason for this is that interpretation of constituent instruments is the primary legal means of knowing the organisation's competences.[100] The very broad and ambiguous language used

100 C. Brölmann, 'Specialized Rules of Treaty Interpretation: International Organizations', in D. Hollis (ed.), *The Oxford Guide to Treaties*, Oxford, Oxford University Press, 2012, 509.

in the Treaty makes the rules of its interpretation all the more important. The relevant interpretation rules are those laid down in the Treaty itself, the rules of the organisation (Article 5 VCLT), the rules promulgated in international case law,[101] and the customary rules of the Vienna Convention on the Law of Treaties.[102] Note that most NATO Member States are also parties to the VCLT. In any case, they are legally bound by the customary rules of the VCLT. This also holds true for the US, which is not a party to the VCLT. Moreover, while NATO is not a party to the 1969 VCLT, it is still subject to the rules of international law, including customary rules, which most Articles of the VCLT are.[103]

In international treaty law, there are generally three methods of interpretation.[104] For multilateral treaties, Articles 31 and 32 VCLT emphasise the textual approach, possibly in combination with the intentional approach.[105] The textual method is generally not very well suited to the interpretation of the constituent treaties of international organisations,[106] and this is certainly the case for the North Atlantic Treaty. NATO's operating environment has changed

---

101 The International Law Commission, *Draft Conclusions on Subsequent Agreements and Subsequent Practice in Relation to the Interpretation of Treaties* will prove useful as a subsidiary means, see ILC 2018, *Draft Conclusions on Subsequent Agreements and Subsequent Practice in Relation to the Interpretation of Treaties with Commentaries*, text adopted by the International Law Commission at its seventieth session, in 2018, and submitted to the UN General Assembly as a part of the Commission's report covering the work of that session (UN Doc. A/73/10). The report, which also contains commentaries to the draft conclusions (para. 52), will appear in *Yearbook of the International Law Commission*, 2018, vol. II, Part Two, *cf.* Article 38(1)(d) Statute ICJ.

102 Vienna Convention on the Law of Treaties, signed on 23 May 1969, entered into force on 27 January 1980, UNTS 1155, 331; G. Hernández, *International Law*, Oxford, Oxford University Press, 2019, 164; ICJ 1974, *Fisheries Jurisdiction (United Kingdom v Iceland)*, Jurisdiction and Admissibility, *ICJ Rep* 1974, 3 and 18; ICJ 2002, *Sovereignty over Pulau Litigan and Pulau Sipidan (Indonesia/Malaysia)*, Judgment, *ICJ Rep* 2002, 625, 645–6.

103 ICJ 1980, *The Interpretation of the Agreement of March 25, 1951 between the WHO and Egypt*, Advisory Opinion, *ICJ Rep* 73, 89–90; P. Sands and P. Klein, *op. cit.*, 456; E. David, *op. cit.*, 95; H. Schermers, 'Les bases juridiques de l'action des organisations internationales', in R. Dupuy (ed.), *op. cit.*, 403.

104 *Cf.* Article 31 and 32 VCLT; O. Corten and P. Klein, *Commentaire article par article des Conventions de Vienne de 1969 et 1986 sur le droit des traités*, Brussels, Bruylant, 2006, 1309–1332; R. Kolb, *The Law of Treaties*, Cheltenham, Edward Elgar, 2016, 134–139; N. Blokker and H. Schermers, *op. cit.*, § 1346, 872; M. Yasseen, 'L'interprétation des traités d'après la Convention de Vienne sur le droit des traités', *Recueil des Cours de l'Académie de Droit International de La Haye* 1976-III, 3–14; C. Brölmann, *op. cit.*, 511–512; R. Gardiner, *Treaty Interpretation*, Oxford, Oxford University Press, 2008, 161–409. Compare to K. Ipsen, *Völkerrecht*, München, Verlag C.H. Beck, 2004, 137–146.

105 C. Brölmann, *op. cit.*, 511. See also ICJ 1952, *Anglo-Iranian Oil Co (United Kingdom v Iran)*, Judgment, *ICJ Rep* 104 and S. Torres Bernárdez, 'Interpretation of Treaties by the International Court of Justice Following the Adoption of the 1969 Vienna Convention on the Law of Treaties' in G. Hafner and others (eds.), *Liber Amicorum Professor Seidl-Hohenveldern*, Leiden, Martinus Nijhoff, 1998, 721–48.

106 N. Blokker and H. Schermers, *op. cit.*, § 1347, 873. See ICJ 1948, *Conditions of Admission of a State to Membership in the United Nations*, Advisory Opinion, *ICJ Rep* 48, 63 and ICJ 1960, *Constitution of the Maritime Safety Committee of the Inter-Governmental Maritime Consultative Organization*, Advisory Opinion, *ICJ Rep* 23, in C. Brölmann, *op. cit.*, 512.

drastically since the Treaty was signed in 1949.[107] Additionally, the Treaty was drafted in not one but two authentic languages (English and French). The teleological interpretation method, which emphasises the object and purpose of the text, is considered the most suitable method for interpretating the constituent treaties of international organisations.[108] The reason for this is that such treaties are considered a special type of multilateral treaty. According to Brölmann, they create both a new subject of law and a separate internal legal order.[109] While the VCLT applies by default to the constituent treaties of international organisations, Article 5 VCLT acknowledges the separate and unique nature of this type of treaty. It is this acknowledgement that prompts a specific interpretative practice in the case of the constituent instruments of international organisations. This practice entails 1) a teleological approach (which requires the interpreter to consider the objects and purposes of the organisation in order to ensure its effectiveness),[110] and 2) a strong regard for the established practice developed by the international organisation. The question that must be answered is: does NATO's power to conduct NA5CROs constitute an implied power and/or an established practice of the Organisation?

3.1. NA5CROS AS AN IMPLIED POWER

The International Court of Justice (ICJ) and the Court of Justice of the European Union (CJEU) have developed a distinctly teleological approach to the interpretation of constituent instruments.[111] In the *Reparations for Injuries*, *Effect of Awards*, and the *Namibia* Opinions, the ICJ prioritised the teleological interpretation of the UN Charter. The *Reparations for Injuries* Opinion is the landmark judgment in which the ICJ, explicitly inspired by the principle of effectiveness, accepted the doctrine of implied powers,[112] which is premised on

---

107 Article 14 North Atlantic Treaty and M. Tabory, *Multilingualism in International Law and Institutions,* Alphen aan den Rhijn, Kluwer Law International, 1980.

108 P. Sands and P. Klein, *op. cit.*, 450; N. Blokker and H. Schermers, *op. cit.*, § 1349, 875 and K. Skubiszewski, 'Remarks on the Interpretation of the United Nations Charter', in R. Bernhardt et al. (eds.), *Völkerrecht als Rechtsordnung, Internationale Gerichtsbarkeit, Menschenrechte, Festschrift für Hermann Mosler*, Berlin, Heidelberg, Springer-Verlag, 1983, 891–902.

109 C. Brölmann, *op. cit.*, 510–511; P. Sands and P. Klein, *op. cit.*, 449. *Cf.* S. Rosenne, *Developments in the Law of Treaties 1945–1986*, Cambridge, Cambridge University Press, 1989, 257–258; M. Ruffert and C. Walter, *Institutionalisiertes Völkerrecht*, München, C.H. Beck, 2009, paras 136–138.

110 Para. 19 ICJ 1996, *Legality of the Use by a State of Nuclear Weapons in Armed Conflict*, Advisory Opinion, ICJ Rep 1996, 66 and see P. Sands and P. Klein, *op. cit*, 450 and C.F. Amerasinghe, *op. cit.*, 44–49.

111 R. Gardiner, *op. cit.*, 2008, 120–122; CJEU, *Van Gend en Loos*, E.C.R. (1963), C-16/62; CJEU, *France v Commission* E.C.R. (1994), I-3658, 3674; C. Brölmann, *op. cit.*, 510; E. David, *op. cit.*, 2016, 136.

112 ICJ 1949, *Reparations for Injuries Suffered in the Service of the United Nations*, Advisory Opinion, *ICJ Rep* 174, 183. *Cf.* S. Rosenne, *op. cit.*, 238.

teleological interpretation.[113] In international institutional law, the doctrine of implied powers entails that an international organisation has the powers necessary to fulfil its function, purposes, and duties, even if its constituent instrument does not explicitly grant it those powers.[114] The ICJ generally accepted the doctrine in its *Reparations for Injuries*, *Effect of Awards*, and *Certain Expenses* Advisory Opinions.[115] The extent of the implied power should be determined on the basis of the extent to which the power is *necessary* and *essential* for the organisation to perform its functions.[116] When the ICJ invokes the doctrine of implied powers, it commonly uses the phrase 'by necessary implication as being essential to the performance of the organisation's duties.'[117]

Is NATO's power to conduct NA5CROs a lawful instance of implied powers, both necessary and essential for the performance of its functions? NATO would probably argue that the answer is yes, based on the following arguments. Speed, effectiveness, functionality, and strategy are essential in the domains of security and defence, and therefore essential to NATO. It could be argued that NA5CROs could prevent conflicts taking place on the periphery of the Alliance's territory from escalating further and may thus prevent an armed attack on its territory, which links back to NATO's primary purpose (Article 5). Moreover, since the decision to carry out a NA5CRO is usually based on classified military intelligence, NATO can easily claim that its intervention was necessary to avoid further escalation, without having to specify any further reason. This is precisely the line of argument that NATO invoked for Bosnia and Herzegovina in the early 1990s and for its 1999 bombing of Kosovo. The argument goes that, if NATO had not intervened, the ethnic and civil conflict being fought on its borders could have escalated to the point that the Alliance's security would have been at stake. One can understand why efficiency and necessity are invoked to justify NA5CROs. NATO officials are convinced that NATO lawfully possesses these implied powers. A statement by the SHAPE OLA Director Andres Mosquera is telling in this regard:

---

113 J. Klabbers, *op. cit.*, 83.

114 C.F. Amerasinghe, *op. cit.*, 47; J. Klabbers, *op. cit.*, 58–61 and N. Blokker and H. Schermers, *op. cit.*, § 232–233A, 194–198.

115 J. Makarczyk, 'The International Court of Justice on the Implied Powers of International Organizations', in J. Makarczyk (ed.), *Essays in International Law in Honour of Judge Manfred Lachs*, The Hague, Brill Nijhoff, 1984, 501–519; B. Rouyer-Hameray, *Les Compétences implicites des organisations internationales*, Paris, Librairie Générale de Droit et de Jurisprudence R. Pichon et R. Durand-Auzias, 1962; D. Simon, *L'interprétation judiciaire des traités d'organisations internationales*, Paris, A. Pedone, 1981, 391; L. Martinez Sanseroni, 'Consentimiento del Estado y Organizaciones Internacionales', *Revista Española de Derecho Internacional* 1985, 45–60.

116 N. Blokker and S. Schermers, *op. cit.*, § 233A, 197 as recognized by the ICJ on multiple occasions. See C.F. Amerasinghe, *op. cit.*, 48.

117 See ICJ *Reparations*, 182, see *Effect of Awards* at 56–58, see *WHO Legality*, 79.

> We now again have a NATO which is in a sort of Cold War. Like NATO in the 1960s and 1970s. Ukraine gave back implied powers to the Supreme Commander that were somehow forgotten in the 1990s, simply because they were not necessary. Why are these powers implied? The idea is that this organisation, in order to *function properly*, needs a military that is capable of giving the best military advice with no interference, sending this advice all the way to the military chains, the Military Committee and then to the NAC.[118]

Interestingly, it would be harder for NATO to argue that its power to conduct NA5CROs is implied by its statutory powers rather than being necessary for its efficient functioning. In *Certain Expenses*, the ICJ broadened its acceptance of implied powers by connecting them to the purposes of the organisation.[119] After all, the North Atlantic Treaty accords only one power, i.e. to collectively defend the North Atlantic Area, a power that sufficed for five decades (1949–1991).

It is clear that efficiency and necessity are arguments in favour of NA5CROs being an implied power. This does not mean, however, that this implied power is lawful or desirable. Importantly, there are limits to the use of the doctrine of implied powers. The doctrine cannot be used to violate fundamental rules and principles of international law. It cannot be used to justify the illegal use of force, for example (Article 2 UN Charter). This means that NATO may have overstepped the limits of its own powers while attempting to overthrow the government in Libya, in addition to having violated UNSC Resolution 1973 and the R2P doctrine, as scholars have argued.[120] It could also be argued that conducting NA5CROs is not necessary to fulfil NATO's function. This argument is inspired by Judge G.H. Hackworth's dissenting opinion to *Reparations for Injuries*.[121] After all, when there is a lawful basis (i.e. self-defence pursuant to Article 51 UN Charter), States can decide to intervene militarily through coalitions of the willing. Moreover, the EU might have developed its defence and security policy at a quicker pace in the 1990s if it had not been for American mistrust. Then, the EU could have exercised greater autonomy in deciding whether to engage in military interventions alongside the US over the past decades. Article 5 would still maintain its value as a solidarity mechanism with a deterring effect, considering the combined capabilities of all NATO Member States. The claim that NA5CROs are essential can also be dismissed, as there will never be *ex ante* or *ex post* proof of the claim that an operation was essential for avoiding further escalation. One could argue it is not essential for NATO to proactively conduct non-Article 5 operations to be able to defend itself efficiently.

---

118 Interview with head of the SHAPE Office of Legal Affairs, Andres Mosquera, online, 10 October 2022. Emphasis added.

119 ICJ 1962, *Certain Expenses of the United Nations*, Advisory Opinion, ICJ Rep 1962, 151.

120 G. Ulfstein and H. Christiansen, 'The Legality of the NATO bombing in Libya', 159–171 and Y. Nahlawi, 'The legality of NATO's pursuit in regime change in Libya', 295–323.

121 Dissenting Opinion by Judge G.H. Hackworth, *Reparation for Injuries*, 198.

NATO proved during the entire Cold War period (and currently *vis-à-vis* Ukraine) that it could do the latter without doing the former. If Judges Winiarski, Koretsky, and Hackworth already dissented from *Certain Expenses* and *Effect of Awards* because they found that even harmless powers, like incurring organisational expenses and creating independent tribunals, were not implied by the UN Charter, it would be difficult to argue that the far-reaching power of conducting NA5CROs is implied by the North Atlantic Treaty.[122] Because the 1949 Treaty describes the purposes of NATO with little precision, it is more difficult to claim that NATO may pursue its purposes using any means possible and that the ends justify the means.[123] Moreover, implied powers are there to give effect to what States have agreed to by becoming parties to the constituent instrument.[124] The North Atlantic Treaty's *travaux préparatoires*, the Cold War Strategic Concepts, and the sole reliance on deterrence during the Cold War support the notion that the signatories had wanted to create an alliance for the purpose of collectively defending themselves. While the *travaux préparatoires* do show that this task was not envisaged solely *vis-à-vis* the Soviet Union but also with regard to 'other potential threats', they make clear that the parties did not intend a fully fledged security organisation.[125] Another argument *a contrario* is that the ICJ agreed in *Certain Expenses* that the UN has the power to create peacekeeping forces even though this power is not mentioned in the Charter. It is important to note that there actually is a provision for this possibility: Article 43 UN Charter. It was because agreement under Article 43 could not be found that the ICJ wanted to safeguard the functioning of the Security Council in an emergency situation.[126] The North Atlantic Treaty, in contrast, contains no similar provision, nor has NATO always conducted its non-Article 5 missions in emergency situations. In addition, the certainty of the explicit powers must trump the uncertainty of the implied powers, writes Blokker.[127] Lastly, the CJEU did not imply in its Opinion 2/94 that the European Commission was competent to accede to the European Convention of Human Rights (ECHR). The CJEU made clear that Article 308 TFEU cannot be used to gain competences which

---

122 Dissenting Opinion by Judge G.H. Hackwort, *Effect of Awards*, 57, Dissenting Opinion by Judge V. Koretsky, *Certain Expenses*, 268 and Dissenting Opinion by Judge Winiarski, *Certain Expenses*, 230.

123 Dissenting Opinion by Judge Winiarski, *Certain Expenses*, 230 and A. Gadkowski, 'The doctrine of implied powers of international organizations in the case law of international tribunals', *Adam Mickiewicz University Law Review* 2016, 55.

124 N. Blokker, 'International Organizations or Institutions, Implied Powers', *Max Planck Encyclopedias of International Law* 2021, § 3.

125 K. Skubiszewski, 'Implied Powers of International Organizations' in Y. Dinstein (ed.), *International Law at a Time of Perplexity: Essays in Honour of Shabtai Rosenne*, Dordrecht, Nijhoff, 1989, 860.

126 ICJ, *Certain Expenses*, 167 and N. Blokker, 'International Organizations or Institutions, Implied Powers', § 6.

127 N. Blokker, 'International Organizations or Institutions, Implied Powers', § 17.

would substantially amount to amendments to the Treaty without following the correct amendment procedures.[128]

3.2. NA5CROS AS AN ESTABLISHED PRACTICE

If the implied powers argument does not apply in the case of NATO, the organisation could, in theory, still resort to the doctrine of established practice. It is accepted that international organisations can create new powers through 'quasi-custom' that post-dates the constitution.[129] In this context, such a custom is referred to as 'established practice' (article 2(b) ARIO, *cf.* Article 5 VCLT).[130] Established practice forms part of the rules of an international organisation, together with its constituent treaty, decisions, and resolutions.[131] The ICJ has, on several occasions, justified its interpretations by using 'the practice of the organisation' as a supporting argument.[132] In its *Wall* Opinion, the ICJ accepted the United Nations General Assembly's (UNGA) practice of making recommendations concerning the maintenance of international peace and security while the matter was still on the United Nations Security Council's (UNSC) agenda.[133] The Court deemed this consistent with Article 12(1) UN Charter. In the *Second Admissions* case, the ICJ found evidence of a practice by the UNGA and UNSC, who had consistently interpreted the UN Charter to mean that the General Assembly can decide to admit a new Member only on the basis of a recommendation by the UNSC.[134] In the *Certain Expenses* case, the ICJ concluded that the phrase 'expenses of the Organization' in Article 17(2) UN Charter refers to all expenses incurred by the UN. The General Assembly had made provision for peacekeeping activities in the same way it had done for other expenses from 1947 to 1959. In *Namibia*, the ICJ decided that the UNSC permanent members

128 CJEU, Opinion 2/94 of 28 March 1996, *Rep.* 1996, I-01759, § 30.

129 H. Schermers and N. Blokker, *op. cit.*, § 1144B and A. Gadkowsi, 'The doctrine of implied powers of international organizations in the case law of international tribunals', *Adam Mickiewicz University Law Review* 2016, 47.

130 P. Reuter, 'Quelques réflexions sur la notion de "pratique internationale" spécialement en matière d'organisations internationales', *Studi in Onore di Giuseppe Sperduti* 1984, 189–207.

131 Article 2(b) ARIO and N. Blokker, 'Beyond Dili: on the Powers and Practice of International Organizations' in G. Kreijen et al. (eds.), *State, Sovereignty and International Governance*', Oxford, Oxford University Press, 307.

132 E. Roucounas, 'Practice as a relevant factor for the responsibility of international organizations' in M. Ragazzi (ed.), *Responsibility of International Organizations: Essays in Memory of Sir Ian Brownlie,* Boston, Nijhoff, 2013, 167–168.

133 ICJ 2004, *Legal Consequences of the Construction of a Wall in the Occupied Palestinian Territory,* Advisory Opinion, *ICJ Rep* 136.

134 ICJ 1950, *Competence of the General Assembly for the Admission of a State to the United Nations,* Advisory Opinion, *ICJ Rep* 1950, 4; C.F. Amerasinghe, *op. cit.*, 50.

had developed an abstention practice in non-procedural matters (Article 27(3) UN Charter).[135]

So, can the power to conduct NA5CROs be considered an established practice of NATO? Are there criteria to establish whether this is so? As the case law indicates, practice can take the form of action, inaction, documents etc.[136] In most cases, there is a certain repetition of the conduct on the part of the organisation, but there is no judicial agreement on whether a practice must effectively consist of repeated conduct. For example, in the *European Commission on the Danube* and the *IMCO* cases, the practice in question had only occurred once. In *Certain Expenses*, the practice had been present for over 12 years.[137] The requirement of a certain degree of consistency—if any, when practice is relied upon to *support* an interpretation—supports NATO's argument that conducting NA5CROs has become an established practice. After all, NATO has been regularly carrying out such operations since the early 1990s, up until this day. Examples are NATO's training missions in Iraq and Afghanistan, its missions in the Balkans, and its support of firefighting in Greece. Until the late 1990s NATO had been defending itself solely on the basis of Article 5. But since 1999 it has regularly been conducting NA5CROs. This consistency supports the notion of NA5CROs being an established practice, as isolated precedents are not sufficient. Note that documents, e.g. the NATO Strategic Concepts, can also form a practice. The German Federal Administrative Court ruled in the *University of Paderborn* case (2009) that

> these texts [the General Comments by the Committee on Economic, Social and Cultural Rights] are not binding under international law. However, [...] they describe in an authorised form the standards in the practice of the Social Committee, thereby serving as an aid to interpretation and thus helping to shape the understanding of contractual legal concepts by the States Parties.[138]

---

135 ICJ 1971, *Legal Consequences for States of the Continued Presence of South Africa in Namibia (South West Africa) notwithstanding Security Council Resolution 276 (1970)*, Advisory Opinion, *ICJ Rep* 16. See C. Stavropoulos, 'The Practice of Voluntary Abstentions by Permanent Members of the Security Council under Article 27, para. 3 of the Charter of the United Nations', *American Journal of International Law* 1967, 737–752.

136 J. Wouters, C. Ryngaert, T. Ruys and G. De Baere, *International Law from a European Perspective*, Oxford, Oxford University Press, 2018, 102.

137 See PCIJ 1927, *Jurisdiction of the European Commission of the Danube Between Galatz and Braila, Advisory Opinion*, PCIJ Publ. Series B, no. 14, 57-58 and ICJ 1960, *Constitution of the Maritime Safety Committee of the Inter-Governmental Maritime Consultative Organization*, ICJ Rep 1960, 167-168. See also Schermers and Blokker's interpretation of ICJ *Namibia* on this point, *op. cit.*, § 1350E, 881.

138 Germany, *Bundesverwaltungsgericht* 29 April 2009, *Students' Union of the University of Paderborn v University of Paderborn*, Case No 6 C 16/08, BVerwGE 134. See B. Brodkorb, 'Analysis of Students' Union of the University of Paderborn v University of Paderborn', *ILDC* 1556 (DE 2009), A8 (own translation from German into English) and J. Wouters, C. Ryngaert, T. Ruys and G. De Baere, *op. cit.*, 102 and R. Gardiner, *op. cit.*, 2015, 257–59.

However, the four ICJ cases mentioned all concern practices in the field of procedure and administration.[139] Arditi convincingly argues that the IMF's power to recognise governments constitutes an established practice, but this, too, is a procedural and organisational matter. It could be argued that acquiring a new substantive power, such as conducting military missions, is just too far-reaching to be eligible for recognition as an established practice. Established practice is usually invoked for (and accepted in the case of) of administrative matters, as the latter are handled by the administrative structure of the organisation rather than by the Member States. One should also note that the reasoning behind the recognition of NA5CROs as an established practice is circular: originally, NATO did not have the power to conduct NA5CROs, because it was not granted this power by its constituent instrument. But by regularly carrying them out anyway over the course of decades, it has thus created an established practice that now forms part of the rules of the organisation (Article 5 VCLT). Also, it is difficult to contend that conducting NA5CROs is a 'rule' that NATO deliberately and consistently abides by. Rather, it is something that NATO does for political, strategic, and military reasons. Even if one were to conclude that NA5CROs cannot be considered an established practice on the part of NATO, it should be remembered that NA5CROs are conducted by the NATO Member States. This contributes to the development of a state practice for the purposes of customary international law.[140] Within NATO itself, practices are created mainly through the conduct of all States acting together in the plenary NAC. The ICJ has stressed the importance of consensus on this point.[141] At the IMF, in contrast, even a unanimous decision cannot form an established practice of its Member States, because the Member States are not represented in the organs of the IMF.[142]

3.3. INTERIM CONCLUSION

Speed, necessity, and efficiency, developed in the case law and legal scholarship, have been invoked to support NATO's claim that the power to conduct NA5CROs is implied by the 1949 Treaty. But these arguments turn out to be

---

139 Although the ICJ in these cases uses 'practice' of the organisation. The Court recognises the notion of 'rules of the organisation' but has not expressly referred to 'established practice'. See L. Arditi, 'The Role of Practice in International Organizations: the Case of Government Recognition by the International Monetary Fund', *International Organizations Law Review* 2020, 578.

140 ILC 1950, Report of the International Law Commission to the General Assembly (Part II): 'Ways and Means of Making the Evidence of Customary International Law More Readily Available', *Yearbook of the International Law Commission,* ILC Doc. A/1316.

141 ICJ *WHO Opinion,* 81 and ICJ 2014, *Whaling in the Antarctic (Australia v Japan: New Zealand intervening),* Judgment, *ICJ Rep* 226, 25.

142 L. Arditi, 'The Role of Practice in International Organizations: the Case of Government Recognition by the International Monetary Fund', 574.

flawed. First of all, it is just a little too convenient for NATO to claim that a NA5CRO was necessary to prevent a non-Article 5 situation from escalating into an Article 5 situation. Referring to speed, necessity and efficiency as arguments is inherently easy in the security and military field, where information tends to be technical and classified. But even if one were to grant the argument, it does not mean that this implied power is lawful or desirable. NATO's power to conduct NA5CROs can be considered unnecessary, as States can already decide to intervene militarily through coalitions of the willing when there is a lawful basis for it (i.e. self-defence pursuant to Article 51 UN Charter). After all, NATO is just the organisational structure facilitating and coordinating the States' capabilities. This power can be said to be inessential, as there will never be *ex ante* or *ex post* proof of the claim that a certain operation was essential to avoid further escalation, precisely because of the speed and secrecy with which such decisions are made. Both during the Cold War and recently in Ukraine, NATO proved it could efficiently defend itself without NA5CROs. Additionally, the ICJ tends to accept only 'harmless' powers of an organisational nature as implied powers. This makes it difficult to argue that a far-reaching power as the one to conduct NA5CROs is implied by the North Atlantic Treaty, especially since its object and purpose is collective self-defence, not collective security.[143] The *travaux préparatoires* make clear that the parties did not intend a fully-fledged security organisation. In addition, conducting NA5CROs is not an administrative, organisational rule that NATO's organisational structure considers itself bound by. But because of NATO's intergovernmental nature, whereby State representatives decide everything by consensus in a plenary organ and where the organisational structure plays a merely facilitating role, the regular carrying out of NA5CROs since the 1990s does contribute to the development of a state practice for the purposes of customary international law. Even if one were to accept that NATO can justify its NA5CROs through the doctrine of implied powers, it would still need to be established that this power is not used to amend the North Atlantic Treaty without following the procedure set forth in Article 12. As has already been pointed out above, the CJEU has declined to recognise an implied power on the part of the European Commission for this very reason. After all, formal amendment procedures are guarantors of legitimacy.[144] If those bound by a legal instrument repeatedly overstep the limits it imposes, the text must either be amended or lose its authority.[145] To this end, it

143 Minutes of the Third Meeting of the Washington Exploratory Talks on Security, July 7, 1948, 10 a. m. in *Foreign Relations of the United States, 1948, Western Europe, Volume III* (U.S. State Department Office of the Historian) and Dissenting Opinion by Judge G.H. Hackwort, *Effect of Awards*, 57, Dissenting Opinion by Judge V. Koretsky, *Certain Expenses*, 268 and Dissenting Opinion by Judge Winiarski, *Certain Expenses*, 230.

144 C. Peters, 'Subsequent Practice and Established Practice of International Organizations: Two Sides of the Same Coin?', *Goettingen Journal of International Law* 2011, 620.

145 L. Arditi, 'The Role of Practice in International Organizations: the Case of Government Recognition by the International Monetary Fund', § 3.1.

must be determined whether the 1999 Strategic Concept constitutes an informal amendment of the North Atlantic Treaty. The German constitutional court has been considering this question for nearly 20 years. In the next section, this case law is examined.

4. THE EXPANSION OF NATO'S POWERS INTERPRETED BY THE *BUNDESVERFASSUNGS-GERICHT*

The distinction between legal amendment and legal interpretation becomes blurred when the text of the constituent instrument is changed by an established practice, as is the case for NATO's NA5CROs.[146] Did the 1999 Strategic Concept, particularly its § 32, in fact constitute an (informal) amendment of the North Atlantic Treaty? This question has been thoroughly examined by the German Constitutional Court. The present section will deal exclusively with German constitutional case law, as this issue has not been the subject of significant judicial (or parliamentary) debate (see below) in any other NATO Member State. To this end, the judicial records of the US, UK, Canada, Belgium, the Netherlands, France, Germany, and Luxembourg in the period from 1990 until 2022 have been consulted.[147] It is crucial to note from the outset that the following cases are all German national constitutional cases, which means that the results of the inquiry in this section will have important limitations in terms of international law. In view of Article 38(1)(d) Statute of the ICJ, the value of these rulings should not be overestimated. Recourse to national case law was made because international courts have never ruled on the North Atlantic Treaty. After all, only States can be parties to an ICJ case. It is unlikely that Allies would bring one another before the ICJ pursuant to Article 36(2)(a) Statute of the ICJ. Moreover, only the UNGA and UNSC can request advisory opinions (Article 91(1) UN Charter). Since there is only one national court that has ever ruled on the issue, this book's conclusions cannot be generalised in terms of international law. With this fact in mind, the choice was made to analyse the four relevant rulings together rather than separately. All cases discussed below are *Organstreit* proceedings. In Germany, the highest federal organs can lodge a case with the Federal Constitutional Court if they find that their rights and obligations provided by the Basic Law (*Grundgesetz*, i.e. Germany's constitution)

---

146 C.F. Amerasinghe, *op. cit.*, 46 and W. Karl, 'Vertragsauslegung – Vertragsänderung' in C. Schreuer (ed.), *Autorität und internationale Ordnung*, Berlin, Aufsätze zum Völkerrecht, 1979, 9–34.

147 The choice of these Member States was made as the author is in a position to read, understand and write in the authentic languages of these case law records.

have been violated.[148] In § 63 of the Federal Constitutional Court Act, the *Bundestag* (parliament) and the political parties are named as high federal organs that can lodge such *Organstreit* proceedings. Applicants must invoke a violation to their constitutional rights or the rights of the constitutional organ of which they form a part.[149] Applicants must also hold these rights towards the respondent. In all cases discussed below, left-wing political parties brought the German Federal Government before the Constitutional Court for violating their parliamentary right to consent to Germany's joining of multilateral treaties, laid down in Article 59 Basic Law. The aim of a successful application is that the *Bundesverfassungsgericht* declares that the respondent has violated a Basic Law provision.[150]

The upcoming analysis is based on the authentic German version of the selected judgments.[151]

4.1. THE *AWACS V. SOMALIA* CASE (1994)

In 1992 the NATO Member States took on the responsibility of monitoring the UNSC-mandated no-fly zone in Bosnia and Herzegovina by deploying NATO AWACS aircraft during the crisis in former Yugoslavia.[152] This happened on the basis of UNSC Resolution 781 (9 October 1992). As the situation worsened, the UNSC adopted Resolution 816 on 31 March 1993, reaffirming Resolutions 781 and 786 (1992), extending the ban to cover flights, and giving permission to use 'all measures necessary' to ensure compliance with the ban, acting under Chapter VII UN Charter.[153] In its decisions taken on 2 and 8 April 1993, the NAC declared its readiness to support the implementation of UNSC Resolution 816 and began enforcing the no-fly zone.[154] The NATO AWACS were operated

148 Article 93(1) Grundgesetz.

149 Germany, *Bundesverfassungsgericht*, Organstreit proceedings, available online at www.bundesverfassungsgericht.de/EN/TheFederalConstitutionalCourt/TypesOfProceedings/OrganstreitProceedings/organstreitproceedings_node.html#:~:text=Organstreit%20proceedings%20allow%20for%20judicial,93(1)%20no. (last accessed January 2025) and D. Kommers, *The Constitutional Jurisprudence of the Federal Republic of Germany*, London, Duke University Press, 1997, 12.

150 Article 20(3) Grundgesetz and Germany, *Bundesverfassungsgericht*, Organstreit proceedings, available online at www.bundesverfassungsgericht.de/EN/TheFederalConstitutionalCourt/TypesOfProceedings/OrganstreitProceedings/organstreitproceedings_node.html#:~:text=Organstreit%20proceedings%20allow%20for%20judicial,93(1)%20no (last accessed January 2025).

151 All translations into English of (parts of) these judgments are the author's own efforts. Certain parts are inspired by the official but non-authentic translations into English issued by the German Constitutional Court.

152 *NATO Encyclopedia* 2018, 407–408.

153 UNSC, Resolution 816, UN Doc. S/RES/816, 31 March 1993.

154 See J. Kriendler, 'NATO's changing role – opportunities and constraints for peacekeeping', *NATO Review* 1993, 16. See also NATO Press Release (1993)029, 12 April 1993, § 1.

by units composed of military personnel from various Member States, including Germany. The German Federal Government had agreed on 2 April 1993 to provide German military personnel to the AWACS operations.[155] Two political parties, the Social Democratic Party (SPD) and the Free Democratic Party (FDP), were troubled by this and filed *Organstreit* applications against the German Federal Government before the Constitutional Court. The SPD and the FDP contended that the German Federal Government's approval of the NAC's decisions to monitor the embargo and enforce flight bans, as well as the government's subsequent decisions to deploy German armed forces, amounted to an implicit modification of the North Atlantic Treaty.[156] This amounted to a circumvention, and thus a violation, of Article 59(2)1 Basic Law.[157] Article 59(2)1 states that 'treaties regulating Germany's political relations or relating to subjects of federal legislation require approval in the form of a federal law adopted by Parliament.'[158] The *Bundesverfassungsgericht* has repeatedly ruled that treaty amendments fall within the scope of this provision of the Basic Law.[159]

According to the SPD and the FDP, the Treaty does grant NATO the power to launch Article 5 collective self-defence countermeasures, but it does not grant other competences. NATO, a collective self-defence organisation, cannot perform peacekeeping tasks at the request of the UN. The constitutionally correct way to achieve the goal of changing the Federal Republic's obligations under the Treaty, according to applicants, was to amend the Treaty in accordance with Article 59(2)(1) Basic Law.[160] The applicants believed that an attempt had been made to achieve the same result under international law by informal means. The Court did not examine whether the 1991 Strategic Concept *in se* constituted an amendment or an interpretation of the Treaty,[161] nor did applicants ask it to. The reason for this was that the 1991 Strategic Concept made no mention of NATO's power to support UNSC peacekeeping operations. This possibility was first expressed in paragraph 5 of the Final Communiqué of the Ministerial Meeting of the NAC in Brussels on 17 December 1992.[162] This awkward political

---

155 Para. 107, Germany, Constitutional Court 1994, *AWACS/Somalia*, BVerfGE 90, 286.

156 Para. 146 *AWACS/Somalia.*

157 Para. 146 *AWACS/Somalia.*

158 Article 59(2)1 Grundgesetz: '*Verträge, welche die politischen Beziehungen des Bundes regeln oder sich auf Gegenstände der Bundesgesetzgebung beziehen, bedürfen der Zustimmung oder der Mitwirkung der jeweils für die Bundesgesetzgebung zuständigen Körperschaften in der Form eines Bundesgesetzes. Für Verwaltungsabkommen gelten die Vorschriften über die Bundesverwaltung entsprechend.*'

159 Para. 261–265 and 270 *AWACS/Somalia.* See § 133 *New Strategic Concept* case; para. 65 *Turkey/AWACS* case and § 45–43 *Tornado* case *(infra).* See H. Sauer, 'Die NATO und das Verfassungsrecht: neues Konzept – alte Fragen', *Zeitschrift für ausländisches öffentliches Recht und Völkerrecht* 2002, 324.

160 Para. 176 *AWACS/Somalia.*

161 In 2001, the Court had the chance to rule on a Strategic Concept as such (that of 1999). See *infra.*

162 Para. 5: 'In this spirit, we are contributing individually and as an Alliance to the implementation of the UN Security Council resolutions relating to the conflict in the former

situation—the fact that NATO felt the need to support its UNSC-authorised measures but lacked the legal basis to do so—was one of the main reasons why the 1991 Strategic Concept was soon revised and why the 1999 Strategic Concept explicitly allowed NA5CROs.[163] NATO's action in former Yugoslavia was a NA5CRO *avant la lettre*. As stated by Jamie Shea, former Spokesperson and Deputy Secretary General for Emerging Security Challenges, at NATO in July 2022:

> In a way the legal basis [for the operation in former Yugoslavia] was encapsulated in the mandate that established UNPROFOR in the UN Security Council in the first place. [...] I'm saying it was not precisely legal, but it certainly gave it the veneer of legality. [...] So that sort of double endorsement by NATO as well as the UN gave it also a sense of legal cover. We are not doing this alone.[164]

In this case, the *Bundesverfassungsgericht* dove into issues of international law, albeit through the lens of the German constitution. In these *Organstreit* proceedings, the Court did not examine whether the government's decision to deploy troops to AWACS violated the North Atlantic Treaty, but only whether it violated Article 59 Basic Law. The Court first made it clear that Article 59(1)2 Basic Law was to be interpreted narrowly.[165] The Court relied heavily on its earlier case law to substantiate this. The Court sees Article 59(2)1 Basic Law as an exception to the constitutional principle of the separation of powers, according to which foreign policy is a function that belongs to the executive branch. The Court pointed out that Article 59(2)1 reflects a trend towards the parliamentarisation of the decision-making process in the domain of foreign affairs. Yet, the Court continued, the parliament's right of participation, granted by Article 59(2)1, is limited by its wording and scope, both in procedural and substantive terms. The Court firmly limits the scope of Article 59(2)1 to formal treaty amendment, excluding dynamic treaty interpretation or subsequent practice:

Yugoslavia. For the first time in its history, the Alliance is taking part in UN peacekeeping and sanctions enforcement operations. The Alliance, together with the WEU, is supporting with its ships in the Adriatic the enforcement of the UN economic sanctions against Serbia and Montenegro and of the arms embargo against all republics of former Yugoslavia. UNPROFOR is using elements from the Alliance's NORTHAG command for its operational headquarters. NATO airborne early-warning aircraft – AWACS – are monitoring the UN-mandated no-fly zone over Bosnia-Herzegovina daily.' The commitment in § 5 of the 1992 Ministerial Communiqué was later confirmed by NATO Heads of State and Government in the 1994 Brussels Summit Declaration (§ 7) and in § 31 of the NATO 1999 Strategic Concept, which talks about non-Article 5 crisis response operations. See S. Bölingen, *op. cit.*, 60.

163 See in the same vein D. Yost, *op. cit.*, 491.

164 Interview with former NATO spokesperson and Deputy Assistant Secretary General for Emerging Security Challenges Dr. Jamie Shea, online, 12 July 2022.

165 Para. 261–65 *AWACS/Somalia*. This has been the repeated position of the Court. See extensively, H. Sauer, 'Die NATO und das Verfassungsrecht: neues Konzept – alte Fragen', 327–329. For Sauer's critical stance see *ibid.*, 339.

> A change in content of an existing treaty requires the consent of the legislative branch under Article 59(2)1 Basic Law *only* if this was done by way of a treaty amendment. Such requires the unanimously expressed will of the contracting parties to change the existing legal situation. The content of an international treaty can also be changed by other legal means. For example, the emergence of a new specific customary law norm applicable between the contracting parties can have a modifying effect on the content of a treaty. Moreover, in modern international law, treaties are often interpreted dynamically in line with changing circumstances. This is especially true for treaties which establish a separate organisation whose members act independently within the framework of the treaty. According to Article 31(1) and (2) VCLT, the object and purpose of the treaty expressed in the text provide essential aids to the interpretation of that treaty. When the legislature consents to an international treaty, it does so in the knowledge of the importance of its preambles and objectives. A further development of treaty law by so-called authentic interpretation or subsequent practice[166] is thus based on the existing treaty and is therefore covered by the consent under Article 59(2)1 of the Basic Law.[167]

The Court is not blind to the realities of international law, however, and recognises that there is a fine line between the interpretation and amendment of treaties in international law.[168] The Court sees the will of the parties as the decisive criterion between interpretation and amendment:

> The interpretation of an existing international treaty, which is merely intended to develop the already existing content of the treaty, or a practice of applying the treaty that is applied consistently by the parties to the treaty, which gains legal significance for the interpretation of an existing treaty, does not constitute an amendment of the treaty because the parties to the treaty do not wish to amend the treaty.[169]

To determine whether the German government had violated the rights of parliament, the Court first had to determine whether a new treaty had arisen under article 59 Basic Law. The Court found that there was not enough evidence to conclude that the government had the will to enter into new treaty obligations by (agreeing to) deploying troops for AWACS operations in Bosnia. The Court stated in a single, simple sentence that there had been no action or declaration by the parties that proved there was any such will. In short, the *Bundesverfassungsgericht* found no violation of Article 59(2)1 Basic Law in *AWACS/Somalia*. It interpreted the constitution narrowly to include formal amendment but exclude informal means of changing treaties. As the German government's decision to deploy AWACS aircraft did not constitute an

166 Orig.: '*eine sich auf dieser Grundlage entfaltende oder jene Rechtsfortbildung allererst bewirkende Vertragspraxis.*'
167 Own translation. Para. 273 *AWACS/Somalia*.
168 Para. 274 *AWACS/Somalia*. See also W. Karl, 'Vertragsauslegung – Vertragsänderung' in C. Schreuer (ed.), *op. cit.*, 9.
169 Own translation. Para. 274 *AWACS/Somalia*.

amendment of the North Atlantic Treaty in the eyes of the Court, parliamentary approval pursuant to Article 59(2)1 Basic Law was not required for the government's decision to participate in the NATO mission. The Court's main argument in this regard was the lack of intent on the part of NATO Member States to amend the Treaty. However, the absence of such intent was explained only very superficially. There were no sources of information disclosed which point to a lack of such a will. This could explain why four Justices dissented. Strikingly, the essential part of the judgment was only backed by four of the eight Justices.[170] The reason why the present judgment prevailed is rather unsophisticated: Article 15(4)3 of the German Federal Constitutional Act stipulates that the Constitutional Court cannot rule that there has been a violation of the Basic Law when the vote is tied. This tells us that there was little agreement on the crux of the matter. The four dissenting Justices found that the actions of the German Federal Government directly endangered the rights of the *Bundestag* under Article 59(2)1 Basic Law and found that the Court should have concluded that Article 59 had been violated.[171] The Justices voiced that:

> Through repeated joint political declarations and participation in the surveillance operations in the Yugoslavian conflict, the Federal Government is participating in a dynamic expansion of the original concept of the North Atlantic Treaty, which cannot be clearly qualified as an amendment in legal terms and which threatens to undermine parliament's rights of participation.[172]

The dissenting Justices pointed to the fact that NATO, according to its founding treaty, is a defensive alliance based on mutual assistance, citing Article 5 of the 1949 Treaty as proof. Undertaking peacekeeping and peace operations in third countries, under the aegis of the United Nations, is not mentioned as one of NATO's tasks in the Treaty.[173] The dissenting Justices made clear that the North Atlantic Treaty's preamble nor its objectives could justify such a mission. This is not to say that the dissenting Justices actually thought that the declarations and decisions extending the scope of NATO's powers amounted (or should have amounted) to an amendment of the Treaty. They agreed with the majority that there had not yet been a revision of the Treaty in the form of an explicit or implied amendment. But it is precisely because the Justices found that the treaty amendment had been *avoided,* that the German government's decisions had hollowed out the rights of parliament.[174] In the opinion of the four dissenting Justices, Article 59 Basic

170 T. Groh, 'Analysis of Parliamentary Group of the Social Democratic Party (SPD) in the German Federal Parliament v Federal government (Germany)', *ILDC* 2750 (DE 1994).

171 Para. 298 *AWACS/Somalia.*

172 Para. 299 *AWACS/Somalia.*

173 Para. 300 *AWACS/Somalia.*

174 Para. 308 *AWACS/Somalia.*

Law requires the consent of parliament not only for formal treaty amendments, but also for more subtle methods of treaty amendment.[175] Examples of the latter are authentic interpretations or dynamic developments that have become legally binding agreements.[176]

4.2. THE *NEW STRATEGIC CONCEPT* CASE (2001)

In the *New Strategic Concept* case, the parliamentary group SPD contended that the German government's approval of the 1999 Strategic Concept, without having initiated the consent procedure in the German parliament, violated Article 59(2)1 Basic Law. Unlike *AWACS/Somalia,* where the Court was asked to consider only the government's singular action of deploying troops for a NATO mission, the Court now had to rule on a NATO Strategic Concept *in se.* Once again the question was whether the government had violated the right of the *Bundestag* to consent to the approval of multilateral treaties and treaty amendments, laid down in Article 59 Basic Law, by having approved the 1999 Strategic Concept. In the *New Strategic Concept* case, the Court was still considering issues of international law mostly through the national, constitutional lens of Article 59(2)1 Basic Law—just like it did in *AWACS/Somalia*—and of Article 24(2) Basic Law. The latter reads that

> with a view to maintaining peace, the Federation may enter into a system of mutual collective security; in doing so it shall consent to such limitations upon its sovereign powers as will bring about and secure a lasting peace in Europe and among the nations of the world.[177]

This must be read in conjunction with Article 59(2)1 Basic Law, meaning that Germany's participation in a system of mutual collective security requires the consent of parliament. First, the Court's arguments pertaining to Article 59(1) will be analysed, then its arguments pertaining to Article 24(2). This time the Court went further than it did in *AWACS/Somalia*, because it assessed the object and purpose of the North Atlantic Treaty itself and the negotiating history of the 1999 Strategic Concept to determine whether the Treaty had been amended. This is permitted because the German Constitutional Court, in its *Lisbon* decision, has recognised 'openness towards international law' (*Völkerrechtsfreundlichkeit*)

---

175 Note how the dissenting judges too gave an interpretation of Article 59 Basic Law rather than of the North Atlantic Treaty.

176 Paras 306–308 *AWACS/Somalia*.

177 Article 24(2) Grundgesetz: '*Der Bund kann sich zur Wahrung des Friedens einem System gegenseitiger kollektiver Sicherheit einordnen; er wird hierbei in die Beschränkungen seiner Hoheitsrechte einwilligen, die eine friedliche und dauerhafte Ordnung in Europa und zwischen den Völkern der Welt herbeiführen und sichern.*'

as an established constitutional principle.[178] German courts, unlike the courts in some other European countries, are competent to apply international treaties as long as they were formally submitted to the legislature before ratification.[179] The hierarchical position of international treaties in the German legal order is defined in Article 59(2) Basic Law. Because the legislature gives its consent to treaties in the form of a statute, treaties like the North Atlantic Treaty have the rank of an ordinary statute.[180] This judicial review of federal governmental acts in the domain of international relations, including multilateral treaties, is permitted because no political question doctrine is applicable (in contrast to the US Supreme Court).[181] However, when a treaty leaves room for multiple interpretations, the Basic Law mandates that the reading compatible with the constitution be chosen.[182]

4.2.1. Does the 1999 Strategic Concept amend the North Atlantic Treaty?

The *Bundesverfassungsgericht* found that:

1. the 1999 Strategic Concept does not demonstrate a willingness on the part of the Member States to formally amend the existing North Atlantic Treaty; and
2. the content of the Concept does not imply such an amendment.[183]

Hence, the Court concluded that the 1999 Strategic Concept is not an amendment to the North Atlantic Treaty. The Court gave two arguments to prove that the parties lacked the will to amend. First of all, as was the case in *ACAWS/Somalia*, the totality of circumstances surrounding the approval of the 1999 Strategic Concept was taken into account.[184] The Court pointed out the generality of the wording used in the Concept, the fact that the text consists mostly of descriptions of the political situation in the Euro-Atlantic area at the time, and the fact that the text contains mostly general declarations of

178 Germany, *Bundesverfassungsgericht*, BVerfGE 123, 267 (347), BVerfGE 6, 309 (362) and BVerfGE 112, 1. See R. Streinz, 'The Role of the German Federal Constitutional Court Law and Politics', *Ritsumeikan Law Review* 2014, 101 and 110.

179 H. Folz, 'Germany' in D. Shelton, *International Law and Domestic Legal Systems: Incorporation, Transformation and Persuasion*, Oxford, Oxford University Press, 2011, 240.

180 H. Folz, 'Germany' in D. Shelton, *op. cit.*, 240.

181 E. Benda and E. Klein, *Verfassungsprozessrecht,* München, Beck, 2012, § 28; K. Schlaich and S. Korioth, *Das Bundesverfassungsgericht*, München, Beck, 2012, § 505; K. Stern, *Staatsrecht,* Vol. II, Berlin, Duncker & Humblot, 1980, 961 and R. Streinz, 'The Role of the German Federal Constitutional Court Law and Politics', *op. cit.*, 101.

182 BVerfGE 36, 1 (14 ff.) and K. Schlaich and S. Korioth, *op. cit.*, § 537 and R. Streinz, 'The Role of the German Federal Constitutional Court Law and Politics', *Ritsumeikan Law Review* 2014, 110.

183 Para. 132 Germany, Constitutional Court 2001, *New Strategic Concept* case, 2 BvE 6/99.

184 Para. 133 *New Strategic Concept* case.

intention.[185] Secondly, the Court also pointed to the lack of a ratification clause in the Concept.[186] The Court did not find that the text implied a wish to amend the treaty. Considering the wording of the Strategic Concept, the expansion of NATO's powers to include NA5CROs should be interpreted as merely a further development of the Treaty, according to the Court.[187] The Court did acknowledge that the 1999 Strategic Concept's new formulation of NATO's fundamental tasks entailed a greater expansion of NATO's powers than the 1991 Strategic Concept did.[188] But it cannot be inferred from this that an objective amendment of the North Atlantic Treaty has taken place.[189] The content of the Strategic Concept must be understood as a development and concretisation of the open wording of the Treaty text. The Court mentioned the fact that the NAC explicitly declared in § 5 of the 1999 Strategic Concept that the purpose and nature of the Alliance remained unchanged.[190] The Court concluded that the North Atlantic Treaty is open to further development and that such flexibility is required to keep the Alliance 'efficient and adaptable' in accordance with its aims.[191] In essence, according to the German Constitutional Court, the 1999 Strategic Concept does not constitute a legal amendment of the 1949 North Atlantic Treaty.

Interestingly, the Court does acknowledge that, by changing the content of a treaty informally—especially when this is done by the Heads of State and Government, the prevailing practice at NATO—there truly is a risk of bypassing parliament. The Court then gave five reasons (four of which are relevant to this book's inquiry) why the *Bundestag* is not 'defenceless' in the face of this risk:

- Article 43(1) Basic Law stipulates that the *Bundestag* and its committees may require the presence of any member of the Federal Government. This assures that the government can be held accountable to parliament for its NATO activities, e.g. through parliament's power of the purse.
- The Accession Protocols of new NATO Member States require ratification by parliament.
- The German Constitution (Articles 87a and 2 Basic Law) requires prior parliamentary approval of any deployment of the *Bundeswehr.*
- If a majority in the German parliament decides that the 1999 Strategic Concept does require an amendment to the North Atlantic Treaty after all, it can exert pressure on the Federal Government's representatives at

185 Para. 133 *New Strategic Concept* case.

186 Para. 134 *New Strategic Concept* case.

187 Para. 139 *New Strategic Concept* case.

188 Para. 142 *New Strategic Concept* case. For the Federal Government's view on this, see Jahresabrüstungsbericht [Annual Disarmament Report, red.], Records of the Bundestag 14/3233, 6.

189 Para. 145 *New Strategic Concept* case.

190 Para. 145 *New Strategic Concept* case.

191 Para. 147 *New Strategic Concept* case.

NATO to initiate such a process.[192] It is true that the right of initiative for treaty amendment is given to NATO Member States (compare Article 12 of the Treaty to Article 32 Constitutive Act of the African Union and to Article XII ASEAN Charter). The Court also refers to debates and answers to parliamentary questions, all concerning Germany's activities within NATO, held in the *Bundestag*. The Court adds that these took place leading up to the 1999 Strategic Concept.[193]

4.2.2. Does the 1999 Strategic Concept depart from the North Atlantic Treaty's purpose?

Having found that the 1999 Strategic Concept does not constitute a treaty amendment, the Court went on to identify a *national* limit to the permissibility of changing a constituent treaty without amending it. This is because, under German constitutional law, the further development of a system of mutual collective security may not exceed the authorisation given under Article 24(2) Basic Law.[194] If that were the case—if, by approving the 1999 Strategic Concept, the Federal Government had transgressed the authorisation granted to it by the Consent Act[195]—the authorisation's constitutional framework and the rights of parliament would be violated. The limit placed on the further development does not lie in the disturbance of a few Articles of the North Atlantic Treaty, the Court finds.[196] No, it is reached only when the dynamic evolution goes against the 'essential structural decisions of the system of treaties',[197] or, in other words, the structural core of the Treaty. In the eyes of the Court, the structural core is found in the Treaty's primary purpose: to preserve peace on a regional level in accordance with the objectives of the UN.[198] The Court came to this conclusion by analysing Articles 1, 2, 6, 10 and 12 of the 1949 Treaty and its preamble, and by taking into account the fact that the Treaty leaves room for interpretation and flexible evolution.[199] The Court found that the German Federal Government did not overstep the national limit because, by maintaining the object of the Treaty,

---

192 See A. Peters, 'L'acte constitutif de l'organisation internationale' in E. Lagrange and J.-M. Sorel (eds.), *op. cit.*, 227–228. Compare Article 12 North Atlantic Treaty to article 32 Constitutive Act of the African Union, article XII ASEAN Charter.

193 Germany, Bundestag, BT- Plenarprotokoll 14/53, Doc. S. 4607C – 4615B, 9 September 1999.

194 Para. 152 *New Strategic Concept* case.

195 The Consent Act to the North Atlantic Treaty defines the integration programme of a system of mutual collective security. This Act was endorsed by the German parliament in accordance with Article 59(1)2 and 24(2) Basic Law. In Germany, a consent act serves as the basis of the ratification of a treaty.

196 Para. 154 *New Strategic Concept* case.

197 Orig.: '*wesentliche Strukturentscheidungen des Vertragswerkes*', § 154 *New Strategic Concept* case.

198 Para. 156 *New Strategic Concept* case.

199 Para. 155 *juncto* 156 *New Strategic Concept* case.

its agreement to the 1999 Strategic Concept was still in line with Article 24(2) Basic Law.[200]

In short: first of all, the Court found that the 1999 Strategic Concept does not constitute an amendment of the Treaty. Secondly, seeing that there had not been any legal amendment, parliamentary approval to further develop the Treaty as a system of mutual collective security was not needed under Article 59 Basic Law. Thirdly, the Federal Government had not overstepped the national constitutional limit imposed on dynamic treaty evolution, laid down in Article 24 Basic Law, because the government's agreement to the 1999 Strategic Concept respects the Treaty's structural core, which the Court defines as the preservation of peace. With this, the Court allowed for the dynamic interpretation of the Treaty without the consent of parliament.[201]

4.3. THE *TORNADO* CASE (2007)

The saga continued with the 2007 *Tornado* case.[202] NATO led the UN-mandated International Security Assistance Force (ISAF) in Afghanistan from August 2003 to December 2014. ISAF's mission was to build the capacity of the Afghan national security forces to ensure that Afghanistan would not fall into the hands of terrorists again. Deployed in 2001 (initially under the lead of individual NATO Allies on a rotational basis), ISAF was tasked, at the request of the Afghan government and under a UN mandate, to assist that government in maintaining security. NATO agreed to take over the command of the force in August 2003 and the UN Security Council subsequently mandated the gradual expansion of ISAF's operations to cover the entire country.[203] The *Tornado* ruling essentially confirmed the rulings in *AWACS/Somalia* and *New Strategic Concept*. The novelty in *Tornado* was that the political party Partei des Demokratischen Sozialismus (PDS)/Die Linke challenged the Federal Government's consent to and participation in a concrete crisis management response operation based on the 1999 Strategic Concept. Unlike the 2001 *New Strategic Concept* case, where the Court ruled on the 1999 Strategic Concept *in abstracto*, the applicant in *Tornado* claimed that ISAF was a case in point of the intolerable expansion of the North Atlantic Treaty. PDS/Die Linke relied on the following arguments. They asserted that, by conducting the ISAF mission, NATO participated in a military operation that no longer had any connection to security in the Euro-Atlantic Area, which is

200 Para. 156 *juncto* 159 *New Strategic Concept* case.

201 What Sauer sees as a bridge too far, see H. Sauer, 'Die NATO und das Verfassungsrecht: neues Konzept – alte Fragen', 341–343.

202 Germany, Constitutional Court 2007, *Tornado* case, 2 BvE 2/07.

203 Paragraph based on A. Verhelst and S. Trifunovska, *op. cit.*, 96 and *NATO Encyclopedia* 2018, 20–27.

the area covered by the Treaty.[204] The declarations made by Member States at the 2006 Riga Summit also pointed in the direction of the alliance reorienting itself towards the role of global security provider.[205] The parliamentary group claimed that the Riga Summit Declaration constituted a treaty amendment.[206] The Court mostly repeated its earlier conclusions. As the Court had already decided in 2001 that crisis response operations pursuant to the 1999 Strategic Concept do not overstep the limits of Articles 59 and 24 Basic Law, it did not really provide anything new in the way of argumentation. The Court dismissed the out-of-area argument, stating that 'the regional connection as the core element of the NATO Treaty integration programme has however not meant that NATO's military operations would have to be restricted to the territory of the member states.'[207] The Riga Summit Declaration cannot be seen as a treaty amendment, as PDS/Die Linke was unable to show how this declaration would be crucially important for the development of the Organisation's constituent treaty.[208] In brief, the Court decided that the application was unfounded, as 'neither the connection of specific NATO military operations to the security of the Euro-Atlantic area has been broken, nor are there any indications that NATO has departed from its objective of maintaining peace.'[209]

4.4. THE *TURKEY/AWACS* CASE (2008)

On 7 May 2008, shortly after the *Tornado* case, the German Constitutional Court issued its latest ruling in the saga, the *Turkey/AWACS* case.[210] The case was factually very similar to *AWACS/Somalia* (1994). Here, for the first time, the Court found that there had been a violation of the rights of parliament under Article 59 Basic Law. As tensions were mounting prior to the March 2003 US-led campaign against Iraq, Turkey invoked Article 4 of the North Atlantic Treaty on 10 February 2003.[211] On 19 February 2003 NATO authorised precautionary defensive measures for Turkey.[212] The political party Free Democratic Party (FDP) argued that the German Federal Government had violated the rights

204 Para. 13 *Tornado* case.
205 Para. 13 *Tornado* case.
206 H. Aust, 'Analysis of Parliamentary Group of the PDS/Die Linke in the German Federal Parliament v Federal Government, 2 Be 2/07', *ILDC* 819 (DE 2007), A6.
207 See § 53–55 and § 59 *Tornado* case.
208 Paras 70–72 *Tornado* case.
209 Para. 50 *Tornado* case.
210 Germany, Constitutional Court, 2008, *Turkey/AWACS*, BvE 1/03.
211 E. Terzuolo, *NATO and Weapons of Mass Destruction: Regional Alliance, Global Threats*, Abingdon, Routledge, 2005, 119.
212 Decision Sheet of the Defence Planning Committee, NATO Support to Turkey within the Framework of Article 4 of the North Atlantic Treaty, Press Release (2003)013, 19 February 2003, available online at www.nato.int/docu/pr/2003/p030216e.htm (last accessed January 2025).

of *Bundestag* by deploying German soldiers in NATO aerial surveillance for the protection of Turkey without having obtained the parliamentary approval mandated by Article 59 Basic Law. The Court found there had indeed been such a violation.[213] This conclusion is less surprising than it might seem. It can be explained almost entirely by a change made to the German national legal order. After *AWACS/Somalia*, in 2005, the Act of Parliamentary Involvement in the Decision of the Deployment of Armed Forces Abroad had entered into force.[214] This Act contained detailed provisions concerning the form and extent of parliamentary involvement therein. It is on the basis of this Act that the Court came to its conclusion. The Court also reiterated what it had ruled in 2001: that the *Bundestag*, for several reasons, is not defenceless against the informal changing of the North Atlantic Treaty.[215]

4.5. AN ANALYSIS OF THE FOUR RULINGS

As things now stand, the expansion of NATO's powers, with the cooperation of the German Federal Government, does not require the involvement of the German parliament, as long as:

1. there is no amendment of the North Atlantic Treaty in the sense of Article 59(2)1 Basic Law;
2. the further development of the North Atlantic Treaty does not depart from its structural core in the sense of Article 24(2) Basic Law, i.e. the purpose of the maintenance of peace.[216]

In all four of its rulings, the *Bundesverfassungsgericht* interpreted Article 59(2)1 Basic Law narrowly, excluding informal amendment from the scope of the Article. The German Court concluded in the *New Strategic Concept* case that the 1999 Strategic Concept is not a treaty amendment under article 59(2)(1) Basic Law because it lacks a ratification clause. A lack of ratification clause strongly indicates there was no wish to create an amendment.[217] But this argument is not convincing in the case of NATO. Article 12 of the 1949 Treaty does not mention any need for ratification. The Court also found that parties lacked the will to amend the North Atlantic Treaty. For the most part,

213 Para. 56 *Turkey/AWACS* case.

214 Germany, Gesetz über die parlamentarische Beteiligung bei der Entscheidung über den Einsatz bewaffneter Streitkräfte im Ausland, Parlamentsbeteiligungsgesetz, ParlBG, *Federal Law Gazette* 2005, 775.

215 Para. 66 *Tornado* case.

216 See also para. 64–67 *Tornado* case.

217 Compare this to Article 108 UN Charter; H. Sauer, 'Die NATO und das Verfassungsrecht: neues Konzept – alte Fragen', 325.

this reasoning had been developed in the *AWACS/Somalia* and *New Strategic Concept* cases. The German Court was correct in attaching importance to the will of the parties. In line with the residual customary international law rules laid down in Article 39 and 40 VCLT, it has to be determined whether parties had agreed to amend the Treaty.[218] This was even more important when considering the broad and vague wording of Article 12 of the 1949 Treaty. Normally, one should first consider whether any of the parties have requested a revision (Article 12).[219] But in the case of NATO this is not straightforward, as Article 12 does not lay down any specific procedure to make such a request. Article 108 UN Charter, in contrast, which says that amendments to the Charter shall come into force when they have been adopted by a vote of two-thirds of the members of the General Assembly and ratified in accordance with their respective constitutional processes by two-thirds of the Members of the UN, including all the permanent members of the Security Council. This provision makes it easier to judge whether an act constitutes an amendment or not. There is no documentation revealing whether the 1999 Strategic Concept drafters referred to Article 12 in their discussions. The reasoning presented by the Court to support the conclusion that no such will existed is therefore too brief and too discretionary. In *AWACS/Somalia*, a single sentence was used to conclude that there had been no action or declaration by the parties that proved there was such a will.[220] Regrettably, the Court did not, in concrete terms, substantiate this lack of evidence.[221] In the *New Strategic Concept* case, the Court elaborated on its argument a little, but not much: parties lacked the will to amend the North Atlantic Treaty, and the content of the 1999 Strategic Concept did not imply a wish to amend, nor could one be inferred from acts of the parties. The 1999 Strategic Concept is a development and concretisation of the open wording of the Treaty. This flexibility is required to keep the Alliance 'efficient and adaptable', in accordance with its aims.[222] Sauer agrees with the

---

218 P. Sands, 'Article 39 – Convention de Vienne de 1969' in O. Corten and P. Klein (eds.), *op. cit.*, 1536–1537; P. Reuter, *Droit international public*, Paris, P.U.F., 1993, 157. As agreed upon by the ILC in *Yearbook of the International Law Commission*, 1966, vol. II, 253.

219 At NATO, the right to initiative for amendment is given to the Member States only. See A. Peters, 'L'acte constitutif de l'organisation internationale', in E. Lagrange and J.-M. Sorel (eds.), *op. cit.*, 227–228.

220 Last sentence para. 274 *AWACS/Somalia*.

221 Para. 271 *AWACS/Somalia*.

222 This language may well be inspired by the teleological interpretation of constituent treaties and by the doctrine of implied powers, both accepted in international law, e.g. *Reparations for Injuries*, 183. Intriguingly, the doctrine of implied powers emerged from the federalist state theory; J. Klabbers, *op. cit.*, 56; J. Becker, *Die Anwendbarkeit der Theorie von den implied power sim Recht der Europäischen Gemeinschaften*, doctoral dissertation, Münster, University of Münster, Faculty of Law, 1976, 1–43; T. Bauer-Savage, 'Die völkerrechtliche Verwandlung der NATO aus Sicht der U.S. Constitution und des deutschen Grundgesetzes' in X. (ed.), *Europäische Hochschulschriften*, Reihe II, Rechtswissenschaft, Frankfurt am Main, 2005; M. Hodun, *Doctrine of Implied Powers as a Judicial Tool to Build Federal Polities: Comparative Study on the Doctrine of Implied powers in the EU and the United States*

Court, pointing out the fact that the NATO Heads of State and Government had endorsed the 1999 Strategic Concept as part of their Summit meetings without any alteration of the stated goals and purposes of the Alliance. According to Sauer, this shows that an amendment was not wanted. It does not exclude that Heads of State and Government might have *wanted* to change the text informally, but it does show there was no willingness to amend formally.[223] According to Klein and Schmahl, on the other hand, the circumstances show that the 1999 Strategic Concept constitutes a treaty amendment because it was the explicit wish of the NATO Member States to expand NATO's aims to include crisis response operations, which fall outside the scope of Article 5. Counterarguments to this are that there is no documented proof that Allies sought to adopt the Strategic Concept under Article 12 and that a Strategic Concept that was less transformative in nature had been adopted eight years before. Given these facts, it is difficult to contend that the 1999 Strategic Concept constitutes a formal treaty amendment. Statements and interviews with NATO officials show that NATO deliberately never opened up the 1949 Treaty for amendment, out of fear of watering down its provisions.[224] Here is a quote by SHAPE OLA Director Andres Mosquara:

> Nations do not have the appetite. Everyone understands that now, in a community of 30—maybe when they were 12 it would have worked—but when you're 30 nations, those nations will try to incorporate their own interests in the discussions on the amendment. [...] We risk to pollute the Treaty and generate a year of discussions, maybe more, referenda, and we risk having Russia interfering in this.[225]

Here is a 2022 quote by a NATO OLA legal adviser:

> The Treaty is beautiful as it is. No need to touch it. And I think everyone feels that. It's a beautiful piece of work. It gives us anything we need. You know how as soon as you open the treaty [...]. That's also the thing at NATO with this whole consensus decision-making: when you have something, don't open it up. Then you risk introducing certain aspects which you managed to avoid when you initially got into the discussion.[226]

Because NATO did not want to amend the Treaty out of fear of 'opening pandora's box' but did want to change its tasks, it chose a Strategic Concept as

---

of America, doctoral dissertation, Reykjavik, Reykjavik University, Faculty of Law, 2015, 253–294; G. Cerexhe, *Les compétences implicites et leur application en droit belge*, Brussels, Bruylant, 1988, 189.

223 H. Sauer, 'Die NATO und das Verfassungsrecht: neues Konzept – alte Fragen', 326.

224 Mentioned by 4/6 interviewees between June 2022 and November 2023.

225 Interview with Andres Mosquera, head of SHAPE Office of Legal Affairs, online, 10 October 2022.

226 Interview with a NATO OLA legal adviser, Tervuren, 11 July 2022.

the document to do so.[227] The Strategic Concept mentions NATO's 'fundamental tasks', something that is usually defined in the constituent instrument of an international organisation, e.g. Article 1 UN Charter and Articles 43 and 45 TEU. If NATO could have formally amended the Treaty to insert crisis management as a task, it would have, as interviews show.[228] All of this goes to show that there was a wish to informally modify the North Atlantic Treaty. Because formal treaty amendment was *avoided*, one can conclude that the German government's decisions did hollow out the rights of parliament. By insisting that informal treaty amendment falls outside the scope of Article 59(2)(a) Basic Law, the German Court failed to appreciate the realities of international law, in which the parliament's right of participation had been hollowed out. The German Constitutional Court found that the national constitutional limit to the dynamic development of the North Atlantic Treaty had not been violated because the government's approval of the 1999 Strategic Concept respected the Treaty's structural core, which, in the eyes of the Court, is the preservation of peace. It is this purported identification of the Treaty's primary purpose that allowed the Court to conclude there had been no violation of the Basic Law. However, what the main purpose of the North Atlantic Treaty is, ultimately lies in the eye of the beholder. The Court saw the preservation of peace as the Treaty's ultimate objective and concluded on that basis that the crisis response operations mentioned in the 1999 Strategic Concept did not constitute a fundamentally new type of operation. Recall the Court's statement that the violation of Article 24(2) Basic Law did not lie in the 'disturbance of some provisions of the North Atlantic Treaty.' In this statement, the Court basically admitted that provisions of the Treaty had been affected (§ 154 *New Strategic Concept* Case). This statement stands in stark contrast to the Court's position on European integration. In the *Maastricht* judgment, the German Court left the question of what constitutes a disturbance of the provisions of the 1949 Treaty open, and even warned the CJEU that it would not recognise any EU legal acts that exceed the EU's competence in the eyes of the German Court.[229] In addition, many commentators consider the Treaty's principal purpose to be collective self-defence rather than the

227 Interview with a NATO legal adviser, Tervuren, 11 July 2022, interview with Dr. Jamie Shea, online, 12 July 2022 and interview with Andres Mosquera, head of SHAPE Office of Legal Affairs, online, 10 October 2022.

228 Interview with a NATO legal adviser, Tervuren, 11 July 2022, interview with Dr. Jamie Shea, online, 12 July 2022, and interview with Andres Mosquera, head of SHAPE Office of Legal Affairs, online, 10 October 2022.

229 A. Paulus, 'Quo vadis Democratic Control? The Afghanistan Decision of the Bundestag and the Decision of the Federal Constitutional Court in the NATO Strategic Concept Case', *German Law Journal* 2002, § 16. See Germany, Constitutional Court 1993, *Maastricht decision*, BVerfGE 89, 155; M. Wiegandt, 'Germany's International Integration: The Rulings of the German Federal Constitutional Court on the Maastricht Treaty and the Out-of-Area Deployment of German Troops', *American University Journal of International Law and Policy* 1995, 889–916.

preservation of peace, based on an analysis of the Treaty, in particular the Preamble and Articles 4, 5, 6, and 7.[230] This claim has merit. The *travaux préparatoires* show that the drafters intended to create an organisation aimed at collective self-defence, not a security organisation tasked with preserving peace.[231] At the time of the Treaty negotiations in Washington D.C., the latter task had already been entrusted to the UN in the Charter of 1945. Furthermore, a military alliance simply cannot exist within international law if it does not commit itself to the preservation of peace, as this would violate Article 2(4) UN Charter.[232] Moreover, a careful reading of the North Atlantic Treaty shows that the Alliance commits itself to acting in accordance with the objectives of the UN, which certainly include the preservation of peace, but no North Atlantic Treaty Article stipulates an aim to preserve international peace and security as such. Quite on the contrary, Article 7 explicitly states that the primary responsibility for the maintenance of international peace and security lies with the UNSC.[233] By mentioning the UN Charter in the Treaty, the parties made clear that they did not wish to extend NATO's powers to include those of the UN, Paulus argues.[234] NATO itself does not articulate the preservation of peace as its essential purpose either. Its own Strategic Concepts identify NATO's core purposes as:

- safeguarding the freedom and security of its Member States (1991 Strategic Concept, § 15);
- safeguarding the freedom and security of all its Members by political and military means (1999 Strategic Concept, § 6);
- safeguarding the freedom and security of its Member States by political and military means (2010 Strategic Concept, § 1);
- safeguarding the freedom and security of Allies. Its key purpose and greatest responsibility is to ensure our collective defence, against all threats, from all directions (2022 Strategic Concept, § 1).

---

230 A. Abbas, *Regional Organisations and the Development of Collective Security: Beyond Chapter VIII of the UN Charter*, Oxford, Hart Publishing, 2004, 14; J. Varwick and W. Woyke, 'NATO 2000, Transatlantische Sicherheit im Wandel', in K. Schubert and G. Wewer (eds.), *Analysen, Politik – Geselschaft, Wirtschaft*, Opladen, 1999, 46; I. Dekker and E. Myjer, 'Air Strikes on Bosnian Positions: Is NATO Also Legally the Proper Instrument of the UN?', *Leiden Journal of International Law* 1996, 414–415. See in a similar vein H. Sauer, 'Die NATO und das Verfassungsrecht: neues Konzept – alte Fragen', 345; see for a nuanced position E. De Wet, 'The Relationship between the Security Council and Regional Organizations during Enforcement Action under Chapter VII of the United Nations Charter', *Nordic Journal of International Law* 2002, 8.

231 Minutes of the Third Meeting of the Washington Exploratory Talks on Security, July 7, 1948, 10 a. m. in *Foreign Relations of the United States, 1948, Western Europe, Volume III* (U.S. State Department Office of the Historian).

232 H. Sauer, 'Die NATO und das Verfassungsrecht: neues Konzept – alte Fragen', *op. cit.*, 322.

233 *Cf.* para. 15 Strategic Concept 1999.

234 A. Paulus, 'Quo vadis Democratic Control? The Afghanistan Decision of the Bundestag and the Decision of the Federal Constitutional Court in the NATO Strategic Concept Case', § 30.

Furthermore, the German Court found the preservation of peace to be the Treaty's core purpose, but it did not explore or define the meaning of the term 'peace', a very vague notion, even though doing so was crucial for the Court's argument to succeed.[235] In addition, a careful and strict reading of Article 24(2) Basic Law reveals that the objective of the maintenance of peace is a requirement for Germany to be able to join and remain in a mutual collective security system; it is not a requirement for that system itself. It is difficult to legitimise NATO's power to conduct NA5CROs with reference to the Preamble alone. Indeed, preambles that commit organisations to the preservation of peace, democracy, and the rule of law are common to many constituent treaties of international organisations. Examples are the preambles of the OSCE, TEU, and WEU. But a preamble is not legally part of the treaty. It serves as an interpretation tool for its treaty (Article 31.2 VCLT).[236] Legally, it is difficult to argue that Article 4 of the Treaty implies the power to conduct NA5CROs, as this Article mentions consultation rather than concrete actions (such as deploying AWACS aircraft).[237] According to Sauer, the artificial outcome of the *New Strategic Concept* case can be partially explained politically. He suspects that the Court may have based its judgment on what it deemed politically opportune. After all, all political parties except the applicant (SPD) wanted the government to approve the Strategic Concept. It would be dire if the reasoning of the Constitutional Court's had been influenced by political considerations.

4.6. INTERIM CONCLUSION

The *New Strategic Concept* ruling leaves one with the impression that the German Court used forced legal reasoning to arrive at its desired conclusion. It did so by knowingly interpreting Article 59(1)2 Basic Law restrictively and by identifying the preservation of peace as the North Atlantic Treaty's primary objective. The Court's reasoning excludes from the scope of Article 24(2) Basic Law almost any shift in powers and fundamental tasks, no matter how profound, as long as NATO remains committed to preserving peace, a vague term if ever there was one. Never mind that neither the North Atlantic Treaty nor the Strategic Concept defines the preservation of peace as NATO's core task, or that the Treaty explicitly states that this task belongs to the UNSC. Aditionally, the reference to international peace in the Preamble is a standard reference in international constituent treaties and a precondition for military alliances to lawfully exist

235 A. Paulus 'Quo vadis Democratic Control? The Afghanistan Decision of the Bundestag and the Decision of the Federal Constitutional Court in the NATO Strategic Concept Case', § 32.

236 J. Wouters, C. Ryngaert, T. Ruys and G. De Baere, *op. cit.*, 100. See also M. Hulme, 'Preambles in Treaty Interpretation', *University of Pennsylvania Law Review* 2016, 1281.

237 S. Bölingen, *op. cit.*, 64–71. See for a slightly different view S. Bumgardner, 'Article 4 of the North Atlantic Treaty', *Emory International Law Review* 2019, 80.

under Article 2(4) UN Charter. With legal reasoning like this, one can be almost certain that the *Bundesverfassungsgericht* will declare any future NATO Strategic Concept as falling within the framework of the North Atlantic Treaty. The rulings reflect a democratic deficit: the decision-making power lies entirely in the hands of the executive, while NATO citizens, represented in their national parliaments, have no means of voicing their opinions or concerns when the Alliance begins to conduct new types of operations. The fact that the Court has no regard for the informal mechanisms of international lawmaking and treaty amendment has resulted in the rights of the *Bundestag* being hollowed out. In the last of the four cases, *Turkey/AWACS*, the Court did finally acknowledge the realities of international lawmaking, but rendered its judgment without actually taking those realities into account:

> The Bundestag will scarcely be able to exercise an effective influence on the NATO system of mutual collective security; it is only the German Federal Government that participates in the decision-making at NATO, and Parliament may not subsequently and unilaterally deviate from the decisions made there without causing political damage to NATO and thus to the Federal Republic of Germany. For this reason, the German Bundestag is often forced to monitor the political actions in an alliance of systems which is shaped by the executive of the Member States, limiting itself to the indirectly exercising its influence.[238]

5. CONCLUSION

The analysis laid out in this chapter has yielded an answer to the research question formulated at its outset: does NATO's expansion of powers to include NA5CROs violate the principle of attributed powers? The power to conduct NA5CROs is not attributed, as it is not mentioned anywhere in the North Atlantic Treaty, nor in any other NATO legal instrument. This does not necessarily mean that the principle has been violated, as the power could be an implied one. The current case law, with its emphasis on the idea that implied powers are those necessary for the efficient functioning of an organisation, is rather convenient for NATO. NATO can easily argue that carrying out a NA5CRO is essential to prevent a situation from escalating into one that would require the invocation of Article 5, as it did when it warned that the Balkan conflict would spread to NATO territory if NATO neglects to intervene. Speed and efficiency are convenient arguments to make in the domain of security. But even if the argument were granted, it does not necessarily mean that this implied power is lawful or desirable. First of all, the cited interviews and the German case law revealed that NATO avoided invoking Article 12 in 1999, so one could argue that NATO violated the higher

---

238 Para. 67 *Turkey/AWACS*.

norm of Article 12 of its own constituent instrument (Articles 5 VCLT and 2(b) ARIO). Moreover, one could argue that it is unnecessary for NATO to have the power to conduct NA5CROs, because its Member States can form coalitions of the willing to carry out these operations if there is a lawful basis for it. One could also argue that this power is unessential because there can never be *ex ante* or *ex post* proof that the operation really was essential to avoid the invocation of Article 5, seeing that these strategic decisions are of a technical, military, and classified nature. Moreover, implied powers are there to give effect to what States agreed to by becoming parties to the constituent instrument. The North Atlantic Treaty's *travaux préparatoires*, the Cold War Strategic Concepts, and the sole reliance on deterrence during the Cold War attest to the fact that the signatories wanted to create an alliance to defend themselves collectively, not a fully-fledged security organisation. Neither can NATO rely on the supporting argument of established practice to support its claim of implied powers. Since conducting NA5CROs is an operational matter and not an administrative or organisational one, NATO cannot pretend that conducting NA5CROs is a rule that it feels obliged to follow, like most practices accepted by the ICJ. Even if one were to agree that conducting NA5CROs is an implied power, in accordance with the principle of attributed powers, it still creates a democratic deficit. It amounts to an informal treaty amendment used to avoid a formal one. The CJEU's Opinion 94/2 demonstrated that implied powers can be denied when they are used to avoid formal treaty amendment. After all, formal amendment is what gives legitimacy to the legal acts of international organisations. Without it, legitimacy must be attained in some other way. Ironically, the case law of the *Bundesverfassungsgericht* demonstrates that NATO Member States wished to informally amend the North Atlantic Treaty by adopting the 1999 Strategic Concept. The only way the Court could avoid the conclusion that Article 59(2)(1) Basic Law had been violated was to firmly limit the Article's scope to formal treaty amendment. In doing so, the court failed to appreciate the realities of international law-making, where practice sometimes replaces treaty amendment. In addition, the Court's argument that the dynamic interpretation of the Treaty does not exceed the limits of the Treaty's structural core does not hold water either. The Court forced its way to the conclusion that the Basic Law had not been violated. It did this by identifying the preservation of peace as the Treaty's structural core, without clarifying this vague term and ignoring the fact that neither the Treaty nor the Strategic Concepts define the preservation of peace as NATO's core task. The 1949 Treaty explicitly gives this task to the UNSC. The reference to international peace in the Preamble is a standard reference in international constituent treaties and a precondition for military alliances to lawfully exist under Article 2(4) UN Charter. By avoiding treaty amendment and expanding NATO's tasks beyond the scope of the Treaty, the 1999 Strategic Concept sidestepped the participation of a billion NATO citizens through their parliaments. In the words of Jan Klabbers, when an organisation transforms itself by bypassing formal amendment and instead developing a practice, 'it may generate a loss of legitimacy of the organisation, affecting its viability.'[239] The German Court's contention that parliament is not defenceless against the risk of exclusion should be criticised too: parliament cannot avoid the expansion of NATO's tasks by approving or disapproving the annual budget. The power of the purse, which the European Parliament has in the domains of security and defence too, is seen as an insufficient form of control. While it is true that accession protocols are ratified by the national parliaments of NATO Member States, these have no bearing whatsoever on the expansion of NATO's tasks. The fact that the German constitution requires prior parliamentary approval for any deployment of the *Bundeswehr* is explained by the unique German context. Such deployment is not the same as the adoption of a Strategic Concept that opens the door to many future deployments. Lastly, it is naive of the Court to claim that the German representatives at NATO can exert pressure to initiate the Article 12 process, as NATO is a consensus-based organisation. Insiders know that opening up the treaty for amendment is a no-go.

[239] J. Klabbers, *op. cit.*, 78–79.

CHAPTER 3

NATO'S INSTITUTIONAL FRAMEWORK: THROUGH THICK AND THIN?

1. INTRODUCTION

In December 2021 the multinational fuel company Supreme brought a case against SHAPE, NATO's military headquarters, before the CJEU. The case had been preceded by years of complicated legal proceedings in which Supreme demanded billions of dollars in damages from SHAPE before multiple Dutch courts. Interestingly, the reason these procedures had been so lengthy and so costly (a SHAPE legal adviser entrusted the author with the knowledge that a person was hired to work on the case full-time)[240] was that NATO has no basic text that grants SHAPE immunity from jurisdiction, even though this is a fundamental protection mechanism in public international law and international institutional law. Supreme, aware of this loophole, continued its lawsuit against SHAPE for years. The Supreme saga is just one manifestation of a broader phenomenon: whereas the North Atlantic Treaty is very 'thin' on institutional issues, NATO's present-day structure is very 'thick'. The 1949 Treaty establishes NATO's institutional framework in exceptionally vague terms. The institutional provisions of constituent treaties of international organisations are usually much more detailed.[241] Examples are Article XIII Modified Brussels Treaty (MBT), Articles 7–31 UN Charter, Article 13–19 TEU, Article 5 Constitution of Interpol, and Article 51 Charter of the Organisation of American States.[242] In its *Articles on the Responsibility of International Organizations*, the International Law Commission (ILC) mentions Article 9 North Atlantic Treaty as the prime

---

240 Interview with head of the SHAPE Office of Legal Affairs, Andres Mosquera, online, 10 October 2022.

241 *Cf.* N. Blokker, 'Constituent Instruments' in J. Cogan, I. Hurd and I. Johnstone (eds.), *op. cit.*, 946 and F. Fabbrini, 'Do NATO Obligations Trump European Budgetary Constraints?', *Harvard National Security Journal* 2018, 131.

242 See footnote 70, Commentary 20 to Article 2 Articles on State Responsibility with Commentaries. Text adopted by the International Law Commission at its sixty-third session, in 2011, and submitted to the General Assembly as a part of the Commission's report covering the work of that session (A/66/10). The report, which also contains commentaries to the Articles (para. 88), appears in *Yearbook of the International Law Commission*, 2011, vol. II, Part Two.

example of an 'economical' institutional provision.[243] Indeed, the only body established by the Treaty is the North Atlantic Council (NAC). Article 9 states:

> The Parties hereby establish a Council, on which each of them shall be represented, to consider matters concerning the implementation of this Treaty. The Council shall be so organised as to be able to meet promptly at any time. The Council shall set up such subsidiary bodies as may be necessary; in particular it shall establish immediately a defence committee which shall recommend measures for the implementation of Articles 3 and 5.[244]

Despite the provision's exceptional brevity, the Alliance has developed a sizable institutional architecture composed of various policy-making bodies, working groups, agencies, military commands, and an International Staff. There is also the little-known NATO Parliamentary Assembly (NATO PA). This multitude of NATO bodies, with its detailed division of decision-making powers, can lead to confused reporting in the media about which NATO organs do what, exactly. The reporting on the war in Ukraine is a recent example of this. The reason for this is that the institutional vacuum left by Article 9 has been filled not by publicly consultable treaty amendments or separate legal instruments, but by NAC decisions and resolutions, multilateral agreements (such as the 1951 Ottawa Agreement), and established practice (such as Article 5 VCLT and Article 2(b) ARIO). It has not yet been investigated whether NATO's institutional transformation took place in accordance with the fundamental principles of international institutional law, specifically 1) the lawful establishment of subsidiary bodies and 2) the lawful delegation of powers to these bodies. This chapter aims to address this lacuna.

2. THE NORTH ATLANTIC COUNCIL

The North Atlantic Treaty has only one institutional provision and it is a brief one. The 1949 Treaty exclusively establishes the NAC, which is endowed with the constitutional power to set up 'such subsidiary bodies as may be necessary' (Article 9). The 2019 NATO Encyclopedia explains that the NAC is the principal political decision-making body within NATO and the ultimate authority at the head of a network of committees.[245] The NAC may discuss and decide on

243 See footnote 70, Commentary 20 to Article 2 Articles on State Responsibility with Commentaries. Text adopted by the International Law Commission at its sixty-third session, in 2011, and submitted to the General Assembly as a part of the Commission's report covering the work of that session (A/66/10). The report, which also contains commentaries to the articles (para. 88), appears in *Yearbook of the International Law Commission*, 2011, vol. II, Part Two.

244 Article 9 North Atlantic Treaty.

245 *NATO Encyclopedia* 2019, 394.

all aspects of the Organisation's activities. Its discussions are often based on reports and recommendations prepared by the committees.[246] Decisions made by the NAC are the expression of the collective will of all Member States, as these decisions are made by consensus.[247] The Secretary General chairs the NAC. Its decisions have the same status and validity, regardless of which level it meets at.[248] The NAC meets at three levels: weekly at the Ambassadorial level (i.e. the Permanent Representatives of the Member States), several times a year at the level of Foreign and Defence Ministers, and occasionally at the level of the Heads of State and Government (the latter meetings are known as NATO Summits). Interestingly—and uniquely—the NAC has no written rules of procedure. The three EU institutions, the UNGA, and the UNSC, in contrast, have their Rules of Procedures.[249] The need for such rules was never felt, said Lord Ismay, the first NATO Secretary General, in 1955.[250] The discussions held between the drafters of the Treaty on whether or not to include a Member suspension or expulsion clause—in the end no such clause was included—show that the negotiators were explicitly opposed to drafting written rules of procedure for the NAC. The aim was to 'keep the body as flexible as possible' and to 'avoid that any potential internal disagreement goes public.'[251] This section will analyse formerly top-secret documents to uncover the drafters' intent behind Article 9 and the institutionalisation of the NAC. The archival records of the Washington Security Talks, which produced the North Atlantic Treaty, show how Article 9 came about during negotiations of Article 4, the Treaty's consultation provision.[252]

---

246 *NATO Encyclopedia* 2019, 394.

247 *Cf.* A. Verhelst and S. Trifunovska, *op. cit.*, 59 and *NATO Encyclopedia* 2019, 162–163.

248 *NATO Encyclopedia* 2019, 394 and ILC 2011, *Comments and observations received from international organizations to the Draft Articles on the Responsibility of International Organizations,* sixty-third session, UN. Doc. A/CN.4/637 and Add. 1, § 1, 139.

249 See European Commission, Rules of Procedure of the Commission, *Official Journal of the European Communities* L. 308–26, 8 December 2000; European Council and the Council, Rules of Procedure of the European Council and the Council, *Official Journal of the European Union* OJ L. 315, 2 December 2009, 52 and OJ L. 325, 11 December 2009, 36, corrigendum, OJ L. 55, 5 March 2010, 83; European Parliament, Rules of Procedure of the European Parliament July 2024, available online at www.europarl.europa.eu/rules/rules20240716/Rules20240716_EN.pdf (last accessed January 2025); UN, Rules of Procedure of the General Assembly (embodying amendments and additions adopted by the General Assembly up to September 2016), UN. Doc. A/520/Rev.18*, 2016. The UN Security Council, by contrast, has only provisional rules of procedure, see UN. Doc. S/96/Rev.7, 1982 (embodying amendments and additions adopted by the Security Council up to December 1982).

250 Lord Ismay, NATO: *The first five years 1949–1954*, Brussels, 1955, 60 (available via the NATO Online Archives).

251 See Telegram of the Ambassador in the U.S. to the Secretary of State for External Affairs, 12 January 1949, in *CDER*, vol. 15, 497.

252 One can divide the intergovernmental meetings held in Washington D.C. that produced the North Atlantic Treaty into four stages. The first stage was the Three Powers Meeting which occurred in the Pentagon between the U.S., the U.K. and Canada (22 March– 1 April 1948). The second stage was the Six Powers Meeting between the U.S., U.K., Canada, France, Belgium and the Netherlands (6 July–10 September 1948). The third stage was the Seven

Having considered a draft version of Article 4, a representative of the Canadian government observed on 13 December 1948:

> The proposed Treaty contemplated consultation between the parties in the event of a threat to peace anywhere in the world. This would be a matter more for Foreign Ministers or their representatives than for Defence Ministers or Chiefs of Staff. There should therefore be, as the senior agency under the treaty, some sort of Council on a ministerial level made up of Foreign Ministers or their deputed representatives. This Council would have the task of creating any other agencies necessary to give effect to the treaty.[253]

The Canadian proposal to provide the parties with a decision-making body made its way into the top-secret Report of the International Working Group to the Ambassadors Committee. The Ambassadors approved the draft and sent it to their respective governments on 24 December 1948.[254] The draft version of Article 8, which is now Article 9, read as follows:

> The Parties hereby establish a Council, on which each of them shall be represented, to deal with matters concerning the implementation of this Treaty. The Council shall be so organized as to be able to meet promptly at any time. The Council shall set up such subsidiary bodies as may be necessary; in particular it shall establish immediately a defence committee which shall recommend measures for the implementation of Articles 3 and 5.[255]

This is identical to the wording of the current Article 9, with the exception of the phrase 'to deal with matters', which was replaced by the phrase 'to consider matters'. Interestingly, the preparatory works show that this institutional provision was one of the two draft articles (out of ten) that were accepted without

---

Powers Meetings that included Luxembourg (10–24 December 1948). The fourth stage was the Seven to Eight Powers Meetings from 10 January–28 March 1949 (Norway joined the discussions on 4 March 1949). Note how it was in principle the bilateral ambassadors to the U.S. who were present at the discussion. See also Minutes of the First Meeting of the Washington Exploratory Talks on Security, 6 July 1948, 11:30 a.m, *Foreign Relations of the United States, 1948, Western Europe, Volume III*. One can find the minutes of nearly all meetings of the Washington Security Talks, detailed as to the AM and PM session on a specific day, in the Office of the Historian of the U.S. State Department. See also E. Reid, *Time of Fear and Hope: the Making of the North Atlantic Treaty*, Toronto, McClelland and Steward, 1977, 71; C. Wiebes and B. Zeeman, 'The Pentagon Negotiations March 1948: The Launching of the North Atlantic Treaty', *International Affairs* 1983, 356 and see S. Bumgardner, 'Article 4 of the North Atlantic Treaty', 73.

253 Minutes of the Ninth Meeting of the Washington Exploratory Talks on Security, 13 December 1948, 2:30 p.m., Doc. 840.20/12-1348, *Foreign Relations of the United States, 1948, Western Europe, Volume III* (U.S. State Department Office of the Historian).

254 Washington Security Talks, Report of the International Working Group to the Ambassadors' Committee, 24 December 1948, Doc. 840.20/12-2448, *Foreign Relations of the United States, 1948, Western Europe, Volume III* (U.S. State Department Office of the Historian).

255 Annex A to the Report of the International Working Group to the Ambassadors' Committee.

comment.[256] The French representatives suggested having an Article 8*bis* to refer disputes to the ICJ, similar to Article 36 ICJ Statute, and to give the NAC powers of conciliation to this end. The French believed the North Atlantic pact deserved the 'appropriate machinery of an organisation'.[257] The suggestion was not warmly welcomed by other representatives. In their words:

> The Council might thus duplicate and perhaps confuse the operation of existing treaties of conciliation between parties to the pact or of permanent agencies already established. Furthermore, the possibility of disputes between parties to the pact of such a serious nature as to defy solutions by these existing agencies or under existing treaties seemed to some members of the Committee so remote as to make it unnecessary to establish a further agency of conciliation as between the parties.[258]

Negotiators also believed that referrals to the ICJ might entail protracted delays in the Treaty negotiations.[259] Ultimately, no conciliatory powers were given to the NAC. On 4 April 1949 the North Atlantic Treaty was signed in Washington D.C. by 12 countries. An analysis of the minutes of the Washington Security Talks, which produced the Treaty, suggests that the Treaty was drawn up with an alliance in mind rather than an international organisation. Nonetheless, the drafters did provide the option of moulding their alliance into an international organisation when they deemed it appropriate, as Smith confirms.[260] This was not a question of 'if', as the Memorandum by the Participants of 6 July–9 September 1948 makes clear.[261] Draft Article 12 of the Memorandum leaves room for a provision to establish agencies necessary for the effective implementation of the Treaty.[262] The Memorandum also stipulates that the arrangement should provide *adequate machinery* for implementing its terms.[263] The passages make clear that the option of institutionalising the Alliance was contemplated from the outset, although the Washington Security Talks were dominated by an 'alliance mindset', as pointed out by SHAPE legal adviser Moquera.[264]

---

256 Annex B to the Report of the International Working Group to the Ambassadors' Committee.

257 Text taken from Annex B to the Report of the International Working Group to the Ambassadors' Committee.

258 Annex B to the Report of the International Working Group to the Ambassadors' Committee.

259 Annex B to the Report of the International Working Group to the Ambassadors' Committee.

260 M. Smith, *NATO in the First Decade after the Cold War*, Dordrecht, Kluwer, 2000, 1.

261 At the time a top-secret document, Memorandum by the Participants in the Washington Security Talks, 6 July 6 to 9 September 9 1948, Submitted to Their Respective Governments for Study and Comment, 9 September 1948, Doc. 840.20/9–945, *Foreign Relations of the United States, 1948, Western Europe, Volume III* (U.S. State Department Office of the Historian).

262 Draft Article 12 Annex A, Memorandum by the Participants in the Washington Security Talks.

263 Para. 8.7 Part III ('Nature of a possible North Atlantic Security Arrangement'), Memorandum by the Participants in the Washington Security Talks.

264 A. Mosquera, 'The North Atlantic Treaty: Article 9 and NATO's Institutionalization', *Emory International Law Review* 2019, 150.

The first meeting of the NAC took place in Washington D.C. on 17 September 1949. The Council was composed of the Foreign Ministers of the 12 signatory States. Interestingly, the NAC declared its terms of reference to be the North Atlantic Treaty.[265] In terms of how far the Council's competencies extend, this is not without implications (see below). To this day the Council (uniquely) has no terms of reference other than the North Atlantic Treaty itself. Concerning its functioning, the Council decided that the NAC would be composed of the Foreign Ministers of the 12 Member States and that it would meet once a year in ordinary session. The Council set up a Defence Committee and a Financial and Economic Committee on the basis of Article 9.[266] However, the existing institutional framework was soon felt to be too cumbersome to deal with everyday issues.[267] New security challenges, like the outbreak of the Korean War and the situation on the European Eastern flank, made Allies on both sides of the Atlantic realise that, to combat the external threat effectively, a fully-fledged political and military organisation was needed.[268] The NAC Ministerial Meeting of February 1952 in Lisbon was important to this end, as it produced far-reaching decisions regarding the reorganisation of the civilian structure of NATO. Two decisions were especially important: first of all, the appointment of Permanent Representatives of the 14 Member States, which meant that the NAC began to function in permanent session,[269] and, secondly, the appointment of a Secretary General and the strengthening of the International Secretariat.[270] On 28 April 1952, three weeks after these changes, the reassembled NAC held its first meeting in Paris.[271]

The sources of the Council's powers are Article 9 and the integral North Atlantic Treaty, which constitute the Council's terms of reference. In line with the principle of attributed powers, the powers of plenary organs are derived from

---

265 Final Communiqué of the first Session of the North Atlantic Council (1949), available online at www.nato.int/cps/en/natohq/official_texts_17117.htm (last accessed January 2025).

266 NATO Directive D-1/4 and Directive D-1/3 (available via the NATO Online Archives); *Documents of the Year 1949–1952, Part II, Series Reviewed*, § 90; NATO, *Facts and Figure* 1989, 36 and L. Schaus, 'Le Conseil de l'Atlantique Nord, son fondement et ses structures, ses compétences et ses missions', 345–346.

267 *NATO Facts and Figures* 1989, 324.

268 L. Kaplan, *op. cit.*, 4–19; A. Mosquera, 'The North Atlantic Treaty: Article 9 and NATO's Institutionalization', 8; NATO, *Facts and Figures* 1989, 37; Z. Barany, 'NATO at Sixty', *Journal of Democracy* 2009, 109. See for the valuable work by historians on this point W. Lafeber, 'NATO and the Korean War: A Context', *Diplomatic History* 1989, 461–77; L. Kaplan, *NATO before the Korean War: April 1949-June 1950*, Kent, Kent University State Press, 2013 and J. Milloy, *The North Atlantic Treaty Organization 1948–1957: Community or Alliance?*, Montreal, McGill-Queen's University Press, 2006 and L. Risso, 'I am the Servant of the Council: Lord Ismay and the Making of the NATO International Staff', *Contemporary European History* 2019, 334.

269 NATO, Final Communiqué of the Ministerial Meeting held in Lisbon, 20–25 February 1952, § 7.

270 Final Communiqué of the Ministerial Meeting held in Lisbon (1952), § 7.

271 Lord Ismay, *op. cit.*, 56; and *NATO Facts and Figures* 1989, 44.

the constituent treaty.[272] These powers can be expressly stated or can be implied on the basis of the doctrine of implied powers.[273] An example of the latter is the Administrative Tribunal of the United Nations, created by UNGA and validated by the ICJ in *Effect of Awards* (see below). The power of an organ to adopt a certain institutional act must be assessed in light of the written rules of the organisation and of its established practice (Articles 5 VCLT and 2(b) ARIO).[274] Significantly, the ICJ has formulated a general presumption of competence with regard to international organs.[275] This presumption, reaffirmed and broadened by both the ICJ and the CJEU, generally applies to the institutional acts adopted in accordance with the rules of procedure of organisations.[276] To understand the extent of the NAC's attributed powers, we turn to Article 9:

> The Parties hereby establish a Council, on which each of them shall be represented, *to consider matters concerning the implementation of this Treaty.*[277] The Council shall be so organised as to be able to meet promptly at any time. *The Council shall set up such subsidiary bodies as may be necessary*[278]; in particular it shall establish immediately a defence committee which shall recommend measures for the implementation of Articles 3 and 5.

Article 9 gives the NAC the power to consider matters concerning the implementation of the Treaty. The 2019 NATO Encyclopedia states that NAC discussions and decisions 'cover all aspects of the Organisation's activities'.[279] Because the 13 other Treaty Articles refer to 'the Parties' and not 'the Council', the NAC can basically do just about anything the contracting parties authorise it to do. This power is limited only by the political and military subject matter of the Alliance itself, as Boeva points out.[280] The terminology used indicates that the contracting parties were expected to take up their roles as States rather than as fully-fledged Member States of the Organisation. One should conclude that Article 9 defines the Council's powers broadly rather than specifically. The only specific power that the North Atlantic Treaty explicitly attributes to the NAC

272 C.F. Amerasinghe, *op. cit.*, 135; N. Blokker and H. Schermers, *op. cit.*, § 209, 165–167 and § 217, 177–178.

273 P. Sands and P. Klein, *op. cit.*, 295; C.F. Amerasinghe, *op. cit.*, 135.

274 P. Sands and P. Klein, *op. cit.*, 295; R. Bernhardt, 'Ultra Vires activities of International Organisations' in J. Makarczyk (ed.), *Theory of International Law at the Threshold of the 21st Century: Essays in Honour of Krzysztof Skubiszewski*, The Hague, Kluwer, 1996, 602 and read the Conclusions of Advocate General Tesauro in case C-327/91 before the CJEU (*France v Commission*, E.C.R. (1994), I-3658, § 29).

275 See ICJ *Certain Expenses*, 168 and P. Sands and P. Klein, *op. cit.*, 295.

276 CJEU, *Consorzio cooperative d'Abruzzo*, E.C.R. (1987), I-1019–1021, C-15/85; CJEU, *Commission v BASF et al.*, E.C.R. (1994), I-2616–2617, C-137/92 and ICJ *Namibia*, 22, § 20.

277 Emphasis added.

278 Emphasis added.

279 *NATO Encyclopedia* 2018, 395.

280 A. Boeva, 'What is NATO HQ', *NATO Legal Gazette* 2013, 21. *Cf.* D. Fleck, *The Handbook of the Law of Visiting Forces*, Oxford, Oxford University Press, 2018, 459.

is the authority to set up subsidiary bodies as may be necessary. Over the past 76 years the Council has created a sizable institutional architecture, composed of a detailed committee system, an International Staff and a NATO Administrative Tribunal. Whether this was done in accordance with the fundamental principles of international institutional law will now be examined.

3. THE NATO SUBSIDIARY BODIES

No body has ever been created within NATO by amending the North Atlantic Treaty. All subsidiary bodies were created by the NAC. This raises a few questions. What is the nature and scope of the NAC's authority to establish subsidiary bodies? While the UN Charter gives the UNGA and the UNSC both the general and the specific authority to set up subsidiary organs (*cf.* Article 7(2), 22, and 29 UN Charter), Article 9 North Atlantic Treaty grants the NAC only the general authority ('as may be necessary'). In any case, the NAC's general authority of establishment is not without limits: as the principal body, the NAC must itself possess, under the constituent instrument, either the expressed or the implied power which it seeks to delegate.[281] This follows from the principle that the authority of principal bodies to establish subsidiary bodies is, in itself, insufficient for the lawful establishment thereof.[282] This section will examine whether the establishment of and the delegation of powers to the committees, the NATO International Staff, and the NATO Administrative Tribunal occurred in accordance with the fundamental principles of international institutional law. Regarding the question of establishment, it is widely agreed upon between international institutional legal scholars what the preconditions are for the lawful establishment of subsidiary bodies.[283] Caution is due, however, as the following analysis draws on case law developed largely in the context of the UN. It should not be assumed that those preconditions can be straightforwardly applied to other international

---

281 D. Sarooshi, 'Delegation to UN Subsidiary Organs', in D. Sarooshi (ed)., *The United Nations and the Development of Collective Security*, Oxford, Oxford University Press, 1999, 93-94 and J. Dutheil de la Rochere, 'Article 7' in J. Cot and A. Pellet (eds.), *La Charte des Nations Unies*, Paris, Economica, 1991, 218.

282 As explained by D. Bowett, *United Nations Forces: a Legal Study of United Nations Practice*, London, Stevens, 1964, 178.

283 The following analysis draws heavily on the valuable work of Sarooshi, namely the article 'The Legal Framework Governing United Nations Subsidiary Organs' published in the *British Yearbook of International Law* 1996 and the chapter entitled 'Delegation to UN Subsidiary Organs', in the book of his hand, *The United Nations and the Development of Collective Security*, published in Oxford with Oxford University Press in 1999. See also R. Higgins, P. Webb et al., *op. cit.*, § 6.04, 154–155; D. Sarooshi, 'The Legal Framework Governing United Nations Subsidiary Organs', *British Yearbook of International Law* 1996, 416–421; D. Sarooshi, 'Delegation to UN Subsidiary Organs', in D. Sarooshi (ed.), *op. cit.*, 89–92; UN, *Repertory of Practice of United Nations Organs*, vol. I, 1966–1969, 224.

organisations. Keeping in mind that the NAC is NATO's principal body, the preconditions can be summarised as follows:

1. The subsidiary body shall be established by the principal body.[284]
2. The subsidiary body shall operate under the authority and control of the principal body.[285] This entails that the principal body can determine the membership, structure, mandate, and the duration of existence of the subsidiary body.[286]
3. The establishment of the subsidiary body may not violate the delimitation of constituent powers between the principal organs.[287] As there is only one principal body within NATO, this issue does not arise and will not be considered in the remainder of this section.

Regarding the issue of delegation, it is largely agreed upon that, when a principal body has the general authority to establish a subsidiary body, it also has the competence to delegate powers to that subsidiary body.[288] In the context of the UN, both practice and case law confirm this.[289] There are two generally accepted limits to the power of delegation:

---

284 D. Sarooshi, 'Delegation to UN Subsidiary Organs' in D. Sarooshi (ed.), *op. cit.*, 119; N. Blokker and H. Schermers, *op. cit.*, § 205, 163 and § 1201, 787; UN, *United Nations Juridical Yearbook*, 2000, 354–358; S. Torres Bernárdez, 'Subsidiary Organs' in R. Dupuy (ed.), *op. cit.*, 148–149 and C. Colliard, *Institutions des relations internationales*, Paris, Dalloz, 1978, 656–657.

285 D. Sarooshi, 'Delegation to UN Subsidiary Organs' in D. Sarooshi (ed.), *op. cit.*, 128–129; R. Higgins, P. Webb et al., *op. cit.*, § 6.06, 155 and § 11.35, 399; Article I.c Ottawa Agreement. For the UN context see UN, *Repertory of Practice of United Nations Organs*, vol. I, 1966–1969, 224; Memorandum to the Representative of the Director General of the International Atomic Energy Agency to the United Nations, *United Nations Juridical Yearbook*, 1982, 164 and 182; Dissenting Opinion by Judge Hackworth to ICJ *Effect of Awards* (p. 79) but see also S. Torres Bernárdez, 'Subsidiary Organs' in R. Dupuy (ed.), *op. cit.*, 112–113 and N. Bentwich and A. Martin, *A Commentary on the Charter of the United Nations*, Abingdon, Routledge, 2002; Memorandum to the Secretary of ECOSOC, *United Nations Juridical Yearbook*, 1984, 135 and 168–169; UN, *United Nations Juridical Yearbook*, 2000, 357.

286 *Cf.* ICJ *Effects of Awards,* 61. See also D. Sarooshi, 'Delegation to UN Subsidiary Organs' in D. Sarooshi (ed.), *op. cit.*, 130 and 133; UN, *United Nations Juridical Yearbook*, 2000, 357; R. Higgins, P. Webb et al., *op. cit.*, § 6.06, 155 and § 11.35, 399.

287 D. Sarooshi, 'Delegation to UN Subsidiary Organs' in D. Sarooshi (ed.), *op. cit.*, 89. According to Sarooshi, an additional element is required in defining a subsidiary organ: the subsidiary organ shall possess a certain degree of independence from its principal organ, *ibid.*, 89. See also R. Higgins, P. Webb et al., *op. cit.*, § 6.06, 155.

288 D. Sarooshi, 'Delegation to UN Subsidiary Organs' in D. Sarooshi (ed.), *op. cit.*, 100; D. Bowett, *op. cit.*, 178; N. Blokker and H. Schermers, *op. cit.*, § 224, 181; F. Seyersted, *Objective International Personality of Intergovernmental Organizations*, Copenhagen, Krohns Bogtrykkeri, 1964, 111; G. Meier, 'Das Recht der Internationaler Organisationen zur Schaffung und Bevollmächtigung einiger Organe', *Archiv des Völkerrechts* 1964/65, 14–33 and J. Makarczyk, 'La création des organes subsidiaires et les statuts des organisations internationales', *Polish Yearbook of International Law* 1972–73, 183–298.

289 D. Sarooshi, 'Delegation to UN Subsidiary Organs' in D. Sarooshi (ed.), *op. cit.*, 100; UN, *United Nations Juridical Yearbook*, 1982, 164–165 and 167–168 and see ICJ *Certain Expenses*, 151 and 167.

1. The principal body cannot implicitly or expressly delegate more powers than it has pursuant to the constituent instrument (*cf.* the general principle of law '*nemo dot quod non habet*').[290]
2. In principle, responsibility cannot be transferred.[291]

3.1. THE NATO COMMITTEES

NATO committees are the advisory bodies doing the preparatory work of exchanging information, consulting, negotiating, drafting reports, recommendations, and decisions, and informing the NAC.[292] Every NATO Member State has a representative at all levels of the committee system, in the fields of NATO activity in which it takes part.[293] This makes all NATO committees plenary in nature. The NAC used its authority, provided by Article 9 of the Treaty, to establish all the currently existing committees.[294] Consequently, all NATO committees are subsidiary bodies, in the sense of Article 9 of the Treaty, Article I.c Ottawa Agreement, and as the term is understood in international institutional law. The committee system in its entirety is subject to the NAC. The committees are part of either the civilian organisation or the military organisation.[295] Strictly speaking, it would be more accurate to use the term 'North Atlantic Council committees.'[296] The NAC has control and authority over all committees. It declares them into existence and can change their composition, issue policy directives to them, demand and receive their reports, abolish or change them (*cf.* the three major committee reforms), and, importantly, is not bound by their decisions or recommendations.[297] This leads us to the conclusion that the preconditions for the lawful establishment of the committees by the NAC are fulfilled. Having considered the powers of the committees and how very broad the powers and competencies of the

290 *Cf.* Article 38.1(c) ICJ Statute.

291 C.F. Amerasinghe, *op. cit.*, 141; J. Dutheil de la Rochere, 'Article 7' in J. Cot and A. Pellet (eds.), *op. cit.*, 218; D. Bowett, *op. cit.*, 178; N. Blokker and H. Schermers, *op. cit.*, § 225–226, 182 and H. Schermers and D. Waelbroeck, *Judicial Protection in the European Union*, Alphen aan den Rhijn, Kluwer Law International, 2001, 361–63.

292 P. Sands and P. Klein, *op. cit.*, 194–195.

293 *NATO Encyclopedia* 2019, 145.

294 *NATO Encyclopedia* 2019, 394; B. Eriksen, *The Committee System of the NATO Council*, New York, Humanities Press, 1967, 66 and P. Sands and P. Klein, *op. cit.*, § 6–69, 194.

295 P. Sands and P. Klein, *op. cit.*, 194.

296 In contrast, once subsidiary organs are lawfully established by a principal UN organ, they become subsidiary organs of the UN as a whole and not just of the particular principal organ, See D. Sarooshi, 'Delegation to UN Subsidiary Organs' in D. Sarooshi (ed.), *op. cit.*, 87; Statement by the Dutch Representative at the San Francisco Conference in the discussion on the current article 7(2) Charter, see UN Doc. WD 60; CO/29, 30 May 1945, vol. 17, 37.

297 Based on *NATO Encyclopedia* 2018, *NATO Handbook* 2006, *Kluwer NATO International Encyclopedia of Laws* 2020 and in-house working experience at NATO HQ (01/01/2018–31/12/2018).

Organisation and the NAC are, the issue of lawful delegation also proves to be unproblematic here.

3.2. THE NATO INTERNATIONAL STAFF

The NATO International Staff (IS) is the civilian body that supports the NAC, executes its decisions, and gives advice and legal and administrative support to the national representatives at NATO Headquarters.[298] The IS seeks to implement the decisions taken at different committee levels and, in doing so, eases the process of consensus-based decision-making within the Alliance.[299] NATO, in contrast to most large international organisations, does not have one unified secretariat.[300] The IS supports the NAC, which means it supports only the civilian branch of NATO. NATO's military branch has its own staff: the International Military Staff (IMS), also housed at HQ. NATO does not have a unified legal office either. The Office of Legal Affairs (OLA) is an independent office within the NATO International Staff. The OLA legal advisers are directly accountable to the Secretary General. As a result, the SHAPE Office of Legal Affairs is not subordinate to the OLA; they are separate entities.[301] Peter Olson, the former Legal Adviser and director of the OLA for the NATO International Staff, explains the situation:

> I am not the Legal Advisor for the whole of NATO and have no hierarchical relationship with the other 100 or so legal professionals throughout the Organisation.

---

298 The NATO Encyclopedia and other official NATO documents define the International Staff as a 'body'. At the UN there is a distinction between the 'Secretariat' (the 'body', a principal organ of the UN, Article 7(2) UN Charter) and the 'Staff' (not an organ of the UN). Such a distinction is not explicitly made at NATO. For the purpose of the present chapter it should be clear that when talking about the International Staff as a 'body' of NATO, reference is made to the International Staff *sensu strictu* (the Office of the Secretary General and the eight divisions) and not to the International Staff *sensu latu* (including all staff, see Article XVII-XXIII Ottawa Agreement). See in this vein R. Jordan, *The NATO international staff / secretariat 1952–1957: a study in international administration,* London, Oxford University Press, 1967, 25–32 and his distinction between 'International Staff/Secretariat'. See *NATO Encyclopedia* 2018, 298–300; A. Verhelst and S. Trifunovska, *op. cit.,* 63; *NATO Legal Deskbook* 2010, 35–36; S. Hill, 'The Role of NATO's Legal Adviser' in A. Zidar and J.-P. Gauci (eds.), *The Role of Legal Advisers in International Law,* Leiden, Boston, Brill Nijhoff, 2016, 219. See more broadly L. Risso, 'I am the Servant of the Council: Lord Ismay and the Making of the NATO International Staff', 342–357. Very little research has been carried out on the topic of the history of the NATO International Staff.

299 *NATO Encyclopedia* 2018, 298; S. Hill, 'The Role of NATO's Legal Adviser' in A. Zidar and J.-P. Gauci (eds.), *op cit.,* 219 and interview with a NATO legal adviser, Tervuren, 11 July 2022.

300 N. Blokker and H. Schermers, *op. cit.,* § 436, 331.

301 X. 'NATO Legal Eagles', *NATO Staff Centre Magazine* 2014, 12; A. Mosquera, 'Some Notes on NATO's Institutionalisation', *NATO Legal Gazette* 2019, 20, footnote 30 and see S. Hill, 'The Role of NATO's Legal Adviser' in A. Zidar and J.-P. Gauci (eds.), *op. cit.,* 219–223 as well as *NATO Legal Deskbook* 2010, 139.

> Most of these are on the military side. [...] This office does not handle all the legal work for the organisation, just the International Staff part of it. I can't tell any other legal office or officer what their policy is or should be.[302]

The International Staff includes the Office of the Secretary General, eight Divisions (each headed by an Assistant Secretary General), and a number of Independent Offices (headed by Directors). The IS was established by the NAC and has its roots in a Memorandum by the Chairman dated 29 January 1951.[303] The 1951 Ottawa Agreement defines the status of the IS in Articles XVII-XXIII. Note that there were two early views on the nature of the International Staff, as described by Risso. The Americans preferred a strong, centralised civil service to support the action of the Secretary General as the leader of the NAC.[304] The British, on the other hand, favoured a leaner secretariat that would leave the nations in the NAC room to manoeuvre. In the end, in 1951, the British vision prevailed because of the support of multiple European States that did not want excessive centralisation to undercut their sovereignty and independence.[305] The above leads one to conclude that the preconditions for the lawful establishment of the IS by the NAC are met. The IS was established by the NAC in January of 1951 and should be classified as a subsidiary body in the sense of Article 9 North Atlantic Treaty, Article I.c Ottawa Agreement, and as the term is understood in international institutional law. The NAC has control and authority over the IS. The NAC can issue policy directives to the IS, receives and demands its reports, and welcomes or dismisses its suggestions.[306] The control that the NATO nations have over the International Staff is greater than in many other international organisations. In the UN or the EU, the Secretariats are true organs of those Organisations. They are freer to chart their own course, independent of the nations. That the NATO International Staff has a facilitating role and not a decision-making one was confirmed by a senior NATO legal adviser and a senior NATO IS member:

---

302 X. 'NATO Legal Eagles', 12.

303 NATO, Memorandum by the Chairman, Establishment of the International Staff and an International Budget for NATO, NATO Doc. D-D(51)30, 29 January 1951.

304 L. Risso, 'I am the Servant of the Council: Lord Ismay and the Making of the NATO International Staff', 345.

305 L. Risso, 'I am the Servant of the Council: Lord Ismay and the Making of the NATO International Staff', 345; NATO, NATO Reorganization – Memorandum by the U.S. Deputy, NATO Doc. DD(52)17, 14 January 1952 and Reorganization of NATO – Memorandum of the U.K. Deputy, NATO Doc. DD(52)19, 15 January 1952.

306 Based on *NATO Legal Deskbook* 2010, 35–36 and 49; S. Hill, 'The Role of NATO's Legal Adviser in A. Zidar and J.-P. Gauci (eds.), *op. cit.*, 219; in-house working experience at NATO HQ (01/01/2018–31/12/2018) and interview with a NATO legal adviser, Tervuren, 11 July 2022.

> The International Staff merely has a serving role. It is there to execute the will of the Member States. Nothing more. And we are all very aware of this limited task.[307]

This was echoed by the head of the SHAPE Office of Legal Affairs, Andres Mosquera:

> The International Staff [...] really reflects what is the feeling of the nations and their intention. They are only there to massage, but not necessarily to change, the opinion of the nations.[308]

This again confirms that, in the NAC, the signatory parties to the North Atlantic Treaty and the Ottawa Agreement tend to act in their capacity as States rather than as Member States of the Organisation. Based on a textual analysis of the Treaty, in-house experience, and interviews with NATO legal advisers, one can conclude that the issue of delegation is unproblematic in this case. The NAC does not delegate more than it has, nor does it delegate responsibility. The main reason is that the NAC keeps most powers to itself and reserves only a facilitating role for the IS.

3.3. THE NATO ADMINISTRATIVE TRIBUNAL

The NATO Administrative Tribunal (AT) may decide on any individual dispute brought by a staff member or a member of the retired NATO staff or his or her legal successor, who is affected by a decision, which is allegedly not in compliance with the Civilian Personnel Regulations or the terms of their appointment with the Organisation, as stated in the Rules of Procedure of the AT.[309] The AT

---

307 Interview with a NATO legal adviser, Tervuren, 11 July 2022, which confirmed the findings of an earlier interview where it was said that the International Staff is 'there to serve, there to support the Members', interview with a senior NATO International Staff Member, NATO Headquarters, 9 June 2022.

308 Interview with head of the SHAPE Office of Legal Affairs, Andres Mosquera, online, 10 October 2022.

309 Rules 9 and 23–30 Rules of Procedure of the Administrative Tribunal, adopted by the NATO Administrative Tribunal in April 2005, last amended in March 2019, available online at www.nato.int/nato_static_fl2014/assets/pdf/pdf_2019_06/20190624_1906-cpr-ROP-eng.pdf (last accessed January 2025). See also *NATO Legal Deskbook* 2010,179; *NATO Encyclopedia* 2018, 371; G. Gilbert, 'La Commission de recours de l'Organisation du Traité de l'Atlantique Nord et sa jurisprudence', *Annuaire français de droit international* 1968, § 8, 325. Remark that '*la commission n'est pas compétente pour connaître de pourvois dirigés contre une décision réglementaire du Conseil de l'Atlantique Nord*' in G. Gilbert, 'La jurisprudence de la Commission de recours de l'Organisation du Traité de l'Atlantique Nord de 1968 à 1972', *Annuaire français de droit international* 1972, § 29, 407; G. Vandersanden, 'La Commission de Recours de l'Organisation du Traité de l'Atlantique Nord: son fonctionnement à la lumière de sa jurisprudence', *Revue Belge de Droit Internationale* 1974, § 8–14, 95–101.

organises oral hearings and produces binding judgments.[310] NATO is not just a political and military alliance; it is also an international organisation, which explains why NATO had to create an AT.[311] On 23 January 2013 the NAC approved amendments to the Civilian Personnel Regulations, which led to the effective establishment of the AT on 1 July 2013. In this regard, Article XXIV.b Ottawa Agreement stipulates that

> the Council shall make provision for appropriate modes of settlement of disputes involving any official or expert of the Organization to whom Part IV of this Agreement applies who by reason of his official position enjoys immunity; if immunity has not been waived in accordance with the provisions of Article XXII.[312]

Strictly speaking, the AT is neither a subsidiary nor a subordinate body, even though it was created by the NAC.[313] The NAC has no direct control over or say in the AT's judgments, hearings, or Rules of Procedure, which are drafted by the AT Members themselves.[314] Strictly speaking, the AT is not an organ of NATO. In this case, the terminological distinction between 'body' and 'organ' in Article I.c Ottawa Agreement does have legal significance. It means that the AT does not represent the Organisation, nor does it express the Organisation's will. The AT can best be described as an 'independent body'.[315] Despite this formal independence, the NAC can, in practice, establish, terminate, and modify the composition of the AT. The NAC also has informal means of control, e.g. when the NAC amends the Civilian Personnel Regulations and appoints the AT Members. These informal means of control were challenged in *Case no. 34* in 1971. A NATO Staff Member (Mr S) argued that the NATO Appeals Board (the AT's predecessor) should have been composed of a judge and two lawyers with no past or present connection to NATO. In its decision of 19 November 1971, the Appeals Board stated that, according to Article 4.11 of its Statute, 'its members shall be appointed [...] outside the staff of the Organisation and of the national delegations to the Council, from among persons of established competence, at least one of whom must have legal competence' and that 'it is not for the Board to question the appropriateness of this rule and of the decisions made by the North Atlantic Council pursuant to the rule.'[316] The Appeals Board

---

310 Rule 25–26 and 27.7 Rules of Procedure NATO Administrative Tribunal.

311 N. Blokker and H. Schermers, *op. cit.*, § 23, 26.

312 Article XXIV.b Ottawa Agreement.

313 *Cf.* C.F. Amerasinghe in *op. cit.*, 142 and C.F. Amerasinghe, *The Law of the International Civil Service*, Oxford, Oxford University Press, vol. II, 1994, 34 but see also Sarooshi's interpretation of ICJ *Effect of Awards* on this point in D. Sarooshi, 'Delegation to UN Subsidiary Organs' in D. Sarooshi (ed.), *op. cit.*, 130, footnote 189.

314 *Cf.* NATO Doc. PO(2013)0356.

315 C.F. Amerasinghe, *op. cit.*, 142.

316 NATO Appeals Board, *Case no. 34*, 19 November 1971 as discussed in G. Gilbert, 'La jurisprudence de la Commission de recours de l'Organisation du Traité de l'Atlantique Nord

rejected the claim made by the NATO Staff Member, ruling that the matters on which it could decide are exhaustively listed in Annex IX to the Civilian Personnel Regulations and that the case therefore fell outside of the scope of that provision.[317] This conclusion is sensible, considering that administrative tribunals are allowed to rule on their own competence (*Kompetenz-Kompetenz*), a basic principle of international procedural law.[318] It is not clear whether the Board used the *Kompetenz-Kompetenz* principle to establish that it was not competent to determine any matter concerning its own competence beyond the topics listed in Annex IX, or that it had assessed its own competence and then, having decided that the list in Annex IX was intended to be exhaustive, came to the conclusion that it was not competent to judge the composition of the Board (which would mean that the Board found it could have declared itself competent if the list in Annex IX had not been exhaustive). In a more recent case before the European Court of Human Rights (ECtHR), two NATO employees sued two NATO Member States, Italy and Belgium, on the grounds that the employment dispute settlement procedure within NATO was 'inadequate'. The applicants argued that AT Members had connections to the Organisation (as they were former Ambassadors to NATO) and that, therefore, the Appeals Board had been improperly appointed by the NAC. More specifically, the appellants argued that Belgium, as the host State, and Italy, the applicants' country of nationality, had failed to ensure the creation by the Organisation of an internal dispute resolution mechanism that complied with Article 6 ECHR. The European Court answered:

> States, when they transfer part of their sovereign powers to an organization of which they are members, are under an obligation to see that the rights guaranteed by the Convention receive within the organization an equivalent protection to that ensured by the Convention mechanism.[319]

The ECtHR found—without providing much fact-based argumentation—that this obligation had not been violated, because the procedure within NATO was not 'manifestly deficient' ('*insuffisance manifeste*', in the original French).[320] The

de 1968 à 1972', § 4, 393 and G. Vandersanden, 'La Commission de Recours de l'Organisation du Traité de l'Atlantique Nord: son fonctionnement à la lumière de sa jurisprudence', *op. cit.*, § 16, 104.

317 *Ibid.*

318 IACtHR 2001, *Hilaire, Benjamin and Constantine and Others v. Trinidad and Tobago*, preliminary objections, Judgment, separate opinion of Judge A. Cançado Trindade, § 2 and 15; UNRWA, Dispute Tribunal Handbook on UN Administrative Law, March 2021, 67 and C. Amerasinghe (ed.), 'La Compétence de la Compétence' in *Jurisdiction of International Tribunals*, Leiden, Brill Nijhoff, 2002, 121.

319 See ECtHR 12 May 2008, *Gasparini v Italy and Belgium*, Admissibility Decision, App. no. 10750/03, as quoted by T. Lock in 'Gasparini v Italy and Belgium' in J. Wouters, C. Ryngaert, I. Dekker and R. Wessel (eds.), *Judicial Decisions on the Law of International Organisations*, Oxford, Oxford University Press, 2016, 328–335 and see ARIO, Commentary 5 to Article 61.

320 ECtHR *Gasparini v. Italy and Belgium*.

Court pointed out that the applicants were entitled to ask that the composition of the Appeals Board be changed for reasons of presumed partiality, but that they had not exercised this right during the proceedings. The Court also found that Belgium and Italy, through their Permanent Representatives in the NAC, were well-positioned to decide whether the NATO Civilian Personnel Regulations, at the time of their adoption, guaranteed a fair trial in accordance with Article 6 ECHR. In its quite far-reaching ruling, the ECtHR considered the conduct of Belgium and Italy separately from NATO's consensus decision-making process and analysed the guarantees in the document that all NATO Member States had agreed to when the AT was created. The Court concluded that Belgium and Italy (and, actually, all NATO Member States) had agreed to provisions that ensure a fair trial under Article 6 ECHR. The Court analysed the conduct of Italy and Belgium as Member States of the Organisation rather than as States acting 'in their external capacity.' As Ryngaert argues (see below), this reasoning opens the door for future rulings in which Member States will be held responsible for the structural lacunae of international organisation's internal procedures.[321]

Since Article 9 of the Treaty is a source of general authority, the NAC may establish subsidiary bodies to carry out functions which it cannot itself perform.[322] In this case, the NAC must either expressly or implicitly possess the power which it seeks to delegate (as mentioned above). Clearly, the NAC does not possess the competence to adjudicate legal disputes. Does this mean that the NAC has unlawfully delegated powers to the AT? To answer this question, one should turn to the ICJ's *Effect of Awards* Advisory Opinion. The case revolves around a decision made by the UN Administrative Tribunal (UNAT), in which compensation was awarded to a UN staff member. The issue at stake in *Effect of Awards* was whether the UNGA could refuse to give effect to this decision. The staff member's employment contract had allegedly been discontinued without his consent. In *Effect of Awards,* the ICJ analysed whether the UNGA effectively disposed of the competence to establish a judicial body to deal with matters of civil staff regulations. The Court made clear that, under the UN Charter, the UNGA does not possess the judicial function which the UNAT was performing.[323] The court stated that 'by establishing the Administrative Tribunal, the General Assembly was not delegating the performance of its

321 C. Ryngaert, 'The European Court of Human Rights' Approach to the Responsibility of Member States in connection with Acts of International Organizations, *International & Comparative Law Quarterly* 2001, 1005.

322 See D. Sarooshi, 'Delegation to UN Subsidiary Organs', ECtHR *Gasparini v. Italy and Belgium*. 93; ICJ *Effect of Awards*, 47 and *supra*.

323 Para. 38 ICJ *Effect of Awards*: 'The Charter contains no provision which authorizes any of the principal organs of the UN to adjudicate upon these disputes and article 105 secures for the UN jurisdictional immunities in national courts.'

own functions.'[324] Rather, the UNGA's power to establish the administrative tribunal was implied by its more general competence to act in the domain of staff affairs.[325] After all, Article 101(1) UN Charter reads that 'the staff shall be appointed by the Secretary-General under regulations established by the General Assembly.'[326] Article 101(3) UN Charter reads that 'the paramount consideration in the employment of the staff and in the determination of the conditions of service shall be the necessity of securing the highest standards of efficiency, competence, and integrity. Due regard shall be paid to the importance of recruiting the staff on as wide a geographical basis as possible.'[327] And so, the Court found that

> in these circumstances, the power to establish a tribunal, to do justice as between the Organization and the staff members, was *essential to ensure the efficient working* of the Secretariat, and to give effect to the paramount consideration of securing the highest standards of efficiency, competence and integrity. Capacity to do this arises by *necessary intendment out of the Charter.*[328]

The Court found that the source of the General Assembly's authority to establish such a subsidiary organ was the general authority laid down in Article 7(2) UN Charter.[329] Accordingly, the ICJ concluded that the UNGA had lawfully exercised its power to establish a tribunal.[330]

Considering the establishment of the NATO AT in light of the reasoning in *Effect of Awards*, the following observations can be made. First of all, the 1949 Treaty, like the UN Charter, does not contain any provision that authorises the NAC to adjudicate disputes between the Organisation and its staff members. In fact, the drafters of the Treaty were explicitly opposed to this (see above). In *Effect of Awards*, the ICJ concluded that the UNGA's power to establish the tribunal was implied by its competence to operate in the domain of staff matters, laid down in Article 101(1) and (3) UN Charter. In its conclusion on this point, the ICJ explicitly stated that the 'capacity to [establish a tribunal] arises by necessary intendment out of the Charter.'[331] The North Atlantic Treaty, however, does not contain any provision on staff regulations. It is the 1951 Ottawa Agreement that gives the NAC the power to regulate the relations between staff members and the

324 Para. 54 *Effect of Awards;* Dissenting Opinion Judge Hackworth to *Effect of Awards*, 81.

325 Paras 36–38 *Effect of Awards*. Compare to the ICJ *Expenses case*, 165 and see C.F. Amerasinghe, *The Law of the International Civil Service*, 27 and J. Gomula, 'The International Court of Justice and Administrative Tribunals of International Organizations', *Michigan Journal of International Law* 1991, 83.

326 Article 101(1) UN Charter.

327 Article 101(3) UN Charter.

328 Para. 39 *Effect of Awards*, emphasis added.

329 Paras 40–42 *Effect of Awards* and D. Sarooshi, 'Delegation to UN Subsidiary Organs' in D. Sarooshi (ed.), *op. cit.*, 95.

330 Para. 42 *Effect of Awards*.

331 Para. 39 *Effect of Awards*.

Organisation. In this regard, Article XXIV.b Ottawa Agreement reads that 'the Council shall make provision for appropriate modes of settlement of disputes involving any official or expert of the Organisation to whom Part IV of this Agreement applies who by reason of his official position enjoys immunity [...].'[332] In contrast to the UNGA, the competence of the NAC to operate in the realm of staff issues does not arise from its constituent document. On the other hand, the language used in Article XXIV.b Ottawa Agreement is clearer and more specific on the matter of dispute settlement than the rather vague Articles 101(1) and (3) UN Charter. In the pivotal paragraph of *Effect of Awards*, the ICJ states that the power to establish a tribunal 'was essential to ensure the *efficient working* of the Secretariat, and to give effect to the paramount consideration of securing the highest standards of efficiency, competence and integrity'[333] before concluding that the capacity to do so arises by necessary intendment from the UN Charter. NATO does not have the same objectives as the UN, nor does the North Atlantic Treaty contain any provisions similar to Articles 1 and 2 UN Charter. All in all, making a case for a lawful delegation of powers to the NATO AT is less straightforward than it was for the UNAT in *Effects of Awards*.

3.4. INTERIM CONCLUSION

Both the committee system and the NATO International Staff were lawfully established by the NAC, which means the two preconditions for lawful establishment under international institutional law had been respected. The following scale depicts, from low to high, the degree of control and authority the NAC exercises over the three entities:

NATO Administrative Tribunal	*International Staff*	*Committees*
lower ←	→	*higher*

Even though the AT was lawfully and formally established, there are also informal means of control. In 1971 a NATO employee criticised the fact that some AT Members had links to NATO. Having applied the principle of international administrative law known as *Kompetenz-Kompetenz*, the AT found itself to be incompetent to judge the NAC decision that established the composition of that AT, as this fell outside of the scope of its competences, which are exhaustively listed in Annex IV to the Civilian Personnel Regulations. The NAC's influence over the appointment of the AT Members (i.e. former NATO Ambassadors) was also questioned by the ECtHR in *Gasparini*. The European

332 Article XXIV.b Ottawa Agreement.

333 Para. 39 *Effect of Awards*, emphasis in the original.

Court found that the establishment of the AT did not violate Article 6 ECHR because applicants had not requested a change in the AT's composition even though they could have done so. By examining the conduct of the Permanent Representatives of Belgium and Italy in the NAC and whether they had been in a position to consider whether the NATO Civilian Personnel Regulations met the requirements of Article 6 ECHR, the Court went quite far. It essentially opened the door to holding Member States accountable for having joined a consensus on a decision. This goes too far, considering the principle that States generally cannot be held liable for the acts of an organisation by virtue of their membership of the organisation alone (see below).[334] Aside from this, the NAC's delegation of powers to the committees and the IS was lawful. This conclusion is further supported by the fact that nations have delegated barely any powers at all to the IS, but rather left it with a facilitating role, the extensiveness of which is unique in international institutional law. The legality of the delegation of powers to the NATO AT, on the other hand, is questionable. As the NAC does not have the competence to adjudicate staff matters, it can only delegate this power if it can be implied from the constituent treaty (*cf. Effect of Awards*). But the North Atlantic Treaty does not contain any clause similar to Articles 101(1) and (3). Moreover, the Treaty does not have objectives similar to those mentioned in Articles 1 and 2 UN Charter that could further justify an implied power. Lastly, the *travaux préparatoires* make it clear that the drafters of the Treaty were against the idea that the NAC should have conciliatory powers. It would be interesting to see this phrase clarified. The ECtHR's *Gasparini* judgment may inspire some to settle the issue and challenge the legality of the delegation of powers to the NATO AT.

4. THE NATO PARLIAMENTARY ASSEMBLY

The previous section made clear that NATO is run by the executive branch. When the governmental bodies within an international organisation take decisions by consensus only, the role of national parliaments is limited to a mere *a posteriori* right of scrutiny, writes Seidl-Hohenveldern.[335] However, the NATO Parliamentary Assembly (NATO PA), though little known, has existed since 1955. Could it be claimed that there has been a process of parliamentarisation in the field of security and defence? If so, does this have an impact on governmental decision-making within NATO? To answer this, the NATO PA's legal status and its relationship to NATO's governmental branches should be clarified, as

334 ILC, Article 62, Commentary no. 2, *Report of the Law Commission on the Work of its Sixty-Third Session*, UN Doc. A/CN.4/L.77, 2009 and C. Ryngaert, 'The European Court of Human Rights' Approach to the Responsibility of Member States in connection with Acts of International Organizations', 997.

335 I. Seidl-Hohenveldern, 'Les organes des organisations internationales' in R. Dupuy (ed.), *op. cit.*, 100.

the Treaty does not mention any assembly. An analysis of the NATO PA is both timely and necessary, especially now that the European Parliament is seeking to obtain more powers in the domains of security and defence, potentially advancing a trend towards the parliamentarisation of those domains.[336] This section will use a comparative methodology. Three bodies will be compared (the NATO PA, the Assembly of the Western European Union (WEU Assembly), and PACE) in order to uncover their similarities and differences.[337] This helps one to identify normative benchmarks and good practices in international institutional law, to see how different organisations have dealt with similar institutional problems, and to contribute to improving the structure and functioning of other international organisations than the ones that will be compared.[338] These are the core objectives of international institutional law, according to Blokker and Schermers.[339] Despite their increased popularity, parliamentary assemblies remain 'remarkably underresearched'.[340] This comparative analysis aims to improve the current state of knowledge about international parliamentary institutions in general. There are multiple positive reasons for choosing these three assemblies. The WEU Assembly and PACE both belong to organisations that, like NATO, have regional membership. The three chosen assemblies were established in the same period (1949–1955) and have partly overlapping membership. The WEU, which ceased to exist in 2011, was a military alliance and international organisation like NATO. Its tasks were similar to NATO's and

---

336 C. Moser and S. Blockmans, *The extent of the European Parliament's competence in Common Security and Defence Policy*, Directorate General for External Policies In-Depth Analysis, Brussels, European Parliament, 2022, 43–44. See also G. Rosen and K. Raube, 'Influence beyond formal powers: the parliamentarisation of European Union security policy', *The British Journal of Politics and International Relations* 2018, 73 and M. Houben, 'On a European War Powers Act', *POLITICO* 2003, 2.

337 The methodology of the present section was to a great extent inspired by the valuable work of Lina Kestemont, *Handbook on Legal Methodology: from objective to method*, Cambridge, Springer, 2018. See also D. Watkins and M. Burton, *Research Methods in Law*, Abingdon, Routledge, 2013, 104–108 and M. Paris, 'The Comparative Method in Legal Research: the Art of Justifying Choices' in L. Cahillane and J. Schweppe (eds.), *Legal Research Methods: Principles and Practicalities*, London, Clarus Press, 2016.

338 L. Kestemont, *op. cit.*, 37; J. Husa, 'Research Designs of Comparative Law – Methodology or Heuristics' in M. Adams and D. Heirbaut (eds.), *The Method and Culture of Comparative Law*, Oxford, Hart Publishing, 2014, 53; J. Vranken, 'Algemeen Deel: een synthese' in J. Vranken (ed.), *Mr. C. Assers Handleiding tot de beoefening van het Nederlands Burgerlijk Recht*, Deventer, Kluwer, 2014, 168; F. Stone, 'The end to be served by comparative law', *Tulsa Law Review* 1950–51, 333; D. Pieters, 'Functions of comparative law and practical methodology of comparing' in *Syllabus Research Master in Law*, Leuven, Tilburg, 2009, 1 and 14 and W. Devroe, *Rechtsvergelijking in een context van europeanisering en globalisering*, Leuven, Acco, 2010, 22.

339 H. Kötz and K. Zweigert, *Introduction to Comparative Law*, Oxford, Clarendon, 1998, 15–31 and N. Blokker and H. Schermers, *op. cit.*, § 6–13, 4–13.

340 C. Kraft-Kasack, 'Transnational Parliamentary Assemblies: A Remedy for the Democratic Deficit of International Governance?', *West European Politics* 2008, 535.

its core provision was similar to Article 5 of the North Atlantic Treaty.[341] The founding of the WEU Assembly by the 1954 Modified Brussels Treaty marked the first time a military alliance was given a permanent parliament.[342] PACE was the first parliamentary assembly to be set up as an organ of a fully fledged international organisation.[343] Since then, PACE has acquired a considerable degree of control and influence over the executive.

4.1. DESCRIPTIVE COMPARISON

4.1.1. *The NATO Parliamentary Assembly*

4.1.1.1. Introduction

The NATO PA brings together members of the parliaments of all NATO Member States to discuss security-related affairs that are of common interest and concern to those Member States.[344] According to the 2019 NATO Encyclopedia, the Assembly's principal objective is to 'foster mutual understanding among Alliance parliamentarians of the key security challenges facing the transatlantic partnership.'[345] In Article 2 of the most recent version of the NATO PA Rules of Procedure (2024), the aims of the Assembly are defined as follows:

> The Assembly, by virtue of its membership drawn from the various national parliaments, provides a link between the NATO authorities and these parliaments. Through its discussions, the Assembly aims to promote a common feeling of Atlantic solidarity in the various legislative assemblies; to strengthen national parliamentary oversight of security and defence; to increase public knowledge of the Alliance and to further the aims and values of the Alliance, in particular support for democracy, individual liberty, and the rule of law.[346]

The NATO PA is made up of parliamentary delegates from all NATO Member States. The size of each delegation is based on the size of the Member State it represents. The composition of each delegation reflects the political composition

---

341 Article V Modified Brussels Treaty.

342 Article IX Modified Brussels Treaty and WEU, *Special supplement: the 50 Anniversary of the Brussels Treaty*, Paris, WEU Publishing, 1998.

343 N. Blokker and H. Schermers, *op. cit.*, § 565, 425–426; C.F. Amerasinghe, *op. cit.*, 133; I. Seidl-Hohenveldern, 'Les organes des organisations internationales' in R. Dupuy (ed.), *op. cit.*, 93 and B. Habegger, 'Democratic accountability of international organizations: Parliamentary Control within the Council of Europe and the OSCE and the prospects for the United Nations', *Cooperation and Conflict* 2010, 187.

344 As stated in the *NATO Encyclopedia* 2019, 382.

345 *NATO Encyclopedia* 2019, 383.

346 Article 2 NATO Parliamentary Assembly, Rules of Procedure, 2024, available online at www.nato-pa.int/documents (last accessed January 2025).

of the national parliament it represents, including opposition parties.[347] Five committees carry out the work of the NATO PA. The NATO PA is headed by a President, who is a member of parliament from a NATO Member State.[348] The NATO PA is supported by its International Secretariat, based in Brussels, which is overseen by a Secretary General.[349]

4.1.1.2. Mode of establishment

The NATO PA is one of the few large international assemblies created by parliamentary initiative rather than on the basis of an intergovernmental treaty.[350] The NATO PA was not created by the North Atlantic Treaty or by any other international act, but originated from a private initiative.[351] The establishment of the NATO PA can be traced back to 18 July 1955, when the first Conference of Members of Parliament from the NATO countries took place at NATO HQ in Paris.[352] Efforts to institutionalise NATO's parliamentary branch followed the start of the Assembly's work in that same year.[353] However, a great majority of subsequent governments and multiple NATO Secretaries General expressed their antipathy towards the idea of a formal NATO PA. Secretary General Spaak said that

> the prominent role which should be played by the Conference is not strictly obliged to be exercised in a juridical framework similar to the one conferred to other international parliamentarian organisations created in Europe.[354]

---

347 Article 1 Rules of Procedure.

348 *NATO Encyclopedia* 2019, 383.

349 S. Charman and K. Williams, *The Parliamentarians' Role in the Alliance: The North Atlantic Assembly 1955–1980*, Suffolk, published by the North Atlantic Assembly, 1981, 174.

350 P. Lellouche, 'Foreword' in X. (ed.), *NATO Parliamentary Assembly 1955–2005*, 10; S. Marschall, 'European parliaments in transnational organisations: Parliamentary cooperation beyond the European Union', *Stiftung Politik und Wissenschaft Conference Paper* 2007, 11.

351 C. Brumter, *The North Atlantic Assembly*, Berlin, Springer, 1986, 223 p.; C. Colliard, *Institutions des relations internationales*, Paris, Dalloz, 1978, 4 and S. Marschall, 'European parliaments in transnational organisations: Parliamentary cooperation beyond the European Union', 11. See also J. Harned, 'Atlantic Assembly – a Genesis', *Journal of Common Market Studies* 1964, 183–189 and L. Hartley, 'The North Atlantic Assembly', *Atlantic Community Quarterly* 1975–1976, 486–491.

352 Z. Sabic, 'Parliamentary Diplomacy and the US Congress: The Case of the NATO Parliamentary Assembly', *The Hague Journal of Diplomacy* 2016, 246.

353 For a detailed overview of the attempts at institutionalization see C. Brumter, *op. cit.*, 17–33 and S. Charman and K. Williams, *op. cit.*, 18–33. See also Report of the Committee of Three on Non-Military Cooperation in NATO, 1956, § 58–59; Report by G. De Freitas, North Atlantic Assembly Doc. no. J 128.PC (66) 43, November 1966 and L. Radoux, 'L'institutionnalisation de l'Assemblée', North Atlantic Assembly Doc no. M 82.PC (69) 5, 1969.

354 Quote taken from C. Brumter, *op. cit.*, 27.

In 1963 Secretary General Stikker said:

> In seeking to formalise its position, your Conference may find itself grasping at the shadow of status only to lose the substance of influence.[355]

In March 1955 UK Prime Minister Winston Churchill stated:

> It is not our policy to establish a parliamentary assembly as part of the North Atlantic Treaty Organisation machinery. We are not alone in this. Our view is shared by a number of other NATO Governments. Her Majesty's Government, however, welcomes parliamentary interest in and support for NATO through unofficial meetings of Members of Parliament from NATO countries.[356]

The governmental animosity towards an institutionalised parliamentary assembly within NATO was strong, as the following statement by a German Ministry of Foreign Affairs official shows:

> One had to keep in mind that raising the status of the Assembly could lead to an intensification of communist interest in the Assembly, which in turn could seriously impair the envisaged political cooperation.[357]

Ultimately, the many proposals to institutionalise the Assembly after 1955 were never successful. The objective of institutionalisation was abandoned in 1979.[358]

4.1.1.3. Position within NATO

The position of the NATO PA is unique. It is not a NATO organ. It functions independently of NATO and has no formal ties with it.[359] Additionally, the NATO PA is not a truly consultative assembly. It has no power of initiative or control, nor does it have any legislative or advisory powers.[360] This is why the NATO PA should be classified as a parliamentary assembly and not as a

355 S. Charman and K. Williams, *op. cit.*, 23 and 25.

356 Quote taken from D. Hobbs, 'The Assembly from 1955 to 1989' in X. (ed.), *NATO Parliamentary Assembly 1955–2005*, 35–36.

357 Quote taken from S. Charman and K. Williams, *op. cit.*, 3 and S. Lunn, 'The Evolving Role of the NATO Parliamentary Assembly' in X. (ed.), *The NATO Parliamentary Assembly 1955–2005*, 18.

358 S. Charman and K. Williams, *op. cit.*, 36 and 161.

359 Z. Selden and L. Oehman, 'The NATO Parliamentary Assembly in parliamentary diplomacy' in K. Raube, M. Müftüler-Baç and J. Wouters (eds.), *Parliamentary Cooperation and Diplomacy in EU External Relations*, Cheltenham, Edward Elgar Publishing, 2019, 208–209 and K. Streit, 'The Diplomatic Potential of NATO', *Annals of the American Academy of Political and Social Science* 1957, 119.

360 C. Kissling, *The Legal and Political Status of International Parliamentary Institutions*, Berlin, Committee for a Democratic U.N. Background Paper, 2011, 31; I. Seidl-Hohenveldern, 'Les organes des organisations internationales' in R. Dupuy (ed.), *op. cit.*, 99.

parliamentary organ. Other examples of parliamentary assemblies that are not formally organs of their international organisations are the EFTA (European Free Trade Association) Parliamentary Committee and the OSCE PA.

4.1.1.4. Legal status

Initially the NATO PA was a *de facto* association, with no legal personality under national or international law. This means that its members could be held responsible without any financial limit. In 1962 host country France provided the NATO PA with a legal basis by decree of 29 January. Pursuant to this decree, the assembly enjoyed the status of a non-profit making foreign association.[361] Its status could be compared to that of Eurocontrol. After France withdrew from the NATO integrated military structure in 1966, the Assembly, along with NATO HQ, was relocated to Belgium. Once there, on 14 August 1974, a federal law granted the Assembly the legal status it still enjoys today.[362] It is often said that the 1974 Belgian law recognised the Assembly as an international organisation without expressing it.[363] This claim requires closer legal scrutiny. Is the NATO PA a public international organisation or a non-governmental one? Sometimes the line between the two can be vague, as the following two illustrations make clear. The Inter-Parliamentary Union (IPU) was created by national parliaments. Its purpose is strictly limited to parliamentary cooperation. Governments do not take part. The IPU is therefore generally classified as a non-governmental organisation, having obtained this status within the UN.[364] Some years ago the IPU looked into the possibility of concluding a convention which would transform it from a private into a public international organisation. Importantly, such a transformation would make it possible to grant privileges and immunities to delegates, IPU meetings, and IPU officials.[365] So far, this possibility has not been actualised. On the other hand, while many NGOs have obtained some sort of official recognition, such recognition has also been given to organisations that do not qualify as NGOs nor as intergovernmental organisations.[366] An example of such a hybrid organisation is the International Committee of the Red Cross (ICRC). The

---

361 C. Brumter, *op. cit.*, 25.

362 Wet van 14 augustus 1974 betreffende het statuut in België van de Noordatlantische Vergadering, *Belgisch Staatsblad* 31 oktober 1974, 13264 (1974 law).

363 C. Brumter, *op. cit.*, 26.

364 N. Blokker and H. Schermers, *op. cit.*, § 35, 42–43; J. Klabbers, *op. cit.*, 214. Compare with the Joint Opinion of Brownlie and Goodwin-Gill in which they defend that the IPU is an international organisation with international legal personality, see I. Brownlie and G. Goodwin, 'Opinion on the Inter-Parliamentary Union', *IPU Archives* 31 May 1999, 27 p. *Cf.* Article 1 Statutes of the Inter-Parliamentary Union, Extensively revised in October 1983 and amended in April 2003, October 2013, March 2016, April 2017, March and October 2018 and October 2019.

365 N. Blokker and H. Schermers, *op. cit.*, § 35, 42–43.

366 N. Blokker and H. Schermers, *op. cit.*, § 47, 52–53.

ICRC was established by private individuals as a private association under Swiss law in 1863. Its governing body is composed of private individuals, not State representatives.[367] For many years the ICRC enjoyed various kinds of privileges and legal immunities within the territory of Switzerland. On 19 March 1993 this special treatment was finally given a legal basis by an agreement between the Swiss government and the ICRC. The agreement established the ICRC's international legal personality, the inviolability of its property, its exemption from domestic taxes, and the staff's immunity from jurisdiction.[368] Nowadays the ICRC's mandate is enshrined in the 1949 Geneva Conventions, their Additional Protocols, and the Statutes of the ICRC and Red Crescent Movement. The ICRC derives international legal personality, privileges, and immunities, the both the international and domestic legal order, directly from its mandate in the Geneva Conventions.[369] Because of all of this, the ICRC is generally recognised as having a legal status equivalent to that of a public international organisation.[370]

Although there is not one universally accepted definition of the term 'public international organisation', legal scholars generally agree on what the elements are that constitute a public international organisation[371]:

- Public international organisations come into being through an international agreement. The vast majority of international organisations are based on a multilateral treaty (Article 1 VCLT), but the agreement can also be expressed in other ways.[372]

---

367 E. Debuf, 'Tools to do the job: the ICRC's legal status, privileges and immunities', *International Review of the Red Cross* 2016, 323.

368 Agreement between the International Committee of the Red Cross and the Swiss Federal Council, *International Review of the Red Cross* 1993, No. 293, 152–160.

369 As argued by E. Debuf in 'Tools to do the job: the ICRC's legal status, privileges and immunities', 324, note 16 and 17 and see J. Crawford, *op. cit.*, 2012, 16. See also D. Bindschedler-Robert, 'Red Cross', *Encyclopedia of Public International Law*, 2000, vol. 4, 56–63; C. Dominicé, 'La personnalité juridique international du CICR', in C. Swinariski (ed.), *Studies and essays on international humanitarian law and Red Cross principles in honour of Jean Pictet*, Leiden, Brill Nijhoff, 1984, 663–673; P. Reuter, 'La personnalité juridique international du Comité international de la Croix-Rouge', in *ibid.*, 783–791 and I. Seidl-Hohenverldern and G. Loibl, *op. cit.*, 5.

370 E. Debuf, 'Tools to do the job: the ICRC's legal status, privileges and immunities', 324 and N. Blokker and H. Schermers, *op. cit.*, § 47, 52–53.

371 *Cf.* N. Blokker and H. Schermers, *op. cit.*, § 33–45, 41–51; P. Sands and P. Klein, *op. cit.*, 16; F. Morgenstern, *Legal Problems of International Organisations*, Cambridge, Grotius, 1986, 19; C.F. Amerasinghe, *op. cit.*, 9–10; P. Reuter, *International Institutional Law*, New York, Praeger, 1958, 215–218; E. Lagrange, 'La catégorie organisation internationale' in E. Lagrange and J.-M. Sorel (eds.), *op. cit.*, 54 and J. Klabbers, *op. cit.*, 9–14.

372 N. Blokker and H. Schermers, *op. cit.*, § 34, 41; J. Crawford, *op. cit.*, 170; I. Seidl-Hohenveldern and G. Loibl, *op. cit.*, 8; ILC 2003, *Draft report of the International Law Commission on the work of its fifty-fifth session: chapter IV (Responsibility of international organizations)*, UN Doc. A/CN.4/L.636/Add.1, 7–8; C.F. Amerasinghe, *op. cit.*, 10; F. Morgenstern, *op. cit.*, 19 and

- They have at least one organ with a will of its own.
- They are established under international law. As international agreements are typically concluded under international law, it can be assumed that this requirement is fulfilled whenever there is an international agreement, according to Blokker and Schermers.[373] The present section therefore disregards this third element and focuses on the first two instead.

At first glance, the NATO PA has many similarities to an NGO, and to the IPU. The NATO PA was created by individual initiative and is not based on an international agreement. Its purpose is parliamentary cooperation. Governments do not take part.[374] However, the 1974 Belgian federal law grants legal personality, privileges, and immunities to the NATO PA's staff and premises, even though States usually grant privileges and immunities only to intergovernmental organisations, i.e. to those organisations based on a treaty and governed by the States party to that treaty.[375] Article 1 of the 1974 law grants the NATO PA legal personality without specifying whether this is to be understood as national or international legal personality. Generally, there are three requirements for international legal personality, which the NATO PA does not meet:

1. the capacity to conclude treaties. For example, the NATO PA has not concluded any Seat Agreement with Belgium.
2. the capacity to enter into diplomatic relations. For example, the NATO PA does not have UN observer status, nor do other international organisations allow the NATO PA to fully participate in multilateral diplomacy.
3. the capacity to operate and entertain claims in its own right in the international legal order. For example, there are no direct and bilateral dispute settlement mechanisms provided in case of disputes between the host State and the NATO PA, and the latter has never intervened directly before international tribunals.[376]

E. Lagrange, 'La catégorie organisation internationale' in E. Lagrange and J.-M. Sorel (eds.), *op. cit.*, 54; J. Klabbers, *op. cit.*, 11.

373 N. Blokker and H. Schermers, *op. cit.*, § 45, 51; I. Seidl-Hohenveldern and G. Loibl, *op. cit.*, 56–59; H. Adam, *Les organismes internationaux spécialisés*, Paris, L.D.G.J., Tome V, 1992 and I. Seidl-Hohenveldern, 'Gemeinsame zwischenstaatliche Unternehmen' in F. Baer-Kaupert, G. Leistner and H. Schwaiger (eds.), *Liber Amicorum Bernhardt C.H. Aubin*, Kehl am Rhein, Strasbourg, 1979, 193–216.

374 Article 1 NATO PA Rules of Procedure 2019.

375 E. Debuf, 'Tools to do the job: the ICRC's legal status, privileges and immunities', 321–322 and as can be deduced from N. Blokker and H. Schermers, *op. cit.*, § 33, 41; § 38, 44; § 44, 48; § 46–47, 51–52; S. Charnovitz, 'Nongovernmental Organizations and International Law', *The American Journal of International Law* 2006, 356.

376 See *a contrario* E. Debuf, 'Tools to do the job: the ICRC's legal status, privileges and immunities', 321–22.

Moreover, the Belgium Seat Policy contains no indication that Belgium adopts a broader and more inclusive definition of what constitutes a 'public international organisation'. The Seat Policy stipulates:

> The criteria commonly used to speak of an international governmental organization are: the organization was established by an international treaty between states or between states and international governmental organizations, or between intergovernmental organizations, which defines the objectives of the organization, its structure and operations; this founding treaty or the organisation's founding documents demonstrate the intention of the contracting parties to grant the organization at least one functional international legal personality, i.e. it is clear that, with a view to achieving its objectives at international level, it exercise the necessary rights and enact necessary legal acts (such as the conclusion of treaties with third countries and with other international organizations); it has bodies distinct from those of the Member States; it has the power to issue optional or binding standards to Member States.[377]

The Policy continues:

> Only international institutions that meet these conditions can claim the privileges and immunities usually accorded to international legal persons under public international and customary law. Consequently, any decision regarding the granting of privileges and immunities to an international organization must be preceded by an examination of its international legal status. [...] This means that the seat policy, as understood here, does not in principle relate to international NGOs, which are private institutions. However, this rule does not apply absolutely. At least two NGOs, namely the International Committee of the Red Cross and the International Federation of Red Cross and Red Sickle Committees, have been specifically mandated by the international community, i.e. through provisions in international treaties, to carry out specific missions under international humanitarian actions. In both cases, an argument could be developed on the basis of this, so that Belgium could assign a form of functional international legal personality to these organizations.[378]

Switzerland, an important host nation to international organisations, defines the term 'international organisations' more broadly. The 2006 Swiss *Loi fédérale sur les privilèges, les immunités et les facilités, ainsi que sur les aides financières accordés par la Suisse en tant qu'Etat hôte* identifies three types

---

377 Belgium, Interministerieel Comité inzake Zetelbeleid, Basisnota Zetelbeleid, available online at https://diplomatie.belgium.be/nl/beleid/interministerieel-comite-zetelbeleid/basisnota#:~:text=Basisnota-,Interministerieel%20Comit%C3%A9%20Zetelbeleid,hebben%20in%20Belgi%C3%AB. (last accessed January 2025).

378 Belgium, Interministerieel Comité inzake Zetelbeleid, Basisnota Zetelbeleid, available online at https://diplomatie.belgium.be/nl/beleid/interministerieel-comite-zetelbeleid/basisnota#:~:text=Basisnota-,Interministerieel%20Comit%C3%A9%20Zetelbeleid,hebben%20in%20Belgi%C3%AB. (last accessed January 2025).

of international organisations to which Switzerland grants privileges and immunities: (1) intergovernmental organisations (e.g. UN, WTO), (2) other international organisations or so-called 'international institutions' (e.g. ICRC, the International Federation of Red Cross and Red Sickle Committees, OSCE), and (3) quasi-governmental international organisations (e.g. International Air Transport Association, World Anti-Doping Agency).[379] The Belgium Seat Policy only makes an exception for the ICRC and the International Federation of Red Cross and Red Sickle Committees. All this suggests that the Belgian government does not consider the NATO PA to be a *de jure* public international organisation. Despite the fact that the NATO PA's establishment has no basis in any treaty, that it has no international legal personality, and that it is not included in the Belgium Seat Policy, the Belgian 1974 law nevertheless grants privileges and immunities to the NATO PA's delegates,[380] its Secretary General,[381] its property and assets,[382] and members of the International Secretariat.[383] The NATO PA Secretary General, for example, shall enjoy the privileges and immunities defined by the rules of international law applicable in Belgium to the members of the diplomatic staff of diplomatic missions accredited in Belgium. This means the NATO PA Secretary General is protected by Article 31 of the 1961 Vienna Convention on Diplomatic Relations. The language of the cited provisions is clearly very similar to the language used in the constituent instruments and headquarters agreements of international organisations.[384] The members of the International Secretariat of the Assembly enjoy functional immunity from jurisdiction for actions, including words spoken or written, performed in their official capacity, which is similar to the immunities granted to NATO International Staff in Article XVIII Ottawa Agreement. The *travaux préparatoires* show that lawmakers deliberately opted for language inspired by the 1951 Ottawa Agreement.[385] By granting the NATO PA these privileges and immunities, Belgium makes it clear that it considers the PA to be more than a *de jure* non-governmental organisation. In essence, the above shows that the NATO PA is not a *de jure* public international organisation, while at the same time being more than a *de jure* non-governmental organisation. The NATO PA

379 Switzerland, Loi fédérale sur les privilèges, les immunités et les facilités ainsi que sur les aides financières accordés par la Suisse en tant qu'Etat hôte, 22 June 2007, 192.12, available online at www.lexfind.ch/tolv/222624/fr (last accessed January 2025). *Cf.* E. Debuf, 'Tools to do the job: the ICRC's legal status, privileges and immunities', 321–322.

380 Article 12 1974 law.

381 Article 13 1974 law.

382 Article 3–11 1974 law of which Articles 9–11 stipulate exemptions from tariffs, direct and indirect taxes and financial control.

383 Article 14 1973 law.

384 N. Blokker and H. Schermers, *op. cit.*, § 325, 269–270.

385 Belgium, Senaat, Wetsvoorstel tot wijziging van de wet van 14 augustus 1974 betreffende het statuut in België van de Noord-Atlantische Vergadering, Toelichting, Zitting 2000–2001, Doc. 2–843/1 of 5 juli 2001.

is a *sui generis* creation, a semi-official institution with an ambivalent legal status. This ambivalent status may seem odd when one tries to understand it from a strictly legal point of view but makes more sense in light of the fact that host nation policy and politics played a significant role in the process. The French government had granted the NATO PA foreign association status on its territory. Once the NATO PA International Secretariat had been relocated, it proved impossible to conclude a seat agreement with an institution that did not have international legal personality under Belgian law.[386] Hence the need for a legislative initiative to comply with the Assembly's request to continue enjoying the benefits it had acquired in France.[387] It would be interesting to see these privileges and immunities tested before national tribunals, as this could shed light on the legal status of the NATO PA, especially if Belgium were to intervene in the proceedings like it did in *El Hamidi v. NATO* (see below).

4.1.1.5. Relation with the governmental branches of the international organisation

In principle, policy actors produce ideas, which political actors then communicate to the public. This is the idea of discursive institutionalism as conceived by Schmidt.[388] In the policy sphere, policy actors (in this case, the NATO Permanent Representatives and the International Staff) engage in a coordinative discourse about how to construct policies, while in the political sphere, political actors (in this case, members of parliament) enter into a communicative discourse with the public about the necessity and appropriateness of such policies.[389] One channel to communicate ideas to the public at the supranational level is via the delegates in parliamentary assemblies.[390] Can it be said that the NATO PA strengthens NATO's communicative discourse? First and foremost, it must be pointed out that the NATO PA does not have any formal relationship with NATO's governmental branches. Former NATO PA Secretary General Lunn described the impact of the NATO PA on governmental decision-making as follows:

---

386 Draft Law 1974, 2; Senate Bill 1974, 2.

387 Draft Law 1974, 2–3; Senate Bill 1974, 2.

388 V. Schmidt, 'Discourse as Framework for Analysis: Policy Construction and Legitimization for Changing Policies and Practices' in V. Schmidt (ed.), *The future of European capitalism*, Oxford, Oxford University Press, 2002, 209–256; V. Schmidt, 'Discursive Institutionalism: The Explanatory Power of Ideas and Discourse', *Annual Review of Political Sciences* 2008, 303–326.

389 V. Schmidt, 'Discursive Institutionalism: The Explanatory Power of Ideas and Discourse', 310.

390 C. Kraft-Kasack, 'Transnational Parliamentary Assemblies: A Remedy for the Democratic Deficit of International Governance?', 535 and G. Rosen and K. Raube, 'Influence beyond formal powers: The parliamentarisation of European Union security policy', 1–2.

> The Assembly has a rather insignificant, indirect influence on the decision-making process at NATO due to NATO's intergovernmental nature and consensus-made decisions under the directive of the capitals of the Member States.[391]

Commentators agree unanimously that the NATO PA has little to no influence, as the term is understood by Rosen, Raube, Russell, and Cowley, on governmental decision-making.[392] Furthermore, a US Senate report mentions how 'the influence of the Assembly is negligible; the assembly's impact on public opinion is extremely limited.'[393] In a 1978 survey conducted by Mower, individual members of parliament were asked to evaluate the impact of Assembly recommendations on their governments. Most said that it was 'fairly minimal'.[394] And so, the fact that there is a NATO Parliamentary Assembly in place does not change the fact that NATO is an intergovernmental organisation *par excellence*, in which the power lies with governments. In this sense, NATO is an organisation which, to an even greater extent than the EU, has a strong coordinative discourse among the policy actors in its governmental bodies, but a weak communicative discourse from the political actors toward the public via the NATO PA.[395]

4.1.2. WEU Assembly[396]

4.1.2.1. Introduction

The WEU Assembly carried out the parliamentary functions arising from the Modified Brussels Treaty. This entailed scrutiny of the implementation of the obligation of collective defence, as stated in Article V MBT.[397] The members of

391 S. Lunn, 'The Evolving Role of the NATO Parliamentary Assembly' in X. (ed.), *op. cit.*, 21. See also S. Charman and K. Williams, *op. cit.*, 166; C. Brumter, *op. cit.*, 89 and N. Blokker and H. Schermers, *op. cit.*, § 576, 441.

392 G. Rosen and K. Raube, 'Influence beyond formal powers: the parliamentarisation of European Union security policy', 3 and M. Russell and P. Cowley, 'The Policy Power of the Westminster Parliament: the 'Parliamentary State' and the Empirical Evidence', *Governance* 2015, 121–137.

393 U.S. Senate, Committee on Foreign Relations, *The role of the North Atlantic Assembly*, 96th Congress, First Session, July 1979, 54.

394 A. Mower, 'The Importance of the North Atlantic Assembly', *Orbis* 1978, 927–945.

395 *Cf.* V. Schmidt, 'Discursive Institutionalism: The Explanatory Power of Ideas and Discourse', 313.

396 This section is largely based on the work of Dumoulin in 'The Statutory Bodies of WEU', *CVCE Luxembourg University* 2016, 1–6.

397 Article 1 Charter WEU Assembly 1955 and Article 1 Charter WEU Assembly 2010 (Charter WEU Assembly 2010/Rules of Procedure WEU Assembly 2010). See Chartre et règlement de l'Assemblée de l'UEO, adoptés le 24 octobre 1955 à Strasbourg, National Archives of the U.K., Records of international organizations, Copies of records of the Brussels Treaty Organisation and Western European Union. For the purpose of the present book, these materials were obtained through the CVCE Online Archives of the University of Luxemburg.

the WEU Assembly were primarily members of PACE (Article IX MBT). There were political parties in the WEU Assembly.[398] The main interparliamentary work within the Assembly was carried out by four committees.[399] The members of the WEU Assembly met twice a year for plenary sessions and throughout the year in committee meetings, conferences, and colloquies.[400] The WEU Assembly had a President and a Secretary General.[401] The functions of the WEU Assembly were wound up in June of 2011, as was the WEU as a whole.[402]

4.1.2.2. Mode of establishment

The WEU Assembly was established by the 1954 Modified Brussels Treaty, the constituent instrument of the WEU, as one of the two statutory organs of the organisation.[403] The MBT established the WEU Assembly with merely a passing reference.[404] Article IX mentions the obligation of the WEU Council to make an annual report on its activities to 'an Assembly composed of representatives of the Brussels Treaty Powers to the Consultative Assembly of the Council of Europe.'[405] A note made by the WEU Secretary General on 19 January 1955 shows that, one year after the signing of the MBT, there was still confusion about Article IX.[406] According to the note, Article IX reads that 'the WEU Council will present an annual report on its activities and in particular concerning the control of armaments to a *consultative assembly of the Council of Europe.*'[407] This point was struck through with a pen and replaced by the current and final phrasing used in Article IX, at the bottom of the note: 'The WEU Council will present to an Assembly composed of representatives of the Brussels Treaty Powers to the Consultative Assembly of the Council of Europe.' The drafting history of the WEU Treaty reveals that the WEU Assembly came into being

398 C. Kissling, *op. cit.*, 45.

399 Article 39 Rules of Procedure WEU Assembly 1955 and article 41 Rules of Procedure 2010.

400 Council of Europe, *Armed Forces and Security Services: what democratic controls?*, Strasbourg, Council of Europe Publishing, 2009, § 349, 228.

401 Article XI Charter and Article 13 and 49 Rules of Procedure WEU Assembly 2010 (*cf.* Article 47 Rules of Procedure 1955).

402 A. Dumoulin, 'The Statutory Bodies of WEU, Decision of the Council Of The Western European Union on the Residual Rights And Obligations of the WEU, 27 May 2011, available online at www.weu.int/documents/Decision_WEU_en.pdf (last accessed January 2025) and S. Gareis, G. Hauser and F. Kerni, *The European Union – A Global Actor?*, Opladen, Berlin, Toronto, Barbara Budrich Publishers, 2013, 50.

403 J. Hovey, *The Superparliaments: Interparliamentary Consultation and Atlantic Cooperation, New York, Washington,* London, Frederick A. Praeger Publishers, 1967, 69–71.

404 Article IX Modified Brussels Treaty and article V First Protocol.

405 Article IX Modified Brussels Treaty.

406 Brussels Treaty Organization, Interim Commission, *Note du Secrétaire Général sur l'organisation de l'Assemblée de l'Union de l'Europe Occidentale*, Doc. IWG/27, 19 January 1955.

407 Emphasis in the original.

more as a kind of 'afterthought'.[408] Still, it was given more consideration than the NATO PA.[409] In view of the rather unpremeditated way in which the WEU Assembly was created, it should come as no surprise that the preparation of a Charter became the Assembly's first order of business—precisely what the NATO PA does not have.[410] The Charter was a sort of preamble to the Assembly's Rules of Procedure. The WEU Assembly was given a certain degree of autonomy in drafting its Rules of Procedure and defining its relationship with the WEU Council.[411]

4.1.2.3. Position within the international organisation

The WEU Assembly is the parliamentary organ of an international organisation. It is one of the two principal statutory organs of the WEU and was established by Article VIII of the Modified Brussels Treaty. The above makes clear that the WEU Assembly is a consultative assembly, not a legislative one. As confirmed by Humblet, a clerk of the WEU Assembly and the Belgian Senate:

> *Nous savons, au surplus, que cette Assemblée n'a qu'un rôle consultatif, c'est-à-dire qu'elle peut seulement formuler des recommandations et résolutions destinées au Conseil des ministres des gouvernements membres de l'U.E.O.*[412]

4.1.2.4. Legal status

The WEU Assembly is the statutory organ of an international organisation. Its legal basis is the Modified Brussels Treaty, the constituent instrument of the international organisation. Being an organ, the Assembly can be assumed to share in the international legal personality of the WEU as a whole.[413] In

408 J. Hovey, *op. cit.*, 68.

409 J. Hovey, *op. cit.*, 68–71; K. Lindsay, *Towards a European Parliament*, Strasbourg, Council of Europe Publishing, 1958, 20.

410 J. Hovey, *op. cit.*, 71.

411 *Note on the organization of the Assembly of Western European Union*, Doc. No. IWG/61, § 8.

412 Interview with F. Humblet, Clerk of the Assembly of WEU and the Belgian Senate in 'Dix ans d'Assemblée de l'UEO', *Le Soir* 17 décembre 1965: 'We know, moreover, that this Assembly has but a consultative role to play, which means it can only formulate recommendations and opinions addressed to the Council of Ministers of the WEU Member State governments.' (translated by the author).

413 N. Blokker and H. Schermers, *op. cit.*, § 1571, 1035–36; A. Miller, 'The Privileges and Immunities of the United Nations', *International Organizations Law Review* 2009, 25; ILC Rep. 1982, UN Doc. A/37/10, 1982, 40. See Agreement on the Status of Western European Union, national representatives and international staff, signed on 11 May 1955 in Paris, entered into force on 19 July 1956, 1258 UNTS 312 (WEU Status Convention). Article 3 WEU Status Convention: '*L'Organisation possède la personnalité juridique; elle a la capacité de contracter, d'acquérir et d'aliéner des biens mobiliers et immobiliers ainsi que d'ester en justice.*' About the legal personality of international organisations in domestic law see e.g. N. Blokker and H. Schermers, *op. cit.*, § 1591–98, 1065–1070; P. Sands and P. Klein, *op. cit.*, 477.

addition, Article 3 of the Agreement on the Status of the WEU of 11 May 1955 grants the WEU legal personality under national law (WEU Status Agreement). The privileges and immunities of WEU Assembly delegates are stipulated in Title V WEU Status Agreement. The immunities enjoyed by the WEU Assembly Secretary General and President should be understood as falling under the privileges and immunities granted to officials of the WEU in Articles 19–25 WEU Status Agreement. The language and structure of the WEU Status Agreement are similar to, and presumably inspired by, the 1951 NATO Ottawa Agreement.

4.1.2.5. Relation with the governmental branches of the international organisation

The language used in Article IX Modified Brussels Treaty implies that the WEU Assembly existed only by virtue of its relationship to the WEU Council. In reaction to this severe statutory limitation, Assembly delegates tried to broaden their own powers through the Charter.[414] The WEU Assembly sent recommendations and opinions to the WEU Council, which was obliged to furnish the Assembly with a written reply.[415] The Assembly could address recommendations or opinions to the Council on any matter that related to the aims of the WEU and fell within the scope of its competences.[416] Article IX MBT obliged governments in the WEU Council to provide Assembly delegates with a written annual report on their security and defence activities. But as Dumoulin and Hovey confirm, these consultative powers do not change the fact that the WEU Assembly had no legislative or budgetary powers and that it had little effect on governmental decision-making.[417] The WEU Assembly did not weigh

Legal personality in municipal law allows the organisation to act as a legal person within the national legal order of each Member State, which generally includes the capacity to contract, to acquire and dispose of immovable and movable property and to institute legal proceedings, see N. Blokker and H. Schermers, *op. cit.*, § 1591, 1065–1066.

414 A. Dumoulin, 'Statutory Bodies of WEU', 4; WEU Assembly, *Changes to the Charter and Rules of Procedure of the Assembly with a view to accommodating associate members and associate partners of WEU*, Fortieth Ordinary Session, WEU Assembly Doc. 1461, 23 May 1995.

415 Council of Europe, *Armed Forces and Security Services: What Democratic Controls?*, § 349, 228.

416 Article V.a Charter 2010: '*L'Assemblée peut adresser aux autorités gouvernementales ou intergouvernementales compétentes des recommandations ou des avis sur toute question se rapportant à la sécurité et à la défense européennes. Elle peut adopter des résolutions dans tous les cas où elle juge cette forme plus appropriée. Sur directive de l'Assemblée, le Président transmet ces résolutions au Conseil de l'UEO, au Conseil de l'Union européenne, aux organisations internationales, aux parlements nationaux et au Parlement européen*'; *cf.* Article V.a Charter 1955.

417 A. Dumoulin, 'Statutory Bodies of WEU', 4–5 and J. Hovey, *op. cit.*, 107. This is in line with the common understanding that consultative assemblies in principle are without true powers, *cf.* N. Blokker and H. Schermers, *op. cit.*, § 576, 441 and C. Kissling, *op. cit.*, 40.

on governmental decision-making within the organisation very much. Further (empirical) research on the effect of WEU Assembly recommendations on the communicative discourse of the parliamentary delegates towards the public should be done from a political science perspective, which, so far, has not been conducted yet.

4.1.3. Council of Europe Parliamentary Assembly (PACE)

4.1.3.1. Introduction

PACE is one of the two statutory bodies mentioned in Article 10 of the 1949 Statute of the Council of Europe (the Statute), the constituent instrument of the Council of Europe. The structure, powers, and composition of PACE are laid down in Articles 22–35 of the Statute.[418] PACE is a deliberative organ, competent to discuss issues that fall within the jurisdiction of the Statute. It presents recommendations to the Committee of Ministers.[419] Article 23 of the Statute makes it clear that the scope of PACE's activities is the same as that of the Council of Europe. PACE consists of representatives of all Council of Europe Member States. Delegations must consist of members of both the ruling parties and the opposition parties.[420] The parliamentary work is carried out by nine committees.[421] In practice, PACE meets about four times a year for a weeklong plenary session in Strasbourg.[422] It has a President and a Secretary General.[423]

4.1.3.2. Mode of establishment

PACE was established by Article 10 of the constituent instrument of the Council of Europe, i.e. the 1949 Statute, as one of the two statutory organs of the organisation. PACE is a principal organ, not a subordinate one. At the 1948 Hague Congress, expression was given to the urgent need to create a 'European

418 Statute of the Council of Europe, signed on 5 May 1949 in London, entered into force 3 August 1949, ETS no. 0001.
419 Article 22 Statute; S. Marschall, 'European parliaments in transnational organisations: Parliamentary cooperation beyond the European Union', 10 and A. Kiss, 'Le Conseil de l'Europe et les suites données par les Etats membres aux textes adoptés par ses organes', *Annuaire français de droit international* 1967, 547–48.
420 C.F. Amerasinghe, *op. cit.*, 133 and I. Seidl-Hohenveldern, 'Les organes des organisations internationales' in R. Dupuy (ed.), *op. cit.*, 93.
421 Article 44.1 Rules of Procedure of the Assembly (2019), Resolution 1202 (1999) adopted on 4 November 1999 with subsequent modifications of the Rules of Procedure, available online at http://assembly.coe.int/nw/xml/RoP/RoP-XML2HTML-EN.asp (last accessed January 2025).
422 See *The Parliamentary Assembly: Practice and Procedure*, Council of Europe, 2009, 190.
423 Article 23.c and 28.a and b Statute; Rule 15, 20 and 68 Rules of Procedure 2019.

Assembly designed to give expression to European public opinion.'[424] The founders saw PACE as a 'means through which the aspirations of the European peoples may be formulated and expressed, the governments thus being kept continually in touch with European public opinion.'[425] There was solid agreement among governments that an assembly should be written into the constituent instrument of what was to become the Council of Europe.

4.1.3.3. Position within the international organisation

PACE is the parliamentary organ of an international organisation. Alongside the Committee of Ministers, it is one of the two principal organs of the Council of Europe (Article 10 of the Statute). PACE was established as a deliberative and consultative assembly by Article 22 of the Statute.[426]

4.1.3.4. Legal status

The 1949 Statute does more than just create the Assembly. It also sets out its purposes, powers, composition, and the scope of its activity (Articles 22–35). Being an organ of the international organisation, PACE should be assumed not to have a separate international legal personality, but to share in the international legal personality of the Council of Europe as a whole, much like the WEU Assembly and unlike the NATO PA. Additionally, Article 1 of the General Agreement on Privileges and Immunities of the Council of Europe (General Agreement) grants the Council of Europe legal personality under national law.[427] The privileges and immunities of PACE representatives are stipulated in Article 40 of the Statute,[428] which the General Agreement gives effect to.

---

424 The Hague, May 1948, Resolutions, *London and Paris: International Committee of the Movements for European Unity* (no date), 7–15, in A. Peters, 'Dual Democracy' in J. Klabbers, A. Peters and G. Ulfstein (eds.), *op. cit.*, 322.

425 Statement issued by the signatories of the Statute of the Council of Europe (5 May 1949), as found in P. Leach, 'The Parliamentary Assembly of the Council of Europe' in S. Schmahl and M. Breuer (eds.), *The Council of Europe: Its Law and Policies*, Oxford, Oxford University Press, 2017, 166.

426 Article 22 Statute; S. Marschall, 'European parliaments in transnational organisations: Parliamentary cooperation beyond the European Union', 10.

427 The General Agreement on Privileges and Immunities of the Council of Europe was signed in Paris on 2 September 1949 and came into force on 10 September 1952, ETS no. 002. The Protocol to the General Agreement was signed on 6 November 1952 in Strasbourg and came into force on 11 July 1956, ETS no. 010.

428 Article 40 Statute: 'The Council of Europe, representatives of members and the Secretariat shall enjoy in the territories of its members such privileges and immunities as are reasonably necessary for the fulfilment of their functions. These immunities shall include immunity for all representatives to the Consultative Assembly from arrest and all legal proceedings in the territories of all members, in respect of words spoken and votes cast in the debates of the Assembly or its committees or commissions.'

Articles 13–15 of the General Agreement specify the immunities enjoyed by PACE representatives.[429]

4.1.3.5. Relation with governmental branches of the international organisation

The relationship between the Committee of Ministers and PACE has several features.[430] During its first two years PACE managed to strengthen its authority *vis-à-vis* the Committee of Ministers. Article 23 of the Statute was amended in 1951 to abolish the requirement that the Assembly agenda had to be approved by the Committee of Ministers. Furthermore, the Statute was amended to stipulate that representatives to the Assembly should not be chosen by the governments but by the national parliaments.[431] PACE can initiate actions to be taken by the Committee of Ministers by adopting a recommendation. These recommendations are not legally binding, but the Committee of Ministers must provide an answer to them.[432] Empirical studies indicate that about one fifth of the decisions adopted by the Committee of Ministers refer to PACE's recommendations.[433] Many of the Council of Europe's conventions owe their existence to PACE initiatives, pursuant to the strongly formulated Article 15 of the Statute.[434] Moreover, in 1951 the Committee of Ministers agreed to consult the Assembly before inviting more States to join the Council of Europe.[435] All

---

429 Including immunity from all official interrogation and from arrest in respect of words spoken in the exercise of their functions (Article 14 General Agreement) and the exemption from arrest and prosecution during PACE sessions on the territory of all Member States (Article 15 General Agreement).

430 What follows should not be construed as a fully comprehensive overview. For more information, see e.g. Article 23.b Statute and Rules 57–61 of Rules of Procedure 2019.

431 J. Hovey, *op. cit.*, 60.

432 Article 15, 22 and 23 Statute and S. Schmahl and M. Breuer, *op. cit.*, § 6.98–99, 16.

433 *Cf.* B. Habegger, 'Democratic accountability of international organizations: Parliamentary Control within the Council of Europe and the OSCE and the prospects for the United Nations', 193 and B. Habegger, *Parlamentarismus in der internationalen Politik: Europarat, OSZE und Interparlamentarische Union*, Baden-Baden, Nomos, 2005, 118. See also Z. Sabic, *International Parliamentary Organs*, Ljubljana, CIR Publications, 1995, 87.

434 Article 15 Statute reads that 'on the recommendation of the Consultative Assembly or on its own initiative, the Committee of Ministers shall consider the action required to further the aim of the Council of Europe, including the conclusion of conventions or agreements and the adoption by governments of a common policy with regard to particular matters.' Empirical studies have shown, for example, that 36% of all Council of Europe conventions have been initiated by PACE. See B. Habegger, 'Democratic accountability of international organizations: Parliamentary Control within the Council of Europe and the OSCE and the prospects for the United Nations', 193; B. Habegger, *op. cit.*, 155 and J. Hovey, *op. cit.*, 63.

435 Council of Europe, Committee of Ministers, Resolution(49)17 and Committee of Ministers Statutory Resolution (51) 30A in Statute of the Council of Europe and Statutory Resolutions, Strasbourg, 2008.

of this shows that the relationship between the Committee of Ministers and PACE goes beyond the merely consultative, but that PACE does not attain the level of a legislative body. PACE is a consultative assembly that has expanded its competences to include certain *de facto* decision-making powers.[436] PACE's *de facto* powers exercised with regard to the accession of new Member States and its initiatives with regard to the Council of Europe's conventions demonstrate that it engages in some communicative discourse with the public through the actions of the PACE representatives. Further research on the effect that PACE has on the communicative discourse with the public should be done, as the initial research is both limited and outdated.[437]

4.2. COMPARATIVE ANALYSIS

The findings for each assembly will now be compared, and the similarities and differences will be identified. The NATO PA was not established by any constituent instrument or other intergovernmental agreement. The WEU Assembly and PACE, on the other hand, were both established as principal organs by their constituent instruments. It is not clear whether the omission of a parliamentary organ in the North Atlantic Treaty was deliberate or not. In any case, the idea of a formal NATO PA was quickly met with hostility, while there had been no fundamental scepticism towards creating a parliamentary organ for the WEU (although there had been no well-thought-out plan for that either). The establishment of PACE was driven by a sense of need and urgency felt by the governments. The NATO PA is not a NATO organ and is in fact fully independent of the Organisation. It is not a consultative parliamentary assembly. The WEU Assembly and PACE, on the other hand, are parliamentary organs of their international organisations and are consultative assemblies. The NATO PA has no formal ties to NATO's governmental branches and has little to no influence on governmental decision-making. Unlike PACE, the WEU Assembly had no palpable effect on governmental decision-making either. Like the WEU Assembly, PACE is a consultative assembly, but its relationship with the governmental Committee of Ministers has been expanded to include certain *de facto* decision-making powers exercised through institutionalised practices,

436 B. Habegger, 'Democratic accountability of international organizations: Parliamentary Control within the Council of Europe and the OSCE and the prospects for the United Nations', 193; C. Kissling, *op. cit.*, 48 and A. Kiss, 'Le Conseil de l'Europe et les suites données par les Etats membres aux textes adoptés par ses organes', 548.

437 M. Lerch and M. Caspar, 'Die Parlamentarische Versammlung des Europarats: Transnationale Vermittlungsprozesse im gesamteuropäischen Kontext' in E. Kuper and U. Jun (eds.), *Nationales Interesse und integrative Politik in transnationalen parlamentarischen Versammlungen,* Leiden, Springer, 1997, 211–263 and C. Kraft-Kasack, Transnational Parliamentary Assemblies: A Remedy for the Democratic Deficit of International Governance?, 534–557.

which renders it the assembly with the strongest influence *vis-à-vis* the executive. But all in all, these three assemblies weigh but lightly on the governmental decision-making process in their organisations. The NATO PA's weight is the lowest, PACE's the highest. PACE's privileges and immunities are listed in Article 40 of the Statute and are worked out in more detail in a separate legal agreement. The WEU Assembly's privileges and immunities are not specified in the constituent instrument, but in a separate legal instrument. The language and structure of the 1955 WEU Status Agreement were inspired by the 1951 Ottawa Agreement. Unlike the WEU Assembly and PACE, the NATO PA does not share in the statutory privileges and immunities given to NATO officials by the Ottawa Agreement. This is why the Belgian government granted the NATO PA privileges and immunities through a federal law. Because the NATO PA is not an organ of NATO, it does not share in NATO's international legal personality either, in contrast to the WEU Assembly and PACE.

4.3. EXPLANATORY ANALYSIS

The fact that the NATO PA was not established by NATO's constituent instrument can be explained by multiple factors. NATO was the first military alliance built on the premise of collective defence, which either suggests that the drafters of the North Atlantic Treaty were neglectful of NATO's political functions, or that they were hostile to the idea of formal parliamentary oversight in the domain of security, which remains a sensitive topic to this day.[438] PACE was established by the Statute just one month after the North Atlantic Treaty had been signed. Some infer from this fact that the European treaty negotiators were predisposed towards consultative assemblies.[439] Like NATO, the WEU is a military alliance and an international organisation, but it came a few years after NATO, had an exclusively European membership (in contrast to the influence of Canada and the US on the NATO PA)[440] and a mandate that was not as unequivocally directed at the 'imminent' Soviet nuclear threat, which explains why the WEU Assembly was established by the constituent instrument. Still, archival research shows that the WEU Assembly came about as an afterthought. PACE, on the other hand, was firmly established by the Statute in 1949. It was the first assembly of its kind. The Council of Europe's strictly European membership, the fact that it is a fully-fledged international organisation, and its mandate, which emphasises human rights and

438 *Cf.* S. Charman and K. Williams, *op. cit.*, 1920; Z. Sabic, 'Parliamentary Diplomacy and the US Congress: The Case of the NATO Parliamentary Assembly', 246; D. Hobbs, 'The Assembly from 1955 to 1989' in X. (ed.), *NATO Parliamentary Assembly 1955–2005*, 33 and I. Straus, 'Atlantic Federalism and the Expanding Atlantic Nucleus', *Peace and Change* 2002, 317.

439 S. Charman and K. Williams, *op. cit.*, 19.

440 J. Hovey, *op. cit.*, 13–23 and 47–57; C. Brumter, *op. cit.*, 6–24 and 26–32. See also N. Blokker and H. Schermers, *op. cit.*, § 569, 431.

the rule of law, made it possible for PACE to be mentioned in the constitution. The NATO PA's unique legal status can be explained by the fact that the idea of a formal, institutionalised NATO PA has always been met with hostility. The policies and politics of the host nations also explain its ambivalent legal status. As the NATO PA is not an organ of NATO, it could not share in the privileges and immunities of the Ottawa Agreement, which is why its privileges, immunities, and national legal personality had to be granted by a national law. The NATO PA has little to no effect on governmental decision-making, but neither did the WEU Assembly, even though it was an organ of the organisation. This is evidence of general hostility towards parliamentarisation in the domains of security and defence, a phenomenon that is resurfacing now that the European Parliament is trying to take on a greater role in those domains. PACE is undoubtedly the most powerful assembly of the three. This is because of the Council of Europe's mandate, which emphasises human rights and the rule of law, its strictly European membership, and the fact that it is a fully-fledged international organisation, in which speedy governmental decision-making is not essential. Lastly, the NATO PA has the weakest communicative discourse of the three, because it is not itself an international organisation, nor is it an organ of one. NATO itself, in the meantime, has a very strong coordinative discourse, due to the highly technical, military, and classified nature of its deliberations, and the fact that the nations tend to fill in their roles within NATO more as States than as Member States. Because decisions within NATO are made by consensus only, it is difficult to communicate anything other than the broad and vague NATO PA resolutions without jeopardising the compromises made to achieve the consensus.[441]

4.4. EVALUATION OF COMPARISON RESULTS[442]

The NATO PA's legal status, mode of establishment, position, and relationship to NATO's other governmental branches prove to be unique. In terms of these benchmarks, the assembly furthest removed from the NATO PA is PACE, which is part of a fully-fledged international organisation. The WEU Assembly is in fact more similar to PACE, despite the fact that the WEU is a military alliance like NATO. This is because (1) the NATO PA is not an organ of its international organisation while the WEU Assembly and PACE are, and (2) the WEU and Council of Europe are both organisations with a more strictly defined regional (read: European) membership, and (3) speed and efficiency in governmental decision-making are paramount at NATO. This can be schematically summarised as follows:

441 V. Schmidt, 'Discourse as Framework for Analysis: Policy Construction and Legitimization for Changing Policies and Practices' in V. Schmidt (ed.), *op. cit.*, 239–250.

442 The evaluation is limited by the scope of the book.

	NATO PA	WEU Assembly	PACE
Mode of establishment	Individual initiative	Constituent instrument	Constituent instrument
Position in the organisation	Not an organ; Not a consultative assembly	An organ; A consultative assembly	An organ; A consultative assembly
Legal status	*Sui generis;* Immunities and privileges in national law	Constituent instrument; Immunities and privileges in Status Convention	Constituent instrument; Immunities and privileges in constituent instrument and Status Convention
Relation to government branches	No powers at all	Some informal powers	Some *de facto* decision-making powers

4.5. INTERIM CONCLUSION

All in all, this chapter's comparative research shows that the WEU Assembly is in fact more similar to PACE when measured against the benchmarks used, despite being a NATO-style military alliance and international organisation. The fact that the WEU Assembly and PACE are organs means they can represent and legally bind their organisations under international institutional law.[443] The NATO PA cannot do this. What is more, no action undertaken by the NATO PA can cause NATO to incur responsibility under international law (Article 6 ARIO *a contrario*). The legal status of the NATO PA under international institutional law can only be categorised as *sui generis*. It is not a *de jure* public international organisation, because it is not based on an international agreement, does not have international legal personality, and does not accord with the definition of an international organisation as formulated in the Belgium Seat Policy. It is not a *de jure* non-governmental organisation either, because the 1974 Belgian federal law grants the NATO PA Secretary General privileges and immunities under international law, and functional immunities to its International Staff. It would be interesting to see these privileges and immunities tested in court, as this could shed light on the legal status of the NATO PA, especially if Belgium were to intervene in the proceedings. In 2016 the Belgian Court of Cassation adopted the ECtHR practice of not examining the proportionality between the

443 *Cf.* J. Klabbers, *op. cit.*, 208; L. Burgorgue-Larsen, 'La structure institutionnelle de l'organisation internationale' in E. Lagrange and J.-M. Sorel (eds.), *op. cit.*, 376; *Dictionnaire de droit international public*, 586, 791 and G. Gaja, 'Introductory note to the Articles on the Responsibility of International Organizations', *United Nations Audiovisual Library of International Law* 2014, 4.

diplomatic immunity of NATO Member State representatives and Article 6 ECHR in concrete terms. Rather, having found that diplomatic immunity serves a necessary and legitimate purpose (i.e. the proper functioning of the mission), the Court did not concretely examine the proportionality. Belgium's lower courts would likely reach the same conclusion, should the immunity of the NATO PA Secretary General be challenged before them. The extent to which NATO PA resolutions and NATO PA delegates strengthen or could strengthen NATO's communicative discourse towards the public merits further research in the political sciences within the analytical framework created by Schmidt, Mutz, Dryzek, and Habermas.[444] To this end, it could be empirically investigated whether and, if so, to what extent the NATO PA delegates communicate NATO PA resolutions to the citizens of their countries. The latest survey of the NATO PA's impact on the public dates back to 1973. This research is important because, through communicative action, discourse could break the elite hold on supranational decision-making, considering, as has been demonstrated in chapter 2, that democratic access to such decision-making is complicated by the lack of formal Treaty amendment.[445] Based on the outcome of this research, the NATO PA could draw inspiration from the European Parliament's informal powers in the domains of EU security and defence.[446] After all, gaining broader formal powers would be unrealistic in the case of the NATO PA, as such institutionalisation would be possible only if the North Atlantic Treaty were amended or if an additional protocol were negotiated, both of which are extremely unlikely. Think of how the Pan-African Parliament unsuccessfully tried to broaden its legislative powers through an amendment of its protocol.[447] There is also no legal alternative to institutionalisation, because States would not accept if the NAC were to establish a parliamentary organ that is subordinate to the governmental structure, on the basis of article 9 North Atlantic Treaty.[448]

---

444 J. Dryzek, *Discursive Democracy: Politics, Policy, and Political Science*, Cambridge, Cambridge University Press, 1990; J. Habermas, *Between Facts and Norms: Contributions to a Discourse Theory*, London, Polity, 1996 and D. Mutz et al., *Political Persuasion and Attitude Change*, Ann Arbor, University of Michigan Press, 1996.

445 V. Schmidt, 'Discursive Institutionalism: The Explanatory Power of Ideas and Discourse', 315.

446 G. Rosen and K. Raube, 'Influence beyond formal powers: The parliamentarisation of European Union security policy', 2–5.

447 O. Nzewi, 'Influence and Legitimacy in African Regional Parliamentary Assemblies: The Case of the Pan-African Parliament's Search for Legislative Powers', *Journal of Asian and African Studies* 2013, 488.

448 See S. Lunn, 'The NATO Parliamentary Assembly', paper presented at the Seminar on the Parliamentary Dimension of the European Security and Defence Policy, The Hague, 14 May 2001, § 37–39.

5. THE IMMUNITY OF NATO HQ AND SHAPE

5.1. INTRODUCTION[449]

Now that the Alliance created by the North Atlantic Treaty has grown into a fully-fledged international organisation, it must be protected from interference by national governments, and the equality of its Member States must be ensured.[450] This is the primary function of privileges and immunities in public international law: to allow them to function independently.[451] After all, if Member States (and especially the host nation, where the organisation has its headquarters) could subject an organisation to the jurisdiction of their courts and their taxation system, they could exert influence on that organisation in ways that are exterior to the agreed framework of the founding treaty.[452] This would make it less likely that an organisation could function in an efficient, effective, and independent way. As recently as December 2021 the multinational fuel company Supreme brought a case against SHAPE, NATO's military headquarters, before the CJEU. The case had been preceded by years of complicated legal proceedings in which Supreme demanded billions of dollars in damages from SHAPE before multiple Dutch courts. Interestingly, the reason these procedures had been so lengthy and so costly (a SHAPE legal adviser entrusted the author with the knowledge that a person was hired to work full-time on the case)[453] was that SHAPE does not enjoy immunity on the basis of any legal text. NATO has no basic text that gives SHAPE immunity from jurisdiction, even though this is a fundamental protection mechanism in public international law and international institutional law. Supreme, aware of this loophole, continued its lawsuit against SHAPE for years. Generally, the privileges and immunities of international institutions

---

449 This section is largely based on a publication by the author entitled 'Zeventig jaar Noord-Atlantisch Bondgenootschap: enkele volkenrechtelijke aspecten', *Rechtskundig Weekblad* 2020, 1202–1216. Translations from Dutch into English are the author's own efforts.

450 Council of Europe, Committee of Ministers, European Committee on Legal Cooperation, *Additional Report of the Eleventh Session of the Committee on Legal Cooperation, Privileges and Immunities of International Organizations and Associated Persons*, Strasbourg, 9 July 1969, 2 and J.-L. Fagnart,'L'Immunité de juridiction des organisations internationales' in *Mélanges Jacques van Compernolle*, Brussels, Bruylant, 2004, 182.

451 ICJ *Reparations*, 183; E. David, *op. cit.*, 630–632; J. Duffar, *Contribution à l'étude des privilèges et immunités des organisations internationales*, Paris, L.G.D.J., 1982, 248; Court of first instance Brussels 22 October 2012, *Journal des Tribunaux* 2014, 156, note by J. Vanderschuren, 'De quelques considérations sur les immunités octroyées aux organisations internationales', 146, § 7 and A. Reinisch, 'Rationales for judicial abstention' in A. Reinisch (ed.), *International Organizations Before National Courts*, Cambridge, Cambridge University Press, 2000, 233.

452 H. Blatt, 'Rechtsschutz gegen die Vereinten Nationen. Internationale Immunitäten und die Streitbeilegung nach Section 29 des Übereinkommens über die Vorrechte und Immunitäten der Vereinten Nationen', *Archiv des Völkerrechts* 2007, 91.

453 Interview with head of the SHAPE Office of Legal Affairs, Andres Mosquera, online, 10 October 2022.

are granted by treaty, and most often by constituent treaty.[454] NATO is an important exception: the North Atlantic Treaty is entirely silent on the matter. In fact, it is Article V of the 1951 Ottawa Agreement that grants NATO HQ its immunity from jurisdiction. One would expect that SHAPE, NATO's military headquarters, is granted the same immunity by the Paris Protocol, but this is not the case. This raises several important questions, particularly whether immunity from jurisdiction can be based on customary law. This is a disputed issue, which was recently brought before Belgian and Dutch courts. These rulings provide interesting insights. The Belgian and Dutch courts have different points of view on the desirability of letting immunity prevail over other human rights. The rulings suggest how future case law on this topic is likely to evolve. The differences between the points of view of the Belgian and the Dutch courts are especially intriguing, because both countries host several international organisations, and the rulings of the ECtHR have a direct effect in both legal systems.[455]

5.2. NATO HQ'S IMMUNITY FROM JURISDICTION

Even though NATO HQ's immunity is treaty-based (but not based on the constituent treaty), it has not gone unchallenged. NATO HQ's immunity from jurisdiction was recently challenged before the Belgian national courts.[456] Mr. Khaled El Hamedi, an Egyptian citizen residing in Libya, filed a claim demanding compensation for the deaths of his family members caused by NATO airstrikes near Tripoli during Operation Unified Protector in 2011. According to Mr. El Hamedi, the fact that he could not sue NATO because of NATO's immunity from jurisdiction constituted a violation of Article 6.1 ECHR. The Brussels Court of First Instance dismissed the claim. The reason: Mr. El Hamidi could not invoke the ECHR before the Belgian courts precisely because of NATO's immunity. The plaintiff then filed an appeal, on which the Brussels

---

454 See e.g. Article 105 UN Charter; article 40 Statute of the Council of Europe; Article VIII WTO Agreement and see J. Wouters, *Internationaal Recht in Kort Bestek*, Antwerpen, Intersentia, 2018, 893.

455 Article 93 and 94 Dutch Constitution (1983); T. Barkhuysen and M. van Emmerik, *European fundamental rights and Dutch administrative law*, Amsterdam, Wolters Kluwer, 2017, 28–32 and V. De Graaf, 'Between dream and deed: review of international law by the Dutch courts' in J. Wouters and D. Van Eeckhoutte (eds.), *Doorwerking van internationaal recht in de Belgische rechtsorde*, Antwerp/Oxford, Intersentia, 2006, 315–334. For Belgium, see J. Velu, 'Les effets directs des instruments internationaux en matière de droits de l'homme', *BTIR* 1980, 293–316; Belgian Constitutional Court 8 May 2014, Ruling No. 74/2014, *Rechtskundig Weekblad* 2014–2015, 779 and M. Bossuyt, 'The enforceability of treaty provisions or what is "direct" about "direct effect"' in J. Wouters and D. Van Eeckhoutte (eds.), *op. cit.*, 111–118.

456 Court of first instance Brussels 22 October 2012, *Journal des Tribunaux* 2014, note by J. Vanderschuren, 'De quelques considérations sur les immunités octroyées aux organisations internationales', 145–149.

Court of Appeal ruled on 23 November 2017.[457] Again Mr. El Hamedi argued that NATO HQ's immunity from jurisdiction had to be set aside to give effect to Article 6.1 ECHR. Unlike the Court of First Instance, the Brussels Court of Appeal concluded that the victim (despite having no territorial or national link to Belgium) could invoke the ECHR.[458] The Court of Appeal first stressed the importance of the distinction between claims relative to the relationship between the international organisation and its employees, on the one hand, and claims between the international organisation and an external party, on the other hand:

> *Les deux situations – litiges contractuels, notamment en raison de relations de travail, d'une part, et responsabilité quasi délictuelle d'autre part – ne soulèvent, à l'estime de la cour, pas les mêmes enjeux et ne s'inscrivent pas dans le même contexte.*[459]

Mindful of this distinction, the Court finds that the immunity granted to international organisations serves a legitimate purpose, and that the operations carried out by NATO and mandated by the UNSC are especially important in the context of global security:

> *Les opérations de maintien de la paix menées par l'OTAN, en particulier lorsqu'elles le sont, comme dans le cas d'espèce, dans le cadre d'une résolution du Conseil de sécurité de l'ONU, sont fondamentales pour les objectifs recherchés de maintien de la paix et de la sécurité internationale; faire relever de telles opérations de la compétence de juridictions nationales reviendrait permettre à des Etats, par le biais de leurs tribunaux, de s'immiscer dans l'accomplissement par l'OTAN d'une mission fondamentale dans ce domaine, [...]; telles sont précisément les interférences que l'immunité de juridiction de l'OTAN vise à légitimement prévenir, pour lui permettre d'agir de manière indépendante.*[460]

So, because the ability to carry out its operations objectively and independently is of fundamental importance to NATO, the Brussels Court of Appeal concluded that the right of access to justice does not justify setting aside NATO's immunity. Keeping in mind the direct applicability of the ECHR in Belgium, the Brussels

---

457 Court of Appeal Brussels 23 November 2017, *Journal des Tribunaux* 2019, 361.

458 Court of Appeal Brussels 23 November 2017, 364, § 28.

459 Court of Appeal Brussels 23 November 2017, 364, 26: 'In the court's view, the two situations – contractual disputes, particularly as a result of employment relationships, on the one hand, and quasi-criminal liability on the other – do not raise the same issues and are not set in the same context.' (translated by the author).

460 Court of Appeal Brussels 23 November 2017: § 31. 'NATO's peacekeeping operations, particularly when, as in the present case, they are carried out under a UN Security Council resolution, are fundamental to the objectives of maintaining international peace and security; to make such operations subject to the jurisdiction of national courts would be tantamount to allowing States, through their courts, to interfere in NATO's performance of a fundamental mission in this field [...]; these are precisely the interferences that NATO's immunity from jurisdiction is legitimately intended to prevent, in order to enable it to act independently.' (translated by the author).

Court of Appeal based its reasoning on the ECtHR's *Mothers of Srebrenica* ruling. In *Mothers of Srebrenica*, the plaintiffs argued that UN peacekeeping forces were complicit in the murders of their family members, victims of the 1995 Srebrenica massacre. Plaintiffs argued that the immunity of the UN violated their right of access to justice as guaranteed by Article 6.1 ECHR. In the end, the ECtHR decided that the immunity enjoyed by the UN serves a legitimate purpose and that it does not achieve this purpose disproportionately. It is striking how closely the Brussels Court of Appeal followed the ECtHR's reasoning in *Mothers of Srebrenica*. The paragraph in which the Court of Appeal concludes that the peace operations carried out by NATO on the basis of a UNSC resolution are of fundamental importance and that States, through their courts, may not interfere in the performance of these fundamental tasks, was almost literally copy-pasted from paragraph 154 of the *Mothers of Srebrenica* ruling.[461] The Court of Appeal added that, in any case, NATO had to honour its obligations towards victims who wished to be compensated for the damage caused by its operations.[462] However, the Court continued:

> *Il n'est pas établi que les appelants ne disposent d'aucun droit de recours, [...], que cela soit notamment devant les tribunaux de Libye – [...] par un recours gracieux, par une plainte auprès de la Commission des droits de l'homme de l'ONU, voire contre l'Etat membre de l'OTAN dont les forces aériennes ont effectué les frappes litigieuses [...] soit [...] les appelants puissent bénéficier de la protection diplomatique de leurs pays pour tenter d'obtenir une indemnisation par la voie diplomatique.*[463]

Because there were still other channels for the victim to assert his grievances, the Court of Appeal concluded that NATO's immunity should be upheld. The Court declared the matter to be outside of its jurisdiction, without having assessed whether these 'alternative channels' constituted judicial or administrative recourse. It follows from *Mothers of Srebrenica* that the unavailability of alternative sanctions does not mean that the immunity of an international organisation is *ipso facto* incompatible with Article 6 ECHR. One

---

461 'Since the operations decided by resolutions of the UN Security Council under Chapter VII of the UN Charter are essential to allowing the UN to take the lead in successfully completing its peacekeeping missions and maintaining international security, [...] the UN Charter should not be interpreted to mean that the acts and omissions of the Security Council are subject to national jurisdiction without the consent of the United Nations. This would allow States, through their national courts, to interfere with the UN's core mission in this area, as well as in the effective conduct of operations.' (translated by the author.) *Cf.* § 154 in *Mothers of Srebrenica*.

462 Court of Appeal Brussels 23 November 2017, § 32.

463 Court of Appeal Brussels 23 November 2017, § 33: 'It has not been established that the appellants have no right of recourse, [...], whether before the Libyan courts – [...] by an ex gratia appeal, by a complaint to the UN Human Rights Commission, or even against the NATO Member State whose air forces carried out the disputed strikes, [...] or [...] the appellants can enjoy diplomatic protection by their countries to try to obtain compensation through diplomatic channels.' (translated by the author).

should compare to the *ENE v. ESA* case, in which the Brussels Court of Appeal upheld the immunity of the European Space Agency (ESA) on the grounds that the plaintiff could have used several alternative methods of dispute resolution, including 'the possibility of bringing the dispute before ESA's ombudsman, asking the Belgian government to come to the plaintiff's defence by intervening in ESA's Industrial Policy Committee and by pursuing a complaint against its main clients', i.e. ESA's main contractors.[464]

The Brussels Court correctly chose *Mothers of Srebrenica* as its inspiration, rather than *Waite and Kennedy* and *Beer and Regan*. After all, the latter concern a claim of employees against their employer, i.e. the international organisation.[465] In contrast, Mr. El Hamidi was a third party suing an international organisation on the basis of its quasi-delictual liability.[466] The Court also correctly referred to paragraph 154 of *Mothers of Srebrenica*, concluding that the peace operations carried out by NATO on the basis of an UNSC resolution are of fundamental importance and that States, through their courts, may not interfere with the performance of these fundamental tasks. Indeed, international organisations require a certain degree of legal protection when carrying out operational activities.[467] Without such protection, international organisations would simply stop carrying them out. But the Brussels Court failed to assess whether its suggested alternatives provided a realistic recourse to justice under Article 6.1 ECHR. The Court of Appeal's reasoning deserves criticism on this point. After all, the majority of the alternatives hardly offer any real perspective (e.g. a complaint to the UN Human Rights Committee) or they are unrealistic (diplomatic protection by Libya). These futile alternatives stand in stark contrast to the dire situation in which Mr. El Hamedi found himself: when, in his position as director of an NGO that provides humanitarian aid in conflict areas, he returned home from a visit to refugee camps in Tripoli, he discovered that his pregnant wife, his four-year-old daughter, his six-year-old cousin, his eight-year-old niece, and his eight-month-old niece had been killed by a NATO bombing raid.[468]

---

464 Note that the issue at stake in this case was the immunity from execution and not the immunity from jurisdiction of ESA. See Court of Appeal Brussels (21st Chamber) 23 March 2011, AR No. 200/AR/1480 (unpublished), reported by P. d'Argent, 'Jurisprudence belge relative au droit international public. (2004–2011)', *BTIR* 2012, 320–321 (author's own translation from French into English).

465 ECtHR 18 February 1999, nr. 28934/95, *Beer and Regan*, § 51. See also Belgium, Court of Cassation 21 December 2009, *RCJB* 2011, 203, 226, note by E. David and J. Wouters, C. Ryngaert en P. Schmitt, 'Het Hof van Cassatie en de immuniteit van internationale organisaties', *Rechtskundig Weekblad* 2011–2012, 678–68.

466 P. Klein, *La responsabilité des organisations internationales dans les ordres juridiques internes et en droit des gens*, Brussel, Bruylant, 1998, 222.

467 P. Bekker, *The Legal Position of Intergovernmental Organizations*, Dordrecht, Brill Nijhof, 1994, 5.

468 X., 'Een slag tegen de NAVO verloren, maar niet de oorlog', *De Morgen* 26 January 2013, online available at www.demorgen.be/nieuws/een-slag-tegen-de-navo-verloren-maar-niet-

5.3. SHAPE'S IMMUNITY FROM JURISDICTION

In contrast to NATO HQ, whose immunity from jurisdiction is laid down in Article V Ottawa Agreement, SHAPE enjoys no such written immunity. This raises fundamental questions, including whether immunity from jurisdiction can have a basis in customary law. If not, SHAPE would have no protection from legal interference before the Belgian courts. Supreme, a fuel supply company, brought a claim against SHAPE in 2017,[469] demanding billions of dollars in damages. Because Supreme also sued the Allied Joint Force Command Headquarters Brunssum (AJFCH Brunssum), the case was brought before the Dutch courts. The facts relate to the ISAF operation in Afghanistan, established by a UN Security Council Resolution in 2001.[470] NATO assumed command of ISAF in August 2003. AJFCH Brunssum was in operational command of this mission, responsible for logistical planning, execution, and fuel supply. In 2006 and 2007 AJFCH Brunssum, on behalf of SHAPE, concluded three so-called 'basic fuel ordering agreements' (BOAs).[471] Two of these were concluded with Supreme. Displeased with the implementation of the contracts, Supreme sued SHAPE and AJFCH Brunssum for allegedly breaching the exclusivity provision in the BOAs. Supreme demanded monetary damages before the Dutch Court of First Instance in Limburg. In response, SHAPE and AJFCH invoked their functional immunity from jurisdiction. No treaty grants SHAPE or AJFCH Brunssum immunity from jurisdiction—not the Ottawa Agreement, not the London Convention, not the Headquarters Agreement, nor the Paris Protocol. So SHAPE and AJFCH argued that there is a widely held principle that it is essential for international organisations to be independent from their Member States and that a Member State cannot, through its judicial power, improperly influence the actions of that organisation.[472] To be on the safe side, they stressed that 'in any case a certain degree of immunity which allows international organisations to operate independently and impartially should be assumed.' SHAPE and AJFCH added that it is a generally accepted fact that international organisations enjoy functional immunity to protect their proper functioning from interference by sovereign States.[473] In sum, SHAPE and AJFCH Brunssum tried to argue that, even if absolute immunity could be granted, they still enjoyed functional immunity. Supreme disagreed with this. Even if immunity must be assumed, Supreme argued that it cannot go beyond what is functionally

---

de-oorlog~bfd86559/?referrer=https%3A%2F%2Fwww.google.com%2F (last accessed January 2025).

469 Court of first instance Limburg 8 February 2017, nr. C/03/217614, *NJF* 2017/125.

470 UNSC, Resolution 1386 on the situation in Afghanistan, UN. Doc. S/RES/1386, 20 December 2001.

471 Court of First Instance Limburg 8 February 2017, § 2.7.

472 Court of First Instance Limburg 8 February 2017, § 4.13.

473 Court of First Instance Limburg 8 February 2017, § 4.13.

necessary for the operation to work effectively and efficiently. The provision of fuel was not functionally necessary for ISAF's operation in Afghanistan, according to Supreme.[474] The Court then considered whether there was a direct link between the conclusion of commercial fuel supply contracts (the BOAs) and the international task assigned to SHAPE and AJFCH Brunssum, which was to carry out the ISAF mission. It did so by examining established case law of the Dutch Supreme Court:

> The Supreme Court in 1985 in *Spaans v. Iran-US Claims Tribunal* ruled that it follows from international law that international organisations enjoy functional immunity regarding the tasks assigned to them, which was confirmed in the *Euratom* judgment and *EOO* judgment. In doing so, the Supreme Court found that Resolution 1386 and the subsequent UN Security Council resolutions authorise the participating states to undertake all necessary activities for the success of ISAF's mission in only very general terms.[475]

Based on a similar argument, referring to the general language of the UNSC resolution which set up ISAF's mission, the Dutch Court found that SHAPE and AJFCH Brunssum had acted within the limits of the tasks assigned to them.[476] The Court held that the signing of the BOAs falls within the functional immunity that SHAPE and AJFCH Brunssum enjoy, even in the absence of a treaty provision.[477] Next, the court had to examine whether that functional immunity was compatible or incompatible with Article 6 ECHR. After all, Supreme had argued that it had not been able to present its case to a judge. The Court noted that the BOAs indeed lacked a dispute resolution mechanism. For this reason, the Court embarked upon an exercise of balancing of interests, examining whether 'reasonable alternatives' to the judicial process had been available. This test stems from the ECtHR's *Waite and Kennedy* ruling. This case law is relevant because it does not concern the activities of peacekeeping and peace enforcement, but rather the failure to carry out contracts for the provision of goods and services.[478] To this end the court analysed *in concreto* whether the internal process that Supreme, SHAPE, and AJFCH had undergone at the US Department of Defense provided sufficient and objective legal safeguards. According to the Court, it did not. The Court therefore concluded that the functional immunity of SHAPE and AJFCH Brunssum was incompatible with Article 6.1 ECHR because no reasonable alternatives to the judicial process had

---

474 Court of First Instance Limburg 8 February 2017, § 4.13–4.14.

475 Translated by author. Court of First Instance Limburg 8 February 2017, § 4.15–4.21.

476 Compare to the 2011 case by the Dutch Court of Appeal which examines whether providing catering is related to the task of the European Patent Office (EPO) after the EPO had invoked its functional immunity. *Cf.* Court of Appeal The Hague 21 June 2011, *European Patent Office* v. *Stichting Restaurant de la Tour*, No. 200.065.887/01, *JAAN* 2011/71.

477 Court of First Instance Limburg 8 February 2017, § 4.23.

478 See also Court of Appeal 's-Hertogenbosch 10 December 2019, § 6.1.14.

been available.[479] And so, the Court pierced the functional immunity of SHAPE and AJFCH Brunssum, declaring by interlocutory judgment that it had the jurisdiction to hear Supreme's claims.

Afterwards, however, the 's-Hertogenbosch Court of Appeal ruled that a reasonable alternative had been available, namely, a voluntary agreement between the parties on how to deal with contractual differences and matters of indebtedness.[480] This alternative, according to the Court of Appeal, withstands the test of Article 6 ECHR. Consequently, the Court decided that the matter fell outside of its jurisdiction and dismissed Supreme's case. Like the Court of First Instance, the Court of Appeal found that SHAPE and AJFCH were entitled to immunity from jurisdiction on the basis of customary international law.[481] To support this decision, the Court referred to the parliamentary archives of the Dutch House of Representatives and to the earlier *Spaans v. Iran–US Claims Tribunal* ruling by the Dutch Supreme Court.[482]

In essence, the Dutch courts are of the opinion that SHAPE and AJFCH Brunssum enjoy functional immunity even in the absence of any treaty provision to that effect. However, it must be pointed out that, regarding the source of immunity from jurisdiction, the position of the Dutch courts has always been isolated. Generally, States rarely take up a position on this matter.[483] The position of the Council of Europe is that organisations do not enjoy privileges and immunities if this is not provided by treaty.[484] The most important Dutch ruling in this regard is *Spaans v. Iran-US Claims Tribunal*. This landmark judgment concerned a Dutch citizen, Mr. Spaans, who sued the Iran-US Claims Tribunal (IUSCT). In 1982 the IUSCT had informed Mr. Spaans that his services as an interpreter and linguist at the IUSCT were no longer needed. In court, Mr. Spaans demanded the continued payment of his wage until the 'lawful termination of his employment.' The IUSCT invoked its immunity from jurisdiction before the lower courts. At the time of the proceedings no Headquarters Agreement between the Netherlands and the IUSCT had been concluded, which explains why the IUSCT did not enjoy immunity on the basis of any treaty. The case eventually reached the Dutch Supreme Court in 1985. The Court found that, even in cases where no treaty provision grants an international organisation any privileges or immunities, it follows from the unwritten rules of international law that an international

479 Court of First Instance Limburg 8 February 2017, § 4.41.

480 Court of Appeal 's-Hertogenbosch 10 December 2019, nr. 200.216.570/01, § 6.8.3.

481 Court of Appeal 's-Hertogenbosch 10 December 2019, § 6.7.1.

482 Court of Appeal 's-Hertogenbosch 10 December 2019, § 6.7.2 and § 6.7.3.

483 P. Cahier, *Le droit diplomatique contemporain*, Genève, Droz, 1962, 46–47.3.

484 Council of Europe, Committee of Ministers, European Committee on Legal Cooperation, Additional Report of the Eleventh Meeting of the Committee on Legal Cooperation, Privileges and Immunities of International Organizations and Associated Persons, Strasbourg, 9 July 1969, 2.

organisation is entitled to immunity from jurisdiction no less than had it been provided by treaty, 'at least in the State in whose territory the organisation is located.'[485] In Belgium, on the other hand, it is much less clear whether international organisations enjoy immunity in the absence of a treaty provision. The official Seat Policy of Belgium sidesteps the issue by using ambiguous wording. It notes that 'because of the exceptional nature of privileges and immunities, the latter in particular should be interpreted restrictively.'[486] The *League of Arab States v. T.M.* case, the most important Belgian ruling on the matter, provides more clarity. In that ruling (12 March 2001) the Belgian Court of Cassation held that 'organisations enjoy immunity *only* when this is provided in a Treaty that has been approved and has entered into force'.[487] Although the *Arab League* case concerned general principles of law rather than customary international law, one can safely assume the reasoning to be equally valid in the case of the latter, considering the hierarchy of norms in international law. This analogous interpretation is also justified by the depth and scrutiny with which the Court of Cassation handled the first plea in *Arab League*. Moreover, in the *El Hamedi* case, the Brussels Court of Appeal noted that, while the immunity of States from jurisdiction is frequently of customary origin, the immunity of international organisations is based on an express text in the form of an international treaty that binds its member states, as in the case of NATO.[488] This indicates that Belgian courts would not accept immunity for SHAPE and AJFCH on the basis of customary law, which would mean that Supreme could successfully bring its claim before the Belgian courts. Still, the language used in *Arab League* is vague and the ruling is very much focused on general principles of law. It would be interesting to see a similar case brought before the Belgian courts. This would have greater importance, relevance, and scope, as Belgium hosts many institutions that might see their immunity challenged at some point. If the case were to be tried in Belgium, host nation to SHAPE, it would, at long

---

485 Hoge Raad voor Justitie 20 december 1985, *Spaans v. Iran-United States Claims Tribunal*, nr. 12627, *NJ* 1986, 428.

486 Interministerial Committee on Seat Policy, Basic Note on Seat Policy, available online at https://diplomatie.belgium.be/nl/beleid/interministerieel-comite-zetelbeleid/basisnota#:~:text=Basisnota-,Interministerieel%20Comit%C3%A9%20Zetelbeleid,hebben%20in%20Belgi%C3%AB. (last accessed January 2025). See also F. Dopagne, 'Bruxelles et ses organisations internationales. Notes sur la politique de siège de la Belgique', *Journal des Tribunaux* 2012, 185–186 and E. De Brabandere, 'Belgian Courts and the Immunity of International Organizations', *International Organizations Law Review* 2013, 467–468.

487 Emphasis added. Belgium, Court of Cassation 12 Maart 2001, *League of Arab States v. T.M.*, *Arr.Cass.* 2001, 395, note by J.F. Leclercq, *APT* 2001, 61 and *RCJB* 2002, 377.

488 Court of Appeal Brussel 23 November 2017, *El Hamidi et al. v. NATO*, 363, § 21. See, in the same vein, E. De Brabandere, 'Belgian Courts and the Immunity of International Organizations', 473 and J. Verhoeven, 'Traités mixtes, assentiments partiels ou rétroactifs et règles non écrites', *RCJB* 2002, 396 and 398–399 (author's own translation from French into English).

last, clarify the Court of Cassation's ambiguous position taken in *Arab League* and the Belgian government's ambivalent position taken in its Seat Policy.

5.4. INTERIM CONCLUSION

NATO HQ's immunity from jurisdiction is based on Article V Ottawa Agreement. Because of the isolated position taken by the Dutch courts in *Spaans v. US-Iran Claims Tribunal*, SHAPE and AJFCH were granted functional immunity from jurisdiction on the basis of customary international law even in the absence of a treaty provision. Had the *Supreme* case been decided in Belgium, it is likely that Belgian judges would not have granted SHAPE and ACJH functional immunity. The Belgian case law and the Belgian Seat Policy would not tolerate such a far-reaching conclusion. This would mean that Supreme could have successfully brought its billion-dollar claim before the Belgian courts, thereby lessening the efficiency with which SHAPE could carry out its missions. If Belgium wants to remain an attractive host nation to the many institutions on its soil, it could consider changing its host nation policy, because legal proceedings would be less lenghty and less costly if an organisation is protected by immunity from jurisdiction. This could be achieved by granting functional immunity from jurisdiction through an amendment to the Paris Protocol or the Belgium-SHAPE Seat Agreement, or by expanding the Belgian Seat Policy to include customary law as a basis for immunity from jurisdiction for international organisations.

6. CONCLUSION

The above analysis allows us to answer the research questions formulated at the outset of this chapter. Was NATO's institutional framework created and transformed in accordance with the fundamental principles of international institutional law concerning the lawful establishment of subsidiary bodies and the lawful delegation of powers to those bodies? The NAC's establishment and competences are in accordance with the principles of international institutional law because the NAC is NATO's only statutory organ and because its competences stem from the North Atlantic Treaty. Since the Treaty Articles speak of 'the Parties' and not 'the Council', the NAC can do just about anything the contracting parties authorise it to do, limited only by the political and military subject matter of the Alliance itself. The committees were lawfully established as well, and the delegation of powers to them occurred lawfully. The same goes for the International Staff. This is attested to by the fact that nations have barely delegated any powers to the International Staff, preferring to limit its role to facilitation. This confirms that, in the NAC, the signatory parties to the North Atlantic Treaty mostly act in their capacity as States rather than as Member States of the Organisation. This is also why, in *Gasparini*, the ECtHR might have gone too far when it opened the door to holding Member States accountable for having joined a consensus on a decision. This is in tension with the principle that, generally, States cannot be held liable for the actions of organisations by mere virtue of their membership of those organisations. Whether the delegation of powers from the NAC to the NATO AT occurred lawfully is questionable. After all, the ICJ allowed the UNGA to delegate judicial powers to the UNAT by implying these powers from Articles 7 and 101(1) and (3) UN Charter. The NAC's judicial powers, however, cannot be implied from the constituent instrument, and the *travaux préparatoires* show that the signatory parties were opposed to the NAC having such conciliatory powers (*nemo dot quod non habet*). Moreover, the North Atlantic Treaty does not have the same objectives as those mentioned in Articles 1 and 2 UN Charter. It would be interesting to see the *Gasparini* case inspiring others to challenge the NATO AT's powers in court, to see whether judges will imply the NATO AT's judicial power from the Ottawa Agreement. Because the NATO PA is not a subsidiary body or organ of NATO, its lawful establishment is not dependent on the aforementioned principles. Regardless, it is worth nothing that Belgium could not conclude an agreement with the NATO PA to grant it privileges and immunities as Switzerland did in the ICRC-Swiss Agreement. This because the NATO PA does not have international legal personality and does not share in the international legal personality of NATO (as opposed to the WEU Assembly and PACE). And so, it is a 1974 Belgian federal law that grants the NATO PA its privileges and immunities, even though, usually, States only grant privileges and immunities to public intergovernmental organisations on the basis of a treaty. The NATO PA does not meet the requirements to be a public international organisation, since its existence is not based on a treaty, nor is it mentioned in the Belgian Seat Policy definition of a public international organisation either. This goes to show that Belgium considers the NATO PA to be more than a *de jure* non-governmental organisation but less than a *de jure* intergovernmental organisation. The NATO PA's legal status can only be categorised as *sui generis*, in terms of international institutional law. Posing a parliamentary question to the Belgian federal parliament should further clarify the matter. After all, if Belgium truly considers the NATO PA to be an international organisation, it should adapt its Seat Policy to the example of the Swiss *Loi fédérale sur les privilèges, les immunités et les facilités*. Furthermore, because the NATO PA is not an organ, it cannot bind the organisation (like the WEU Assembly or PACE can), nor can the conduct of the NATO PA cause NATO to incur responsibility under international law (Article 6 ARIO *a contrario*).

The institutionalisation of NATO created the need for immunities, which, for NATO HQ, are laid down in Article V Ottawa Agreement. The 2017 *El*

Hamedi ruling deserves to be criticised, as the majority of the alternative dispute settlement mechanisms suggested by the Brussels Court are either unrealistic (e.g. diplomatic protection by Libya) or offer hardly any real chance of justice. In contrast to NATO HQ, SHAPE does not enjoy immunity from jurisdiction based on a written clause. Had a Belgian court ruled on the *Supreme* case, the contractor would probably have been able to sue SHAPE for billions of dollars in damages, because Belgian judges do not recognise customary law as a basis for immunity from jurisdiction. Although the Dutch courts eventually did recognise SHAPE's immunity on the basis of customary law—on this point the position of the Dutch courts has always been isolated—the lack of any written basis in law still led to extremely long and costly proceedings for SHAPE. It would be advisable for the Belgian government to consider changing its host nation policy in this regard if it wants to keep being an attractive host for the many institutions on its soil. This could be done by granting immunity from jurisdiction by amending the Paris Protocol or the Belgium-SHAPE Seat Agreement, or by following the example of the Netherlands and expanding the Belgian Seat Policy to include customary law as a basis for immunity from jurisdiction.

CHAPTER 4
NATO'S DECISION-MAKING: LEGALLY FORMALISED OR UNCONSTRAINED?

1. INTRODUCTION[489]

Imagine that today is 22 March 1999. The North Atlantic Council is meeting to decide on the launch of air operations in Kosovo. All NATO Member States are represented in the NAC. You are the Greek representative. Your government and the Greek public are opposed to these air operations. What would you, as Greece's representative in the NAC, do during this decision-making round? Would you:

A. vote against the NATO decision to intervene in Kosovo?
B. block the decision by raising objections?
C. join the consensus decision but opt out of taking part in the air operations?
D. convince fellow NATO Member States to undertake air operations outside of the context of NATO?

This quiz question was presented to the expert audience during the author's second doctoral seminar on 4 October 2021.[490] The results of the poll were as follows: 52% voted for option A, 38% for B, 10% for C, and 0% for D.[491] This chapter will show that option A is actually incorrect, and that option D is one of the correct answers. This goes to show that, even in an expert setting, NATO's decision-making is misunderstood. Remarkably little is known about it. This is because the North Atlantic Treaty nor any other NATO basic document lays down any decision-making procedure or voting formula.[492] In contrast, almost

---

489 Parts of this Chapter were published in an at-a-glance note entitled 'The comparison of Article 5 North Atlantic Treaty to Article 42.7 TFEU', published online by the *European Parliament Research Service* 2023.

490 The audience consisted of 22 people, including Belgian and Dutch professors of international institutional law, current and former NATO legal advisers, KU Leuven international law PhD researchers and one diplomat.

491 Doctoral seminar by Anne Verhelst, KU Leuven, online, 4 October 2021. All answers except for a. are correct.

492 *Cf.* A. Payton, 'Consensus Procedures in International Organizations', 1; E. Posner and A. Sykes, 'Voting Rules in International Organizations', *University of Chicago Public Law and*

all international organisations have official voting rules in their constituent instruments. Think of Article 16.3 TEU, Article 231 TFEU, Article 27 UN Charter, Article 6 OECD Convention, Article 59 OAS Charter, Article 16.2 ILO Constitution, Article 9.2 ECOWAS Treaty, Article 20 Statute of the Council of Europe, and Article IX.1 WTO Agreement. Apart from the 'unanimity' requirement for the accession of new parties to the North Atlantic Treaty (which is not a voting formula but pertains to the ratification of accession protocols), the North Atlantic Treaty does not prescribe any decision-making rule. And apart from Article 9 ('The parties hereby establish a Council [...] *to consider matters concerning the implementation of this Treaty*'[493]), the Treaty says nothing about the legally binding nature of NATO decisions. The 1949 Treaty does not provide NATO decision-making bodies with any rule or procedure to be followed when adopting acts, nor does it specify what the legal and normative status of such acts is. This is remarkable, seeing that decision-making is ultimately the most important activity of international organisations.[494] Taking decisions is how international organisations put their objectives into action. The decisions of international organisations need to be made in accordance with established procedures and within the confines of the constituent instrument. The rules of decision-making also influence the extent to which States retain their sovereignty within the international organisation and the extent to which they will seek to control the powers of the organisation, as Schermers and Blokker point out.[495] They impact the extent to which NATO States act as States rather than

Legal Theory Working Paper 2014, 2–27 and E. McIntyre, 'Weighted Voting in International Organizations', *International Organization* 1954, 484–497.

493 Emphasis in the original.

494 'Decision-making' as described by Blokker and Schermers, *op. cit.*, § 703, 529, where reference is made to Ustor's definition of 'decision-making': 'what takes place in a given body of the organization when the will of its members is coordinated and moulded into one which can and shall be considered under the relevant law of the organization as the expression of the will of the organization.' The present Chapter adheres to this definition of decision-making, see E. Ustor, *Decision-making in the Council for Mutual Economic Assistance*, Leiden, Martinus Nijhoff Publishers, 1971, 174. See also I. Dekker and R. Wessel, 'Governance by International Organizations: Rethinking the Normative Force of International Decisions' in I. Dekker and W. Werner (eds.), *Governance and International Legal Theory*, Leiden, Nijhoff, 2004, 215; J. Klabbers, *op. cit.*, 154; P. Klein, 'International Organizations or Institutions: Decision-Making Process' in X (ed.), *Max Planck Encyclopedia of Public International Law*, Oxford, Oxford University Press, 2019, § 1; J. D'Aspremont and D. Ventura, 'La composition des organes et le processus décisionnel' in E. Lagrange and J.-M. Sorel (eds.), *op. cit.*, § 796, 404.

495 N. Blokker and H. Schermers, *op. cit.*, § 918, 632; K. Honkanen, 'The Influence of Small States on NATO Decision-Making: the Membership Experiences of Denmark, Norway, Hungary and the Czech Republic', *Swedish Defence Research Agency Paper* 2002, 23. E.g. according to Blokker and Schermers, the voting rules in many organizations are attempts to balance State sovereignty with the factual inequality of States (*op. cit.*, § 923, 633). See *infra* on what this entails for NATO.

as Member States within the Organisation.[496] The following analysis will help to better understand NATO's role as an international organisation in relation to its Member States in light of the latter's decision-making sovereignty and responsibility.[497] The veil of mystery, secrecy, and bureaucracy that surrounds NATO, and the lack of any database containing NATO decisions, explain why no fundamental legal research has yet been done on NATO's decision-making. Little is known about the chain, process, and procedure of NATO decision-making. In the academic literature and even in official NATO documents, there is often confusion around the formula with which NATO adopts decisions. They tend to blur the lines between the concepts of unanimity, consensus, and veto in international institutional law.[498] This is why the present chapter aims to clarify what precisely constitutes a 'NATO decision', which actors can initiate the decision-making process, and how NATO's decisions are prepared and adopted.

2. NATO DECISIONS: DEFINITION AND THE ROLE OF CONSULTATION

In the absence of a legal basis in the North Atlantic Treaty or any other NATO basic agreement, one must resort to the definition of a 'NATO decision' given in the 2010 NATO Legal Deskbook and in the 2019 NATO Encyclopedia: the 'expression of the individual and collective will of all the sovereign states that are members of the Alliance.'[499] This definition immediately reveals an ambiguity: NATO decisions reflect both the collective and the individual will of the Member States. The decisions adopted by NATO, together with the constituent instrument and the established practice of the organisation, form part of its internal law, known as the 'rules of the organisation' in Article 5 VCLT[500] and

---

496 I. Dekker and R. Wessel, 'Identities of States in International Organizations', *International Organizations Law Review* 2015, 293–318. Compare to C. Bickerton, 'From Nation States to Member States in European Union Foreign Policy' in C. Bickerton (ed.), *European Integration: From Nation-States to Member States*, Oxford, Oxford University Press, 2012, 151.

497 M. Virally, 'La valeur juridique des recommandations des organisations internationales', *Annuaire français de droit international* 1956, 67.

498 See e.g. T. Gazzini, 'NATO's Role in the Collective Security System', *Journal of Conflict and Security Law* 2003, 243; A. Sari, 'The Mutual Assistance Clauses of the North Atlantic and EU Treaties: The Challenge of Hybrid Threats', *Harvard National Security Journal* 2019, 431; A. Lindstrom, 'Consensus Decisionmaking in NATO: French Unilateralism and the Decision to Defend Turkey', *Chicago Journal of International Law* 2003, 579–580; J.C.S., 'Problèmes juridiques de l'Organisation du Traité de l'Atlantique Nord', *Politique Étrangère* 1955, 698; F. Beer, *Integration and Disintegration in NATO: Processes of Alliance Cohesion and Prospects for Atlantic Community*, Ohio, Ohio State University Press, 1969, 13; E. Buckley, 'Invoking Article 5', *NATO Review* 2006, 2. See *NATO Encyclopedia* 2018, 265, 377 and 394–95.

499 *NATO Legal Deskbook* 2010, 47; *NATO Encyclopedia* 2019, 162, 165 and 394.

500 As an international legal person, NATO is bound by the customary provisions of the VCLT. *Cf.* ICJ *Namibia (South West Africa)*, § 94, 18; ICJ 1997, *Gabčikovo-Nagymaros Project*

Article 2.1(j) VCLTIO.[501] NATO generates thousands of decisions every year. In terms of subject matter, these decisions fall into five broad categories (some exceptions notwithstanding), according to Michel[502]:

1. broad political and military strategies, which are reflected in documents such as the Strategic Concept and in decisions regarding expansion;
2. military structure and planning functions, covering areas such as the NATO command and force structure, capabilities development, and contingency and operational planning related to potential military missions;
3. authorising, monitoring, and adjusting collective defence and crisis management operations;
4. organisational and management concerns, e.g. defining the responsibilities and overseeing the operations of the International Staff, International Military Staff, and various NATO agencies;
5. resource and budgeting issues involving NATO collective assets, personnel, and infrastructure.

Strikingly, the North Atlantic Treaty nor any other NATO basic document prescribes a procedure or voting formula for the adoption of decisions. In this regard, NATO is unique. The North Atlantic Council, during its first meeting in September 1949, issued no formal procedure for decision-making and has never done so since. How, then, are NATO decisions prepared and adopted? The power to initiate an international organisation's decision-making

(Hungary v. Slovakia), Judgment, *ICJ Rep* 1997, 7; J. Wouters, C. Ryngaert, T. Ruys and G. De Baere, *op. cit.*, 62.

501 Ostensibly, Article 2.1(j) VCLTIO distinguishes between 'decisions' and 'resolutions'. The commentaries to the VCLTIO inform that the International Law Commission opted for a descriptive approach employing the words 'decisions' and 'resolutions' while the adverbial phrase 'in particular' shows that the adoption of a 'decision' or of a 'resolution' is only one example of the kind of formal act that can give rise to rules of the organisation. For reasons of clarity, this Chapter employs the term 'NATO decisions' and disregards the use of the term 'resolutions'. See Commentary 25 to article 2 VCLTIO, ILC 1982, *Draft articles on the law of treaties between States and international organizations or between international organizations, with commentaries*, 1982, Text adopted by the International Law Commission at its thirty-fourth session, in 1982, and submitted to the General Assembly as a part of the Commission's report covering the work of that session (at para. 63). The report, which also contains commentaries on the draft articles, appears in *Yearbook of the International Law Commission*, 1982, vol. II, Part Two. Note how the VCLTIO has not yet entered into force, see Vienna Convention on the Law of Treaties between States and International Organizations or between International Organizations, adopted on 20 March 1986, not yet entered into force, UN. Doc. A/CONF/129/15, *cf.* J. Wouters, C. Ryngaert, T. Ruys and G. De Baere, *op. cit.*, 63; see also M. Virally, 'La valeur juridique des recommandations des organisations internationales', 66.

502 L. Michel in 'NATO Decisionmaking: How the "Consensus Rule" Works', *Croatian International Relations Review* 2006, 8–9.

machinery is usually limited to certain specific instances.[503] Strikingly, the North Atlantic Treaty does not have built-in provisions regarding the right of initiative. The initiation of the decision-making process at NATO relies on practice. Generally, NATO Member States are the most important initiators of decisions of international organisations.[504] This power of governments is limited by the competence of the organisation itself: a government is permitted to take only those initiatives related to decisions the organisation is competent to take (*cf.* chapters 2 and 3).[505] Any NATO Member State government can provoke discussion on a certain subject matter by means of continuous consultations that take place in the hallways of NATO HQ, in the NATO HQ lobby, within groups of like-minded States, during the informal weekly NAC lunches hosted by the individual Member States on a rotating basis[506] etc.[507] Having decided to take an initiative, a national delegation will rarely submit a detailed proposal for discussion, preferring to propose to study a particular problem, ask fellow Member States to consider the question at a future meeting, or request a report from another NATO body.[508] In practice, the NATO International Staff is able to initiate decisions too, despite lacking formal power of initiative.[509] For example, members of the IS can initiate new activities by persuading national delegations

503 N. Blokker and H. Schermers, *op. cit.*, § 710, 532 and P. Klein, 'International Organizations or Institutions: Decision-Making Process' in X. (ed.), *op. cit.*, § 6.

504 Interview with a NATO legal adviser, Tervuren, 11 July 2022 and P. Klein, 'International Organizations or Institutions: Decision-Making Process' in X. (ed.), *op. cit.*, § 6; J. D'Aspremont and D. Ventura, 'La composition des organes et le processus décisionnel' in E. Lagrange and J.-M. Sorel (eds.), *op. cit.*, § 827, 420.

505 Interview with a senior NATO International Staff Member, NATO Headquarters, 9 June 2022. Note that this interview was conducted in Dutch, and that all translations provided in this book are the author's own efforts. See also N. Blokker and H. Schermers, *op. cit.*, § 711, 533 and P. Klein, 'International Organizations or Institutions: Decision-Making Process' in X (ed.), *op. cit.*, § 6.

506 Based on in-house working experience at NATO HQ (1 January 2018 – 31 December 2018) and see K. Honkanen, 'The Influence of Small States on NATO Decision-Making: the Membership Experiences of Denmark, Norway, Hungary and the Czech Republic', 25.

507 Based on in-house working experience at NATO HQ (1 January 2018 – 31 December 2018) and an interview with a senior NATO International Staff Member, NATO Headquarters, 9 June 2022 and an interview with a NATO legal adviser, Tervuren, 11 July 2022. See also F. Kirgis, 'NATO Consultations as a Component of National Decisionmaking', *The American Journal of International Law* 1979, 372; *NATO Encyclopedia* 2018, 162 and see N. Blokker and H. Schermers, *op. cit.*, § 711, 533 and compare to the importance of informal consultation in the UNSC context, L. Feuerle, 'Informal Consultation: A Mechanism in Security Council Decision-Making', *New York University Journal of International Law and Politics* 1985, 267–306 and F. Delon, 'La concertation entre les membres permanents du Conseil de sécurité', *Annuaire français de droit international* 1993, 53–64.

508 Based on in-house working experience at NATO HQ (1 January 2018 – 31 December 2018) and an interview with a senior NATO International Staff Member, NATO Headquarters, 9 June 2022 and a NATO legal adviser, Tervuren, 11 July 2022. See also N. Blokker and H. Schermers, *op. cit.*, § 710, 532 and § 726, 539.

509 Based on in-house working experience at NATO HQ (1 January 2018 – 31 December 2018) and an interview with a NATO legal adviser, Tervuren, 11 July 2022.

of their necessity. They may also draw the attention of the governing bodies to issues related to their field of responsibility.[510] Consultations allow Allies to exchange views and information on a certain topic, and discuss issues prior to reaching a consensus and undertaking action.[511] Consultation has always been seen as crucial to the achievement of NATO's purposes.[512] Moreover, almost all major NATO statements on cooperation within the Alliance underline the importance of consultation.[513] NATO Secretaries General regularly ask Member States to conduct timely consultations when formulating decisions that affect the Alliance.[514] Continuous consultations take place in a variety of fora, including bilateral and multilateral discussions in Allied capitals, at national delegations in NATO HQ, within the NAC, in committees, and in working groups.[515] The principal formal forum for political consultation is the North

---

510 N. Blokker and H. Schermers, *op. cit.*, § 713, 533 and § 461, 343 and A. Boeva, 'What is NATO HQ', 23 as well as an interview with a senior NATO International Staff member, NATO Headquarters, 9 June 2022.

511 Interview with a senior NATO International Staff Member, NATO Headquarters, 9 June 2022 and interview with a NATO legal adviser, Tervuren, 11 July 2022. See also *NATO Encyclopedia* 2018, 164.

512 F. Kirgis, 'NATO Consultations as a Component of National Decision-making', 372. Note how the North Atlantic Treaty was negotiated by way of preceding consultations and consensus, K. Honkanen, 'The Influence of Small States on NATO Decision-Making: the Membership Experiences of Denmark, Norway, Hungary and the Czech Republic', 23 and S. Kay, *NATO and the Future of European Security*, Maryland, Rowman & Littlefield, 1998, 32.

513 NATO, Report of the Committee of Three on Non-Military Cooperation in NATO, 1956, § 4, 15, 29 and 42; The Future Tasks of the Alliance, Report of the Council – 'The Harmel Report', 1967, § 7 and 15 (Harmel Report); Declaration on Atlantic Relations issued by the North Atlantic Council (The Ottawa Declaration), 1974, para. 11 and see also para. 20 of the 1991 Strategic Concept; para. 10 of the 1999 Strategic Concept and para. 5 of the 2010 Strategic Concept.

514 For a detailed overview of the efforts and pronouncements of the first four NATO Secretaries General see F. Beer, *op. cit.*, 30–37; F. Kirgis, 'NATO Consultations as a Component of National Decisionmaking', 373; NATO, NATO Letter: Ten Years of Atlantic Cooperation, 1959, 1 and 4, available online at https://archives.nato.int/uploads/r/null/1/3/137362/0098_NATO_Letter_Ten_Years_of_Atlantic_Co-operation_1949-1959_ENG.pdf (last accessed January 2025); P.-H. Spaak, 'The Atlantic Alliance and its Future', Text of a speech given by Secretary General Paul-Henri Spaak at the closing session of the Conference on the North Atlantic Community, 14 September 1957, available online at www.nato.int/cps/en/natolive/opinions_17588.htm (last accessed November 2023); P.-H. Spaak, *Why NATO?*, Middlesex, Penguin Books, 1959, 33; J. Luns, 'Introduction' in J. Godson (ed.), *Transatlantic crisis: Europe and America in the 70s*, London, Alcove Press, 1974, 12; see also more recently A. Rasmussen, 'New NATO – new Turkey', Text of a speech given by Secretary General Anders Fogh Rasmussen held in Ankara, Turkey, 17 February 2012, available online at www.nato.int/cps/en/natohq/opinions_17588.htm?selectedLocale=en (last accessed January 2025) and J. Stoltenberg, Remarks by NATO Secretary General Jens Stoltenberg on launching #NATO2030 – Strengthening the Alliance in an increasingly competitive world, 8 June 2020, available online at www.nato.int/cps/fr/natohq/opinions_176197.htm (last accessed January 2025).

515 L. Michel, 'NATO Decisionmaking: How the "Consensus Rule" Works', 8 and interviews with a senior NATO International Staff Member, NATO Headquarters, 9 June 2022; a NATO legal adviser, Tervuren, 11 July 2022 and with Dr. Jamie Shea, former NATO spokesperson and

Atlantic Council.[516] Consultations also take place informally, e.g. within groups of like-minded Member States, in the hallways or in the lobby of NATO HQ.[517] Interestingly, certain elements of NATO's informal consultation process have been partly institutionalised. Since the 1960s, Permanent Representatives have had lunch together every week, usually on the day before the formal NAC.[518] This lunch is hosted by the individual national delegations on a rotating basis, which allows each delegation to provoke discussion on a subject matter that is of interest to it. These weekly informal lunches have restricted attendance and are off-the-record, to allow a truly free exchange of thoughts.[519] The fact that all national delegations are located at NATO HQ makes consultation easier. In this regard NATO is unique, being the only international organisation in the world to have all its national delegations located in the same building. The consultations continuously taking place in the aforementioned fora allow the NATO Member States to define their positions, either with their own governments or with groups of like-minded states within NATO HQ. On the basis of the consultations, written proposals are brought forward, which are then negotiated and drafted within NATO decision-making bodies at the various committee levels, all the way up to the North Atlantic Council.[520] In brief, NATO decisions are prepared through consultations, whether formal or informal, and they are taking place continuously. As explained before, such consultation has no legal basis in the North Atlantic Treaty or in any other NATO basic document. Considering all this, one can safely say that consultation constitutes an established practice of the Organisation (Article 5 VCLT *juncto* Article 2.b ARIO and Article 2.1(j) VCLTIO).[521] One must distinguish between consultation as part of the preparatory phase of the NATO decision-making process *versus* consultation as an emergency measure in Article 4 North Atlantic Treaty. This distinction is

---

Deputy Assistant Secretary General for Emerging Security Challenges, online, 12 July 2022. See also *NATO Encyclopedia* 2018, 164.

516 *NATO Encyclopedia* 2018, 167 and E. Shuckburgh, 'Political Consultation' in X. (ed.), *NATO Letter: Ten Years of Atlantic Cooperation*, 1959, 11.

517 Interviews with a senior NATO International Staff Member, NATO Headquarters, 9 June 2022; a NATO legal adviser, Tervuren, 11 July 2022 and Dr. Jamie Shea, online, 12 July 2022. See also L. Michel, 'NATO Decisionmaking: How the "Consensus Rule" Works', 7–9 and K. Honkanen, 'The Influence of Small States on NATO Decision-Making: the Membership Experiences of Denmark, Norway, Hungary and the Czech Republic', 25.

518 K. Honkanen, 'The Influence of Small States on NATO Decision-Making: the Membership Experiences of Denmark, Norway, Hungary and the Czech Republic', 25 and based on in-house working experience at NATO HQ (1 January 2018 – 31 December 2017).

519 Based on in-house working experience at NATO HQ (1 January 2018 – 31 December 2017).

520 Note that all Member States are represented at all levels of the committee structure in the fields of NATO activity in which they participate (*cf. supra* Chapter 3).

521 *Cf. supra* Chapter 2 and see C. Peters, 'Subsequent Practice and Established Practice of International Organizations: Two Sides of the Same Coin?', 641; P. Sands and P. Klein, *op. cit.*, 456; UN, *Yearbook of the International Law Commission*, 1972, vol. II, 198 and W. Karl, 'Die spätere Praxis im Rahmen eines dynamischen Vertragsbegriffs', in R. Bieber and G. Ress (eds.), *op. cit.*, 90–91.

often misunderstood and could do with some clarification. Article 4 of the North Atlantic Treaty states:

> The Parties will consult together whenever, in the opinion of any of them, the territorial integrity, political independence or security of any of the Parties is threatened.

The first kind, consultation as an integral part of the NATO decision-making process, refers to the process of discussions, negotiations, and deliberations that continuously takes place, both formally and informally, in order to reach a consensus on a decision within NATO. The second kind, consultation in the context of Article 4 North Atlantic Treaty, occurs when a Member State invokes that Article, which is more or less an emergency measure.[522] This distinction is substantiated by the fact that the NAC, during its first ever meeting, announced that invocations of either Article 4 or Article 5 would necessitate extraordinary Council meetings. Bumgardner points out that, in the last days of the North Atlantic Treaty negotiations, Article 4 became a 'useful early reference for distinguishing emergency consultations from political consultations', which is confirmed in Article 4's *travaux préparatoires*.[523] In 1951 the Committee on the North Atlantic Community assumed the phrase 'frequent consultation', mentioned in the Committee's terms of reference, to mean, in general, exchanges of views on policy matters with a view to possible coordinated action, rather than interpreting it in the more technical sense of Article 4 of the Treaty, where the term 'clearly refers to situations of emergency.'[524] The 1969 NATO Information Service Pamphlet points out that special attention must be paid to matters of 'urgent and immediate importance to the members of NATO, and to emergency situations where it may be necessary to consult closely on national lines of conduct affecting the interests of the members of NATO as a whole', something Article 4 explicitly recognises.[525] As soon as Article 4 is invoked, the situation is discussed and can potentially lead to some sort of collective decision or action on behalf of the Alliance. Since the birth of the Alliance in 1949, Article 4 has

---

522 See Final Communiqué of the First Session of the North Atlantic Council (1949).

523 S. Bumgardner, 'Article 4 of the North Atlantic Treaty', 79–80 and Minutes of the Fifteenth Meeting of the Washington Exploratory Talks on Security, *Foreign Relations of the United States, 1949, Western Europe, Volume IV.*

524 The Committee on the North Atlantic Community in 1951 considered the phrase 'frequent consultation' in the terms of reference of the Committee to have the general meaning of exchanges of views on policy matters with a view to possible coordinated action, rather than the technical meaning of the word consultation as used in article 4 of the Treaty where it 'clearly refers to situations of emergency', see NATO, Interim Report by the Committee on the North Atlantic Community, NATO Doc. C8-D/6, 26 November 1951, of which the text can be found in NATO, *The Evolution of NATO political consultation 1949–1962*, Brussels, NATO Archives, 1963, §VI.9.

525 *NATO Encyclopedia* 2018, 165 and J. Olsen, 'Understanding NATO', *The RUSI Journal* 2020, 65.

been invoked seven times,[526] most recently by eight NATO Member States (Bulgaria, the Czech Republic, Estonia, Latvia, Lithuania, Poland, Romania, and Slovakia) on the day Russia invaded Ukraine, which led to consultations in the NAC and, indirectly, to the measures taken, including the deployment of NATO Response Force elements.[527] However, it should be clear, on the basis of the language ('will' rather than of 'shall' or 'undertake'),[528] the preparatory works, and the historical practice of Article 4[529] that the other NATO Member States are under no obligation to discuss the situation invoked by a fellow Member.[530] As confirmed by Sloan, Article 4 'promises nothing' (as the Allied debate over the war in Iraq made clear), but 'invites the treaty parties to work together to defend their interests from threats emanating from any source, anywhere in the world.'[531] However, if a NATO Member State does decide to join the discussion about the situation that has been raised—which, out of unity and solidarity towards the other Member States, is usually the case—it must do so in good faith. After all, NATO Member States are parties to the North Atlantic Treaty and in that capacity they are bound to perform Article 4 in good faith, an obligation that stems from Article 26 VCLT. The latter provision is binding on all NATO Member States, both as customary law and as a general principle of international law.[532]

---

526 NATO, *Aspects of NATO: Political Consultation*, Brussels, NATO Information Division, 1969, 18.

527 S. Clapp, 'Russia's war on Ukraine: NATO response', *European Parliament Research Service Briefing* 2022, 2 and speech by NATO Secretary General Jens Stoltenberg at the online Summit of the International Crimea Platform, 23 August 2022, text available at www.nato.int/cps/en/natohq/opinions_198268.htm (last accessed January 2025).

528 R. Kolb, *op. cit.*, 20; D. Hollis, 'Defining Treaties' in D. Hollis (ed.), *op. cit.*, 27 and A. Aust, 'Alternatives to Treaty-Making: MOUs as Political Commitments' in D. Hollis (ed.), *op. cit.*, 48–50. Do note how the use of language is an indication and not a definitive measure, *ibid.*, 49.

529 See *NATO Encyclopedia* 2018, 165.

530 For a different opinion see E. Brüel, 'Die juristische Bedeutung des Atlantikpaktes', *Archiv des Völkerrechts* 1954, 294 and see also S. Bumgardner, 'Article 4 of the North Atlantic Treaty', 71.

531 S. Sloan, 'Negotiating Article 5', *NATO Review* 2006, 2.

532 Article 38(1)(c) Statute of the ICJ. Good faith is one of the most important general principles of law and it underlies numerous international rules of law. The ICJ emphasised the importance of the principle in the *Nuclear Tests case* and has repeatedly confirmed it since. See ICJ 1974, *Nuclear Tests Case (Australia v. France)*, Judgment, *ICJ Rep* 253, § 46; see also e.g. *The North Atlantic Coast Fisheries Case (Great Britain v. United States of America)*, 1910 (Award), *UNRIAA* 169, vol. XI, § 188; ILC, *Yearbook of the International Law Commission*, 1964, vol. II, 7ss; M. Shaw, *International Law*, Cambridge, Cambridge University Press, 2017, 103; J. Wouters, C. Ryngaert, T. Ruys and G. De Baere, *op. cit.*, 158; M. Virally, 'Review Essay: Good Faith in Public International Law', *American Journal of International Law* 1983, 130; E. Zoller, *Bonne Foi en Droit International Public*, Paris, Pedone, 1977; R. Ziegler and J. Baumgartner, 'Good Faith as a General Principle of (International) Law' in A. Mitchell, M. Sornarajah and T. Voon (eds.), *Good Faith and International Economic Law*, Oxford, Oxford University Press, 2015, 9–36. However, note that, as found by the ICJ, good faith is not in itself a source of obligations when no other obligation exists, see ICJ 1988, *Borders and Transborder Armed Actions (Nicaragua v. Honduras)*, Judgment, *ICJ Rep* 105; ICJ *Nuclear Weapons*, 26

3. THE ADOPTION OF NATO DECISIONS: CONSENSUS

Because no NATO basic document provides any voting formula, one must turn to policy documents. The 2019 NATO Encyclopedia explains that consensus is NATO's decision-making principle at all levels, for all decisions.[533] But if this is not grounded in any NATO basic text, what does 'consensus' mean, precisely? First of all, one should note that consensus, in contrast to other methods of decision-making, can refer to both process and outcome.[534] Process consensus is a negotiating style of which the end goal is to produce a universally agreed upon measure among the negotiating parties, as explained by Payton.[535] Outcome consensus refers to whether and, if so, how many Member States object to a proposal under consideration, according to the same author.[536] It replaces a formal vote. As shown, both process consensus and outcome consensus are characteristic to NATO decision-making. This present section will focus on outcome consensus, while the previous section essentially discussed process consensus. In the context of decision-making in international organisations, consensus is most often defined negatively, as the absence of any objections.[537] The 1999 Berlin Resolution of the Institute of International Law states that 'a text should be considered as adopted by consensus when upon its presentation to participants, none of them expresses an objection thereto which distracts from or affects essential or fundamental provisions of that text.'[538] In Rule 69 of the Final Recommendation of the Helsinki Consultations of the Conference

and ICJ 1969, *North Sea Continental Shelf (Federal Republic of Germany v Denmark and the Netherlands)*, Judgment, *ICJ Rep* 3, 46–47.

533 *NATO Encyclopedia* 2018, 162 and J. D'Aspremont and D. Ventura, 'La composition des organes et le processus décisionnel' in E. Lagrange and J.-M. Sorel (eds.), § 840, 425.

534 A. Payton, 'Consensus Procedures in International Organizations', 2 and B. Buzan, 'Negotiating by Consensus: Developments in Technique at the United Nations Conference on the Law of the Sea', *American Journal of International Law* 1981, 324–348.

535 A. Payton, 'Consensus Procedures in International Organizations', 2 and E. Suy, 'Rôle et signification du consensus dans le processus législatif des Nations Unies' in M. Boisard and E. Chossudovsky (eds.), *Multilateral Diplomacy*, Alphen aan den Rijn, Kluwer Law International, 1998, 206.

536 A. Payton, 'Consensus Procedures in International Organizations', 2.

537 N. Blokker and S. Schermers, *op. cit.*, § 772, 561–62; *United Nations Juridical Yearbook*, 1982, at 177 and *United Nations Juridical Yearbook*, 1987, at 174–75. *Cf.* W. Chen, 'Issues on Consensus and Quorum at International Conferences', *Chinese Journal of International Law* 2010, 718; Rules of Procedure of the Conference on Security and Cooperation in Europe, Rule 69.4.9; UN, Official Records of the Third Law of the Sea Conference, vol. 1, 44, Summary Records of the 17th Meeting of the Plenary, UN Doc. A/CONF.62 (1973), § 2.

538 Article 1 Resolution, 'The Role and Significance of Consensus in the Forming of International Law' in *Annuaire de l'Institut de droit international*, Session de Berlin, vol. 68, II, 1999, 156. See also the definition provided in the revised resolution (Article 3, *ibid.*, 182): 'a statement shall be deemed to have been approved by consensus if, at a meeting expressly held for that purpose, no State present formally objects to its approval by consensus, and the presiding person officially notes that fact and announces that the statement has been approved by consensus.'

on Security and Co-operation in Europe, for example, consensus is defined as 'the absence of any objection expressed by a representative and submitted by him as constituting an obstacle to the taking of the decision.'[539] According to Article 161.8(e) UN Convention on the Law of the Sea, consensus is the 'absence of any formal objection.'[540] The WTO Agreement stipulates that a consensus is reached when 'no Member present at the meeting where the decision is taken, formally objects to the proposed decision.'[541] Authoritative definitions can be found in legal scholarship as well. Suy gives the following definition, which reflects the distinction between process consensus and outcome consensus:

> *Une technique de négociation et de prise de décision caractérisée par l'absence, tout au long du processus, de recours au vote – bien qu'il puisse y avoir des sondages informels – ainsi que l'absence d'objections fondamentales.*[542]

D'Aspremont and Venture define consensus as

> *un mode décisionnel déformalisé (i.e. en dehors de tout scrutin et en l'absence d'objection formelle rédhibitoire par un participant au processus décisionnel traduisant un accord général entre les Etats membres leur permettant d'obvier à certaines divergences de points de vue sur des aspects précis et délimités.*[543]

---

539 Rule 69, OSCE, Final Recommendations of the Helsinki Consultations, adopted on 8 June 1973 in Helsinki, available online at https://www.osce.org/mc/40213 (last accessed January 2025).

540 Article 161.8(e) United Nations Convention on the Law of the Sea, signed on 10 December 1982, entered into force on 16 November 1994, 1833 UNTS 397.

541 Article IX WTO Agreement, Marrakesh Agreement Establishing the World Trade Organization, signed on 15 April 1994, entered into force on 1 January 1980, 1867 UNTS 154.

542 E. Suy, 'Rôle et signification du consensus dans le processus législatif des Nations Unies' in M. Boisard and E. Chossudovsky (eds.), *op. cit.*, 206 and see E. Suy, 'Consensus' in R. Bernhardt (ed.), *Encyclopedia of Public International Law,* Amsterdam, North Holland, 1992, vol.I, 759; 'A negotiation and decision-making technique characterised by the absence, throughout the entire process, of voting—though informal polls may still be held—as well as the absence of fundamental objections.' (translation by the author).

543 J. D'Aspremont and D. Ventura, 'La composition des organes et le processus décisionnel' in E. Lagrange and J.-M. Sorel (eds.), *op. cit.*, § 840, 425. In addition, see the definitions provided by H. Cassan, 'Le consensus dans la pratique des Nations Unies', *Annuaire français de droit international* 1974, 456–485; M. Virally, 'Sources of International Law: Unilateral Acts of International Organisations' in M. Bedjaoui (ed.), *International Law: Achievements and Prospects*, Dordrecht, Nijhoff, 1991, 250; H. Ballreich, 'Wesen und Wirkung des Konsens im Völkerrecht' in R. Bernard, W. Geck, G. Jaenicke et al. (eds.), *Völkerrecht als Rechtsordnung, Internationale Gerichtsbarkeit, Menschenrechte, Festschrift für Hermann Mosler,* Berlin, Heidelberg, Springer, 1983, 2–6 and M. Brinkmann, 'Einstimmigkeit und Konsensverfahren: Zur Notwendigkeit und Entwicklung des konsensualen Abstimmungsverfahrens in der Generalversammlung', *Vereinte Nationen: German Review of the United Nations* 1979, 201–205: 'A deformalised decision-making process (i.e. outside of any vote and in the absence formal objection by any participant in the decision-making process) reflecting a general agreement between member states, enabling them to overcome certain differences of opinion on specific, delimited aspects' (translation by the author).

Schermers and Blokker describe a consensus process as

> debates that are frequently continued until general agreement is reached. Decisions are then taken not by voting, but by consensus (acclamation). In such cases, the chairperson of an organ asks whether (s)he may take it that it is the wish of this organ to adopt the proposal concerned (or similar language). If this is followed by silence, the proposal is adopted. If it is followed by one or more objections raised by members of this organ, or by a request for a vote, the proposal is not adopted.[544]

The 2010 NATO Legal Deskbook provides a definition with both positive and negative elements:

> The principle of consensus means that there is no voting on a matter, but rather that a decision can be made only if all Member States are in agreement. Agreement is reached by common consent, meaning that decisions are accepted by each member country, without having any formal objection and which is still in line with the member country's (national) policies.[545]

In the academic literature, and even in official NATO documents, the legal difference between the concepts of unanimity and consensus sometimes becomes blurred by the inaccurate claim that the NAC makes its decisions by 'unanimity'.[546] Consensus and unanimity are not the same thing in international institutional law. Unanimity entails the full and active support of all Member States for the measure under consideration, whereas consensus leaves room for those parties that do not fully support the measure but prefer not to oppose its execution.[547] Decision-making by consensus, as opposed to by unanimity, does

---

544 Compare to P. Sands and P. Klein, *op. cit.*, 266. See N. Blokker and S. Schermers, *op. cit.*, § 771, 561 and *United Nations Juridical Yearbook*, 2003, 533.

545 *NATO Legal Deskbook* 2010, 47.

546 See e.g. T. Gazzini, 'NATO's Role in the Collective Security System', 243; A. Sari, 'The Mutual Assistance Clauses of the North Atlantic and EU Treaties: The Challenge of Hybrid Threats', 431; A. Lindstrom, 'Consensus Decisionmaking in NATO: French Unilateralism and the Decision to Defend Turkey', 579–580; J.C.S., 'Problèmes juridiques de l'Organisation du Traité de l'Atlantique Nord', 698; F. Beer, *op. cit.*, 13; E. Buckley, 'Invoking Article 5', 2. And see *NATO Encyclopedia* 2018, 265, 377 and 394–95 and www.nato.int/cps/bu/natohq/topics_49178.htm (last accessed January 2025).

547 U. Benecke, *Reconsidering NATO's Decision Making Process*, Philadelphia, U.S. Army War College, 2007, 4; P. Gallis, *NATO's Decision-Making Procedure – CRS Report to Congress*, Washington D.C., Congressional Research Service, 2004, 2; J. D'Aspremont and D. Ventura, 'La composition des organes et le processus décisionnel' in E. Lagrange and J.-M. Sorel (eds.), *op. cit.*, § 839, 424–25; P. Sands and P. Klein, *op. cit.*, 266; W. Jenks, 'Unanimity, The Veto, Weighted Voting, Special and Simple Majorities and Consensus as Modes of Decisions in International Organizations' in A. McNair (ed.), *op. cit.*, 48–63; E. Suy, 'The Meaning of Consensus in Multilateral Diplomacy' in R. Akkerman and B. Röling (eds.), *Declarations on Principles, A Quest For Universal Peace: Liber Amicorum Discipulorumque B.V.A. Röling*, Leiden, Sijthoff, 1977, 259–74 and N. Blokker and S. Schermers, *op. cit.*, § 787, 575.

not require the positive consent of all participants.[548] In other words, passive agreement suffices. A consensus could be arrived at even when some parties remain neutral towards the draft decision, have reservations, or dislike it, as long as they do not insist on having a vote or do not object to the adoption of the decision without a vote.[549] Simply put, unanimity means everyone agrees (which may be established by vote or by a raising of hands), while consensus means no one disagrees. In a commentary on Article 63 ARIO, NATO itself declares the principle of consensus decision-making to be an established practice of the organisation under Article 2(b) ARIO:

> With reference to the phrase special rules of international law, including rules of the organization applicable to the relations between the international organization and its members, it may be observed that the fundamental internal rule governing the functioning of the organization—that of consensus decision-making—is to be found neither in the treaties establishing NATO nor in any formal rules and is, rather, the result of the practice of the organization.[550]

Moreover, the NATO archives and library contain no documents proving that any other decision-making formula has ever been used in NATO committees. Five out of six interviewees stated in clear and robust terms that NATO has never deviated from its practice of consensus at any time during their years at the Organisation (a period spanning from 1990 to the present).[551] A few quotes to this end:

> Consensus is the golden rule.[552]

> At the end of the day everybody wants consensus at NATO. Nobody challenges it, because if you challenge consensus it means I can outvote you, but then a year later you can outvote me! And nobody wants that. So there's a sense that, oh okay I don't like consensus because it is stopping things, but I could be in a situation next year where I would really like to say look guys, give this to me, like Greece did with North Macedonia.[553]

548 D. Akande, 'What is the Meaning of Consensus in International Decision Making', *European Journal of International Law Talk* 2013 and W. Chen, 'Issues on Consensus and Quorum at International Conferences', 719.

549 W. Chen, 'Issues on Consensus and Quorum at International Conferences', 719.

550 Commentary by NATO to Article 63 of the ARIO in *Comments and observations received from international organizations on the Responsibility of International Organizations*, 168.

551 Interviews with a senior NATO International Staff Member, NATO Headquarters, 9 June 2022; with a NATO legal adviser, Tervuren, 11 July 2022 and with Dr. Jamie Shea, online, 12 July 2022.

552 Interview with a NATO legal adviser, Tervuren, 11 July 2022.

553 Interview with Dr. Jamie Shea, online, 12 July 2022.

> Nobody would question it [the consensus rule]. And I never, never have I been confronted by a situation where they'll say there's an appetite to change that.[554]

As archival and empirical research and NATO's statement to the ARIO show, consensus has been the exclusive decision-making principle behind all NATO decisions, at all levels, for about seven decades. It is to be labelled as an established practice of NATO (Article 5 VCLT *juncto* Article 2.1(j) VCLTIO and Article 2(b) ARIO).[555] The condition that the practice must showcase a certain regularity is met. This means that consensus is part of NATO's internal law and that bypassing it would violate this internal law. Some authors have questioned whether NATO violated this established practice during the 2003 decision-making deadlock following Turkey's request for NATO defensive aid.[556] On 15 January 2003, the US requested that NATO begin planning to defend Turkey against potential counterstrikes by Iraq. France, Belgium, and Germany refused because of national resistance and objections in light of the UN Charter and other international law.[557] In response, Turkey formally invoked Article 4 North Atlantic Treaty on 10 February 2003. Upon this, Secretary General Robertson sent around a decision sheet, whereupon France, Belgium, and Germany broke their silence. For almost a month the three Allies continued to block any decision that would authorise NATO to lend defensive aid in the form of AWACS surveillance aircraft and Patriot missiles to Turkey.[558] The consensus rule rendered any preparation in defensive support of Turkey unattainable. What happened next is that the decision-making process was moved from the NAC into the Defence Planning Committee (DPC).[559] In 2003, France did not participate in the DPC, following that country's famous 1996 withdrawal from NATO's integrated military structure.[560] Belgium and Germany agreed to move the issue to the DPC as a diplomatic compromise, after critical public remarks

554 Interview with Head of SHAPE OLA Andres Moquera, online, 10 October 2022.

555 See F. Beer, *op. cit.*, 13, 33, 52, 135, 168, 174, 178–79 and 204. See also A. Lindstrom, 'Consensus Decisionmaking in NATO: French Unilateralism and the Decision to Defend Turkey', 580 and see *NATO Legal Deskbook* 2010, 47–50.

556 A. Lindstrom, 'Consensus Decisionmaking in NATO: French Unilateralism and the Decision to Defend Turkey', 580 and P. Shishkin, 'Head of NATO admits standoff has hurt Alliance', *Wall Street Journal* 2003, § 12.

557 A. Lindstrom, 'Consensus Decisionmaking in NATO: French Unilateralism and the Decision to Defend Turkey', 579; J. Dempsey, 'Allies' Broken Silence over Turkey Brings Crisis of Credibility for NATO', *Financial Times* 11 February 2003, 6; P. Shishkin, 'Head of NATO Admits Standoff Has Hurt Alliance', § 12 and P. Gordon, 'The Crisis in the Alliance', *Brookings Institution Report* 2003, 1.

558 A. Lindstrom, 'Consensus Decisionmaking in NATO: French Unilateralism and the Decision to Defend Turkey', 579–83 and L. Michel, 'NATO Decisionmaking: How the "Consensus Rule" Works', 11.

559 L. Michel, 'NATO Decisionmaking: How the "Consensus Rule" Works', *op. cit.*, 11 and A. Lindstrom, 'Consensus Decisionmaking in NATO: French Unilateralism and the Decision to Defend Turkey', 579.

560 A. Verhelst and S. Trifunovska, *op. cit.*, 125; *NATO Encyclopedia* 2018, 357.

by the US Ambassador to NATO.[561] And so, the DPC—not the NAC—granted Turkey the defensive measures in February 2003.[562] Some authors interpret this move as a circumvention of France's veto and question whether bypassing France contradicts the North Atlantic Treaty by violating established practice.[563] Had NATO suddenly introduced a voting requirement or a strict unanimity rule to decide on the defensive measures for Turkey, this could arguably be considered a violation of NATO's internal law (Article 5 VCLT *juncto* Article 2(b) ARIO). On the other hand, an international organisation is free to choose its own bureaucratic structure and the structure and scheme of its decision-making chain.[564] The DPC had the same level of authority as the NAC in matters within its competence and it had the authority to draw up defensive plans when there was a consensus among the Member States to do so.[565] In addition, one should bear in mind that France had agreed to the DPC's taking decisions without its input or acceptance when it withdrew from NATO's integrated military structure in 1966, which is in line with the importance of consent in international law.[566] While the move was surely opportunistic, relocating the decision from the NAC to the DPC and deciding on it by consensus does not violate any NATO internal law.

NATO's decision adoption process will now be explained. The process is similar at all committee levels, including the NAC, to which all other committees report. Decisions pass through different committees, moving up through various levels of seniority until they reach the NAC, NATO's highest decision-making

561 L. Michel, 'NATO Decisionmaking: How the "Consensus Rule" Works', 11; A. Lindstrom, 'Consensus Decisionmaking in NATO: French Unilateralism and the Decision to Defend Turkey', 579 and P. Shishkin, 'Head of NATO Admits Standoff Has Hurt Alliance', § 12.

562 Decision Sheet of the Defence Planning Committee, NATO Support to Turkey within the Framework of Article 4 of the North Atlantic Treaty, Press Release (2003)013, 19 February 2003, available online at www.nato.int/docu/pr/2003/p030216e.htm (last accessed January 2025) and I. Black, 'NATO crisis over veto on plans to defend Turkey', *The Guardian* 11 February 2003.

563 A. Lindstrom, 'Consensus Decisionmaking in NATO: French Unilateralism and the Decision to Defend Turkey', 580 and P. Shishkin, 'Head of NATO Admits Standoff Has Hurt Alliance', § 12.

564 *Cf.* J. Klabbers, 'Checks and Balances in the Law of International Organizations' in M. Sellers (ed.), *Autonomy in the Law*, London, Springer, 2008, 153 and his interpretation of ICJ *Admissions II* in this regard.

565 *NATO Handbook* 2001, 151; NATO Archives Online, Subfonds DPC – Defence Planning Committee, Administrative History, available online at https://archives.nato.int/defence-planning-committee (last accessed January 2025).

566 F. Beer, *op. cit.*, 49; A. Lindstrom, 'Consensus Decisionmaking in NATO: French Unilateralism and the Decision to Defend Turkey', 581 and see also PCIJ 1927, *Lotus' Case (France v Turkey)*, Judgment, *PCIJ Rep Series* A No 10, 18; H. Thirlway, 'The Sources of International Law' in M. Evans (ed.), *International Law*, Oxford, Oxford University Press, 2006, 115–44; D. Bodansky and J. Watson, 'State Consent and the Sources of International Obligation', *Proceedings of the Annual Meeting (American Society of International Law)* 1992, 108–113 and G. Fitzmaurice, 'The Foundations of the Authority of International Law and the Problem of Enforcement', *Modern Law Review* 1956, 1–13.

body. A committee meeting is usually chaired by an IS official, i.e. the (Deputy) Secretary General at the level of the NAC and a (Deputy) Assistant Secretary General at the committee level.[567] On the basis of the consultations, discussions, negotiations, and the draft work in the committee, the chairperson may inquire whether the body wishes to adopt the proposal concerned[568] or may suggest a way forward (as it is often the case that one or more Allies do not yet have a position at the time of the meeting and have to consult their capitals first).[569] Based on the verbal agreement on the way forward,[570] the IS prepares a new or altered draft text, which is then circulated among all national delegations, after which the 'NATO silence procedure' follows. As explained by the 2010 NATO Legal Deskbook, national representatives can take the following actions (usually communicated by email to the (Assistant) Secretary General) in response to a silence procedure set up by the IS:

- silence, no response (which is considered a formal response agreeing with the proposal);
- requesting an extension to the silence deadline;
- expressing an interpretation or understanding of the document in question, thereby commenting but not breaking the silence (such comments may then not be included in a revision of the document);
- breaking the silence, e.g. by raising objections or proposing amendments. In principle, the latter entails that a follow-up meeting will be set up at the relevant committee level.[571]

If, at the time of the deadline, no delegation has raised any written objections to the proposal ('broken the silence'), the text is considered to have been adopted by consensus and can move further up the committee decision-making chain until it reaches the highest decision-making body, the NAC.[572] In principle, all NATO decisions can be subject to the silence procedure at all levels.[573] The NATO silence procedure gives Member States the time (usually 24, 48, or 72 hours) to consult with their national governments about the positions the

567 See *supra* Chapter 3.

568 Based on in-house working experience at NATO HQ (1 January 2018–31 December 2018) and see N. Blokker and S. Schermers, *op. cit.*, § 771, 561 and J.C.S., 'Problèmes juridiques de l'Organisation du Traité de l'Atlantique Nord', 692.

569 L. Michel, 'NATO Decisionmaking: How the "Consensus Rule" Works', *op. cit.*, 8 and F. Beer, 14.

570 Meaning met by silence or no objections raised on the part of Member States.

571 Based on *NATO Legal Deskbook* 2010, 47–48; L. Michel, 'NATO Decisionmaking: How the "Consensus Rule" Works', 8 and substantiated by in-house working experience at NATO HQ (1 January 2018–31 December 2018) and interviews with a senior NATO International Staff Member, NATO Headquarters, 9 June 2022 and a NATO legal adviser, Tervuren, 11 July 2022.

572 P. Ochmannova, 'NATO: Evolution and Legal Framework for the Conduct of Operations', *NATO Legal Gazette* 2016, 123; U. Benecke, *op. cit.*, 5 and P. Gallis, *op. cit.*, 3.

573 *Cf. NATO Legal Deskbook* 2010, 47–8.

Allies around the table have expressed.[574] As a rule, NATO does not make public which countries break the silence (although sometimes, if the matter is contentious, national positions do get leaked to the press—sometimes by the country breaking silence).[575] To understand why NATO's consensus-based decision-making process amounts to a *de facto* veto power, one must understand the *ratio legis* behind this decision-making process. NATO embraced the two principles that underpinned the negotiations of the North Atlantic Treaty: consultation and consensus.[576] The requirement of consensus gives each NATO Member State *de facto* veto power, regardless of its size, power, or financial or military contribution.[577] Legally speaking, NATO's decision-making process does not discriminate between large and small States.[578] This shows the formal equality of NATO Member States. This formal equality can be explained by the fact that States cannot be expected to compromise on something as fundamental as national defence. In the international community, decisions to use force are politically sensitive.[579] A Member State's size, power, or military contribution do matter informally, of course, and there have been NATO decisions that were controlled by the larger Member States, but attempts to institutionalise the special position of larger Allies in NATO's decision-making structure have never been successful, as four of the six interviewees have confirmed.[580] In practice, the consensus principle guarantees that a NATO

574 Based on in-house working experience at NATO HQ (1 January 2018–31 December 2018) and U. Benecke, *op. cit.*, 5.

575 L. Michel, 'NATO Decisionmaking: How the "Consensus Rule" Works', 8.

576 The principles of consensus and consultation characterized the Washington Exploratory Talks. This 'NATO spirit' of consensus and consultations was felt as essential to the success of the treaty negotiations, so that it was adopted as the decision-making principle for the NAC and other bodies. See K. Honkanen, 'The Influence of Small States on NATO Decision-Making: the Membership Experiences of Denmark, Norway, Hungary and the Czech Republic', 23; T. Achilles, 'The Omaha Milkman: The role of the United States' in A. de Staercke et al. (eds.), *NATO's Anxious Birth: The Prophetic Vision of the 1940's*, London, C. Hurst & Company, 1985, 34–35 and S. Kay, *op. cit.*, 32.

577 K. Honkanen, 'The Influence of Small States on NATO Decision-Making: the Membership Experiences of Denmark, Norway, Hungary and the Czech Republic', 23 and L. Traugutt, 'Is Consensus Still Necessary Within NATO?', *NATO Defense College Research Paper* 2016, 2–3.

578 Bearing in mind that (military) power and politics do so informally. Yost writes that Allies' mutual equality has sometimes been imperiled by a tendency towards informal groupings of larger States (D. Yost, *op. cit.*, 183). Think of the historical examples of the Standing Group and the Berlin Four and see K. Honkanen, 'The Influence of Small States on NATO Decision-Making: the Membership Experiences of Denmark, Norway, Hungary and the Czech Republic', 29.

579 Interview with a senior NATO International Staff Member, NATO Headquarters, 9 June 2022. See also L. Michel, 'NATO Decisionmaking: How the "Consensus Rule" Works', 8; L. Traugutt, 'Is Consensus Still Necessary Within NATO?', 2.

580 In addition, when in 1958, French President De Gaulle suggested that France, the U.K. and the U.S. form a tripartite Directorate, U.S. President Eisenhower replied that 'we cannot afford to adopt a system which would give our other Allies the impression that basic decisions affecting their vital interests are being made without their participation,' quote taken from R. Jordan, *op. cit.*, 79, see U.S., *The Atlantic Alliance: Hearings Before the Subcommittee on*

Member State will never be compelled to undertake (military) action against its will and that, at the same time, no Member State can stop the others from taking collective action. A *de facto* veto by a Member State simply prevents NATO bodies from adopting a decision that would legitimise the undertaking by rendering it a 'NATO operation'. After all, NATO Member States are not prevented from acting unilaterally or in groups of like-minded States outside of the organisation, as long as their actions are in line with international and domestic law, e.g. based on Article 51 UN Charter.[581] The reason the 1949 Treaty and the Organisation exist in the first place, according to the NATO Legal Deskbook itself, is to have a political guarantee of the collectiveness, of the unity of policies and efforts, as well as to have the technical means and organisational structure that facilitate the implementations and exercise of collective self-defence.[582] All of the above should make clear that NATO is an intergovernmental organisation *par excellence*.[583] The consensus rule reflects how NATO is structured as an alliance of independent and sovereign states, not as a supranational entity.[584] As the archival and empirical research makes clear, it is rare for a NATO Member State to fully, continuously, and obtrusively exercise its *de facto* veto power. This is so because there is a more common and constructive alternative to blocking a consensus: the opt-out. A NATO Member State can join the consensus decision but opt out of taking part in its implementation. The matter arose prominently during the 1999 NATO decision-making process concerning Kosovo. In Greece, public opinion was heavily opposed to NATO action against the Federal Republic of Yugoslavia.[585] Greece ultimately did not block the NATO action, as it would have been the

---

National Security and International Operations of the Senate Committee on Government Operations, 89th Congress, 2nd session, 1966, p. 230, pt. 7 and see D. Yost, *op. cit.*, 183 and F. Kirgis, 'NATO Consultations as a Component of National Decisionmaking', 378.

581 K. Honkanen, 'The Influence of Small States on NATO Decision-Making: the Membership Experiences of Denmark, Norway, Hungary and the Czech Republic', 24; A. Sari, 'The Mutual Assistance Clauses of the North Atlantic and EU Treaties: The Challenge of Hybrid Threats', 415; U. Benecke, *op. cit.*, 3–4 and T. Achilles, 'The Omaha Milkman: The role of the United States' in A. de Staercke et al. (eds.), *op. cit.*, 39.

582 *NATO Legal Deskbook* 2010, 241.

583 K. Honkanen, 'The Influence of Small States on NATO Decision-Making: the Membership Experiences of Denmark, Norway, Hungary and the Czech Republic', 24; J.C.S., 'Problèmes juridiques de l'Organisation du Traité de l'Atlantique Nord', 694 and B. Eriksen, *op. cit.*, 46.

584 Reflected in the NATO Legal Deskbook definition of a 'NATO decision' as being 'the expression of the individual and collective will of all the sovereign states that are members of the Alliance'; see L. Traugutt, 'Is Consensus Still Necessary Within NATO?', 1–4.

585 C. Migdalovitz, 'Greece' in K. Donfried (ed.), *Kosovo: International Reactions to NATO Air Strikes – CRS Report for Congress* (Congressional Research Service, Washington D.C., 1999), 4; X. (Specialist in Middle Eastern Affairs, Foreign Affairs, Defense and Trade Division) (ed.), *Kosovo: Greek and Turkish Perspectives – CRS Report for Congress* (Congressional Research Service, Washington D.C., 1999), 2–4; H. Dellios, 'While government backs NATO, Greek hearts go with Serbs', *Chicago Tribune* 1999 and L. Michel, 'NATO Decisionmaking: How the Consensus Rule Works', 9: 'polls showing that about 95% of Greek public opposed NATO intervention.'

only Member State to do so. However, the country did not actively take part in the 78-day bombing campaign either.[586] This is where the nuance between consensus-based decision-making and a voting formula proves its significance. The former allows a State to acquiesce to a NATO collective decision despite its public or private reservations.[587] Imagine, for contrast, that national representatives had been required to vote in favour of Operation Allied Force. It is very likely that domestic political pressure in Greece would have translated into a vote against the operation.[588] In turn, this would have made it easier for other hesitating Allies to do the same.[589] Legally, though, by having acquiesced to the NATO consensus decision, Greece was estopped from later challenging the lawfulness of the Allies' resort to force. This means that, by having agreed to the operation, it could no longer begin a legal trial against one or more of its fellow Allies for embarking on the 78-day bombing campaign in Kosovo. NATO views the possibility of opt-out as one of the major advantages of its consensus-based process, as SHAPE legal adviser Andres Mosquera confirms.[590]

While the consensus principle is the cornerstone of the Alliance, NATO must ensure that it remains capable of taking and implementing decisions in a timely manner, especially now that it has 32 Members. The recent (perceived) inability of NATO to arrive at strongly supported decisions and the increased frequency of single-country deadlocks involving external bilateral disputes (i.e. Turkey blocking the accession of Sweden over the recognition of the Kurdistan Workers' Party (PKK) suggest that NATO should consider ways to make its decision-making process more timely and effective.[591] The NATO Secretary General has

586 G. Kostakos, 'The Southern Flank: Italy, Greece, Turkey' in A. Schnabel and R. Thakur (eds.), *op. cit.*, 167–168 and K. Honkanen, 'The Influence of Small States on NATO Decision-Making: the Membership Experiences of Denmark, Norway, Hungary and the Czech Republic', 24 and Interview with Greek Minister of Foreign Affairs Mr. Papandreou, *India Times* 21 December 2000, available online at www.elinepa.org/a-greek-you-can-understand-interview-with-george-a-papandreau-foreign-minister-greece (last accessed January 2025).

587 *Cf.* Article 45(b) VCLT; ICJ 1984, *Case concerning the Delimitation of the Maritime Boundary in the Gulf of Maine Area (Canada v. United States of America),* Judgment, *ICJ Rep* 305, § 130; V. Rodríguez Cedeño (Special Rapporteur), *Unilateral Acts of States: Seventh report on Unilateral Acts of States* (Doc. A/CN.4/542), 2004, paras 190–92; I. Sinclair, 'Estoppel and Acquiescence' in V. Lowe and M. Fitzmaurice (eds.), *Fifty Years of the International Court of Justice: Essays in Honour of Sir Robert Jennings*, Cambridge, Cambridge University Press, 1996, 104–20 and J. Barale, 'Acquiescement dans la jurisprudence internationale', *Annuaire français de droit international* 1965, 389–427.

588 *Cf.* L. Michel, 'NATO Decisionmaking: How the "Consensus Rule" Works', 9.

589 *Cf.* L. Michel, 'NATO Decisionmaking: How the "Consensus Rule" Works', 9.

590 Interview with Andres Mosquera, online, 10 October 2022.

591 L. Michel, 'NATO Decision making: Au Revoir to the Consensus Rule?', *Strategic Forum* 2003, 1; A. Hivert, 'Reasons for Sweden's NATO membership deadlock', *Le Monde* 5 February 2023, available online at www.lemonde.fr/en/international/article/2023/02/05/reasons-for-sweden-s-nato-membership-deadlock_6014453_4.html (last accessed January 2025) and NATO 2030: United For a New Era, Reflection Group, Expert Report, 2020, 60, available online at www.nato.int/nato_static_fl2014/assets/pdf/2020/12/pdf/201201-reflection-group-final-report-uni.pdf (last accessed January 2025).

initiated a reflection process to arrive at a stronger and more effective alliance by 2030. The experts who drafted the NATO 2030 reflection report suggested to alter the consensus principle by:

- bolstering the NATO Secretary General's chief executive role in order to allow him/her to make decisions on routine matters and to bring difficult issues into the open at an early stage;
- creating a more structured mechanism to support the establishment of coalitions inside the existing Alliance structures and examining ways to place a time-limit on decision-making in crisis situations;
- considering raising the bar for single-country blockages to the Ministerial level.[592]

These suggestions were dismissed by the NATO Heads of State and Government at the 2021 Brussels Summit.[593] The reasons for this have already been discussed. Moreover, chapter 3 showed that the NAC deliberately delegated few powers to the IS and that a merely facilitating role was always intended for it. NATO Member States do not want a bigger role for the Secretary General, as this would make NATO a less intergovernmental organisation. In addition, the current chapter revealed that coalitions of the willing outside of NATO are legally possible as long as there is an international legal basis for the action, so that there is no need to have them within NATO. They can even exist within NATO, as the opt-out ensures that States can join the decision to launch an action but opt-out of its implementation. Chapter 3 also showed that important defence decisions taken by the NAC are later endorsed at Ministerial meetings (which is mostly a matter of lip service), which is why it is not realistic to limit blockages to the Ministerial level and higher. This would invite States to wait until the decision-making process has reached those levels before blocking, rather than first resolving them internally. This would harm the credibility of the Alliance in the eyes of the outside world. A less far-reaching option would be for NATO to heed the calls to replace unanimity with qualified majority voting (QMV).[594] In contrast to the EU, this would not require a treaty amendment, but a sustained

592 NATO 2030: United For a New Era, Reflection Group, Expert Report, 2020, § 13.

593 NATO, NATO 2030 Agenda, adopted at the 2021 Brussels Summit, available online at NATO2030 (last accessed January 2025).

594 A. Baerbock, H. Lahbib, J. Asselborn, W. Hoekstra et. al., 'It's time for more majority decision-making in EU foreign policy', *POLITICO* 12 June 2023, 2; R. Wessel et. al., 'The future of EU Foreign, Security and Defence Policy: Assessing legal options for improvement', *European Law Journal* 2021, 385; European Commission, State of the Union Address by President von der Leyen at the European Parliament Plenary, Brussels, 16 September 2020; C. Navarra, L. Jančová and I. Ioannides, 'Qualified majority voting in common foreign and security policy A cost of non-Europe report', *European Parliament Research Service Study* 2023, available online at www.europarl.europa.eu/thinktank/en/document/EPRS_STU(2023)740243 (last accessed January 2025).

change in practice.[595] On the other hand, it would render the decision-making process less intergovernmental and move NATO in the direction of further integration.[596] This is why NATO should, for now, consider introducing QMV into administrative decisions only. Limiting QMV to administrative decisions would avoid issues for outvoted Member States as well as potential issues with enforcement and implementation.[597] Allies do not want to give up the consensus principle when it comes to the core sensitive issues of security and defence, where they want to retain their full sovereignty. This is why it is written in the Treaty on the European Union (TEU) that, within the EU CFSP and CSDP, decisions that have military or defence implications can only be taken by unanimity (Article 31(4) TEU). Overall, introducing QMV could ensure faster, more transparent, more flexible, and more efficient decision-making, and change the perception that Member States can at all times put political pressure on each other with the threat of a *de facto* veto.[598] In order to be realistic, QMV for administrative and routine matters should be complemented with an EU-inspired 'emergency brake' (Article 31(2) TEU). In the context of NATO, this would mean that a Member State should still be able to resort to breaking the silence by declaring its intention to oppose a decision. Just like with Article 31(2) TEU, no voting would take place, and the NATO Secretary General could try to find a solution with the Member State involved. The Secretary General has proven skilled at this in the past.[599] If the Secretary General does not succeed, the NAC can, by qualified majority, request that the matter be decided upon by consensus. The Allies themselves could, by consensus, designate the types

595 N. Blokker, 'Beyond Dili: on the Powers and Practice of International Organizations' in G. Kreijen et al. (eds.), *op. cit.*, 307. *Cf.* Stiftung Wissenschaft und Politik, 'More EU Decisions by Qualified Majority Voting – but How?', SWP Comment 2022/C, 2, available online at www.swp-berlin.org/10.18449/2022C61/ (last accessed January 2025).

596 E. Lazarou, L. Tothova, 'Implementation of the common foreign and security policy (CFSP)', *European Parliament Research Service* 2022; R. Wessel, 'Lex Imperfecta: Law and Integration in European Foreign and Security Policy', *European Papers* 2016, 439 and R. Wessel and V. Szep, *The implementation of Article 31 of the Treaty on European Union and the use of Qualified Majority Voting: Towards a more effective Common Foreign and Security Policy?*, Policy Department for Citizens' Rights and Constitutional Affairs, Directorate-General for Internal Policies, European Parliament, November 2022.

597 R. Wessel et. al., 'The future of EU Foreign, Security and Defence Policy: Assessing legal options for improvement', 386 and C. Navarra, L. Jančová and I. Ioannides, 'Qualified majority voting in common foreign and security policy A cost of non-Europe report', IV.

598 R. Wessel et. al., 'The future of EU Foreign, Security and Defence Policy: Assessing legal options for improvement', 386 and C. Navarra, L. Jančová and I. Ioannides, 'Qualified majority voting in common foreign and security policy A cost of non-Europe report', IV and V. Szep, 'Making EU Foreign Policy More Effective: Qualified Majority Voting on the Horizon?', *Carnegie Europe Article* 2023, available online at https://carnegieendowment.org/europe/strategic-europe/2023/05/making-eu-foreign-policy-more-effective-qualified-majority-voting-on-the-horizon?lang=en (last accessed January 2025).

599 NATO – News: Military de-confliction mechanism between Greece and Turkey established at NATO, 1 October 2020, available online at https://www.nato.int/cps/en/natohq/news_178523.htm (last accessed January 2025).

of decisions, committees, or working groups to which they want the QMV rule to apply. This should, as a matter of principle, exclude decisions on military or defence matters, including the launch of crisis response operations, decisions to invoke Article 4 or 5, and decisions about accession pursuant to Article 10. Examples of administrative matters that would benefit from QMV are logistics, IT, procurement, and procedural and ceremonial matters. Inspired by Michel's classification, QMV would best be applied to the decision areas 4 and 5 (see above). However, applying QMV to NATO administrative decisions is not an easy fix–all solution. As Pomorska and Wessel have warned (regarding the CSFP, but their warning is relevant to NATO as well), introducing QMV could mean negotiations would then take place 'under the shadow of QMV, without a need to keep everyone on board as long as there is a voting majority.'[600] But this is currently an underexplored suggestion which merits investigation as NATO is growing in both membership and importance, with a view to its 2030 agenda. That there may be an opening for this can be derived from the following statement by a NATO HQ OLA legal adviser:

> Nobody would question it [the consensus rule]. And I never, never have been confronted by a situation where they'll say there's an appetite to change that. Maybe in another context when there's a link to for example the more administrative decisions for example like choosing a chair. Sometimes that will be by majority, they will do like votes, but usually that's only for very, very kind of administrative things.
>
> Follow-up question: So in your experience it [voting] has happened before, for choosing a chair for example?
>
> Interviewee: Things like that, yes, but very basic things that have no political nature. Where you really need a sense [...] when there's a split, when you need like three candidates, and there's an American, a French, a Turk, you know you will have a vote. I've seen it done before, but very, very rarely.[601]

The idea of applying QMV to NATO administrative decisions, coupled with the option to break the silence, merits more academic research in the fields of political science and policy, inspired by the European Parliament Research Service study on QMV in the EU CSFD. This should include research on the formula behind QMV, as a population-based formula is not likely to be accepted by the smaller Allies, many of whom are among the most solid contributors to NATO operations and defence spending.[602] Decision-making

---

600 K. Pomorska and R. Wessel, 'Qualified Majority Voting in CFSP: A Solution to the Wrong Problem?', *European Foreign Affairs Review* 2021, 354.

601 Interview with a NATO legal adviser, Tervuren, 11 July 2022.

602 L. Michel, 'NATO Decision-Making: The 'Consensus Rule' Endures Despite Challenges' in S. Mayer (ed.), *NATO's Post-Cold War Politics*, London, Palgrave-Macmillan, 2014, 121–122.

rules have an important impact on the identity of an organisation (i.e. intergovernmental or integration-orientated), so these questions should not be treated lightly.

Aside from this, NATO's consensus principle is not entirely fit to be implemented in other existing organisations, as many already have treaty-based consensus rules, like the WTO, GATT, the Executive Board of the IMF, and some specialised agencies of the UN. Moreover, the following rules already apply in organisations whose mandates entail security and defence:

- EU: The Council decides by 'unanimity' in CSDP matters (Article 31(1) TEU), but, in practice, this is mostly interpreted as an 'absence of disagreement'.[603] Coupled with the emergency brake (Article 31(2)) and the practice of constructive abstention (which is also possible in defence matters), this requirement of unanimity is, in practice, quite similar to NATO's consensus-based decision-making, although more regulated. Transposing the consensus principle to the EU CSDP or the EU CFSP is not something scholars or the EU itself have considered.
- The OSCE decides by consensus, based on Article II.a.2 Rules of Procedure.
- The UNSC decides by voting (Article 27 UN Charter). It is unrealistic to think that the five Permanent Members would give up their veto right.

In general, NATO's consensus principle could be made to apply in new intergovernmental organisations acting in domains in which State sovereignty is crucial (e.g. foreign policy, defence policy, or social security). Those organisations could take the following advantages and disadvantages, learned from NATO, into account, reflected in the following SWOT-analysis[604]:

603 E. Bartolini, 'Simple Abstention and Constructive Abstention in the Context of International Economic Sanctions: Two Too Similar Sides of the Same Coin?', *European Papers* 2023, 1121–1130.

604 L. Demeyere, 'Swot Analysis for Cross-Border Litigation', *International Business Law Journal* 2005, 449.

Internal	**Strengths**	**Weaknesses**
	Consensus respects the formal equality of States.	Consensus is a secretive and opaque way of making decisions.
	Consensus means that Member States retain their sovereignty in sensitive policy domains.	Consensus can lead to decision-making deadlocks.
	Member States can decide not to voice opinions they feel uncomfortable with, to maintain their reputation towards their constituents.	Consensus bars the further integration of the organisation.
	Member States cannot be compelled to take part in a certain action, nor can they prevent other Members from undertaking such action outside the remit of the Organisation if there is a legal basis for doing so.	
	Consensus allows Member States to speak with one voice and reflect the credibility of the Organisation.	
External	**Opportunities**	**Threats**
	Consensus eases implementation because Member States have already agreed to the measure.	Consensus may tempt countries to insert bilateral issues into the discussion and threaten to veto if a national interest is not met.
	Consensus may lead to diplomatic bargaining and compromise, which makes it more likely that the final decision will be well-balanced.	Consensus may slow down decision-making when dealing with the day-to-day running of affairs.
	In principle, consensus should make it more difficult to hold Member States accountable for their individual conduct within the organisational context.	Member States may be estopped from later challenging the lawfulness of a certain decision they had previously acquiesced to.
	Decisions can be agreed to swiftly at Ministerial and Summit levels because the contents and ideas have already been agreed to at the technical level.	Consensus may endanger the reputation of the Organisation when it is used for political bargaining in external bilateral disputes.
	Consensus allows for acquiescence and acceptance, so that violations of the internal legal order will not readily arise.	

NATO's consensus principle, as an established practice, cannot be applied as such in other international organisations. The paradox of Article 2(b) ARIO is that each organisation has its own established practice, because each organisation has its own functions and objectives.[605] Established practice is not 'shared'. In the absence of a treaty provision, however, the flexibility that established practice offers as a source of law could inspire new intergovernmental organisations to allow their decision-making rule(s) to develop by practice, like NATO did. This flexibility allows organisations to adapt to changing circumstances, because an established practice can be altered by developing a new one without treaty amendment.[606] Keeping in mind the hierarchy suggested in Article 5 VCLT, this transposition would only work for new organisations whose legal texts do not lay down decision-making rules, because in that case practice might constitute an interpretation that goes against the constituent instrument.[607] Developing decision-making rules through practice without any textual basis has the further advantage of not having to stay too close to the (potentially outdated) intent of the drafters, but it may come at the expense of legal certainty and transparency.[608]

4. NATO'S CONSENSUS-BASED DECISION-MAKING: A DEFLECTION OF THE INTERNATIONAL RESPONSIBILITY OF STATES?

4.1. THE *FYROM V. GREECE* CASE (2011)

As we have suggested, the rules on decision-making influence the extent to which States remain sovereign within the international organisation.[609] NATO's consensus principle means States retain virtually all decision-making sovereignty within NATO. Do they also retain their full decision-making responsibility? Can NATO Member States be held individually responsible for having objected to a consensus? The issue arose when the Former Yugoslavian Republic of Macedonia (FYROM, now North Macedonia) instituted proceedings against Greece before the ICJ in 2011.[610] At the time FYROM was an aspiring NATO Member State, while Greece had been a Member State since 1952.

605 L. Arditi, 'The Role of Practice in International Organizations: The Case of Government Recognition by the IMF', 578.

606 L. Arditi, 'The Role of Practice in International Organizations: The Case of Government Recognition by the IMF', 560.

607 L. Arditi, 'The Role of Practice in International Organizations: The Case of Government Recognition by the IMF', 578.

608 E. Roucounas, 'Practice as a Relevant Factor for the Responsibility of International Organizations', *op. cit.*, 170.

609 N. Blokker and H. Schermers, *op. cit.*, § 918, 632 and K. Honkanen, 'The Influence of Small States on NATO Decision-Making: the Membership Experiences of Denmark, Norway, Hungary and the Czech Republic', *Swedish Defence Research Agency Paper* 2002, 23.

610 ICJ 2011, *Application of the Interim Accord of 13 September 1995 (the former Yugoslav Republic of Macedonia v. Greece)*, Judgment, *ICJ Rep*, 644.

FYROM's candidacy was considered during the NATO Bucharest Summit of April 2008. At the end of the Summit the country was not invited to begin accession talks. The Bucharest Summit Communiqué stated that an invitation would be extended to FYROM 'as soon as a mutually acceptable solution to the name issue has been reached.'[611] Importantly, FYROM realised that the ICJ would not be inclined to pierce NATO's institutional shield—as confirmed by Barros and Ryngaert—which is why the country directed its application, not against the NATO Bucharest decision to refuse to begin accession talks, but against Greece's individual conduct,[612] which allegedly violated obligations stemming from international law.[613] These obligations were laid down in the Interim Accord of 1995, a bilateral agreement.[614] In particular, FYROM sought to establish that, by objecting to the country's admission to NATO, Greece had breached Article 11 § 1 Interim Accord,[615] which reads:

> Upon entry into force of this Interim Accord, the Party of the First Part agrees not to object to the application by or the membership of the Party of the Second Part in international, multilateral and regional organizations and institutions of which the Party of the First Part is a member; however, the Party of the First Part reserves the right to object to any membership referred to above if and to the extent the Party of the Second Part is to be referred to in such organization or institution differently than in paragraph 2 of United Nations Security Council resolution 817 (1993).[616]

Greece contested both the ICJ's jurisdiction and the admissibility of the application. The country asserted that the issue at stake was a 'collective decision taken by NATO and its organs, wherein Greece has no individual or autonomous role to play.'[617] In doing so, Greece was clearly trying to use NATO's consensus principle as a shield, arguing before the Court that a NATO decision reflects

611 Para. 20 NATO Bucharest Summit Declaration.

612 *ICJ FYROM v. Greece*, Memorial of FYROM, 69–70, 87 and 123; A. Barros and C. Ryngaert, 'The Position of Member States in (Autonomous) Institutional Decision-Making Implications for the Establishment of Responsibility', *International Organizations Law Review* 2014, 77; N. Blokker and S. Schermers, *op. cit.*, § 67, 68.

613 The disagreement over the constitutional name of Macedonia dates back to the Republic of Macedonia's declaration of independence in 1991. Greece argues that the name 'Macedonia' is linked to the historical Kingdom of Macedon and that including it in the name of a neighbouring country would appropriate a vital aspect of Greece's culture and heritage. Additionally, Greece maintains that the use of the name 'Macedonia' suggests potential territorial claims over a northern Greek region that shares this name. See the website of the European Stability Initiative: www.esiweb.org/macedonias-dispute-greece.

614 Interim Accord between Greece and the Former Yugoslav Republic of Macedonia, signed on 13 September 1995, available online at www.mfa.gr/images/docs/fyrom/interim_accord_1995.pdf (last accessed January 2025); ICJ *FYROM v. Greece*, Application instituting proceedings filed in the Registry of the Court on 17 November 2008, 14–15 and Memorial of FYROM, 37–42.

615 Memorial of FYROM, 72–84 and 85–113.

616 Article 11 § 1 Interim Accord and ICJ *FYROM v. Greece*, 654.

617 Para. 39 ICJ *FYROM v. Greece*.

the will of the organisation and not the will of a certain Member State.[618] Such collective decisions are 'by definition not attributable to any individual State.'[619] The ICJ did not agree with Greece's reasoning. The Court decided it could exercise its jurisdiction. It also declared Greece's individual conduct as relevant and analysed it in view of Greece's obligations under international law, i.e. the bilateral Interim Accord of 1995.[620] Contrary to what Greece had argued, the ICJ found that the issue before the Court 'did not concern the conduct of NATO or the Member States of NATO, but rather solely the conduct of Greece.'[621] The Court vehemently isolated Greece's conduct and saw no relevance in determining whether 'the decision taken by NATO at the Bucharest Summit with respect to FYROM's candidacy was due exclusively, principally or marginally to Greece's objection.'[622] The ICJ investigated Greece's obligations under Article 11 § 1 of the Interim Accord and analysed whether Greece had effectively objected to FYROM's admission to NATO. It found that Greece, through diplomatic correspondence and statements of its senior officials before, during, and after the Bucharest Summit, made clear that the naming issue was the 'decisive criterion' in rejecting FYROM's admission. The ICJ concluded that Greece had violated Article 11 § 1 of the 1995 Interim Accord.[623]

This conclusion is rather unsurprising, as Article 11 § 1 contains a clear black letter law obligation for Greece not to object to FYROM's membership to any international organisation on the grounds of the naming issue. However, the *FYROM v. Greece* case does mark the first time the ICJ has so confidently isolated the individual conduct of a Member State from the organisation's decision-making process, as Barros and Ryngaert point out.[624] This is why this case warrants comparison to the ICJ's 1948 *Admissions* Advisory Opinion. There, the ICJ scrutinised the refusal by UNSC Members of other States' UN membership application, based on conditions other than those laid down in

---

618 ICJ *FYROM v. Greece*, Counter Memorial of Greece, 119. For more on the institutional veil, see N. Blokker, 'International Organizations and their Members', *International Organizations Law Review* 2004, 144; A. Barros and C. Ryngaert, 'The Position of Member States in (Autonomous) Institutional Decision-Making Implications for the Establishment of Responsibility', 57; C. Ryngaert and H. Buchanan, 'Member State Responsibility for the Acts of International Organizations', *Utrecht Law Review* 2011, 131; C. Brölmann, 'Member States and International Legal Responsibility: Developments of the Institutional Veil', *International Organizations Law Review* 2015, 359–360 and C. Brölmann, 'Introduction' in C. Brölmann (ed.), *The Institutional Veil in Public International Law: International Organizations and the Law of Treaties*, London, Hart Publishing, 2007, 4–6.

619 ICJ *FYROM v. Greece*, Counter Memorial of Greece, 120.

620 Para. 42 and 64 ss. *FYROM v. Greece*.

621 Para. 42 *FYROM v. Greece*.

622 Para. 70 *FYROM v. Greece* and A. Barros and C. Ryngaert, 'The Position of Member States in (Autonomous) Institutional Decision-Making Implications for the Establishment of Responsibility', 78.

623 Para. 113 *FYROM v. Greece*.

624 A. Barros and C. Ryngaert, 'The Position of Member States in (Autonomous) Institutional Decision-Making Implications for the Establishment of Responsibility', 75.

Article 4 UN Charter. The request for the Advisory Opinion did not pertain to the actual votes cast by the UNSC Member States, but was limited to the question whether the conditions laid down in Article 4(1) UN Charter were exhaustive or not.[625] Regardless, as Barros and Ryngaert state, the issue of Member State autonomy still simmered through[626]:

> All the conditions [for admission] are subject to the judgment of the Organization. The judgment of the Organization means the judgment of the two organs mentioned in Article 4(2), and, in the last analysis, that of its Members. The question is concerned with the individual attitude of each Member called upon to pronounce itself on the question of admission.[627]

By isolating Greece's conduct from NATO's decision-making process, the ICJ submits that States retain responsibility for their discretionary actions, even for those taken in an institutional context.[628] Indeed, *FYROM v. Greece* makes clear that a NATO Member State cannot simply do away with its responsibility stemming from international law by shielding itself with a NATO collective decision. However, it is the existence of a clear external legal obligation in the 1995 bilateral agreement which explains why the ICJ could arrive at its conclusion. This is an important caveat. Had the Interim Accord not existed, it is extremely doubtful that the Court would have considered piercing NATO's institutional veil and would have held Greece accountable for the Bucharest decision not to invite FYROM to accession talks. As parties to the North Atlantic Treaty, NATO Member States are not obliged to admit a candidate Member State once certain conditions are met, a fact that makes it difficult to pinpoint a wrongful act under international law.[629] NATO is not a party to the Interim Accord, so there was no question of NATO, as an organisation, having committed one. Had the Interim Accord not existed and had Greece made no public remarks, the Court would not have been in a position to assume—and should not have assumed—that Greece had objected to the consensus, as there is no way of knowing whether other Member States (and, if so, which Member States) broke the silence behind closed doors. One should also critically remark

---

625 ICJ 1948, *Conditions of Admission of a State to Membership in the United Nations (Article 4 of Charter)*, Advisory Opinion, *ICJ Rep* 1948, 57–58; A. Barros and C. Ryngaert, 'The Position of Member States in (Autonomous) Institutional Decision-Making Implications for the Establishment of Responsibility', 74–75 and Y. Liang, 'Conditions of Admission of a State to the Membership in the United Nations', *The American Journal of International Law* 1949, 288.

626 A. Barros and C. Ryngaert, 'The Position of Member States in (Autonomous) Institutional Decision-Making Implications for the Establishment of Responsibility', 75.

627 ICJ 1948, *Conditions of Admission of a State to the Membership in the United Nations*, Advisory Opinion, ICJ Rep 1948, 62.

628 A. Barros and C. Ryngaert, 'The Position of Member States in (Autonomous) Institutional Decision-Making Implications for the Establishment of Responsibility', 80.

629 *Cf.* Article 10 North Atlantic Treaty and see *infra* Chapter 5 on the absence of clear legal conditions for NATO membership.

that, had there been no Interim Accord, it would be unfair for Greece to incur all the blame for NATO's decision not to invite FYROM, as there might have been other countries that blocked the consensus but could hide behind Greece's public opposition. In this case, the Court limited itself to investigating whether Greece had objected to FYROM's admission in violation of Article 11 § 1 Interim Accord. It did not consider the obligations that Greece may have had as a NATO Member State under the North Atlantic Treaty, under international human rights law, or under the general principles of international law (e.g. good faith).[630] It is telling that Judges Basdevant, Winiarski, McNAir, and Read dissented to the 1948 *Admissions* Advisory Opinion and reviewed the conduct of States in their internal capacity as members of the UN, mentioning the obligation of UN Member States to use their voting power in accordance with the principle of good faith.[631] Scholars such as White and, to a certain extent, Amerasinghe, are also of the opinion that States, in their capacity as voting members of an international organisation, should perform their duties in line with the purposes and principles of the organisation's founding document and should further the organisation's objectives in accordance with the general principle of good faith.[632] So far, the ICJ has been able to avoid speaking out on this issue in both *Admissions* and *FYROM v. Greece*. A concluding remark pertains to the practical implications of the *FYROM v. Greece* judgment. In her dissenting opinion, Judge Xue agreed with the majority that the relevant issue was whether Greece had breached its obligations under the Interim Accord as a result of its own conduct.[633] Nevertheless, she critically remarked that, by constructing FYROM's request so narrowly, the judgment could have no effect on NATO's decision not to begin accession talks. Judge Xue wrote:

> NATO's decision remains unchanged, while there are only two possible ways for FYROM to regain its status as a candidate for NATO: one is the settlement of the

630 A. Barros and C. Ryngaert, 'The Position of Member States in (Autonomous) Institutional Decision-Making Implications for the Establishment of Responsibility', 80.

631 ICJ *First Admissions*, Dissenting Opinions of Judges Basdevant, Winiarski, McNair and Read, 83, § 4; 91, § 20; and 92, § 21, in A. Barros and C. Ryngaert, 'The Position of Member States in (Autonomous) Institutional Decision-Making Implications for the Establishment of Responsibility', 79. See also A. Barros, 'Application of the Interim Accord of 13 September 1995 (The Former Yugoslav Republic of Macedonia v Greece)' in A. Barros (ed.), *Governance As Responsibility: Member States as Human Rights Protectors in International Financial Institutions*, Cambridge, Cambridge University Press, 2019, 65.

632 N. White, 'Decision-making' in J. Klabbers and A. Wallendahl (eds.), *Research Handbook on the Law of International Organizations*, Cheltenham, Edward Elgar, 2011, 243–245 and C.F. Amerasinghe, *op. cit.*, 177–184. *Cf.* A. Barros and C. Ryngaert, 'The Position of Member States in (Autonomous) Institutional Decision-Making Implications for the Establishment of Responsibility', 79.

633 ICJ *FYROM v. Greece*, Dissenting Opinion by Judge Xhue, 717.

> name issue between the Parties; the other is a reversal of NATO's decision. The Court's declaratory judgment is apparently intended to eschew the latter.[634]

There was a happy ending to *FYROM v. Greece*, if you will: in 2020, NATO welcomed North Macedonia as its 30th Member State, after the successful resolution of the naming dispute.

4.2. INTERIM CONCLUSION

This chapter made clear that the consensus principle, coupled with the options of breaking the silence and opt-out, allow NATO Member States to retain virtually all their decision-making sovereignty. The last section showed that Member States also retain virtually all decision-making responsibility.[635] Contrary to what Greece had hoped for, NATO's collective decisions do not shield Member States from their individual international responsibility based on bilateral treaties, even if the decisions were taken in an institutional context. Had the bilateral Interim Accord not existed, the Court would probably not have come to the conclusion that Greece had violated its obligations. This would have been only fair, as the Court should not have assumed Greece to be the only Member State that broke the silence, and because neither NATO nor its Member States are obliged to admit a candidate State when a certain number of criteria have been met. The ICJ did not review the conduct of Greece in its capacity as a Member State of the international organisation. Below, in this chapter's conclusion, it will be explained how the ICJ's position in *FYROM v. Greece* is different to, and preferable over, the ECtHR's in *Gasparani*.

5. THE EFFECT AND LEGAL NATURE OF NATO DECISIONS

5.1. NATO OPERATIONAL ACTS

The North Atlantic Treaty does not mention any rules with regard to decision-making, nor does it indicate what the legal or normative value of NATO decisions is. It is a basic principle of international institutional law that the power that the organs of international organisations have to perform

---

634 ICJ *FYROM v. Greece*, Dissenting Opinion by Judge Xhue, 717.

635 See this confirmed in the General comment by NATO to the ARIO, in Comments and observations received from international organisations on the Responsibility of International Organizations, 139; NATO Legal Deskbook 2010, 47 and NATO Encyclopedia 2018, 396.

acts is explicitly or implicitly derived from the constituent instrument (*cf.* chapter 3).[636] Consequently, the legal effect of these acts depends primarily on the constitutional provisions in question.[637] To this end, it is necessary to first determine the powers of the North Atlantic Council. Article 9 of the North Atlantic Treaty merely gives the NAC the power to '*consider* matters concerning the implementation of the Treaty' (emphasis added) and to set up a defence committee which 'shall *recommend measures* for the implementation of Articles 3 and 5'.[638] From Article 9's preparatory works,[639] NATO's highly intergovernmental nature, and the fact that the NAC has the authority to 'consider matters', it follows that its powers are, in principle, advisory. This is confirmed by legal scholarship[640] and by the NATO Encyclopedia's definition of the NAC's powers: the NAC's essential purpose is 'to make recommendations to governments and to assist them in reaching coordinated decisions.'[641] The legal effect of its decisions, on the other hand, must be sought in the basic texts. The 1949 Treaty does not explicitly prescribe the legal effect of NATO's decisions, in contrast to Article 25 UN Charter, Article 9(a) Constitution of the WMO, Article 22 WHO Constitution, and Article 9.4 ECOWAS Treaty.[642] This is why,

---

636 C.F. Amerasinghe, *op. cit.*, 135; N. Blokker and H. Schermers, *op. cit.*, § 209, 165–167 and § 217, 177–178; P. Sands and P. Klein, *op. cit.*, 295 and P. Klein, 'Les compétences et pouvoirs de l'organisation international' in E. Lagrange and J.-M. Sorel (eds.), *op. cit.*, § 1411–1420, 714–721.

637 C.F. Amerasinghe, *op. cit.*, 162; G. Ulfstein, 'Les activités normatives de l'organisation internationale', in E. Lagrange and J.-M. Sorel (eds.), *op. cit.*, § 1451, 739 and § 1466, 747 and J. Klabbers, *op. cit.*, 154–55.

638 Emphasis added.

639 Based on a reading of the Minutes of the Eighteenth Meeting of the Washington Exploratory Talks on Security, 15 March 1948, *Foreign Relations of the United States, 1949, Western Europe, Vol. IV* (U.S. State Department Office of The Historian), 223–224; Minutes of the Ninth Meeting of the Washington Exploratory Talks on Security, 13 December 1948, 2:30 p.m., Doc. 840.20/12-1348, *Foreign Relations of the United States, 1948, Western Europe, Volume III* (U.S. State Department Office of the Historian); Washington Security Talks, Report of the International Working Group to the Ambassadors' Committee, 24 December 1948, Doc. 840.20/12-2448, *Foreign Relations of the United States, 1948, Western Europe, Volume III* (U.S. State Department Office of the Historian); Annex A and B to the Report of the International Working Group to the Ambassadors' Committee as well as the legal doctrine by NATO legal adviser A. Mosquera, 'The North Atlantic Treaty: Article 9 and NATO's Institutionalization', 154 and by E. Reid, *op. cit.*, 267.

640 F. Wilcox and T. Kalijarvi, 'The Organizational Framework of the North Atlantic Treaty', *American Journal of International Law* 1949, 157 and A. Boeva, 'What is NATO HQ?', 22–23.

641 As stated in the *NATO Encyclopedia* 2019. See more generally P. Sands and P. Klein, *op. cit.*, 284–286.

642 Article 9(a) Convention of the World Meteorological Organization, signed on 11 October 1947 and entered into force on 23 March 1950; Article 22 Constitution of the World Health Organization, signed on 22 July 1946 and entered into force on 7 April 1948 and Article 9.4 Economic Community of West African States Treaty, signed on 28 May 1975 and entered into force provisionally on 28 May 1975 in respect of certain States. Subsequently, the Treaty came into force in respect of the following States on the date of ratification: Benin (24 June 1975), Sierra Leone (26 June 1975), Togo (27 June 1975), Niger (2 July 1975), Guinea-Bissau

in this chapter, the following distinction will be made. In terms of legal effect, international organisations take two sort of decisions[643]:

1. Institutional acts (or 'household' acts), such as approving the administrative budget, appointing the NATO Secretary General, creating NATO subsidiary bodies, agreeing on staff regulations, establishing the NATO Administrative Tribunal, etc. According to Stein, Carreau, Sands, and Klein, these acts may be presumed to be binding by nature because it is the reasonable interpretation of the constituent text that they should have this effect.[644] Caution is due, however, because institutional acts may not always be decisively binding.[645] Because of their administrative nature and because this type of decision has already been subject to analysis in chapter 3, they will be disregarded here.
2. Operational acts, which relate to achieving the objectives of the organisation.[646] In other words, the acts to carry out the direct and substantive operations of an international organisation.[647] Examples (given by Amerasinghe) are decisions by the UNSC under Chapter VI or VII UN Charter related to peacekeeping, decisions by the IMF implementing the provisions of its Articles of Agreement, particularly those concerning the drawing of and exchange rates, etc.[648] As an example of a NATO operational act, Schermer and Blokker mention the NAC decision of 9 February 1994

(15 March 1976), Mauritania (15 March 1976). The 1949 Treaty was revised on 24 July 1993. *Cf.* C.F. Amerasinghe, *op. cit.*, 162 and J. Klabbers, *op. cit.*, 175.

643 Note that this division is simplified. See C.F. Amerasinghe, *op. cit.*, 163–187; J. Klabbers, *op. cit.*, 156–158 and 174; N. Blokker and S. Schermers, *op. cit.*, § 1196–1205, 785–790 and § 1216, 796; P. Sands and P. Klein, *op. cit.*, 455–56 and G. Ulfstein, 'Les activités normatives de l'organisation internationale' in E. Lagrange and J.-M. Sorel (eds.), *op. cit.*, § 1466–1480, 747–755.

644 E. Stein and D. Carreau, 'Law and Peaceful Change in a Subsystem: "Withdrawal" of France from the North Atlantic Treaty Organization', 608; P. Sands and P. Klein, *op. cit.*, 279–280; J. Klabbers, *op. cit.*, 156 and 174; C.F. Amerasinghe, *op. cit.*, 163–164; N. Blokker and S. Schermers, *op. cit.*, § 1201–1203, 787–789; UN, *United Nations Juridical Yearbook*, 1982, 182–183; A. Basak, *Decisions of the United Nations Organs in the Judgments and Opinions of the International Court of Justice*, Wrocław, Zakład Narodowy im. Ossolińskich, 1969, 209; J. Castañeda, 'Valeur juridique des résolutions des Nations Unies', *Recueil des Cours de l'Académie de Droit International de La Haye* 1970, 227. See also ICJ *Expenses*, 163 about article 18 UN Charter and 169–170 about Article 17(2) UN Charter.

645 C.F. Amerasinghe, *op. cit.*, 166 and his analysis of ICJ *Second Admissions*, 7–9. See also the Separate Opinions of Judge Lauterpacht (*ICJ Voting Procedure case*) and Judge Klaestad (*ICJ Voting Procedure* case). See ICJ 1955, *Voting Procedure on Questions relating to Reports and Petitions concerning the Territory of South West Africa*, Advisory Opinion, ICJ Rep 1955, 67.

646 As defined by C.F. Amerasinghe, *op. cit.*, 168; E. Stein and D. Carreau, 'Law and Peaceful Change in a Subsystem: "Withdrawal" of France from the North Atlantic Treaty Organization', 608–609; J. Klabbers, *op. cit.*, 156–58; P. Sands and P. Klein, *op. cit.*, 280–283 and N. Blokker and S. Schermers, *op. cit.*, § 1216, 796–97.

647 C.F. Amerasinghe, *op. cit.*, 168.

648 C.F. Amerasinghe, *op. cit.*, 168.

that heavy weapons belonging to any of the parties found within the Sarajevo exclusion zone will be subject to NATO air strikes (unless they are controlled by UNPROFOR).[649]

As a side note, Klabbers identifies a third category of decisions which he calls 'amorphous instruments.'[650] These are acts adopted by Member States rather than by organs of the organisation, or by its organs but ostensibly outside of the ordinary decision-making process.[651] These types of decisions are attractive instruments precisely because of their 'legally nebulous status', as it is not always clear whether they are acts of the organisation or acts of the Member States *en groupe*.[652] Because NATO decides by consensus, its decisions adopted at Ministerials and Summits have a nebulous status a well; they are both acts of the Organisation and acts of the States *en groupe*.[653] NAC decisions have the same status and validity regardless of the level at which they are adopted. One can readily understand how this vague legal status liberates decision-makers: the Organisation can shift responsibility to the Member States while the Member States can shift responsibility to the Organisation.

It is a general rule of modern international institutional law that international organisations cannot make binding operational decisions unless their constitutions expressly provide this competence, which the North Atlantic Treaty does not.[654] There are very few international organisations that can issue acts that bind their Members in the operational sphere.[655] That the NAC's operational acts are, in principle, non-binding is substantiated by official NATO documents stating that the responsibility for making final decisions

---

649 See N. Blokker and S. Schermers, *op. cit.*, § 1323, 859. The decision can be found in *NATO Press Release* (94)15, 9 February 1994 as quoted by J. Headley in 'Sarajevo, February 1994: the first Russia-NATO crisis of the post-Cold War era', *Review of International Studies* 2003, 217–218.

650 J. Klabbers, *op. cit.*, 157–158.

651 Klabbers gives as examples the UNSC Declaration adopted at the level of Heads of State and Government rather than at the regular ambassadorial level in January 1992, and the EU Charter on Fundamental Rights.

652 J. Klabbers, *op. cit.*, 157–158.

653 This can be explained by the fact that the North Atlantic Council was initially construed as a non-permanent Ministerial body to meet only when deemed necessary. Later on, the possibility of meeting at the level of Heads of State and Government was introduced. In 1952, the NAC became a permanent body at ambassadorial level (see *supra* Chapter 3).

654 N. Blokker and S. Schermers, *op. cit.*, § 1320, 857; P. Sands and P. Klein, *op. cit.*, 280; K. Skubiszewski, 'The Elaboration of general multilateral conventions and of non-contractual instruments having a normative function or objective – Resolutions of the General Assembly of the United Nations', *Annuaire de l'Institut de droit international* 1985, 35; G. Ulfstein, 'Les activités normatives de l'organisation internationale' in E. Lagrange and J.-M. Sorel (eds.), *op. cit.*, § 1466, 747 yet see also C.F. Amerasinghe, *op. cit.*, 169.

655 Noteworthy exceptions are laid down in Article 25 UN Charter and Article 288 TFEU. See N. Blokker and S. Schermers, *op. cit.*, § 1320–1330, 857–860 and P. Sands and P. Klein, *op. cit.*, 280–281.

rests with the respective governments rather than with the NAC itself.[656] In the 1967 Harmel Report, the NAC stressed that 'as sovereign States, the Allies are not obligated to subordinate their policies to collective decision. Each Ally can decide its policy in the light of close knowledge of the problems and objectives of others.'[657] Add to this the fact that the NAC has advisory powers only and the fact that NATO moves from Summit to Summit and Ministerial to Ministerial.[658] The non-binding nature of the NAC's operational acts was confirmed by two IS officials in 2022. The more senior of the two stated:

> We don't regulate, we don't legislate. So all you can do as NATO is to map out what's going on. And that applies in more areas. I also saw this with the drafting of a strategy for AI, in which we all agreed on principles of responsible use. But those are not regulations, those are not laws. Does that hinder things? I don't think so. Because by agreeing on soft law together, it will go faster, and the soft law can then be used by the individual Member States or by the EU to change into regulation or hard law.[659]

This does not mean, however, that NATO operational acts cannot have any legal effect.[660] The norms articulated in a NATO operational act may become binding on its addressees when they are attached to a traditional source of international law.[661] The unilateral acts of States,[662] treaties (including

---

656 General comment by NATO to the ARIO in *Comments and observations received from international organizations on the Responsibility of International Organizations*, 139; *NATO Legal Deskbook* 2010, 47; *NATO Encyclopedia* 2018, 396 and see R. Heindel, T. Kalijarvi and F. Wilcox, 'The North Atlantic Treaty in the United States Senate', *American Journal of International Law* 1949, 647.

657 Para. 7 Harmel Report, NATO, Report of the Council on the Future Tasks of the Alliance, 1967, online available at https://www.nato.int/cps/en/natohq/official_texts_26700.htm (last accessed January 2025).

658 Similarly, see P. Sands and P. Klein, *op. cit.*, 286–287; K. Skubiszewski, 'The Elaboration of general multilateral conventions and of non-contractual instruments having a normative function or objective – Resolutions of the General Assembly of the United Nations', 35; I. Detter, 'The effect of resolutions of international organisations' in J. Makarczyk (ed.), *Theory of international law at the threshold of the 21st century: essays in honour of K. Skubiszewski*, The Hague, Kluwer, 1996, 389–390 but see also G. Tunkin, 'The Role and resolutions of international organisations in creating norms of international law' in W. Butler (ed.), *International law and the international system*, Dordrecht, Nijhoff, 1987, 6.

659 Interview with a senior NATO International Staff member, NATO Headquarters, 9 June 2022, building upon the interview with a NATO legal adviser in Tervuren on 11 July 2022.

660 T. Gazzini, 'NATO's Role in the Collective Security System', 243; P. Sands and P. Klein, *op. cit.*, 286–287; N. Blokker and S. Schermers, *op. cit.*, § 1220–1261, 798–822 and § 1320, 857; S. Sloan, *United Nations General Assembly Resolutions in Our Changing World*, Leiden, Brill Nijhoff, 1991, 105–118 and B. Conforti, 'Le role de l'accord dans le système des Nations Unies', *Recueil des Cours de l'Académie de Droit International de La Haye* 1969(II), 257–288.

661 P. Sands and P. Klein, *op. cit.*, 287–288.

662 *Cf.* ILC, *Unilateral acts of States: Seventh report on unilateral acts of States, by Mr. Víctor Rodríguez Cedeño, Special Rapporteur*, UN Doc. A/CN.4/542, 22 April 2004 and ICJ *Nuclear Tests* case, § 43–60.

international agreements in simplified form),[663] and international customary law are of particular importance in this respect. For example, the part of a NATO decision that prohibits the use of force is binding because the prohibition reflects customary international law (Article 2.4 UN Charter). This especially applies to NATO because it makes decisions by consensus, meaning that all Member States have at least passively agreed to the decision. In international treaty law, the ultimate criterion of distinction between a political commitment and a legally binding agreement is intent.[664] The intent to be legally bound must be ascertained on the basis of various elements, including the language of the decision, the surrounding circumstances, and the constitutional intention (see ICJ, *Namibia*, § 114).[665] Recall how the German *Bundesverfassungsgericht* correctly analysed the intent of the parties in order to determine whether the 1999 Strategic Concept constituted a legally binding amendment (Article 39 VCLT). Keeping in mind the importance of intent, one cannot categorically deduce legally binding force from the fact that NATO decides by consensus. This was incorrectly claimed by former NATO HQ Legal Adviser Boeva, who said that 'collective decisions of the Alliance, once taken, are binding on the members of the Alliance.'

The only argument Boeva used to substantiate this claim was that

> the binding character of Council decisions [...] derives, in a very real sense, from the way those decisions are taken. [...] It is the practice of consensus—with its critical corollary that any Ally has the power to block the taking of any decision—combined with the right of every Ally to participate in the Council, that makes it politically

663 J. Wouters, C. Ryngaert, T. Ruys and G. De Baere, *op. cit.*, 70; Commentary 3 to Article 2 of the Draft Articles on the Law of Treaties with Commentaries; ILC, First report by Sir H. Lauterpacht, in *Yearbook of the International Law Commission*, 1953, vol. II, 101–106; P. Gautier, *Essai sur la définition des traités entres Etats. La pratique de la Belgique aux confins du droit des traités*, Brussels, Bruylant, 1993, 149 and F. Hamzeh, 'Agreements in Simplified Form - Modern Perspective', *British Yearbook of International Law* 1968, 179. See also ICJ 1994, Maritime Delimination and Territorial Questions between Qatar and Bahrain (*Qatar v. Bahrain*), Judgment, ICJ Rep 1994, § 25 and ICJ 2010, Pulp Mills on the River Uruguay (*Argentina v. Uruguay*), Judgment, ICJ Rep 2010, § 138.

664 ICJ 1978, *Aegean Sea Continental Shelf (Greece v. Turkey)*, Judgment, *ICJ Rep* 1978, 39, § 96; ICJ *Qatar v. Bahrain*, § 25; ICJ *Pulp Mills*, § 138. See R. Kolb, *op. cit.*, 19–20, 25–26; D. Hollis, 'Defining Treaties' in D. Hollis (ed.), *op. cit.*, 26; A. Aust, *op. cit.*, 17–18 and J. Pauwelyn, 'Is it International Law or Not and Does it Even Matter?' in J. Pauwelyn, R. Wessel and J. Wouters (eds.), *Informal International Lawmaking*, Oxford, Oxford University Press, 2012, 134.

665 The ICJ in *Namibia* held that the 'legal effect of UNSC resolutions is to be determined having regard to the terms of the resolution to be interpreted, the discussions leading to it, the Charter provisions invoked and in general, all circumstances that might assist in determining the legal consequences of the resolution of the UNSC' (ICJ *Namibia*, § 114). See also D. Hollis, 'Defining Treaties' in D. Hollis (ed.), *op. cit.*, 27; O. Schachter, 'The Twilight Existence of Nonbinding International Agreements', *American Journal of International Law* 1977, 297; R. Kolb, *op. cit.*, 19–20; Switzerland, *Guide de la pratique en matière de traités internationaux*, Bern, Swiss Department of Foreign Affairs, 2015, 7–8.

as well as legally possible for NAC decisions to be binding on every member of the Alliance.[666]

In the same vein, Sari inaccurately claimed that 'since the North Atlantic Council proceeds by unanimity, its decisions may, in principle, constitute international agreements in simplified form that are legally binding on the member states.'[667]

These statements disregard the legal distinction, in international institutional law, between unanimity and consensus (see above). Moreover, in the context of NATO, a consensus means that no one disagrees with the proposed measure. This is amplified by NATO's silence procedure, its opt-out option, and there being no consistent way of knowing whether, or if so, which Member State broke the silence or opted out of the collective decision. Because these factors make it difficult or even impossible to know the intent of the parties, NATO's exclusively consensus-based decisions cannot be reliably dissected into individual Member State decisions. Admittedly, making a case for acquiescence or estoppel in this context may be relatively straightforward.[668] When a Member State consents (in other words: acquiesces) to a NATO decision to undertake a NATO operation but does not participate in the execution of that operation, the country may be estopped from later challenging the lawfulness of the military operation (Article 45(b) VCLT). This is what happened when Greece joined the 1999 NATO decision to intervene in Kosovo but opted out of participating in the actual bombing campaign. In essence, considering the language of the North Atlantic Treaty, its preparatory works, historical practice and legal scholarship, it must be concluded that NATO operational acts are non-binding in principle, although lawyers should always ascertain the parties' intent to be bound. This theoretical

666 A. Boeva, 'What is NATO HQ?', 22.

667 A. Sari, 'The Mutual Assistance Clauses of the North Atlantic and EU Treaties: The Challenge of Hybrid Threats', 431. Although Sari puts the statement into perspective by claiming that 'to determine whether or not NAC decisions are binding on the Member States, regard must be had to the terms of each relevant decision and the circumstances of its adoption, and this to establish whether they reveal an intent to enter into binding commitments.' (p. 431).

668 J. Barale, 'L'acquiescement dans la jurisprudence internationale', *Annuaire français de droit international* 1965, 389–427; Paras 190–92 of *Unilateral acts of States: Seventh report on unilateral acts of States, by Mr. Víctor Rodríguez Cedeño, Special Rapporteur*; J. Salmon, 'Les accords non formalisés ou "solo consensu"', *Annuaire français de droit international* 1999, 15; I. Sinclair, 'Estoppel and Acquiescence' in V. Lowe and M. Fitzmaurice (eds.), *op. cit.*, 104–120. For case law, see ICJ 1984, *Case concerning the Delimitation of the Maritime Boundary in the Gulf of Maine Area (Canada v. United States of America)*, Judgment, *ICJ Rep* 305, § 130; ICJ *Fisheries Jurisdiction*, 138. On estoppel, see P. Sands and P. Klein, *op. cit.*, 288; E. Stein and D. Carreau, 'Law and Peaceful Change in a Subsystem: "Withdrawal" of France from the North Atlantic Treaty Organization', 613 and more generally W. Friede 'Das Estoppel-Prinzip im Völkerrecht', *Zeitschrift für ausländisches öffentliches Recht und Völkerrecht* 1935, 517–545; F. Mosconi, 'La dottrina dell' "Estoppel" in diritto internazionale', *Rivista di Diritto Internazionale* 1962, 388–341; ICJ *North Sea Continental Shelf*, § 30; ICJ 1998, *Case concerning the Land and Maritime Boundary between Cameroon and Nigeria (Cameroon v. Nigeria: Equatorial Guinea Intervening)*, Preliminary Objections, *ICJ Rep* 275, § 57 and § 71.

conclusion will now be tested by applying it to the most essential type of decision the NAC can take: invoking Article 5 North Atlantic Treaty. This exercise is relevant because the first Trump administration had cast doubt on the legally binding force of Article 5 (in the context of coming to the collective defence of Montenegro)[669] and because discussions on the invocation of the mutual defence clauses in Article 5 of the North Atlantic Treaty and Article 42.7 TEU features more prominently on the international agenda since the war in Ukraine began. Article 5 reads as follows:

> The Parties agree that an armed attack against one or more of them in Europe or North America shall be considered an attack against them all and consequently they agree that, if such an armed attack occurs, each of them, in exercise of the right of individual or collective self-defence recognized by Article 51 of the Charter of the United Nations, will assist the Party or Parties so attacked by taking forthwith, individually and in concert with the other Parties, such action as it deems necessary, including the use of armed force, to restore and maintain the security of the North Atlantic area. Any such armed attack and all measures taken as a result thereof shall immediately be reported to the Security Council. Such measures shall be terminated when the Security Council has taken the measures necessary to restore and maintain international peace and security.

Article 5 has only been invoked once in NATO's history, in the wake of 9/11. The negotiations that ultimately produced Article 5 may have been long and difficult, but NATO was quick to invoke it in the aftermath of 9/11.[670] During the evening of 11 September, senior members of the IS prepared a memorandum for NAC approval. According to NATO officials and legal advisers, these preparations were mostly unguided and were not made according to any clear policy or formal process.[671] On the day of 9/11 there had been no structured consultation with national delegations. The personal efforts of NATO IS members had been very influential, as Buckley testifies.[672] The IS members opted for a plain reading

669 E. Sullivan, 'Trump Questions the Core of NATO: Mutual Defense, Including Montenegro', *New York Times* 18 July 2018, 3.

670 M. Goldberg, 'Mirage of Defense: Reexamining Article Five of the North Atlantic Treaty After the Terrorist Attacks on the United States', *Boston College International and Comparative Law Review* 2003, 86.

671 E. Buckley (former Assistant Secretary General for Defence Planning and Operations) in 'Invoking Article 5', 1 and S. Fournier (former Legal Adviser at the International Military Staff) and S. Bumgardner (former Legal Adviser of Allied Command Transformation Staff Element Europe) in 'Article 5 of the North Atlantic Treaty: The Cornerstone of the Alliance', *NATO Legal Gazette* 2014, 29.

672 As he describes the events of that day: 'We had not even discussed the way ahead or options with the Secretary General or his Private Office. There had been no 'steer' from any capital. I first raised the possibility of a statement invoking Article 5 at a meeting in Günter Altenburg's office in the early evening. As Assistant Secretary General for Political Affairs, Günter would also be involved in advising the Secretary General and we needed to be united. I took the text of the Washington Treaty with me. Ted Whiteside, head of NATO's Weapons

of the North Atlantic Treaty, 'untrammeled by reference to the judgments of the ICJ or the 1974 UNGA Resolution 3314 on the Definition of Aggression.'[673] The IS members agreed that there had indeed been an armed attack in the sense of Article 51 UN Charter. The aircraft had been used as missiles.[674] To distinguish the 9/11 attacks from domestic terrorism, the IS members used two criteria: the scale of the attacks and whether they had been directed from abroad.[675] They deemed the scale of the attacks important enough for the purposes of Article 51 UN Charter 'because the Washington Treaty had been written to deal with threats to peace and security in the North Atlantic area.'[676] To judge whether the attacks had been directed from abroad, prior NAC decisions were researched.[677] This led to the conclusion that the characterisation of the attacks as coming from abroad was necessary to place the Alliance's response within the scope of the North Atlantic Treaty.[678] Members of the IS went through the draft together and presented their work to NATO Secretary General Lord Robertson on the morning of 12 September.[679] With the support and approval of the United States, Lord Robertson called the NAC into session to invoke Article 5. During the Council session a few nations asked Baldwin DeVidts, NATO's Legal Adviser, to inform them whether, in his view, Article 5 should be interpreted in the sense that each nation must determine individually what action it would take and whether collective action by the Alliance would be undertaken only after

of Mass Destruction Centre, was also present and questioned whether the attack that day had been 'armed': Article 5 contemplated an 'armed attack' against any NATO Ally, but was an aircraft a weapon? [...] I went back to my office and called in Holger Pfeiffer, my deputy, and Steve Sturm, head of defence policy. We went through all the issues on our own. We agreed that there had indeed been an armed attack. An hour later, we met again and went through the draft together. [...] We finished our work and had a typed draft ready to present to the Secretary General early the next morning' in E. Buckley, 'Invoking Article 5', 1–2.

673 In the words S. Fournier and S. Bumgardner, 'Article 5 of the North Atlantic Treaty: The Cornerstone of the Alliance', 29.

674 E. Buckley, 'Invoking Article 5', 1; *cf.* ICJ 1984, Military and Paramilitary Activities in and against Nicaragua (*Nicaragua v. United States of America*), Judgment, ICJ Rep 1984, § 176-195 and see T. Ruys, 'The armed attack requirement ratione materiae' in T. Ruys (ed.), *Armed Attack and Article 51 of the UN Charter: Evolutions in Customary Law and Practice*, Cambridge, Cambridge University Press, 2011, 126–249; A. Sari, 'The Mutual Assistance Clauses of the North Atlantic and EU Treaties: The Challenge of Hybrid Threats', 411–415 and C. Stahn, 'International Law at Crossroads? The Impact of September 11', *Zeitschrift für ausländisches öffentliches Recht und Völkerrecht* 2002, 189.

675 E. Buckley, 'Invoking Article 5', 1 and S. Fournier and S. Bumgardner, 'Article 5 of the North Atlantic Treaty: The Cornerstone of the Alliance', 29.

676 E. Buckley, 'Invoking Article 5', 1. See for information ICJ *Nicaragua v. United States of America*, § 195; A. Constantinou, *The Right of Self-Defence under Customary International Law and Article 51 of the UN Charter*, Athens, Sakkoulas, 2000, 63–64 and C. Greenwood, 'Self-Defence' in X. (ed.), *Max Planck Encyclopedias of International Law*, Oxford, Oxford University Press, 2011, § 11–12.

677 S. Fournier and S. Bumgardner, 'Article 5 of the North Atlantic Treaty: The Cornerstone of the Alliance', 29.

678 S. Fournier and S. Bumgardner, 'Article 5 of the North Atlantic Treaty: The Cornerstone of the Alliance', 29 and M. Goldberg, 'Mirage of Defense: Reexamining Article Five of the North Atlantic Treaty After the Terrorist Attacks on the United States', 82.

679 E. Buckley, 'Invoking Article 5', 2.

additional specific consultation.[680] While the full text of DeVidts' memorandum is classified, former NATO officials report that DeVidts assured the Member States it was up to each of them to judge what should be done, adding 'whatever actions States were to take' should be appropriate to the scale of the attack, the means of each country and the steps necessary to restore peace and security', and that additional consultation was necessary for collective action by the Alliance.[681] In October 2021, Baldwin DeVidts publicly stated that

> the aim of my work that day was not to see on the basis of what legal arguments we could invoke article 5, but how we could convince allies to join, since it had already become clear that article 5 was going to be invoked anyway, after phone conversations amongst allied leaders and foreign ministers.[682]

In comparison, after the EU Member States first invoked Article 42(7) TEU in 2015, they made clear that 'no formal decision or conclusion by the Council will be required to implement Article 42(7).'[683] The EU High Representative stressed that 'no further formality' was needed to begin providing mutual assistance.[684] Thus, in practice, no formal requirement has been established to adopt the decision to trigger Article 42(7).[685] After the legal memorandum had been provided to all national representatives, the NAC (without having broken the silence) reached a consensus on the fact that, if it were to be determined that the attack had been directed from abroad, that attack would be considered an action covered by Article 5.[686] Clearly, the insertion of the word 'if' is legally important. On 2 October 2001, after being briefed on the results of the investigation into the 9/11 attacks, the NAC determined that the attacks had been directed from abroad.[687] Consequently, the NAC was able to confirm the invocation of Article 5 (because the 'if' requirement was satisfied). The NAC decided on the following individual and collective measures to implement Article 5[688]:

---

680 S. Fournier and S. Bumgardner, 'Article 5 of the North Atlantic Treaty: The Cornerstone of the Alliance', 29 and E. Buckley, 'Invoking Article 5', 2.

681 S. Fournier and S. Bumgardner, 'Article 5 of the North Atlantic Treaty: The Cornerstone of the Alliance', 29 which refers back to E. Buckley, 'Invoking Article 5', 2.

682 Comments by former NATO Legal Adviser Baldwin DeVidts at the doctoral seminar of the author, KU Leuven, online, 4 October 2021.

683 Council of the EU, Foreign Affairs Meeting, 16–17 November 2015, Doc. 14120/15.

684 S. Anghel and C. Cirlig, 'Activation of Article 42(7) TEU?', *European Parliament Research Service Briefing* 2016, 2.

685 S. Clapp and A. Verhelst, 'A comparative analysis of Article 5 Washington Treaty (NATO) and Article 42(7) TEU (EU)', 1.

686 Statement by the NAC, Press Release (2001) 124 of 12 September 2001, second sentence; *NATO Encyclopedia* 2018, 21; S. Fournier and S. Bumgardner, 'Article 5 of the North Atlantic Treaty: The Cornerstone of the Alliance', 29.

687 *NATO Encyclopedia* 2018, 21 and M. Goldberg, 'Mirage of Defense: Reexamining Article Five of the North Atlantic Treaty After the Terrorist Attacks on the United States', 83.

688 Statement to the Press by NATO Secretary General Lord Robertson on the NAC Decision on Implementation of Article 5 of the Washington Treaty following the 11 September Attacks

- enhance intelligence sharing and cooperation, bilaterally and in the appropriate NATO bodies, relating to the threats posed by terrorism and the actions to be taken against it;
- provide collective or individual, as appropriate and according to their capabilities, assistance to Allies and other States which are or may be subject to increased threats of terrorism;
- take measures to provide increased security for US and other Allied facilities on their territory;
- backfill selected Allied assets in NATO's area of responsibility required to directly support operations against terrorism;
- provide blanket overflight clearances for the aircraft of the US and other Allies in accordance with the national procedures;
- provide access for the US and other Allies to ports and airfields on the territory of NATO Member States for operations against terrorism, as well as for refuelling.

In addition, the NAC expressed the readiness of the NATO Member States to:

- deploy elements of the Standing Naval Forces to the Eastern Mediterranean aimed at providing NATO presence and at demonstrating resolve in the campaign against terrorism;
- deploy elements of the NATO Airborne Early Warning and Control Force to support operations against terrorism.[689]

This historic illustration raises important legal questions: 1) What is the legal effect of a NATO decision to invoke Article 5 and implement it? 2) What is the scope of obligation(s) for Member States under Article 5?

5.2. AN ANALYSIS OF THE PREPARATORY WORKS FOR ARTICLE 5

An analysis of the preparatory works for Article 5 yields the following observations. First of all, there had been a difference of opinion between the American and European negotiators over the strength of the security guarantee and the legally binding force of the collective self-defence provision.[690] At the

against U.S., 4 October 2001 and B. Grady, 'Article 5 of the North Atlantic Treaty: Past, Present, and Uncertain Future', *Georgia Journal of International and Comparative Law* 2002, 169.

689 Statement to the Press by NATO Secretary General Lord Robertson on the NAC Decision on Implementation of Article 5 of the Washington Treaty following the 11 September Attacks against the U.S., 4 October 2001.

690 T. Ireland, *Creating the Entangling Alliance: The Origins of the North Atlantic Treaty Organization*, Santa Barbara, Praeger Security International, 1981, 83; A. Verhelst and

time of the North Atlantic Treaty negotiations, the Western European nations, ravaged by two world wars and feeling exposed to an imminent Communist threat, favoured a formulation of Article 5 that would ensure an automatic and unqualified commitment on the part of the United States to defend Western Europe with military action in the case of an armed attack.[691] The Western European nations demanded strong, precise, formally and legally binding guarantees from the US.[692] The US, on the other hand, feared that a strongly formulated Article 5 would automatically engage them in a war in Europe.[693] From the outset of the discussions, the mandatory provisions of the Brussels Treaty were unacceptable to the US and Canada.[694] The Americans favoured the language of the 1947 Rio Pact, in which an armed attack against an American country was considered an attack against all, the measures taken in response

J. Wouters, 'Zeventig jaar NAVO: juridische kanttekeningen bij een bijzondere internationale organisatie', 243.

691 L. Kaplan, *The United States and NATO, The Formative Years*, Lexington, The University Press of Kentucky, 1984, 1; A. Verhelst and J. Wouters, 'Zeventig jaar NAVO: juridische kanttekeningen bij een bijzondere internationale organisatie', 240–242. See, for instance, Prime Minister Churchill's telegram to President Truman of 12 May 1945, expressing his immense concern about the expanding Soviet threat while the Allied forces demobilised in W. Churchill, *Triumph and Tragedy*, New York, Houghton-Mifflin Books, 1953, 679; S. Fournier and S. Bumgardner, 'Article 5 of the North Atlantic Treaty: The Cornerstone of the Alliance', 20 and *NATO Encyclopedia* 2018, 262.

692 S. Sloan, 'Negotiating Article 5', 1; M. Schmitt, 'The North Atlantic Alliance and Collective Defense at 70: Confession and Response Revisited', 97; L. De Brabander and G. Spriet, *Als de NAVO de passie preekt*, Berchem, EPO, 2009, 50.

693 'U.S. negotiators were well-aware that such a provision would immediately be seen by Congress as undercutting its constitutional powers for declaring war and would therefore have no chance of winning Senate consent' in S. Sloan, 'Negotiating Article 5', 1; S. Fournier and S. Bumgardner, 'Article 5 of the North Atlantic Treaty: The Cornerstone of the Alliance', 20–21; A. Verhelst and J. Wouters, 'Zeventig jaar NAVO: juridische kanttekeningen bij een bijzondere internationale organisatie', 242 and see Dean Acheson, the U.S. Secretary of State who signed the North Atlantic Treaty on behalf of the U.S., *Broadcast on Atlantic Accord*, Radio Address to the Nation, 18 March 1949, *The New York Times* 19 March 1949, available online at https://archive.nytimes.com/www.nytimes.com/library/world/global/031949nato-acheson-text.html (last accessed January 2025).

694 The signing of the Brussels Treaty (1948) marked the determination of five Western European countries (Belgium, France, Luxembourg, the Netherlands and the U.K.) to develop a common defence system and to strengthen ties in a manner that would enable them to resist threats to their security. The treaty provided for the organisation of military, economic, social and cultural cooperation among Member States as well as a mutual defence clause. The mutual defence clause laid down in Article IV Modified Brussels Treaty (1954) read as follows: 'If any of the High Contracting Parties should be the object of an armed attack in Europe, the other High Contracting Parties *will*, in accordance with the provisions of Article 51 of the Charter of the United Nations, afford the Party so attacked *all the military and other aid and assistance in their power*' (emphasis added), *cf. NATO Handbook* 2001, 29; M. Schmitt, 'The North Atlantic Alliance and Collective Defense at 70: Confession and Response Revisited', 97 and S. Fournier and S. Bumgardner, 'Article 5 of the North Atlantic Treaty: The Cornerstone of the Alliance', 21.

to that attack were to be individually determined by each country.[695] Unlike the Brussels Treaty, the Rio Pact did not specify that the response had to be armed. The vague wording of the Rio Pact was unattractive to the Europeans because they feared that, without the guarantee of a military response, the North Atlantic Treaty would be useless.[696] The US, on the other hand, favoured an Article 5 that would allow each party to decide for itself, using its own honest judgment, which actions it deems necessary to restore and maintain the security of the North Atlantic area and take those actions accordingly.[697] The treaty negotiations ended with a compromise: the security guarantee was laid down in a formal treaty (a European demand),[698] but embedded in an Article 5 that does not imply the automatic involvement of the US in an armed conflict (an American demand). Article 5 reflects this compromise to the present day.

5.3. AN ANALYSIS OF THE LANGUAGE OF ARTICLE 5

5.3.1. *'Will assist the Party or Parties so attacked'*

This phrase in Article 5 expresses the pledge of assistance.[699] The language used (especially when compared to Article IV Modified Brussels Treaty), taken

695 Article 3 of the Rio Pact provided that: 'An armed attack by any State against an American State shall be considered as an attack against all the American States, and consequently, each one of the said Contracting Parties undertakes to assist in meeting the attack in the exercise of the inherent right of individual or collective self-defense recognized by Article 51 of the Charter of the United Nations. On the request of the State or States directly attacked and until the decision of the Organ of Consultation of the Inter-American System, each one of the Contracting Parties *may determine the immediate measures which it may individually take* in fulfilment of the obligation contained in the preceding paragraph and in accordance with the principle of continental solidarity. [...]' (emphasis added). The Inter-American Treaty of Reciprocal Assistance ('Rio Pact') was signed on 2 September 1947 in Rio de Janeiro and entered into force on 12 March 1948. See M. Schmitt, 'The North Atlantic Alliance and Collective Defense at 70: Confession and Response Revisited', 97 and G. Schwarzenberger, 'The North Atlantic Pact', *Western Political Quarterly* 1949, 313–314.

696 S. Sloan, 'Negotiating Article 5', 1 and M. Schmitt, 'The North Atlantic Alliance and Collective Defense at 70: Confession and Response Revisited', 97.

697 U.S. Senate Foreign Relations Committee, *Senate Executive Report* No. 8, 81st Congress., 1st session, 1949, 13–14.

698 And not a presidential declaration e.g. see A. Verhelst and J. Wouters, 'Zeventig jaar NAVO: juridische kanttekeningen bij een bijzondere internationale organisatie', 243 and T. Ireland, *op. cit.*, 83.

699 As put by former NATO legal advisers S. Fournier and S. Bumgardner, 'Article 5 of the North Atlantic Treaty: The Cornerstone of the Alliance', 26. Sed also A. Sari, 'The Mutual Assistance Clauses of the North Atlantic and EU Treaties: The Challenge of Hybrid Threats', 429 and see Memorandum by the Director of the Policy Planning Staff, 24 November 1948 in *Foreign Relations of the United States, 1948, Western Europe, Volume III*, 1974, 283–84 and Minute from Mr. Bevin (then British Foreign Secretary) to Mr. Attlee (then Prime Minister of the UK), 6 April 1948 in T. Insall and P. Salmon (eds.), *The Brussels and North Atlantic Treaties, 1947–1949*, Abingdon, Routledge, 2014, 146.

together with Article 5's *ratio legis* as expressed in the preparatory works, expresses an obligation, i.e. a duty to assist when the NAC has determined that an armed attack in the sense of Article 51 UN Charter has taken place within the geographical scope of Article 6 North Atlantic Treaty. This interpretation has been confirmed by two former NATO legal advisers.[700] There is, however, a caveat (phrase (b), see below), which leaves the nature of the commitment undefined.[701] This is why phrase (a) uses the less committal word 'will' instead of 'shall' or 'undertake', words that have different meanings in international law.[702] Article 42(7) TEU, in contrast, uses the more committal word 'shall'. Note that the bar for invoking an armed attack under international law is higher than the bar for invoking armed aggression under Article 42(7) TEU.[703] Not every act of armed aggression can trigger the right to self-defence under Article 51 UN Charter. Its scope is limited to armed attacks.[704]

5.3.2. *'Such action as it deems necessary, including the use of armed force'*

This phrase in Article 5 gives each NATO Member State the opportunity to determine, as it deems necessary, which action it takes, which may or may not include the use of armed force. Unlike the 1948 draft text, which called for 'such military or other action *as may be necessary*' (emphasis added), the final text demands only such action as the individual contracting parties *themselves* deem necessary.[705] It is up to each contracting party to determine how it will respond in the case of an armed attack. The text leaves the parties a wide margin

---

700 S. Fournier and S. Bumgardner, 'Article 5 of the North Atlantic Treaty: The Cornerstone of the Alliance', 26; E. Perot, 'The art of commitments: NATO, the EU and the interplay between law and politics within Europe's collective defence architecture', *European Security* 2019, 51–53; M. Schmitt, 'The North Atlantic Alliance and Collective Defense at 70: Confession and Response Revisited', 113–114 and A. Sari, 'The Mutual Assistance Clauses of the North Atlantic and EU Treaties: The Challenge of Hybrid Threats', 411.

701 M. Schmitt, 'The North Atlantic Alliance and Collective Defense at 70: Confession and Response Revisited', 113–114; R. Heindel, T. Kalijarvi and F. Wilcox, 'The North Atlantic Treaty in the United States Senate', 636; S. Fournier and S. Bumgardner, 'Article 5 of the North Atlantic Treaty: The Cornerstone of the Alliance', 27 and S. Sloan, 'Negotiating Article 5', 2.

702 R. Kolb, *op. cit.*, 20; D. Hollis, 'Defining Treaties' in D. Hollis (ed.), *op. cit.*, 27 and A. Aust, 'Alternatives to Treaty-Making: MOUs as Political Commitments' in D. Hollis (ed.), *op. cit.*, 48–50.

703 T. Ruys, 'The armed attack requirement ratione materiae' in T. Ruys (ed.), *op. cit.*, 126–249 and Y. Dinstein, 'Aggression', *Max Planck Encyclopedia of International Law* 2015, § 33.

704 A naval blockade by a warship would constitute armed aggression, without necessarily constituting an armed attack, according to J. Rehrl in 'Invoking the EU's Mutual Assistance Clause. What it says, what it means', *Egmont Paper* 2015, 2.

705 *Cf.* Article 11 North Atlantic Treaty and A. Sari, 'The Mutual Assistance Clauses of the North Atlantic and EU Treaties: The Challenge of Hybrid Threats', 428 and R. Heindel, T. Kalijarvi and F. Wilcox, 'The North Atlantic Treat in the United States Senate', 649–651.

of discretion.[706] In contrast, the EU's mutual assistance pledge, expressed in Article 42(7) TEU, is more strongly formulated. Member States have an explicit obligation to come to the defence of a victim state by 'all means' in their power, not just the means they deem necessary.[707] For NATO Member States, the action could, in theory, be as minimal as sharing information or providing fuel for aircraft.[708] Phrase (a) is less committal, allowing each party to determine which action it takes.[709] On the other hand, the discretionary element in Article 5 should not be overestimated.[710] The assistance provided must be reasonable in light of Article 5's express purpose, which is to restore and maintain the security of the North Atlantic area and to fulfil the overall obligations of States as parties to the 1949 Treaty.[711] Indeed, NATO Member States, as parties to the Treaty, are bound to perform Article 5 in good faith. If the response is manifestly

---

706 Lord Ismay, *op. cit.*, 13. See also J.C.S., 'Problèmes juridiques de l'Organisation du traité de l'Atlantique Nord', 691 (who links this to article 3 North Atlantic Treaty); A. Orakhelashvili, *Collective Security*, Oxford, Oxford University Press, 284 and P. Potter, 'The Proposed North Atlantic Pact', *World Affairs* 1949, 5–6. See also Germany, Constitutional Court, 1984, *Atomwaffenstationierung*, 2 BvE 13/83, 159. Interestingly, Brüel calls this discretionary freedom a legal reality more so than a political and policy one: '*Die Freiheit jeder Partei zu bestimmen, welches Mittel sie als Reaktion gegen einen Angriff anwenden will, ist mehr juristischer und theoretischer als praktischer und politischer Natur. Greift aber eine Großmacht zur Gewaltanwendung, so wird die Situation sich leicht so entwickeln können, dass auch ein kleiner Partner, der vielleicht gar nicht zur Gewaltanwendung hatte greifen wollen, in einen Krieg hineingezogen wird*' in E. Brüel, 'Die juristische Bedeutung des Atlantikpaktes', *op. cit.*, 295.

707 S. Clapp and A. Verhelst, 'A comparative analysis of Article 5 Washington Treaty (NATO) and Article 42(7) TEU (EU)', 1.

708 See S. Sloan, 'Negotiating Article 5', 2. but see A. Sari, 'The Mutual Assistance Clauses of the North Atlantic and EU Treaties: The Challenge of Hybrid Threats', 430.

709 Some argue that the phrase 'such action as it deems necessary' leaves so much discretion in the hands of Member States that there can be no legal obligation under Article 5. These authors essentially question whether a commitment which its addressees may dismiss at their discretion can constitute a binding legal obligation. Amongst others, John Bolton—former U.S. National Security Advisor—has defended this position in J. Bolton, 'Is There Really Law in International Affairs', *Transnational Law and Contemporary Problems* 2000, 5. This statement can be explained by a specific, limited and narrow view on international law: since international law lacks traditional compliance mechanisms, some are of the opinion that there can be no 'hard' obligations in international law. Note how Lauterpacht, specifically on Article 5 North Atlantic Treaty, has said that 'the fact that the interested State is the sole judge of the existence of the obligation is, while otherwise of considerable importance, irrelevant for the determination of the legal character of the instrument', in ILC, Report on the Law of Treaties by Mr. H. Lauterpacht - Special Rapporteur, Doc. A/CN.4/63 in *Yearbook of the International Law Commission*, 1953, vol. II, 97.

710 As defended by a.o. Sari (p. 429–432), Lindstrom (p. 584), Fournier and Bumgardner (p. 27) and Schmitt (p. 115).

711 Statement by NATO Legal Adviser DeVidts during the 12 September 2001 meeting of the NAC on the invocation of Article 5 North Atlantic Treaty, as quoted in S. Fournier and S. Bumgardner, 'Article 5 of the North Atlantic Treaty: The Cornerstone of the Alliance', 29 which refers back to E. Buckley, 'Invoking Article 5', 2; A. Sari, 'The Mutual Assistance Clauses of the North Atlantic and EU Treaties: The Challenge of Hybrid Threats', 430; A. Lindstrom, 'Consensus Decisionmaking in NATO: French Unilateralism and the Decision

unreasonable, or inadequate in nature or scale, it could constitute a violation of Article 5.[712] As parties to the North Atlantic Treaty, NATO Member States are obliged to use their honest judgment to determine such action as they deem necessary and consequently take such action (Article 26(4) VCLT).[713] This must be done in good faith. The meaning of the phrase 'aid and assistance by all the means in their power' in Article 42(7) TEU, on the other hand, remains uncertain. The provision is still young. Whether 'all the means in their power' should be interpreted as a strong obligation can only be revealed in practice.

5.4. INTERIM CONCLUSION

In principle, the NAC's operational decisions, including the decision to invoke Article 5, are non-binding. The NAC's powers are merely advisory, and the North Atlantic Treaty does not endow its decisions with legally binding effect. Moreover, NATO itself confirms in its commentary to the ARIO that the effect of the NAC's operational acts is non-binding. This does not mean, however, that NATO's operational acts cannot have any legal effect. The norms articulated in them may become binding on Member States when they also emanate from a traditional source of international law, such as unilateral State acts, agreements in simplified form, or international customary law. The intent of parties to be bound is still the most important criterion. The fact that NATO

---

to Defend Turkey', 584; M. Reichard, *The EU-NATO Relationship: a Legal and Political Perspective*, Aldershot, Ashgate, 2006, 184.

712 Lauterpacht states that the determination of Article 5 must take place in accordance with the implied obligation to act in good faith and sees no ground for questioning the instrument's legal character as a treaty, in ILC, Report on the Law of Treaties by Mr. H. Lauterpacht – Special Rapporteur, Doc. A/CN.4/63 in *Yearbook of the International Law Commission*, 1953, vol. II, 97. See Article 26 VCLT, Article 38(1)(c) Statute of the ICJ and general principle of law of good faith, *cf.* ICJ *Nuclear Tests Case,* § 46; *The North Atlantic Coast Fisheries Case (Great Britain v. United States of America),* 1910 (Award), *UNRIAA* 169, vol. XI, § 188; ILC, *Yearbook of the International Law Commission*, 1964, vol. II, 7ss; M. Shaw, *op. cit.*, 103; J. Wouters, C. Ryngaert, T. Ruys and G. De Baere, *op. cit.*, 158. See A. Sari, 'The Mutual Assistance Clauses of the North Atlantic and EU Treaties: The Challenge of Hybrid Threats', 430; M. Reichard, 184; A. Lindstrom, 'Consensus Decisionmaking in NATO: French Unilateralism and the Decision to Defend Turkey', 584: 'More reasonable is that article 5 implies good faith efforts to take a reasonable level of action' and see B. Cardozo in U.S., New York Court of Appeals 4 December 1917, *Wood v Lucy, Lady Duff-Gordon*, 222 NY 88, 118 N.E. 214, 91.

713 Former U.S. Secretary of State Dean Acheson emphasised that 'each nation is committed to do what in its honest judgment is necessary to restore and maintain the security of the North Atlantic area, taking into account the gravity of the armed attack and the action believed to be necessary to achieve this end' in D. Acheson, 'The Meaning of the North Atlantic Pact', *U.S. Department of State Bulletin* 1949, 387 as quoted by Sari in 'The Mutual Assistance Clauses of the North Atlantic and EU Treaties: The Challenge of Hybrid Threats', 430. See also Article 5, 6, 11 and Preamble of the North Atlantic Treaty, Article 2(2) UN Charter, Article 26 VCLT and general principle of good faith, *cf.* Article 38(1)(c) Statute of the ICJ.

decisions are adopted in the plenary NAC, at Ministerials and Summits, leaves their legal status deliberately nebulous. It is not always clear whether it was the Organisation or the Member States *en groupe* that took the decision. When Article 5 is invoked, the parties to the North Atlantic Treaty have a legal duty to assist. A caveat to this obligation is the fact that it is up to each treaty party to determine how exactly it will respond, whether by using force or by merely sharing information. This stands in contrast to the more strongly formulated Article 42(7) TEU, according to which the EU Member States are explicitly obliged to come to a victim state's defence by all means within their power. But the discretionary element in Article 5 does not do away with the fact that the parties to the North Atlantic Treaty are still bound by Article 26 VCLT and by the general principle that they must, in good faith, use their honest judgment to determine the action they deem necessary and to consequently take such action.

6. CONCLUSION

NATO decisions are prepared by consultation and adopted by consensus. This constitutes an established practice of the organisation (Article 5 VCLT and Article 2(b) ARIO), which means that the decisions are made within the confines of the constituent instrument, even though the North Atlantic Treaty does not provide any decision-making formula. Contrary to what some commentators have claimed, this internal law was not violated in 2003, when the DPC approved defensive aid to Turkey, instead of the NAC. After all, France had consented to not being in the DPC and organisations are free to choose their own bureaucratic structure. Had the defensive aid been granted on the basis of unanimity or majority voting, it could have constituted a violation of NATO's internal law. NATO decisions are legally formalised only to a small extent. This is because procedural and substantive violations of NATO's limited internal legal order, even if they do arise, would be neutralised by acceptance, acquiescence, or estoppel, so that even purely *ultra vires* decisions are likely to be upheld.[714] NATO nations have retained their decision-making sovereignty and act as States rather than as Member States of the Organisation in this respect. Considering NATO's perceived inability to make decisions quickly, its growing membership, and the increased frequency of single-country vetoes, NATO should explore ways to ensure more efficient and transparent decision-making. The underexplored idea of applying qualified majority voting to administrative decisions merits further academic research in the field of political science. In this chapter, it was explained why other suggested changes to the consensus rule

714 R. Bernhardt, 'Ultra Vires Activities of International Organizations' in J. Makarczyk (ed.), *op. cit.*, 599–609.

were unsuccessful. Besides retaining their decision-making sovereignty, NATO Member States also retain their decision-making responsibility. The ICJ in FYROM v. Greece correctly pointed out that Member States cannot use NATO's consensus rule as a shield to protect them from their external obligations (i.e. external to NATO) under international law. Courts should indeed be allowed to establish a Member State's responsibility under international law if the individual conduct of that Member State can be isolated (e.g. on the basis on publicly made objections like in *FYROM v. Greece*) and when that conduct violates an external legal obligation. In contrast and more problematic, the ECtHR, in its *Gasparini* ruling, opened the door to holding Member States responsible for the acts of the Organisation. This is difficult to reconcile with the principle that States should not be held responsible for merely being Members of an Organisation. The Court, in *Gasparini*, should not have isolated the institutional conduct of Italy and Belgium from NATO's decision-making process, because it is perfectly possible that other Member States had voiced concerns or had broken the silence with regard to NATO's decision to establish the NATO AT. Moreover, no clear Member State action could be identified, as required by *Bosphorus*, as *Gasparini* concerned an alleged structural institutional deficiency within NATO.[715] It is difficult to claim that Italy and Belgium, by simply agreeing to establish the NATO AT, had sought to evade their obligations under international law.[716] Being an established practice, NATO's consensus principle is not entirely fit for application in other international organisations that have codified consensus rules, nor is it fit to apply in the EU CSDP or the UNSC. It could be applied in new intergovernmental organisations, however, if they are willing to accept the advantages and disadvantages of consensus-based decision-making identified in the SWOT-analysis above. If such an organisation does not want to move in the direction of more integration, it could consider introducing NATO's silence procedure or its opt-out practice. If a new intergovernmental organisation plans to introduce consensus-based decision-making, it is advisable to express this in a basic legal text, perhaps coupled with a passerelle clause, to avoid Member States contesting the established practice like persistent objectors do in customary international law, unless that organisation wants to maintain as much flexibility as possible. To answer the last research question: the NAC's operational decisions, including the invocation of Article 5, are non-binding, in principle, the intent of the parties to be bound still being the most important criterion in this regard. Policymakers, judges, and academics should not conclude that NATO decisions have legally binding force on the sole basis of consensus, but should establish the intent of the parties to be bound.

715 ECtHR 2006, *Bosphorus v Ireland*, Application No 4036/98, 42 EHRR 1, § 137.

716 *Cf.* ARIO, Commentary (2) to Article 62, 267 and C. Ryngaert, 'The European Court of Human Rights' Approach to the Responsibility of Member States in connection with Acts of International Organizations', 1004.

CHAPTER 5

NATO MEMBERSHIP FROM ADMISSION TO EXPULSION: A MATTER OF LAW OR POLITICS?

1. INTRODUCTION

In several ways, the name 'NATO' is actually self-describing. Its Member States are all North Atlantic. This has not changed over the past 70 years, despite the fact that NATO has grown from 12 to 32 Member States since 1949, currently acting on behalf approximately a billion people. Since the fall of the Berlin Wall, NATO's approach to expansion changed fundamentally. NATO has, for example, been pursuing its (in)famous open-door policy.[717] This has resulted in a doubling of its membership, from 16 Member States in 1999 to 32 in 2025.[718] Whereas, typically, an international organisation will lay out its membership conditions and accession procedure in its constituent instrument, the legal aspects of admission to NATO are obscure. This was demonstrated in the news coverage preceding the Ukraine crisis. Upon closer scrutiny, it is clear that Article 10 of the North Atlantic Treaty does not contain very specific legal conditions for NATO membership, instead providing a brief overview of what is expected

---

717 *NATO Encyclopedia* 2019, 217–219; *NATO 2030: United for a New Era – Analysis and Recommendations of the Reflection Group Appointed by the NATO Secretary General*, 25 November 2020, 8; J. Eichler, *NATO's Expansion after the Cold War: Geopolitics and Impacts for International Security*, Cham, Springer International, 2021, 9–32; R. Asmus, *Opening NATO's Door: how the Alliance remade itself for a New Era*, New York, Columbia University Press, 2004, 134–174 and T. German, 'NATO and the enlargement debate: enhancing Euro-Atlantic security or inciting confrontation?', *International Affairs* 2017, 291–308.

718 During the Cold War, four countries became NATO Member States: Turkey and Greece (1952), the Federal Republic of Germany (1955) and Spain (1982). The Czech Republic, Poland and Hungary were the first former members of the Warsaw Pact to join NATO in 1999. In the largest enlargement round yet, Bulgaria, Estonia, Latvia, Lithuania, Romania, Slovakia and Slovenia joined NATO in 2004. In 2009, Albania and Croatia became NATO Member States, while Montenegro was admitted in 2017. North Macedonia became NATO's thirtieth Member State in 2020 after the successful resolution of the naming dispute. After the invasion of Ukraine, Finland and Sweden became NATO's newest members, in 2023 and 2024 respectively.

from candidates.[719] Despite the brevity of Article 10's conditions, NATO does actually evaluate candidate Member States on their compliance with quite a few specific requirements. Nowadays, candidates are explicitly expected to adhere to the principles of democracy, individual liberty, and the rule of law, and to demonstrate a commitment to promoting stability and well-being through economic liberty, social justice, and environmental responsibility, to settle ethnic disputes etc.[720] Strikingly, Article 10 has never been amended to this end. The provision reads as follows:

> The Parties may, by unanimous agreement, invite any other European State in a position to *further the principles of this Treaty*[721] *and to contribute to the security of the North Atlantic area*[722] to accede to this Treaty. Any State so invited may become a Party to the Treaty by depositing its instrument of accession with the Government of the United States of America. The Government of the United States of America will inform each of the Parties of the deposit of each such instrument of accession.[723]

In the French version, Article 10 reads:

> *Les parties peuvent, par accord unanime, inviter à accéder au Traité tout autre Etat européen susceptible* de favoriser le développement des principes du présent Traité et de contribuer à la sécurité de la région de l'Atlantique Nord.[724] *Tout Etat ainsi invité peut devenir partie au Traité en déposant son instrument d'accession auprès du gouvernement des Etats-Unis d'Amérique. Celui-ci informera chacune des parties du dépôt de chaque instrument d'accession.*

The 1949 Treaty's negotiators understood from the outset that an accession provision was needed. They believed that a North Atlantic security system, if it was to be fully effective, should provide both its own security and that of other countries in the general North Atlantic area whose security is interdependent with their own.[725] At the same time, the negotiators agreed that not all States fitting that description would automatically become part of the Alliance.[726] The final wording of Article 10 reflects these divergent concerns. Now the question arises whether this expansion of the accession conditions, which

---

719 A. Duxbury, *op. cit.*, 129 and as inspired by N. Minogue, 'The North Atlantic Treaty at 70: Article 10', 171–72.

720 Following a decision by the Foreign Ministers in December 1994, the Allies decided to examine the why and how of future admissions, which translated into the 1995 Study on NATO Enlargement. See § 5–6 of the 1994 Ministerial Communiqué. See also Article I.1 MAP 1999.

721 'First limb of Article 10'.

722 'Second limb of Article 10'.

723 Emphasis added.

724 Emphasis added.

725 As quoted by N. Minogue, 'The North Atlantic Treaty at 70 – Article 10', 166.

726 N. Minogue, 'The North Atlantic Treaty at 70 – Article 10', 166.

has caused them to drift further and further away from the text of Article 10, constitutes a tolerable interpretation of the Treaty or an unlawful imposition of new conditions.[727] And inversely, what if a Member State, once admitted to NATO, violates the provisions of the North Atlantic Treaty? While it is often the case that the constituent instrument of an international organisation provides the option of suspending a Member State's rights (e.g. Article 5 UN Charter, Article 8 Statute of the Council of Europe, Article 7 TEU, and Article XXIII IMF Articles of Agreement)[728] and, under certain circumstances, even allows it to be expelled,[729] the North Atlantic Treaty does not. What legal tools, then, are available to States in their capacity as Members of NATO when they want to suspend or expel another Member State? Do the political threats of expelling a NATO Member State, which occasionally surface on the political agenda and in the media, have a foundation in international law?

2. A(N) (UN)LAWFUL EXPANSION OF NATO'S ACCESSION CONDITIONS?

Article 10 North Atlantic Treaty does not contain very specific legal conditions for NATO membership. Instead, writes Duxbury, it gives a brief overview of what is expected from a candidate Member State.[730] First of all, the candidate must be in a position to 'further the principles of the Treaty' (first limb of the Article 10 test). Secondly, the candidate must be in a position to 'contribute to the security of the North Atlantic Area' (second limb of the Article 10 test). The first limb reflects a political requirement, while the second entails both the candidate's capacity to contribute to common defence of the Alliance (as well as other activities) and the military and security implications of its accession for the North Atlantic Area in a broader sense, as Minogue summarises it.[731] Despite the brevity of Article 10, NATO does actually evaluate candidate Member States on their compliance with quite a few specific requirements. Over the last 70 years NATO has expanded its accession conditions, which has caused them to drift increasingly further and further away from the text of Article 10, without ever formally amending it. Instead, NATO has been expanding its membership conditions through a succession of policy decisions, of which the 1995 Study on NATO Enlargement is the most important. According to the 1995

---

727 *Cf.* A. Duxbury, *op. cit.*, 137 and ICJ *First Admissions*, 62.

728 *Cf.* Article 5 UN Charter, Article 8 Statute of the Council of Europe, Article 7 TEU, and Article XXIII IMF Articles of Agreement.

729 *Cf.* Article 6 UN Charter, Article 16 League of Nations Covenant and to a certain extent Article 8 Statute of the Council of Europe.

730 A. Duxbury, *op. cit.*, 129.

731 N. Minogue, 'The North Atlantic Treaty at 70: Article 10', 169. For the aforementioned reasons, the former falls outside of the scope of this work.

Study, countries seeking NATO membership must be able to demonstrate that they fulfil a variety of requirements. According to Nick Minogue, NATO Legal Adviser, the following criteria, listed in the Study, give expression to the first limb of Article 10 ('the principles of the North Atlantic Treaty'):

- adhering to and promoting the purposes and principles of the United Nations Charter, and conforming to the principles of democracy, individual liberty, and the rule of law[732];
- demonstrating a commitment to promoting stability and well-being through economic liberty, social justice, and environmental responsibility[733];
- having established appropriate democratic and civilian control of their defence force[734];
- committing to the peaceful resolution of conflicts and, specifically, settling, by peaceful means, any international disputes in which they may be involved[735];
- resolving, by peaceful means and in accordance with OSCE principles, any ethnic disputes, external territorial disputes, or internal jurisdictional disputes. The resolution of such disputes is specifically identified as a factor to be taken into account before issuing an invitation to accede, and not solely as a future commitment.[736]

The following criteria, listed in the Study, give expression to the second limb of Article 10 ('the security of the North Atlantic Area'):

- a commitment to maintaining the effectiveness of the Alliance by sharing roles, risks, responsibilities, costs, and benefits of assuring common security goals and objectives[737];
- how aspirants intend to contribute to NATO's collective defence, and how they will participate in the integrated military structure and collective defence planning process[738];
- assimilation into NATO force structures and stationing, taking into account the imperative of achieving, as swiftly as possible, at least the minimum level of interoperability required for military effectiveness[739];
- contributing to peacekeeping and other missions.[740]

---

732 Articles 4 and 70 Study on NATO Enlargement.
733 Article 72 Study on NATO Enlargement.
734 Article 72 Study on NATO Enlargement.
735 Article 5 Study on NATO Enlargement.
736 Articles 6 and 72 Study on NATO Enlargement.
737 Article 5 Study on NATO Enlargement.
738 Articles 45 and 47 Study on NATO Enlargement.
739 Articles 53–61 and 78 Study on NATO Enlargement.
740 Articles 42–46 Study on NATO Enlargement and N. Minogue, 'The North Atlantic Treaty at 70: Article 10', 171–72.

2.1. INTERPRETING THE IMPOSITION OF CONDITIONS IN THE NORTH ATLANTIC TREATY

Having identified these criteria, Duxbury believes that NATO has redefined its membership conditions more expansively than any other international organisation ever has without amending its constitutional instrument. This is in comparison to other international organisations, such as the EU and the Council of Europe.[741] Do the criteria listed in the 1995 Study merely elaborate upon the conditions of Article 10, which render those criteria an interpretation of vague constitutional provisions, or do they create new membership requirements, which would raise issues of legality, according to Duxbury?[742] The latter conclusion would also inflict an unfair burden on the States that have joined NATO since the fall of the Berlin Wall. A natural reading of Article 10 in both authentic versions ('The Parties may [...] invite any other European State in a position to [...]' and '*Les parties peuvent [...] inviter à accéder tout autre Etat européen susceptible de [...]*') suggests that those conditions are exhaustively listed.[743] This conclusion seems all the more likely when one compares Article 10 to Article 4 UN Charter, which also lists its conditions exhaustively: 'Membership in the United Nations is open to all other peace-loving States *which*' and '*Peuvent* devenir Membres des Nations unies tous autres États pacifiques qui' (emphasis added). Compare this *a contrario* to the non-exhaustively listed conditions in Article 1.4 ILO Constitution, Article 6 WHO Agreement, Article 2.2 FAO Constitution, and Article XXII ESA Convention. The same goes for Article 237 EEC Treaty, which reads that 'the conditions of admission and the adjustments to this Treaty necessitated thereby shall be the *subject of an agreement* between the Member States and the applicant State. This *agreement* shall be submitted for *ratification* by all the Contracting States in accordance with their respective constitutional requirements'.[744] In *Lothar Mattheus v. Doego Fruchtimport and Tiefkühlkost*, the CJEU interpreted Article 237 EEC Treaty to mean that it expressly enables the authorities to define the legal conditions for accession without to the possibility of defining them in advance.[745] In contrast, the preparatory works for the North Atlantic Treaty confirm that the membership conditions in Article 10 are listed exhaustively. If drafters had meant to leave NATO Member States the freedom to import unconnected conditions, they would have opted for the wording used in the September 1948 accession provision:

---

741 A. Duxbury, *op. cit.*, 136.

742 A. Duxbury, *op. cit.*, 137. See also ICJ *First Admissions* Opinion, 63.

743 See the relevance of the textual analysis on this point reflected in *ICJ First Admissions*.

744 Emphasis added.

745 CJEU, *Lothar Mattheus v. Doego Fruchtimport und Tiefkühlkost*, E.C.R. (1978), 2203, 2211.

> Provision should be made by which the parties may by agreement invite any other state in or bordering upon Western Europe, the maintenance of whose territorial or political integrity is of direct concern to the security of the parties, to accede to the treaty *on conditions to be agreed between them and the state so invited.*[746]

This wording is similar to the wording in the open-ended Article 237 EEC Treaty. In *Admissions,* the ICJ found the conditions for admission in Article 4 UN Charter to be listed exhaustively. The Court added, however, that their exhaustive nature does not forbid that other factors be taken into account.[747] But this must be done in a reasonable way, in good faith, and in connection with the conditions of Article 4 UN Charter. According to the Court, the fact that other factors can be taken into account is already implied by the broadness and elasticity of the prescribed conditions. But adding the informal criterion that UN Member States can be admitted to UN membership together is incompatible with the 'letter and spirit' of Article 4, the Court held, because it prevents Members from exercising their judgement with complete liberty on a case-by-case basis.[748] When one applies the *Admissions* reasoning to NATO, it can be seen that 'the principles of the treaty' and 'the contribution to security' mentioned in Article 10 are very broad and very elastic concepts as well, much like the conditions in Article 4 UN Charter conditions are (being a State, being peace-loving, accepting the obligations of the Charter, being able to carry out these obligations, and being willing to do so). The preparatory works for the North Atlantic Treaty confirm that the drafters preferred the wording to be 'elastic' on this point. In the early drafts of Article 10, a candidate was expected to be able to contribute to the 'security' of the North Atlantic area in a broad sense. The December 1948 and January 1949 accession provisions even omitted conditionality altogether. The reference to the 'principles of the treaty' was only added to Article 10 near the end of the negotiations, without any ambassadorial discussions.[749] Chapter 2, which discussed the case law of the German

---

746 Emphasis added. See Memorandum by the Participants in the Washington Security Talks, 6 July to 9 September, Submitted to Their Respective Governments for Study and Comment, 9 September 1948, 241.

747 ICJ *First Admissions*, 63.

748 ICJ *First Admissions*, 65.

749 There is no record available of the changes made to the accession provision after January 1949. As a consequence, the drafters' intention behind including the first limb near the end of the negotiations remains somewhat of a mystery. See Minutes of the Fourth Meeting of the Washington Exploratory Talks on Security, July 8, 1948, 164–165; Minutes of the Fifth Meeting of the Washington Exploratory Talks on Security, July 9, 1948, 179; Memorandum of the Ninth Meeting of the Working Group Participating in the Washington Exploratory Talks on Security, August 9, 1948, 210–212; Memorandum of the Fourteenth Meeting of the Working Group Participating in the Washington Exploratory Talks on Security, September 7, 1948, 234–235; Memorandum by the Participants in the Washington Security Talks, 6 July to 9 September, Submitted to Their Respective Governments for Study and Comment, 9 September 1948, 241; Minutes of the Tenth Meeting of the Washington Exploratory Talks,

Bundesverfassungsgericht, showed how broad the concept of 'security' is. The *Admissions* test (i.e. that the exhaustive nature of a provision does not mean that other conditions cannot be taken into account, but that those conditions must, reasonably and in good faith, be connected with the conditions laid down in the existing provision) should be applied to the conditions listed in the 1995 Study that are furthest removed from the Treaty's object and purpose: environmental responsibility and economic liberty (*qui peut le plus, peut le moins*).

The interconnection between peace, security, and the environment is well established by now, in the opinion of the UN, the EU, and NATO.[750] As climate change accelerates, it risks exacerbating existing social, economic, and environmental drivers of insecurity, both locally and internationally. The EU and UNEP had established a five-year long partnership (2017–2022) with the aim of strengthening the capacity of nations to identify environment- and climate-related security risks.[751] As described by Lazarou and Tethova, the 2020 World Climate and Security Report identifies five main risks that climate change poses to security:

1. water insecurity exacerbated by climate change;
2. the increased likelihood of conflict affected by climate change;
3. the effects of climate change on military infrastructure and military operations;
4. the potential second-order negative effects of climate mitigation strategies (such as geoengineering) on global security if not implemented carefully;
5. the rise of authoritarianism, protectionism, and nationalism, which undermines the international cooperation needed to address the security risks generated by climate change.[752]

NATO affirms the interconnectedness of security and the environment in its 7th proposal in the recent NATO 2030 Report:

December 22, 1948, 326–332, all found in *Foreign Relations of the United States, 1948, Western Europe, Volume III.*

750 United Nations Environment Programme, EU-UNEP Climate Change and Security Partnership Project 2017–2020, Final Report, September 2022, available online at https://wedocs.unep.org/handle/20.500.11822/40549 (last accessed January 2025) and E. Lazarou and L. Tothova, 'Climate change considerations for EU security and defence policy', *European Parliamentary Research Service Briefing* 2022, 2.

751 United Nations Environment Programme, Final Report, September 2022.

752 International Military Council on Climate and Security, The World Climate and Security Report, February 2020, available online at https://imccs.org/wp-content/uploads/2021/01/World-Climate-Security-Report-2020_2_13.pdf (last accessed January 2025) and E. Lazarou and L. Tothova, 'Climate change considerations for EU security and defence policy', 2.

> The security implications of climate change are being felt in NATO's neighborhood, be it in the Sahel, Middle East and North Africa, or the Arctic, as well as within NATO Allied territory. By understanding this challenge, adapting, and mitigating where possible, NATO will be better placed to fulfil its three core tasks.[753]

The same sentiment was expressed in the 2010 and 2022 Strategic Concepts.[754] The interconnectedness of security and the environment is also confirmed in the Studies commissioned by the NATO Science for Peace and Security Committee[755] and in scholarship.[756] Thus, the 1995 Study's requirement of promoting environmental responsibility can be said, reasonably and in good faith, to be connected to the second limb of Article 10, as environmental responsibility is now a crucial component of security. The requirement of promoting economic liberty is implied by Article 2 of the Treaty, which commits parties to encourage economic collaboration between any or all of them. This condition can therefore also be said, reasonably and in good faith, to be connected to the principles of the Treaty. Duxbury points out that NATO now expects candidate Member States to respect the principles of human rights and democracy but has not consistently demanded the same of earlier candidates. It is true that Portugal was an original signatory to the North Atlantic Treaty and that Turkey and Greece became Member States in 1952 without so much as a whisper about the democratic situation in those countries. It is also true that NATO does currently take the democratic track records of candidate Member States into account.[757] However, the principles of democracy, individual liberty, and the rule of law are mentioned in the Preamble to the North Atlantic Treaty. Although a preamble is not legally part of a treaty, it does serve as an interpretation tool, providing context in the sense of Article 31(2) VCLT.[758] It gives further meaning to the broad 'principles' referred to in the first limb of Article 10, and thus constitutes a tolerable interpretation of

753 Main finding no. 8 in the *NATO 2030 Report.*

754 NATO Strategic Concept 2022, § 15 and 36.

755 B. Slay, 'Environment, Security and Development Challenges in the 21st Century' in S. Stec and B. Baraj, *Energy and Environmental Challenges to Security*, Dordrecht, Springer, 2009, 33–37 (part of the NATO Science for Peace and Security Series C: Environmental Security book series) and O. Nikolov and S. Veeravalli, 'Implications of Climate Change and Disasters on Military Activities' in *Building Resiliency and Mitigating Vulnerability in the Balkan Region*, Conference proceedings, 2017, 1–158 (part of the NATO Science for Peace and Security Series C).

756 E. Chalecki, 'Environment and Security', *International Studies* 2010 and E. Page, Theorizing the Link Between Environmental Change and Security', *RECIEL* 2000, 33–44.

757 NATO Bucharest Summit Declaration, § 2, speech by NATO Secretary General Jaap Hoop de Scheffer at the Albanian parliament, available online at www.nato.int/cps/fr/natohq/opinions_22479.htm (last accessed January 2025) and U.S., Senate Executive Report 116-5, Protocol to the North Atlantic Treaty of 1949 on the accession of the Republic of North Macedonia, 18 September 2019, 116th Congress, 1st session, 2.

758 M. Hulme, 'Preambles in Treaty Interpretation', *University of Pennsylvania Law Review* 2016, 1281.

the Treaty. If the two criteria that are furthest removed from the text of Article 10 constitute a lawful interpretation of the North Atlantic Treaty, the other conditions mentioned in the 1995 Study on NATO Enlargement must be considered to do so as well. This is why it is not necessary to analyse them separately. Moreover, the 1995 Study had been consensually agreed upon by NATO Member States and has since served as NATO's conceptual enlargement framework for four decades.[759] Thus, the 1995 Study constitutes an established practice of the organisation (Article 5 VCLT *juncto* Article 2(b) ARIO) and shall be taken into account when interpreting Article 10 (Article 31(3)(2) VCLT).[760] Overall, the Study's criteria can be said to be implied by the broadness and the elasticity of the conditions prescribed in Article 10. In sum, the expansion of NATO's accession conditions, while certainly far-reaching, does not contravene the purposes of the North Atlantic Treaty, but appears to constitute a permissible interpretation of Article 10. This conclusion, however, reveals the circularity of using established practice as an interpretation tool. Pursuant to Article 31(3)(b) VCLT, established practice is taken into consideration when interpreting Article 10, but, at the same time, NATO can broaden the meaning of Article 10 by developing an established practice. If the ICJ were to formulate its *Admissions* Opinion today, or had it done so in the 1950s instead of the 1940s, and if the UN Members would have developed the established practice of admitting countries together to UN membership, the ICJ would probably (have) permit(ted) such a practice. After all, after 1949 the Court began to accept established practice as a tool to interpret treaties in the organisational context (*Second Admissions* and *Certain Expenses*).[761] Although established practice is widely accepted as a corollary of the theory of functionalism, which prevails in the law of international organisations, this does not change the fact that its reasoning is circular.[762] Critical reflection is due, especially when organisations expand their powers through practice, which bypasses the ratification of treaty amendments by national parliaments even though such acquisition of new powers has consequences for citizens (*cf.* chapter 2). Recourse to established practice is more defensible in the case of accession, as the decision to admit

759 *NATO Encyclopedia* 2019, 216; NATO Fact Sheet, NATO Enlargement, 2009, available online at www.nato.int/summit2009/topics_en/05-enlargement.html (last accessed January 2025) and J. Goldgeier and J. Shifrinson, 'Evaluating NATO enlargement: scholarly debates, policy implications and roads not taken', 296.

760 ICJ 1950, *Competence of the General Assembly for the Admission of a State to the United Nations*, Advisory Opinion, *ICJ Rep* 1950, 9; ICJ *Certain Expenses*, 157; ICJ *Namibia* 22; ICJ *WHO Legality*, 76 and C. Brölmann, *op. cit.*, 515 and C. Peters, 'Subsequent Practice and Established Practice of International Organizations: Two Sides of the Same Coin?', 629.

761 ICJ *Second Admissions*, 4.

762 L. Gasbarri, 'Functionalism' in L. Gasbarri (ed.), *The concept of an International Organization in International Law*, Oxford, Oxford University Press, 2021, 17 and J. Klabbers, 'Towards a Political Economy of International Organizations Law', *International Organizations Law Review* 2023, 82–101.

a new NATO Member State is a highly political one, which might necessitate adapting the interpretation of Article 10 to changing circumstances. Article 10 is nearly 76 years old, after all. This was already advocated by Judge Alvarez in his individual opinion and by Judges Basdevant, Waniarski, McNair, and Read in their dissenting opinions to *Admissions*.[763] It is also more defensible because NATO's admission process has many procedural safeguards. The fact that accession to NATO is a highly political matter is reflected in the first three words of Article 10 ('The Parties *may*...' and 'les parties *peuvent*' (emphasis added)) and in the first five words of the second sentence ('Any State *so* invited may' and 'Tout Etat *ainsi* invité peut' (emphasis added)).[764] The ICJ stressed the importance of textual analysis on this point in its *First Admissions* ruling.[765] The preparatory works for Article 10 confirm that the drafters sought to give the parties the broadest possible discretion, and did so by drawing inspiration from Article IX of the 1948 Brussels Treaty.[766] They were of the opinion that not all States would be able to join the Alliance 'due to lack of agreement amongst the seven governments themselves', without providing a further explanation.[767] The 1949 Treaty does not oblige NATO Member States to admit a country as soon as a certain number of conditions have been met. This is why NATO's decision not to invite FYROM in 2008 did not constitute an internationally wrongful act. Greece had wrongly tried to hide behind NATO's consensual shield, and it was a smart move on FYROM's part to direct its lawsuit against Greece rather than against the discretionary 2008 Bucharest decision. In addition, NATO accession protocols must be ratified by all national parliaments ('by unanimous agreement'), although they typically do not contain any substantive conditionality. National parliaments generally ratify

763 Individual Opinion by Judge Alvarez, 69 and Dissenting Opinion by Judge Basevant, Waniarski, McNair and Read, 82–140.

764 However, from a political and pragmatic perspective, Simon's observations are interesting: 'We need to recognize that as NATO moves down the MAP road we are slowly embedding ourselves in an implicit contractual relationship with the [...] aspirants that will increasingly limit political choices. In other words, as NATO encourages MAP governments to implement political, economic, and defence reforms, it is increasingly obliged to choose new members based on these criteria to justify their choices. NATO will find it difficult to decline a MAP partner that clearly has succeeded in implementing serious reforms or to invite one that has not fulfilled them. If NATO were to disregard these criteria, it would undermine the credibility and legitimacy of MAP for those partners who did,' in J. Simon, 'The next round of NATO Enlargement', *Strategic Forum* 2000, 1.

765 See Article 38(1)(d) ICJ Statute; A. Duxbury, *op. cit.*, 134, and J. Wouters, C. Ryngaert, T. Ruys and G. De Baere, *op. cit.*, 159.

766 Memorandum by the Participants in the Washington Security Talks, 6 July to 9 September, Submitted to Their Respective Governments for Study and Comment, 9 September 1948, 247 and Memorandum of the Sixth Meeting of the Working Group Participating in the Washington Exploratory Talks on Security, 26 July 1948, 201–204, both in *Foreign Relations of the United States, 1948, Western Europe, Volume III.*

767 As quoted by N. Minogue, 'The North Atlantic Treaty at 70: Article 10', 166.

an accession protocol without much substantive debate.[768] There had been, for example, no substantive parliamentary debate on NATO's recent Accession Protocol for North Macedonia in the following countries: Belgium, the Netherlands, Germany, France, Luxemburg, the UK, and Canada. In the US, one senator initially voted against the protocol due to doubts concerning North Macedonia's military spending and capacity.[769] Moreover, the NATO accession procedure is invitation-based and open only to 'European' States (albeit in a fairly broad sense). This makes NATO a closed international organisation rather than a universal one.[770] Article 10 makes clear that NATO's membership is regional. The fact that NATO defines itself as an international organisation does not change this. It is in the Organisation's best interest to define itself as an international organisation, in view of its legal relationship with the UN. The drafters of the North Atlantic Treaty deliberately omitted any reference to Chapter VIII UN Charter, which deals with regional arrangements. That way, they made clear that they consider NATO to be an international organisation under Chapter VII UN Charter. Consequently, NATO does not have to take the conditions spelled out under Chapter VIII into account. The opposite would entail that all NATO enforcement activities would be subject to authorisation by the UNSC, and thus to the veto power of Russia and China.[771] The procedural bar for joining NATO is also high because it requires consensus at every stage

---

768 These eight Member States were selected since the author is in a position to read, understand and write in the authentic languages of their parliamentary records. See Belgium, Kamer van Volksvertegenwoordigers, Wetsontwerp houdende instemming met het Protocol voor de toetreding van de Republiek Noord-Macedonië tot de Noord-Atlantische Verdragsorganisatie, Doc. 54 3717/001, 19 April 2019; the Netherlands, Goedkeuring van het op 6 februari 2019 te Brussel tot stand gekomen Protocol bij het Noord-Atlantisch Verdrag betreffende de toetreding van de Republiek Noord-Macedonië; Germany, Bundestag, Entwurf eines Gesetzes zu dem Protokoll vom 6. Februar 2019 zum Nordatlantikvertrag über den Beitritt der Republik Nord Mazedonien, Doc. 19/10418, 17 May 2019; France, Assemblée nationale, Rapport fait au nom de la commission des affaires étrangères sur le projet de loi autorisant la ratification du protocol au traité de l'Atlantique nord sur l'accession de la République de Macédoine du Nord, Doc. 2344, 20 November 2019; Luxemburg, Commission des Affaires étrangères et européennes, Procès-verbal de la réunion du 6 mai 2019, Doc. P-2018-O-AEECA-24-01, 6 May 2019, 3; the U.K., U.K. Parliament, Written Statements of the Foreign and Commonwealth Office, Prespa Agreement and North Macedonia's NATO Accession, vol. 655, 26 February 2019 and U.S., Senate Executive Report 115–116, Protocol to the North Atlantic Treaty of 1949 on the accession of the Republic of North Macedonia, 18 September 2019, 116th Congress, 1st session, 2. No records of any debate on the North Macedonian accession protocol were found in the database of the Canadian House of Commons.

769 U.S., Senate Executive Report 115–116, Protocol to the North Atlantic Treaty of 1949 on the accession of the Republic of North Macedonia, 18 September 2019, 116th Congress, 1st session, 2.

770 ICJ *FYROM v. Greece*, Dissenting Opinion by Judge Roucounas, 734. See Memorandum by the Participants in the Washington Security Talks, 6 July to 9 September, Submitted to Their Respective Governments for Study and Comment, 9 September 1948, 247.

771 See S. Mayer, *NATO's Post-Cold War Politics: the Changing Provision of Security*, London, Palgrave Macmillan, 2014, 2–27; A. Verhelst en J. Wouters, 'Zeventig jaar NAVO: juridische

of the accession procedure, which means that every Member State must refrain from using its *de facto* veto power. In sum, one could say that the procedural bar for becoming a NATO Member State is higher than the substantive bar.[772]

2.2. INTERIM CONCLUSION

The expansion of NATO's accession conditions, while far-reaching, does not contravene the purposes of the North Atlantic Treaty, but rather seems to constitute a permissible interpretation of Article 10. The exhaustive nature of Article 10, compared to the CJEU's *Lothar Mattheus v. Doego Fruchtimport* ruling, does not exclude that other conditions may be taken into account. Like the conditions listed in Article 4 UN Charter, the wording of the criteria in Article 10 is intentionally broad and vague (*cf. Admissions*). Because the link between environmental responsibility and security is now well-established in academic research and recognised in NATO policies, such as Strategic Concepts, demanding a sense of environmental responsibility from candidate Member States constitutes a tolerable interpretation of Article 10's 'security' requirement. Moreover, economic liberty is implied in Article 2 and the principles of individual liberty, democracy, and the rule of law, mentioned in the Preamble, serve to interpret the North Atlantic Treaty (Article 31(2)(b) VCLT). Moreover, the 1995 Study constitutes an established practice of NATO and should be taken into account as such (Article 5 VCLT). If the *Admissions* case were to be opined on today and if the UN Members would have developed the practice of admitting several UN Member States together, it is likely that the ICJ would not conclude that Article 4 UN Charter has been violated. The acceptance of established practice as an interpretation tool for treaties is circular, though: established practice is taken into consideration when interpreting Article 10, but, at the same time, NATO can broaden the meaning of Article 10 by developing an established practice. The 1949 Treaty does not oblige NATO Member States to admit a country once a certain number of conditions are met. The preparatory works show that it was the intent of the drafters that the Member States would be able to make such decisions with absolute discretion. This is why NATO did not commit an internationally wrongful act in 2008 when it decided not to invite FYROM. This chapter also established that almost nothing is publicly known about which criteria are decisive for NATO when it invites or does not invite a country to join. There are various reasons for this lack of information:

kanttekeningen bij een bijzondere internationale organisatie', 244 and D. Yost, 'NATO and International Organizations', 33.

772 E. Rubinson, 'Flexible democratic conditionality? The role of democracy and human rights adherence in NATO enlargement decisions', *Journal of International Relations and Development* 2021, 696–725.

1. NATO decides behind closed doors, and the Summit and Ministerial Declarations reveal nothing about membership conditionality.
2. As a rule, Membership Action Plans (MAPs), Annual National Programs (ANPs), letters of intent, and other documents used to prepare for a country's accession are not made public.
3. The NATO accession protocol is a procedural document which does not reveal the substantive conditions that were taken into account.
4. National parliaments generally ratify accession protocols without much, if any, substantive debate. The extent to which national parliaments actually scrutinise accession protocols is a good topic for future research in the political sciences.

3. THE SUSPENSION AND EXPULSION OF NATO MEMBER STATES

3.1. INTRODUCTION

On 13 October 2019 US Defence Secretary Mark Esper warned Turkey that, if it were to proceed with its offensive into north-eastern Syria, it would 'damage US relations with Turkey, their staying in NATO.'[773] In the same vein, US Senator Lindsey Graham promised to 'call for Turkey's suspension from NATO if they attack Kurdish forces who assisted the US in the destruction of the ISIS Caliphate.'[774] In May of 2003 the US Senate asked the Bush administration to raise the possibility of changing the consensus rule and 'suspending a NATO member before the NAC.'[775] This request was fuelled by concerns over the functioning of the Alliance in view of the fifth round of expansion and over intra-Alliance divisions over the war in Iraq. In light of the latter, Belgium, France, and Germany were obstructing the consensus on providing defensive aid to Turkey.[776] A US Senate resolution recommended that the US President place the following topic on the NAC's agenda by late 2004: 'the merits of establishing a process for suspending the membership in NATO of a member country that no longer complies with the NATO principles of democracy,

[773] M. Esper, Interview with Chris Wallace on Fox News, 13 October 2019, available online at www.youtube.com/watch?v=E6dKmovvFQc (last accessed January 2025).

[774] C. Riotta, 'Lindsey Graham turns on Trump over disaster Syria move', *Independent* 7 October 2019, available online at www.independent.co.uk/news/world/americas/us-politics/trump-syria-turkey-lindsey-graham-twitter-pomepo-isis-assad-iran-middle-east-a9146161.html (last accessed January 2025).

[775] L. Michel, 'NATO Decisionmaking: Au Revoir to the Consensus Rule', 1.

[776] US Senate, NATO Expansion Treaty, Executive Session, Congressional Record, Vol. 149, 8 May 2003, S5882, as quoted in L. Michel, 'NATO Decisionmaking: Au Revoir to the Consensus Rule', 2.

individual liberty, and the rule of law.'[777] US Senator Kay Bailey Hutchison, who became the US Ambassador to NATO in 2016, had advocated for the possibility of expelling a NATO Member State in the 80s and 90s.[778] While many international organisations provide the option of suspending a Member State's rights in their constituent instruments, the North Atlantic Treaty does not. The reason for this absence can be found in the preparatory works. From the outset it was clear that Canada, more than any other negotiating party, wanted the North Atlantic community to be more than a military alliance.[779] The country had expressed misgivings over Spain's potential NATO membership during the Franco regime and had actively advocated for including a suspension or expulsion mechanism into the draft Treaty to ensure that the Alliance would remain dedicated to the principles of democracy, liberty, and the rule of law. Consequently, the 1948 September draft of the North Atlantic Treaty included the following note:

> The question of including a provision for *disqualification* under certain circumstances of any of the signatories from *enjoying the benefits of the Treaty* requires further consideration.[780]

The circumstances that would have justified a disqualification at the time were limited to the rise of communist governments. Such disqualification was not intended for treaty parties that violated the North Atlantic Treaty or the principles of democracy, liberty, and the rule of law, mentioned in the Preamble.[781] In the draft North Atlantic Treaty of 17 December 1948, Canada proposed a provision which would entitle the NAC to suspend or expel a Member State from the privileges of membership.[782] But the other negotiating parties were opposed to any provision that would raise questions about the NAC's voting processes, preferring *in camera* discussions.[783] The British Foreign

777 US Senate, NATO Expansion Treaty, Executive Session, Congressional Record, Vol. 149, 8 May 2003, S5886, as quoted in L. Michel, 'NATO Decisionmaking: Au Revoir to the Consensus Rule', 2.

778 Interview with Dr. Jamie Shea, online, 12 July 2022.

779 The next section was inspired largely by the valuable work done by Aurel Sari in his article 'Can Turkey be Expelled from NATO? It's Legally Possible, Whether or Not Politically Prudent', *Just Security* 15 October 2019.

780 Memorandum by the Participants in the Washington Security Talks, 6 July to 9 September, Submitted to Their Respective Governments for Study and Comment, 247. Emphasis added.

781 Canada, Commentary on the Washington Paper, 6 December 1948, as quoted in A. Sari, 'Can Turkey be Expelled from NATO? It's Legally Possible, Whether or Not Politically Prudent', 2.

782 A. Sari, 'Can Turkey be Expelled from NATO? It's Legally Possible, Whether or Not Politically Prudent', 2.

783 Canadian Ambassador in the U.S. to Secretary of State for External Affairs, 4 January 1949, in *CDER*, Vol. 15, 483.

Secretary, Ernest Bevin, also disapproved of any attempts to grant the NAC conciliatory powers:

> I really do not see any advantage in disputes which we may have in the future with the Americans or indeed with the French being discussed in the open and in the presence of the Italians, the Scandinavians and the Portuguese.[784]

In the draft treaty of 24 December 1948, which was sent to the national governments, the idea was struck down with the following brief note:

> Various forms of an article which would provide for the expulsion from the treaty of any signatory under certain circumstances were discussed. This proved difficult to express and on balance it was decided to recommend that no such article be included.[785]

After this, Canada's ambitions had been tempered. Eventually, the North Atlantic Treaty was signed on 4 April 1949 without any suspension or expulsion clause. The question of how the Alliance should deal with an Ally that was no longer fit to be part of the club, was left unanswered.[786] In a statement to the Senate Committee on Foreign Relations in 1949, US Secretary of State Dean Acheson took the view that such a member could be kicked out even in the absence of a formal provision:

> This draft, Mr. Chairman, starts out with a preamble, and one of the purposes of this preamble was to see if we could in some way describe a democratic non-Communist country. The purpose of that was, if, for instance, Italy becomes a member of such a treaty and then by any chance should go Communist, a question has arisen in people's minds about what happens then. You do not want to have provisions in such a treaty saying that you can throw them out, because that indicates you are rather doubtful about them before you start; but if you can describe the sort of objectives that are shared by all of these countries, and one of them should no longer be able to be seeking those objectives, then the basis is laid for a separation.[787]

---

784 Mr. Bevin to Sir O. Franks, UK Ambassador to Washington, 12 January 1949, in *Documents on British Policy Overseas*, Series I, Vol. X, 334.

785 Report of the International Working Group to the Ambassadors' Committee, 24 December 1948, 339.

786 A. Sari, 'Can Turkey be Expelled from NATO? It's Legally Possible, Whether or Not Politically Prudent', 3.

787 U.S. Senate, The Vandenberg Resolution and the North Atlantic Treaty, Hearings held in executive session before the Committee on Foreign Relations, Eightieth Congress, 93, as quoted in A. Sari, 'Can Turkey be Expelled from NATO? It's Legally Possible, Whether or Not Politically Prudent', 3.

The same sentiment was expressed by Senator George:

> We can say, no, it [the North Atlantic Treaty] does not provide for expulsion or suspension of rights, but clearly if they get into a hostile position, they will no longer be beneficiaries.[788]

This is reflected further down in the US Senate report as well:

> The treaty has been criticized in some quarters because it contains no provision for expulsion or the suspension of rights of a recalcitrant member *which might fail to carry out its obligations* as a result, for example, of its succumbing to communism. Given the nature of the pact and the close community of interests of the signatory states, the committee believes that such a provision would be both unnecessary and inappropriate. Obviously, however, if a member persistently violates the principles contained in the pact, the *other members will no longer be obligated to assist that member.* A country suffering such a fate would be in no position either to carry out its own obligations under the treaty or to expect assistance from the other parties.[789]

The preparatory works show that not much consideration, if any, was given to the issue of the legal permissibility of suspension and expulsion. The statement in the US Senate Report that 'if a member persistently violates the principles contained in the pact, the other members will no longer be obligated to assist that member' reflects the idea of *exceptio non adimpleti contractus*.[790] In *FYROM v. Greece*, Greece relied on this exception to justify its refusal to perform the Interim Accord. In Greece's view, FYROM had failed to comply with the Accord first by making use of symbols that were deemed part of Greece's cultural identity, by using its constitutional name when signing multilateral treaties, by not negotiating in good faith over the naming issue, by allowing for propaganda etc. Greece insisted that the conditions for the termination or suspension of the Interim Accord were met and that its behaviour could not be considered wrongful because the exception of non-performance applied.[791] FYROM denied that the exception could apply independently in public international law. As the Court found

788 U.S. Senate, The Vandenberg Resolution and the North Atlantic Treaty, Hearings held in executive session before the Committee on Foreign Relations, Eightieth Congress, 306, as quoted in A. Sari, 'Can Turkey be Expelled from NATO? It's Legally Possible, Whether or Not Politically Prudent', 3.

789 U.S. Senate, The Vandenberg Resolution and the North Atlantic Treaty, Hearings held in executive session before the Committee on Foreign Relations, Eightieth Congress, 379, as quoted in A. Sari, 'Can Turkey be Expelled from NATO? It's Legally Possible, Whether or Not Politically Prudent', 3. Emphasis added.

790 *Cf.* ICJ *Namibia*, § 96.

791 ICJ *FYROM v. Greece*, Countermemorial by Greece, 33, 37, 43, 52 and 163.

no connection between FYROM's one and only breach of the Interim Accord (i.e. using the symbol of the Vergina Sun in official documents in 2004) and Greece's behaviour (objecting to FYROM's NATO membership in 2008), it deemed it unnecessary to determine whether the exception of non-performance forms part of contemporary international law.[792] This was a missed opportunity to gain more judicial clarity on the legal status of the exception. Legal scholarship finds that the exception of non-performance still has an independent (i.e. not covered by Article 60 VCLT) but nonetheless limited role as a reaction to the lawful non-performance of international treaties.[793] Because of the Court's stance in *FYROM v. Greece*, the exception of non-performance will be disregarded as an independent legal ground. Now, in the absence of any provision in the North Atlantic Treaty, is there a basis in international law for the suspension or expulsion of a NATO Member State? In public international law, the suspension or expulsion of a NATO Member State would be possible only 1) if the North Atlantic Treaty is amended, 2) if NATO has an implied power in this regard, 3) if it is a countermeasure in the context of State responsibility, or 4) on the basis of Article 60 VCLT. These four grounds will now be discussed *in abstracto* and applied to the example of a NATO Member State acquiring weapon systems from Russia. This is based on the real-life case of Turkey purchasing Russian S-400 missile weapon systems in 2017, which was sanctioned by the US. This example was selected for several reasons:

- It provides insight into the object and purpose of the North Atlantic Treaty, because these type of agreements could be said to undermine NATO's collective defence.
- It provides insight into the more general compatibility of bilateral arms deals and agreements with the North Atlantic Treaty, which is relevant, considering a changing security landscape in which such agreements may become more prevalent.
- It provides insight into how the Treaty obligations under the little-known Articles 3 and 8 of the North Atlantic Treaty should be interpreted and when they are violated.

The S-400 issue was widely covered in the media in 2017 and resurfaces regularly, which is why it warrants legal clarification.

792 ICJ *FYROM v. Greece*, 161.

793 S. Forlati, 'Reactions to Non-Performance of Treaties in International Law', *Leiden Journal of International Law* 2012, 759; M. Xiouri, 'The Exceptio Non Adimpleti Contractus in Public International Law', *International Community Law Review* 2019, 90–91 and J. Crawford and S. Olleson, 'The Exception of Non-performance: Links between the Law of Treaties and the Law of State Responsibility', *Australian Yearbook of International Law* 2000, 55–57.

3.2. AMENDMENT OF THE NORTH ATLANTIC TREATY

The preparatory works show that the Treaty's drafters did not want a formal provision for the suspension and expulsion of Member States. Chapter 2 explained that NATO always deliberately avoided constitutional amendments, out of fear of opening up the document and watering down its provisions. It is extremely unlikely, if not unthinkable, that the Treaty will be amended to this effect, especially considering that all NATO Member States—including the one the others want to suspend or expel—would have to consent to this amendment.[794] It is difficult, if not impossible, to imagine any Ally willing to endorse the notion, 'however masked, that a policy disagreement with Washington could be grounds for suspending or expelling a member from the Alliance', as Michel points out.[795] As a legal ground, formal treaty amendment is thus unsuitable for the suspension or expulsion of a NATO Member State.

3.3. SUSPENSION OR EXPULSION AS AN IMPLIED POWER

Most writers deny that the doctrine of implied powers can be used as a basis for suspending or expelling a Member State from an international organisation.[796] Even if one were to use the broad approach formulated in the ICJ's *Reparations* ruling, it would be difficult to justify the existence of implied power to suspend, let alone expel a Member State.[797] After all, the doctrine of implied powers concerns an organisation's powers and competences, not its relationship to its Member States as such (*cf.* chapter 2).[798] The object and purpose of an alliance pact also suggest the opposite of such a power.[799] Moreover, each NATO Member State would have to agree that such an implied power exists, thereby risking its own suspension and expulsion. An exception to the rule, according to Schermers and Blokker, is expulsion to protect the organisation, which would be permitted. For example, if a NATO Member State no longer participates in the activities of the organisation while continuing to accept its services, or if it adopts a completely negative attitude and blocks all decisions (a fairly easy thing to do

794 Article 5 VCLT *juncto* Article 2(b) ARIO and Article 39 VCLT.

795 L. Michel, 'NATO Decision-Making: Au Revoir to the Consensus Rule', 8.

796 P. Sands and P. Klein, *op. cit.*, 545–546; J. Klabbers, *op. cit.*, 108; A. Duxbury, *op. cit.*, 273; N. Singh, *Termination of Membership*, London, Stevens & Sons, 1958, 79–80 and K. Magliveras, *Exclusion from Participation in International Organisations*, The Hague, Kluwer Law International, 1999, 254–255.

797 See F. Zeidler, *Der Austritt und Ausschluss von Mitgliedern aus den Sonderorganisationen der Vereinten Nationen*, Berlin, Peter Lang Publishing, 1990, 152–170; J. Klabbers, *op. cit.*, 108–109; N. Blokker and H. Schermers, *op. cit.*, § 148, 127; P. Sands and P. Klein, *op. cit.*, 549–552 and C. Jenks, 'Some Legal Aspects of the Financing of International Institutions', *Transactions of the Grotius Society* 1943, 111.

798 K. Magliveras, *op. cit.*, 254–255.

799 *Cf.* Dean Acheson's remarks and the 1949 US Senate report in this regard (see above).

in NATO because of its consensus rule), an expulsion on the basis of an implied power may be in the interest of the organisation, although caution is due.[800] Concluding a one-time deal to purchase weapon systems does not necessarily mean that the Member State is blocking NATO's activities and decisions.

3.4. SUSPENSION AND EXPULSION AS COUNTERMEASURES

The suspension of a defaulting Member State's rights and privileges can be invoked as a countermeasure, on the condition that that Member State has committed an internationally wrongful act.[801] An internationally wrongful act must consist of the violation of an obligation stemming from international law and must be attributable to the State.[802] The acquisition of a weapon system is, in principle, attributable to the government.[803] But does a NATO Member State's purchasing of weapons from Russia violate an obligation stemming from international law? NATO Member States are bound by Article 8 of the North Atlantic Treaty, which reads:

> Each Party declares that none of the international engagements now in force between it and any other of the Parties or any third State is in conflict with the provisions of this Treaty, and undertakes not to enter into any international engagement in conflict with this Treaty.[804]

The wording of Article 8 ('undertake') implies a legally binding obligation not to conclude any engagements that are in conflict with the obligations under the Treaty.[805] Importantly, NATO legal advisers interpret Article 8 to include

---

[800] N. Blokker and H. Schermers, *op. cit.*, § 141, 122. Compare to Jenks' opinion on the expulsion clause in the League of Nations Covenant, C. Jenks, 'Expulsion from the League of Nations', *British Yearbook of International Law* 1935, 156.

[801] Articles 1, 2, 12, and 22 ASR, ILC, Articles on State Responsibility, text adopted by the International Law Commission at its fifty-third session, in 2001, and submitted to the General Assembly as a part of the Commission's report covering the work of that session (UN Doc. A/56/10). The report, which also contains commentaries on the draft articles, appears in the *Yearbook of the International Law Commission*, 2001, vol. II, Part Two, as corrected.

[802] Article 2 ASR.

[803] Article 4 ASR and Reuters, 'Timeline: Turkey's path to buying Russian air defense systems and possible US sanctions', 22 July 2019, available online at www.reuters.com/article/us-turkey-security-usa-timeline-idUSKCN1UH1RB (last accessed January 2025) and J. Marcus, 'Turkey signs deal to get Russian S-400 air defence missiles', *BBC News* 12 September 2017, available online at www.bbc.com/news/world-europe-41237812 (last accessed January 2025).

[804] Article 8 North Atlantic Treaty.

[805] R. Kolb, *op. cit.*, 20; D. Hollis, 'Defining Treaties' in D. Hollis (ed.), *op. cit.*, 27; A. Aust, 'Alternatives to Treaty-Making: MOUs as Political Commitments' in D. Hollis (ed.), *op. cit.*, 48–50 and see K. Vegh, 'The North Atlantic Treaty and its Relationship to Other Engagements of Its Parties: A Commentary on Article 8', *Emory International Law Review* 2019, 141.

private legal or commercial engagements, including with regard to military technology or capability development, as long as they bind the Member State's government.[806] Interestingly, Vegh discovered that one of the intentions behind Article 8 was precisely to replace an expulsion clause.[807] If the acquisition concerns a matter of military capability and it is a private engagement between the NATO Member State and the third State, it falls under Article 8. Consequently, it shall not be in conflict with the Member's obligations under the North Atlantic Treaty. Article 3 merits closer scrutiny in this regard. It reads as follows:

> In order more effectively to achieve the objectives of this Treaty, the Parties, separately and jointly, by means of continuous and effective self-help and mutual aid, will maintain and develop their individual and collective capacity to resist armed attack.[808]

This Article can reasonably be interpreted to mean that interoperability is a crucial capability, as confirmed by the article's drafting history.[809] NATO's interoperability policy defines this notion as 'the ability of Allies to act together coherently, effectively and efficiently to achieve tactical, operational and strategic objectives.'[810] Based on its wording and drafting history, Article 3 at least refers to the military capacity to resist an armed attack.[811] For example,

---

806 K. Vegh, 'The North Atlantic Treaty and its Relationship to Other Engagements of Its Parties: A Commentary on Article 8', 141.

807 See Foreign Office Brief for the Fourth Meeting of the Consultative Council of the Brussels Treaty Powers, 27 January 1949, in *Documents on British Policy Overseas,* Series I, Vol. X., 360 and Letter from Mr. Henderson to Mr. Russell, 2 February 1949, in *British Policy Overseas,* Series I, Vol. X. 367–68, as referenced to by K. Vegh in 'The North Atlantic Treaty and its Relationship to Other Engagements of Its Parties: A Commentary on Article 8', 137.

808 Article 3 North Atlantic Treaty.

809 See the analysis by NATO International Staff member Matjaz Kacic in his, 'Commentary on Articles 2 and 3 of the Washington Treaty', *Emory International Law Review* 2019, 57–59 and 62, which was written with the advice and comments of Steven Hill, NATO legal adviser and then Director of the NATO International Staff Office of Legal Affairs, as well as Lone Kjelgaard and Nadia Marsan, both NATO Senior Assistant legal advisers. See the archival sources quoted there as well as the Telegram by the Acting Secretary of State to the Embassy in France, 22 November 1948 in *Foreign Relations of the United States, 1948, Western Europe, Vol. III* (US State Department Office of The Historian) and Policy paper approved by the Foreign Assistance Correlation Committee, 20 May 1949 in *Foreign Relations of the United States, 1949, National Security Affairs, Foreign Economic Policy, Vol. I* (US State Department Office of the Historian).

810 See 'NATO, Interoperability: Connecting NATO Forces', available online at www.nato.int/cps/em/natohq/topics_84112.htm (last accessed January 2025).

811 Matjaz Kacic in his, 'Commentary on Articles 2 and 3 of the Washington Treaty', 57–59 and Telegram by the Acting Secretary of State to the Embassy in France, 22 November 1948 in *Foreign Relations of the United States, 1948, Western Europe, Vol. III* (U.S. State Department Office of The Historian) and Policy paper approved by the Foreign Assistance Correlation Committee, 20 May 1949 in *Foreign Relations of the United States*, 1949, National Security Affairs, Foreign Economic Policy, Vol. I (US State Department Office of the Historian).

American officials have long warned that the S-400 system is incompatible with NATO equipment and that this poses a threat to the US military. They find the S-400 missile system to be non-interoperable with NATO capabilities.[812] However, there is currently too little evidence available to say whether that is actually true. But if there were sufficient evidence, Articles 3 and 8 of the North Atlantic Treaty would be violated, and the weapons purchase would be an internationally wrongful act that, in theory, justifies countermeasures under the ASR. One of those countermeasures could be the suspension of the defaulting State's membership rights, but that would be incompatible with the doctrine's core limitations. After all, countermeasures must be directed at the defaulting State and must try to induce that State to fulfil its obligations, with the aim of changing the behaviour that led to the breach (Article 49 ASR).[813] In *FYROM v. Greece* (2008), the ICJ found Greece's objection to FYROM's membership to be unjustified as a countermeasure because it was not aimed at stopping FYROM's wrongful conduct, i.e. using Greek symbols in official correspondence. This is a sensible conclusion, as FYROM had already stopped using the Greek symbols in 2004.[814] Comparing this judgment to the case study makes it clear that, if a Member State were to suspend another Member State's rights within NATO (whatever that means in practice, considering that the North Atlantic Treaty generates more membership obligations than rights; there are no voting rights to suspend), the defaulting State would not change its behaviour. It would feel subjected to a hostile action by its Allies, removing the country from NATO's sphere of influence instead of persuading it not to go ahead with the arms acquisition. In addition, if the acquisition happened only once, it would be difficult to claim that the suspension is aimed at stopping (or preventing) the Member State from acquiring further weapon systems later, and that it is not inspired by other political or strategic reasons. Expulsion as a countermeasure is even more out of the question. After all, the limitations of the doctrine of countermeasures are that countermeasures cannot be punitive in nature and must be reversible (Articles 49–51 ASR).[815] The expulsion of a Member State would also punish other Member States if that Member State is a security provider for them. Nor would the expulsion be easily reversible. The Member State would have to accede to NATO again, pursuant to Article 10 and the MAP process. All this confirms the observation, made in scholarship, that countermeasures are ill-fitted tools in an institutional context.[816]

812 See R. Ellehuus and P. Morcos, 'Lifting Up our Values at Home: How to Revitalize NATO's Political Cohesion', *CSIS Commentary* 2021, 3; A. Macias, 'U.S. sanctions Turkey over purchase of Russian S-400 missile system', *CNBC News* 14 December 2020 and M. Lee, 'US Sanctions NATO ally Turkey over purchase of Russian missile defense system', *Defense News* 14 December 2020.

813 As explained by J. Wouters, T. Ruys, C. Ryngaert and G. De Baere, *op. cit.*, 553.

814 ICJ, *FYROM v. Greece*, 164.

815 J. Wouters, T. Ruys, C. Ryngaert and G. De Baere, *op. cit.*, 553.

816 K. Magliveras, *op. cit.*, 254.

3.5. ARTICLE 60 VCLT

There is another legal ground for suspension or expulsion that circumvents the *de facto* veto power of the defaulting NATO Member State: the partial or complete suspension or termination of the North Atlantic Treaty *vis-à-vis* the defaulting Member State, based on the international law of treaties. If the conditions of Article 60 VCLT are satisfied, i.e. a Member State has committed a material breach of the Treaty, all NATO Member States minus the defaulting one would be entitled to suspend the operation of the North Atlantic Treaty, in whole or in part, or to terminate it either in their relations with the defaulting State or amongst themselves as a whole. The bar Article 60 sets for a 'material breach' is high, however, as the case law (*Namibia* and *South West Africa*) and legal scholarship confirm.[817] This high bar aims to ensure the stability of treaty-based relationships, which was considered essential during the Vienna Conference. To commit a material breach of the North Atlantic Treaty in the sense of Article 60.3 VCLT, the Member State would have to violate a provision *essential to the accomplishment of the object or purpose* of the Treaty.[818] If the acquisition of the weapon system is a one-time deal rather than a bilateral treaty or agreement, and if there is no hard evidence of its non-interoperability with NATO systems, the acquisition cannot be said to go against the Treaty's object and purpose of collective defence. The ICJ concluded that FYROM's only breach of the Interim Accord (i.e. having used a Greek sun symbol in official documents until 2004) was merely an 'incident' rather than a material breach in the sense of Article 60 VCLT.[819] Although arguably more substantial than the use of a symbol in official documents, the one-time acquisition of weapon systems from Russia is also 'an incident' rather than a structural breach, which would not meet Article 60's threshold in the eyes of the ICJ. Compare this to the 1979 suspension by the Organisation of Islamic Cooperation (OIC) of Egypt's membership, even in absence of a suspension clause in the constituent document. Egypt had allegedly infringed upon the OIC Charter by agreeing to the Camp David Accords. The Organisation found that Egypt's behaviour constituted a material breach of the OIC Charter in the sense of Article 60 VCLT.[820] Magliveras agrees with this organisational decision. He finds that Egypt's ratification of the Camp David Accords breached the OIC Charter. Article 2(a)(6) of the Charter reads that:

---

817 B. Simma, 'Reflections on Article 60 of the Vienna Convention on the Law of Treaties and its Background in General International Law', *Austrian Journal of Public and International Law* 1970, 5.

818 Article 60.3 VCLT, emphasis added.

819 ICJ *FYROM v. Greece*, § 163.

820 K. Magliveras, *op. cit.*, 237 and see in the same line T. Bouachba, 'L'Organisation de la Conférence Islamique', *Annuaire Français de Droit International* 1982, 274.

> Members undertake to support the fight of all Moslem people in order to protect their honor, independence and national rights and are obliged to assist the Palestinian fight against Israel.

By entering into a unilateral peace treaty, Egypt had violated the strict political solidarity that was essential for bringing about the solution to the Palestinian question put forward by the OIC Charter, and thus its core objectives.[821] Similarly, if a Member State were to conclude more structural bilateral trade agreements for non-interoperable weapon systems with a hostile nation, this could be a violation of Articles 3 and 8. It could be argued that this violation crosses the threshold of a 'material breach' in the sense of Article 60 VCLT, as systematic non-interoperability could risk undermining the objective and purpose of the North Atlantic Treaty, i.e. the task of collective defence and the solidarity between the Allies, which is essential to provide credible deterrence.[822] In any case, the suspension or termination of the North Atlantic Treaty on the basis of Article 60 VCLT would bring about very undesirable results. If the defaulting Member State is a security provider for other Member States, suspending or terminating the North Atlantic Treaty would result in an important *realpolitik* loss for the Allies. If the defaulting Member State is suspended or terminated in its entirety, that country is no longer obliged to come to the collective defence of the Allies on the basis of Article 5.

3.6. INTERIM CONCLUSION

There are four grounds in international law that in theory could allow for the suspension or expulsion of a NATO Member State in the absence of a constitutional provision to that effect. But as our analysis has shown, none of those four grounds is suitable for NATO. Amending the 1949 Treaty is unrealistic and so is the claim that suspension or expulsion is an implied power, as both of these options require the consent of the defaulting party. Given the reputational/political damage the alliance could incur if a Member is suspended or expelled, the other Members to the alliance pact have a strong incentive not to do so. Should a NATO Member State enter into a structural weapons trade agreement with a hostile nation rather than a one-time deal, which the ICJ would consider a mere 'incident' (*FYROM v. Greece*),[823] this could constitute a

821 K. Magliveras, *op. cit.*, 237. See in the same vein H. Moinuddin, *Die Organisation der Islamischen Konferenz als Forum politischer und wirtschaftlicher Kooperation*, Bochum, Studienverlag Brookmeyer, 1984, 100–101.

822 In chapter 2 we demonstrated that the task of collective self-defence is still considered to be the primary object and purpose of the North Atlantic Treaty. This was also demonstrated in the the German case law discussed there and in the recent 2022 Strategic Concept, which emphasises that collective defence is the Alliance's number one task.

823 ICJ, *FYROM v. Greece*, 162.

violation of Articles 3 and 8 and thus constitute an internationally wrongful act. The other Member States are then entitled to suspend that Member State from NATO as a countermeasure. However, such countermeasure would probably be unlawful, because the suspension would not induce the defaulting Member State to comply with the obligations of the 1949 Treaty, as it will interpret the suspension as a hostile act by the Allies. Keeping in mind the ICJ's conclusion in *FYROM v. Greece* (i.e. that Greece's objection to FYROM's NATO membership in 2008 was not aimed at stopping FYROM from using Greek symbols in its official documents), it would be difficult to prove that a certain Member State was suspended as a reaction to an arms agreement alone. Lastly, if that Member State were to conclude structural bilateral trade agreements with a hostile nation for weapon systems that were demonstrated to be non-interoperable, this could constitute a violation of Articles 3 and 8. It could be argued that this violation crosses the threshold of a 'material breach' in the sense of Article 60 VCLT, as systematic non-interoperability could risk undermining the objective and purpose of the North Atlantic Treaty, i.e. the task of collective defence and the solidarity between the Allies, which is essential to provide credible deterrence. A one-time deal does not reach this high bar. In any case, the suspension or termination of the North Atlantic Treaty on the basis of Article 60 VCLT would also bring about very undesirable results. If the defaulting Member State is a security provider, suspension or termination would weaken the collective defence promised in Article 5. The North Atlantic Treaty generates more membership obligations than it does rights. Invoking the *exceptio non adimpleti contractus* to suspend obligations *vis-à-vis* a defaulting State, as US lawmakers had suggested in the early years of the Treaty, was not considered by the ICJ in *FYROM v. Greece*. The ICJ found no connection between FYROM's one and only breach of the Interim Accord in 2004 and Greece's objection to FYROM's NATO membership in 2008. The Court did not delve deeper into the issue, unfortunately missing an opportunity to provide some much-needed clarity on the independent status of that doctrine in public international law.

4. CONCLUSION

The analysis developed in this chapter provides answers to the research questions formulated at its outset. As NATO's accession conditions expanded, they drifted increasingly further away from the text of Article 10 of the 1949 Treaty. Can this be considered a tolerable interpretation of the 1949 Treaty or does it constitute an imposition of new conditions that oversteps the limits set in the ICJ's *Admissions* Opinion? The expansion of NATO's accession conditions does not contravene the purposes of the 1949 Treaty. It constitutes a permissible interpretation of Article 10. The exhaustive nature of the conditions listed in

Article 10 does not exclude that other conditions may be taken into account. The broadness and vagueness of Article 10's criteria are intentional. Because the link between environmental responsibility and security is now well-established in academic research and recognised in NATO policies, e.g. the Strategic Concepts, demanding environmental responsibility from a candidate Member State can be said to constitute a tolerable interpretation of the security requirement in Article 10. NATO's expansion policy is thus future-proof and in accordance with *Admissions*. The ICJ would probably accept the 1995 Study criteria as a lawful interpretation of Article 10 and, if it were to rule on the *Admissions* Opinion today, would probably not conclude that there had been a violation of Article 4 UN Charter. Even though the expansion of NATO's membership conditions is lawful, it is still far-reaching, and close to nothing is publicly known about which criteria are decisive to NATO when it decides (not) to invite a country to join. The extent to which national parliaments actually scrutinise accession protocols is a good topic for future research in the field of political science. It appears that NATO accession protocols are barely debated in the national parliaments, if they are even debated at all. It should also be investigated whether citizens know what (some of) NATO's membership conditions are. This could be done through a comparative empirical research project conducted in the field of political science. In the absence of a provision in the North Atlantic Treaty, is there a basis in international law for the suspension or expulsion of a NATO Member State? No, the four grounds provided in international law are all unsuitable for NATO. The only legal option left, then, would be for all Allies *minus* the defaulting one to withdraw from the North Atlantic Treaty on the basis of its Article 13 and Article 56 VCLT, and start a new Alliance on the basis of a new multilateral treaty. The Dutch government proposed this option several years ago, but confirmed that it was unlikely, improbable, and undesirable.[824] Calls to suspend or expel a NATO Member State are political; they have no grounds in international law.

[824] Interview with a senior NATO International Staff member, NATO Headquarters, 9 June 2022.

CHAPTER 6
CONCLUSION AND RECOMMENDATIONS

The above analysis provides answers to the research questions formulated in chapter 1.

Does NATO's expansion of powers to include non-Article 5 crisis response operations (NA5CROs) violate the principle of attributed powers? (chapter 2)

Conducting NA5CROs is not an attributed power because it is not mentioned anywhere in the North Atlantic Treaty or in any other NATO legal instrument. But this does not necessarily mean that the principle has been violated. The power could still be implied. The current international case law, with its emphasis on necessity and efficiency, seems favourable to NATO. The Organisation can quite easily argue that conducting NA5CROs is both necessary and essential to prevent a conflict from escalating to an Article 5 situation. In fact, that is exactly what NATO argued during the Balkan conflict. This does not mean that the invocation of the doctrine of implied powers is necessarily lawful or even desirable. One could argue that NATO's power to conduct NA5CROs is unnecessary because the Member States could form coalitions of the willing, outside of the NATO framework, to carry out these operations if there is a lawful basis for it. One could also say that the power to conduct NA5CROs is unessential, as there will never be *ex ante* or *ex post* proof that the operation really was essential to avoid the invocation of Article 5. Such strategic decisions are, after all, of a technical and military nature, and therefore classified. Moreover, implied powers are there to give effect to what States have agreed to by becoming parties to the constituent instrument. According to the North Atlantic Treaty's *travaux préparatoires* and the Cold War Strategic Concepts, the signatories wanted to create an alliance, not a collective security organisation. In addition, it is difficult for NATO to justify its implied powers interpretation by invoking established practice (Article 5 VCLT). NA5CROs are occasional operational actions, not administrative, organisational ones that create a rule that Allies feel obliged to follow, like the majority of practices accepted by the ICJ are. Even if one were to believe that conducting NA5CROs is an implied power in accordance with the principle of attributed powers, it still lacks the legitimacy of treaty amendment and creates a democratic deficit. The CJEU's *Opinion 94/2* demonstrated that implied powers can be denied when they are invoked merely to avoid informal treaty amendment. The case law of the *Bundesverfassungsgericht* and expert interviews demonstrate that NATO States wanted to amend the North Atlantic Treaty informally by adopting the 1999 Strategic Concept. The German Court's assertion that parliament is not defenceless against the risk of informal amendment holds no water. The German parliament cannot use its power of the purse to prevent NATO's tasks from expanding. In the European context, such parliamentary control is increasingly seen as an insufficient. Furthermore, the accession protocols ratified by the national parliaments have no bearing on the expansion of NATO's tasks. By avoiding treaty amendment and expanding NATO's task beyond the scope of Article 5, the 1999 Strategic Concept sidestepped the parliamentary participation of NATO citizens. This could be remedied with the following legal and policy recommendations:

- NATO Member States could anchor NATO's three fundamental tasks, including crisis management, in a separate legal instrument, such as an amendment to the Ottawa Agreement, or an accord or protocol to the 1949 Treaty, which can then be ratified by the national parliaments. Since NATO's three core tasks have remained unchanged since the 1999 Strategic Concepts, this could presumably be done without much controversy. It would give NATO's power to conduct NA5CROs the legitimacy of a legal instrument. Inspiration could be drawn from the tasks listed in the Petersberg Declaration, which were incorporated in the TEU by transferring them to the European Security and Defence Policy during the 1997 European Summit in Amsterdam.[825]
- Through academic scholarship and education, greater awareness should be fostered of this lack of legitimacy and the democratic deficit that results from it, so that citizens and political parties will ask parliamentary questions concerning the legality of NATO's expansion of powers.
- National judges should be aware of the realities of international law-making and the importance of informal treaty amendment when they interpret national constitutional provisions requiring the consent of parliament to enter into, or amend, multilateral treaties.

[825] In the Petersberg Declaration, the WEU Member States expressed their commitment to provide military units to the WEU, NATO, and the EU. The tasks were formulated as humanitarian, rescue, and peacekeeping tasks, and the tasks of combat forces in crisis management, including peacemaking.

Was NATO's institutional framework created and transformed in accordance with the fundamental principles of international institutional law concerning the lawful establishment of subsidiary bodies and the lawful delegation of powers to them? (chapter 3)

The NATO committees and the International Staff were lawfully established and the delegation of powers to them occurred lawfully as well. Nations delegated few powers to the IS, preferring to assign it a facilitating role. Although the NATO Administrative Tribunal is not a subsidiary body in the strict sense, the lawful delegation of powers to it should still be questioned. After all, the ICJ, in *Effect of Awards*, allowed the UNGA to delegate judicial powers to the UN Administrative Tribunal because it implied these powers from Articles 7 and 101(1) and (3) UN Charter, but the NAC's judicial powers cannot be implied from NATO's constituent instrument. With *Gaspirini* in mind, it would be interesting to see more cases in which those powers are questioned instead of the NATO AT's composition, to see whether courts imply these judicial powers from the North Atlantic Treaty or from the Ottawa Agreement.

Is the NATO Parliamentary Assembly a public international organisation? (chapter 3)

Because the NATO PA does not have international legal personality and does not share in the international legal personality of NATO (in contrast to the WEU Assembly and PACE), the NATO PA was granted its privileges and immunities by a 1974 Belgian federal law. States usually grant privileges and immunities only to public intergovernmental organisations whose existence is based on a treaty. The NATO PA's existence is not based on a treaty, nor on any other agreement, and therefore does not meet the requirements to be a public international organisation. Nor is the NATO PA mentioned in the Belgian Seat Policy's definition of a public international organisation. We can conclude that Belgium considers the NATO PA to be something more than a *de jure* non-governmental organisation but less than a *de jure* intergovernmental organisation. The NATO PA's legal status can only be categorised as a *sui generis* case under international institutional law.

What is the legal basis of NATO's immunity from jurisdiction? (chapter 3)

The *El Hamedi* ruling by the Brussels Court of Appeal, which addressed the question of NATO HQ's immunity as laid down in Article V Ottawa Agreement, deserves to be criticised. The majority of the alternative dispute settlement mechanisms suggested by the Court are either unrealistic (e.g. diplomatic protection by Libya) or offer hardly any real chance of justice for the victim. SHAPE, in contrast to NATO HQ, does not enjoy immunity from jurisdiction on the basis of a written clause. This led to long and costly legal proceedings against it in the Netherlands. Moreover, had the *Supreme* case taken place in Belgium, the appellant would have been able to sue SHAPE for billions of dollars in damages over the course of many years, hampering the efficient and independent working of the military headquarters in the process. The Belgian Seat Policy and national case law do not currently recognise customary law as a basis for immunity from jurisdiction. This leads us to the following recommendations:

- The Belgian Federal Government should grant SHAPE immunity from jurisdiction through an amendment of either the Paris Protocol or the Belgium-SHAPE Seat Agreement, or by expanding the Belgian Seat Policy to recognise customary law as a basis for immunity from jurisdiction, as is the case in the Netherlands.
- National judges who rely on the ECtHR's *Mothers of Srebrenica* ruling to interpret an international organisation's immunity from jurisdiction should duly justify the assertion that the alternative dispute settlement mechanisms available under Article 6 ECHR are a realistic means to justice.
- Greater clarity on the legal status of the NATO PA should be achieved, either by challenging the NATO PA's privileges and immunities before national tribunals or by asking the Belgian federal parliament a parliamentary question. If Belgium actually considers the NATO PA to be an international organisation, it should adapt its Seat Policy to the example of the Swiss *Loi fédérale sur les privilèges, les immunités et les facilités.*
- The effect that NATO PA recommendations have on the communicative discourse towards the public should be researched more in the field of political science. This could inspire the NATO PA to gain more informal powers, which should not be achieved through treaty amendment or additional agreements (because these options are unrealistic), but in other ways than through institutionalisation, e.g. strengthening the NATO PA's legal position and, with it, its public visibility and the role of its secretariat.

To what extent are NATO decisions made within the confines of the constituent instrument and of established practice? (chapter 4)

In the absence of a treaty provision, NATO has been preparing its decisions by consultation and adopting them by consensus for decades, which makes the process an established practice of the Organisation (Articles 5 VCLT and 2(b) ARIO), thus within the confines of the constituent instrument. NATO's internal law was not violated in 2003, when the DPC granted defensive aid to Turkey instead of the NAC, as France had consented to not being part of the Defence Planning Committee and because organisations are free to choose their own bureaucratic structure. Although NATO's decision-making procedure, as an established practice, does not exceed the confines of its constituent instrument, the process has been legally formalised to only a small extent. This is because procedural and substantive violations of NATO's limited internal legal order, even if they were to arise, would be neutralised by acceptance, acquiescence, or estoppel, thanks to the consensus principle. Even strictly *ultra vires* decisions are likely to be upheld.

To what extent do NATO Member States retain their decision-making sovereignty and responsibility? (chapter 4)

Because of the consensus rule, coupled with the option of breaking the silence and the opt-out, NATO Member States virtually retain full decision-making sovereignty. States in NATO also retain decision-making responsibility. The ICJ pointed out in *FYROM v. Greece* that Member States cannot use NATO's consensus rule as a shield from their own responsibility stemming from their external obligations in international law. The ECtHR's *Gasparini* ruling may have opened the door for holding Member States responsible for the acts of the Organisation, which is difficult to reconcile with the principle that States should not be held responsible for merely being members of an organisation. The Court in *Gasparini* should not have isolated the institutional conduct of Italy and Belgium from NATO's decision-making process, because one cannot be sure that a Member State did not voice any concerns or objected to the NATO decision to establish the NATO AT. Moreover, no clear Member State action could be identified, as required by *Bosphorus*, because *Gasparini* concerned an alleged structural institutional deficiency within NATO. The case law on this point should be followed closely as it develops, as it may endanger the effectiveness of multilateralism.

What is the legal effect of NATO operational decisions in light of the rule of international institutional law that international organisations cannot take binding operational decisions unless their constitutions expressly permit this? (chapter 4)

In principle, NATO operational decisions, including the invocation of Article 5, are non-binding, because the Treaty only accords the NAC advisory powers. However, the intent of parties to be bound remains the most important criterion. Policymakers, judges, and academics should not the deduce the legally binding force of NATO decisions from consensus alone, but should scrutinise the intent of the parties to be bound. This does not mean that NATO operational acts never have legal effect. The norms articulated in them may become binding on Member States when they also from a traditional source of international law, such as unilateral State acts, agreements in simplified form, or international customary law. To strengthen the position of NATO's decision-making in the law of international organisations:

- International and national courts should hold Member States responsible for their individual conduct when that conduct violates an external obligation stemming from international law.
- International and national courts should not hold NATO Member States responsible for simply having joined the consensus on a decision that resulted in the creation of a structural deficiency within the Organisation.
- In court, Member States should not use NATO's consensus rule as a shield against their own international responsibility when they violated an external legal obligation.
- In the field of political science, more research should be done on the application of qualified majority voting to NATO administrative decisions. This option could help to make NATO's decision-making process faster, more efficient, and more transparent, now that the Organisation is growing in both membership and importance, and single-country vetoes are increasingly frequent.
- States should be aware that, if they acquiesce to a NATO consensus-based decision, they may be estopped from later challenging the lawfulness of that decision.

As NATO's accession conditions were expanded, they have away drifted increasingly further away from the text of Article 10 North Atlantic Treaty. Can this expansion be considered a tolerable interpretation of the Treaty, or does it impose new conditions that overstep the limits set in the ICJ's Admissions Opinion? (chapter 5)

The expansion of NATO's accession conditions does not contravene the purposes of the North Atlantic Treaty, but rather constitutes a permissible interpretation of Article 10. Because the link between environmental responsibility and security is now well-established in academic research and NATO policies, such as the Strategic Concepts, demanding environmental responsibility from candidate Member States constitutes a tolerable interpretation of the (intentionally) broad 'security' requirement in Article 10. Moreover, economic liberty is implied in Article 2 of the North Atlantic Treaty. The principles of democracy, individual liberty, and the rule of law, mentioned in the Preamble, serve to interpret the North Atlantic Treaty (article 31(2)(b) VCLT). NATO's expansion policy, based on the 1995 Study, is thus both future-proof and in accordance with the ICJ's *Admissions* Opinion. It makes sense to accept the 1995 Study as an established practice of the organisation, because accession conditions occasionally need to be adapted to changing circumstances. A further democratic check is provided by the rule that NATO accession protocols must be ratified by all the Member States' national parliaments. Even though the far-reaching expansion of NATO's membership conditions is lawful, it has not been legitimised by legal amendment. Additionally, close to nothing is publicly known about which criteria are decisive for NATO when it decides (not) to invite a country to join. These criteria are not written down in the accession protocols and are not discussed during NATO Summits and Ministerials. The internal decisions to move forward with accession on the basis of the 1995 Study are made behind closed doors, by consensus, and sometimes verbally. For this reason, NATO should start publishing executive summaries of the annual MAPs or ANPs again. Three executive summaries of Annual National Programs (Slovenia, Latvia, and Bulgaria) were published but have since been taken offline. These summaries could be inspired by the Country Reports published annually by the European Commission but should take into account the fact that NATO is not merely an international organisation, but a military and strategic alliance as well, in which speed and political discretion are important to the decision-making process. Even if these reports were brief, they would still provide greater transparency and legal certainty in the sensitive and topical matter of accession to NATO, a matter susceptible to misinformation, as the Ukraine crisis proves.

In the absence of a provision in the North Atlantic Treaty, is there a basis in international law for the suspension or expulsion of a NATO Member State? (chapter 5)

There are four possible grounds in international law for the suspension or expulsion of a NATO Member State in the absence of a constitutional provision: 1) the amendment of the North Atlantic Treaty, 2) the doctrine of implied powers, 3) the doctrine of countermeasures in the context of State responsibility, and 4) a material breach of the Treaty in the sense of Article 60 VCLT. In *FYROM v. Greece*, the ICJ disregarded the exception of non-performance as an independent legal ground. The analysis showed that all four grounds are unsuitable in the case of NATO. Treaty amendment is unrealistic because policymakers and lawmakers have been avoiding it for over 70 years, and the defaulting State would have to consent to it. The defaulting State would also have to recognise the existence of an implied power to suspend or expel. The object and the purpose of an alliance pact imply the opposite of such a power, and suspension or expulsion are not necessary or essential to carry out the functions of the Organisation. Article 60 VCLT is unsuitable as well because the bar for a material breach is so high (the conduct cannot consist of a mere incident) and because its effects are undesirable, as it would suspend the defaulting Member State's obligation to come to the defence of the others. Lastly, even if an internationally wrongful act is established on the part of a Member State, suspension or expulsion would not be lawful as a countermeasure because it is not reversible and most likely not aimed at stopping the illegal conduct. All in all, the arguments for the assertion that suspension and expulsion are generally ill-fitted tools in the law of international organisations are even stronger in the case of NATO, as NATO is not just an international organisation but an alliance of like-minded States. To remedy the issues identified, we recommend that:

- NATO publish executive summaries of the annual MAPs or ANPs and make them available on the NATO website;
- States not bring NATO or its Member States before the courts for not having admitted them as Members, as there is no automatic right to NATO membership as soon as certain conditions are met;
- political science research be conducted on the extent to which national parliaments actually scrutinise accession protocols and on the citizens' awareness of NATO membership conditions;
- the potential harm posed by political threats of suspending or expelling a NATO Member State should be put into perspective by journalists and academics, as they have no basis in international law;
- NATO Member States realise that they might be internationally responsible on the basis of Articles 3 and 8 North Atlantic Treaty when they enter into commercial agreements for (weapon) systems that prove to be non-interoperable with NATO systems, although suspending or expelling the defaulting Member State as a countermeasure would not be a lawful reaction.

CONCLUDING OBSERVATIONS

This book made clear that little of NATO's legal order is written down in the North Atlantic Treaty. Not one text lays down the international legal personality of NATO. This book offers the unique opportunity to determine in its conclusions whether NATO has international legal personality on a deductive basis. Much has been written about this in scholarly work, but this has never been preceded by such an in-depth legal analysis of the North Atlantic Treaty. According to the prevailing objective theory, international organisations have international legal personality when this status is explicitly or implicitly given to them.[826] Just like the UN (see *Reparations for Injuries*), NATO is equipped with organs and special tasks, and its privileges and immunities are granted to its Members by the Ottawa Agreement. NATO HQ has diplomatic representation on its premises and can mobilise international forces.[827] Larsen finds that the International Criminal Tribunal for the former Yugoslavia (ICTY), in the *Simic* case, acknowledged NATO's international legal personality by scrutinising SFOR rather than each NATO Member State individually.[828] NATO Member States have also asserted NATO's international legal personality in the ICJ's *Legality of the Use of Force* case.[829] In its submission to an ILC consultation on the definition of an international organisation, NATO itself remarked that 'NATO is an international organisation [...] and as such a subject of international law. It possesses international legal personality as well as treaty-making power' (*cf.* Article 2(a) DARIO).[830] Moreover, NATO concluded an agreement with Belgium regarding the legal status of the International Military Staff Personnel,

---

826 H. Schermers and N. Blokker, *op. cit.*, § 1566, 989 and ICJ *Reparation for injuries*, 178–179.

827 H. Schermers and N. Blokker, *op. cit.*, § 1566, 989.

828 ICTY 2000, *Decision on the Defence Motion for Judicial Assistance to be provided by SFOR and others (Prosecutor v. Simic et al)*, Doc. IT-95-99, § 48, K. Larsen, *The Human Rights Treaty Obligations of Peacekeepers*, Cambridge, Cambridge University Press, 2014, 96, as mentioned in L. Tinel, *Should I stay or should I go? An analysis of the NATO decision to withdraw from Afghanistan based on the theoretical framework of international responsibility of international organizations*, Leuven, KU Leuven, Faculty of Law, 2023, 18.

829 As defended by L. Tinel, *op. cit.*, 19 and ICJ 5 July 2000, *Case Concerning Legality of Use of Force (Yugoslavia v. Netherlands)*, Preliminary objections of the Kingdom of The Netherlands, para. 7.2.7, and Preliminary objections of the Republic of France, para. 23.

830 ILC 2011, Draft Articles on Responsibility of International Organizations, with Commentaries in ILC, Report of the ILC on the work of its sixty-third session, UN Doc. A/66/10, 11, § 2 and D. Grütters, 'NATO, International Organizations and Functional Immunity', *International Organizations Law Review* 2016, 221.

which was enacted into law.[831] In 2022 the NATO Secretary General concluded an arrangement with Belgium concerning the status of temporary personnel engaged by and serving in a NATO body located on the territory of the Kingdom of Belgium.[832] In contrast, Belgium could not enter into an agreement with the NATO PA because of the latter's lack of international legal personality. In addition, NATO and the Islamic Republic of Afghanistan concluded an agreement on the Status of NATO Forces and NATO Personnel conducting mutually agreed-on NATO-led activities in Afghanistan.[833] This leads to the conclusion that NATO has international legal personality. Some commentators suggest that NATO does not have international legal personality, using the consensus rule as an argument.[834] However, as shown in the case of NATO, consensus does not necessarily imply the consent of each State. It implies merely the absence of disagreement. International legal personality is considered to imply that an international organisation has a separate legal position.[835] It shows the *volonté distincte* of NATO HQ.[836] The book showed that the signatory parties act at times as real Member States, proving the distinct will and the personality of the organisation. They participate in a consensus on a certain decision, which implies that they should not be held responsible for the acts of the Organisation when those acts end up creating a structural deficiency without this being clearly attributable to State conduct (cf. *Gasparani*). Here, the State is protected by its status as a NATO Member State (chapter 4). Instead of concluding agreements, NATO makes decisions, which is an argument for NATO being a distinct and autonomous person towards its members (chapter 4).[837] Moreover, the analysis of the suspension and expulsion of Members showed that the Member States very much behave like Member States in this realm, which explains why the four grounds provided by international law are unsuitable (chapter 5). On the

---

[831] Law 28 april 1970, Arrangement entre le Royaume de Belgique et l'OTAN concernant le Statut du Personnel de l'Etat Major Militaire International du Comité Militaire de l'OTAN installé sur le territoire de Belgique, *Belgisch Staatsblad* 1970, 7297–7298.

[832] Arrangement between the North Atlantic Treaty Organization and the Kingdom of Belgium Concerning the Status of Temporary personnel engaged by, and serving in, a NATO body located on the territory of the Kingdom of Belgium, Brussels, 7 February 2022, available online at 1267_Regeling in het Engels.pdf (fdfa.be) (last accessed January 2025).

[833] See the Agreement between NATO and the Islamic Republic of Afghanistan, 30 September 2014, available online at NATO – Official text: Agreement between the North Atlantic Treaty Organization and the Islamic Republic of Afghanistan on the Status of NATO Forces and NATO personnel conducting mutually agreed NATO-led activities in Afghanistan (last accessed January 2025) as quoted by K. Daugirdas, 'How and Why International Law Binds International Organizations', *Harvard International Law Journal* 2016, 348.

[834] T. Gazzini, 'NATO Coercive Military Activities in the Yugoslav Crisis (1992–1999)', *European Journal of International Law* 2001, 391–436.

[835] R. Wessel, 'Reparation for Injuries Suffered in the Service of the United Nations' in C. Ryngaert, I. Dekker, R. Wessel and J. Wouters (eds.), *op. cit.*, 11–18.

[836] Part of the definition of a public international organisation as given by Schermers and Blokker, *op. cit.*, § 44, 44.

[837] R. Wessel and I. Dekker, 'Identities of States in International Organizations', *op. cit.*, 310.

other hand, the book showed that the signatory parties also often behave more like States than as Member States of the Organisation. First of all, the fact that NATO decides only by consensus, coupled with the option of breaking the silence and the opt-out, in plenary organs only, means that they very much retain their identity as States. This book has shown that few powers were given to the International Staff and that this was done intentionally in order to avoid further integration (chapter 2). Moreover, signatory parties to the Treaty act in their capacity as States when they decide on the accession of a new Ally to the Alliance on the basis of Article 10 North Atlantic Treaty, as States have complete discretion in this decision (chapter 5). Furthermore, international case law showed that States retain their full decision-making responsibility at NATO. States should not try to use NATO's consensus rule, and thus their NATO membership, as a shield against their own international responsibility for the violation of an external legal obligation, as Greece unsuccessfully tried to do in *FYROM v. Greece* (chapter 4). This book allows for an answer to the two research questions posed in chapter 1: the North Atlantic Treaty is the constituent instrument of the Alliance. It has the necessary characteristics: it establishes the objectives of the Alliance, its core task of self-defence, and the principles that guide the cooperation between the signatory parties. The 1949 Treaty was concluded for an indefinite period and has both a revision and a withdrawal clause.[838] In Article 8, it establishes the priority of the Treaty over other international engagements, following the example of Article 103 UN Charter, although it has no internal priority rule.[839] The Treaty falls within the ILC's wide definition of a 'constitution'.[840] However, the North Atlantic Treaty lacks certain elements which are typical for a constituent instrument, such as the international legal personality of NATO, the privileges and immunities of the different bodies, HQ International Staff, and the Member State representatives. It does not provide for the judicial settlement of disputes either. All of this is to be found in the 1951 Ottawa Agreement. In addition, while Article 10 of the North Atlantic Treaty regulates State accession to the Treaty, and thus to the Alliance, it leaves out accession to the Organisation in the capacity of Member State. This is because the North Atlantic Treaty does not create the Organisation. For this reason, the Ottawa Agreement should be seen as the constituent instrument of the NATO HQ, the International Staff, Agencies, and the National

---

838 R. Monaco, 'Le caractère constitutionnel des actes institutlfs d'organisations internationales' in *La Communauté International: Mélanges offerts à Charles Rousseau*, Paris, Pedone, 1974, 154 and N. Blokker, 'Constituent Instruments' in J. Cogan, I. Hurd and I. Johnstone, *op. cit.*, 943961.

839 Like for example Article XVI.3 of the WTO Agreement, according to Schermers and Blokker, *op. cit.*, § 1145, 726. See also S. Tetsuo, 'Constituent Instruments of International Organizations and Their Interpretative Framework – Introduction to the Principal Doctrines and Bibliography', *Hitotsubashi Journal of Law and Politics* 1986, 6.

840 Report of the ILC, 17th session, Suppl. No 9 (A/5209), 7, commentary to Article 3, § 3.

Representations. The constitutional rules of NATO can thus be found both in the North Atlantic Treaty and in the Ottawa Agreement.[841] Together, they form the 'constitutional texts' of NATO that provide its organisational features. This is strengthened by the findings in chapter 2 that the Treaty's drafters left the door open for the Alliance to further institutionalise itself. Based on all of the above, it should be concluded that, while NATO has developed its powers, institutional structure, decision-making process, and membership conditions mostly in accordance with the principles of international institutional law, they have been legally formalised and constrained to a remarkably small extent.

841 And in the NATO SOFA and the Paris Protocol for the military side.

BIBLIOGRAPHY

LEGISLATION

Agreement between the International Committee of the Red Cross and the Swiss Federal Council, *International Review of the Red Cross* 1993, No. 293.

Agreement on the Status of Western European Union, National Representatives and International Staff, signed on 11 May 1955 in Paris, entered into force on 19 July 1956, 1258 UNTS 312.

Articles on State Responsibility, text adopted by the International Law Commission at its fifty-third session, in 2001, and submitted to the General Assembly as a part of the Commission's report covering the work of that session (A/56/10). The report, which also contains commentaries on the draft articles, appears in the *Yearbook of the International Law Commission*, 2001, vol. II, Part Two, as corrected.

Articles on the Responsibility of International Organizations with Commentaries, text adopted by the International Law Commission at its sixty-third session, in 2011, and submitted to the General Assembly as a part of the Commission's report covering the work of that session (A/66/10). The report, which also contains commentaries to the articles (para. 88), appears in *Yearbook of the International Law Commission*, 2011, vol. II, Part Two.

Agreement concerning the legal status of the North Atlantic Treaty Organization, National Representatives and International Staff, signed in Ottawa on 20 September 1951, entered into force on 18 May 1954, 200 UNTS 3.

Belgium, Kamer van Volksvertegenwoordigers, Wetsontwerp betreffende het statuut in België van de Noordatlantische Vergadering, Verslag namens de Commissie voor de Buitenlandse Zaken en de Ontwikkelingssamenwerking, Buitengewone zitting van 10 juli 1974, Doc. No. 187 B.Z. 1974.

Belgium, Kamer van Volksvertegenwoordigers, Wetsontwerp houdende instemming met het Protocol voor de toetreding van de Republiek Noord-Macedonië tot de Noord-Atlantische Verdragsorganisatie, Zitting van 19 April 2019, Doc. 54 3717/001.

Belgium, Senaat, Wetsvoorstel tot wijziging van de wet van 14 augustus 1974 betreffende het statuut in België van de Noord-Atlantische Vergadering, Zitting van 5 juli 2001, Doc. 2–843/1.

Belgium, Wet van 14 augustus 1974 betreffende het statuut in België van de Noordatlantische Vergadering, *Belgisch Staatsblad* 31 oktober 1974, Doc. 13264.

Belgium, Wet 28 april 1970, Arrangement entre le Royaume de Belgique et l'OTAN concernant le Statut du Personnel de l'Etat Major Militaire International du Comité Militaire de l'OTAN installé sur le territoire de Belgique, *Belgisch Staatsblad* 1970, 7297–7298.

Charter of the United Nations and Statute of the International Court of Justice, signed in San Francisco on 26 June 1945, entered into force on 24 October 1945.
Convention on the Prohibition of the Development, Production, Stockpiling and Use of Chemical Weapons and on their Destruction (1992), signed on November 1993, entered into force on 29 April 1997, 974 UNTS 45.
Convention of the World Meteorological Organization, signed on 11 October 1947, entered into force on 23 March 1950, 77 UNTS 143.
Draft Articles on the Law of Treaties between States and International Organizations or between International Organizations, with commentaries, 1982. Text adopted by the International Law Commission at its thirty-fourth session, in 1982, and submitted to the General Assembly as a part of the Commission's report covering the work of that session (at para. 63). The report, which also contains commentaries on the draft articles, appears in *Yearbook of the International Law Commission*, 1982, vol. II, Part Two.
Economic Community of West African States Treaty, signed on 28 May 1975, entered into force provisionally on 28 May 1975, 595 UNTS 287.
Final Agreement for the settlement of the differences as described in the United Nations Security Council Resolutions 817 (1993) and 845 (1993), the termination of the Interim Accord of 1995, and the establishment of a Strategic Partnership between the Parties, signed in Psarades on 17 June 2018, entered into force on 12 February 2019.
France, Loi du 1er juillet 1901 relative au contrat d'association, *Journal Officiel Republique française*, 2 juillet 1901, Doc. 4025.
Germany, Bundestag, Entwurf eines Gesetzes zu dem Protokoll vom 6. Februar 2019 zum Nordatlantikvertrag über den Beitritt der Republic Nordmazedonien, Doc. 19/10418, 17 May 2019.
Germany, Bundestag, BT- Plenarprotokoll 14/53, Doc. S. 4607C – 4615B, 9 September 1999.
Germany, Gesetz über die parlamentarische Beteiligung bei der Entscheidung über den Einsatz bewaffneter Streitkräfte im Ausland, Parlamentsbeteiligungsgesetz, ParlBG, *Federal Law Gazette* 2005.
Inter-American Treaty of Reciprocal Assistance ('Rio Pact'), signed on 2 September 1947 in Rio de Janeiro, entered into force on 12 March 1948, 21 UNTS 77.
Optional Protocol to the Convention on the Rights of the Child on the Involvement of Children in Armed Conflict, signed on 25 May 2000, entered into force on 12 February 2002, 2173 UNTS 222.
Protocol to the North Atlantic Treaty on the Accession of the Federal Republic of Germany, signed in Paris on 23 October 1954, entered into force on 5 May 1955, available online at www.nato.int/cps/cn/natohq/official_texts_17411.htm (last accessed January 2025).
Protocol to the North Atlantic Treaty on the Accession of Greece and Turkey, signed in London on 17 October 1951, entered into force on 15 February 1952, available online at www.nato.int/cps/in/natohq/official_texts_17245.htm (last accessed January 2025).
Statute of the Council of Europe, signed on 5 May 1949, entered into force 3 August 1949, ETS no. 0001.

The General Agreement on Privileges and Immunities of the Council of Europe, signed on 2 September 1949, entered into force on 10 September 1952, ETS no. 002.
The Treaty for Collaboration in Economic, Social and Cultural Matters and for Collective Self-Defence (Treaty of Brussels), signed on 17 March 1948, entered into force on 25 August 1948, as amended by the Protocol modifying and completing the Brussels Treaty, signed in Paris on 23 October 1954, entered into force on 6 May 1955, 211 UNTS 342.
UN, Security Council Resolution 1973, 17 March 2011, UN Doc. S/RES/1973.
UN, Security Council Resolution 1970, 26 February 2011, UN Doc. S/RES/1970.
UN, Security Council, Resolution 1386, 20 December 2001, UN Doc. S/RES/1386.
UN, Security Council, Resolution 816, 31 March 1993, UN Doc. S/RES/816.
Vienna Convention on the Law of Treaties, signed on 23 May 1969, entered into force on 27 January 1980, UNTS 1155.
Vienna Convention on the Law of Treaties between States and International Organizations or between International Organizations, adopted on 20 March 1986, not yet entered into force, UN Doc. A/CONF/129/15.

DOCTRINE

A. Barros, 'Application of the Interim Accord of 13 September 1995 (The Former Yugoslav Republic of Macedonia v Greece)' in A. Barros (ed.), *Governance As Responsibility: Member States as Human Rights Protectors in International Financial Institutions*, Cambridge, Cambridge University Press, 2019, 61–65.
A. Barros and C. Ryngaert, 'The Position of Member States in (Autonomous) Institutional Decision-Making Implications for the Establishment of Responsibility', *International Organizations Law Review* 2014, 53–82.
A. Basak, *Decisions of the United Nations Organs in the Judgments and Opinions of the International Court of Justice*, Wrocław, Zakład Narodowy im. Ossolińskich, 1969, 223 p.
A. Boeva, 'What is NATO HQ?', *NATO Legal Gazette* 2013, 7–12.
A. Buchan, 'The Reform of NATO', *Foreign Affairs* 1962, 165–182.
A. Buchanan and E. Keohane, 'The Legitimacy of Global Governance Institutions', *Ethics and International Affairs* 2006, 405–437.
A. Constantinou, *The Right of Self-Defence under Customary International Law and Article 51 of the UN Charter*, Athens, Sakkoulas, 2000, 225 p.
A. Cragg, 'A New Strategic Concept for a new era', *NATO Review* 1999, 19–22.
A. Dumoulin, 'Statutory Bodies of WEU', *CVCE Luxemburg University* 2016, 1–8.
A. Duxbury, *The Participation of States in International Organizations: The Role of Human Rights and Democracy*, Cambridge, Cambridge University Press, 2011, 382 p.
A. Gadkowski, 'The doctrine of implied powers of international organizations in the case law of international tribunals', *Adam Mickiewicz University Law Review* 2016, 45–59.
A. Galletta, *Mastering the Semi-Structured Interview and Beyond*, New York, New York University Press, 2013, 245 p.

A. Kiss, 'Le Conseil de l'Europe et les suites données par les Etats membres aux textes adoptés par ses organes', *Annuaire français de droit international* 1967, 695–708.
A. Lindstrom, 'Consensus Decisionmaking in NATO: French Unilateralism and the Decision to Defend Turkey', *Chicago Journal of International Law* 2003, 579–585.
A. Macias, 'U.S. sanctions Turkey over purchase of Russian S-400 missile system', *CNBC News* 14 December 2020, 1–4.
A. Miller, 'The Privileges and Immunities of the United Nations', *International Organisations Law Review* 2009, 169–257.
A. Mosquera, 'The North Atlantic Treaty: Article 9 and NATO's Institutionalization', *Emory International Law Review* 2019, 149–164.
A. Mosquera, 'Some Notes on NATO's Institutionalisation', *NATO Legal Gazette* 2019, 13–26.
A. Mower, 'The Importance of the North Atlantic Assembly', *Orbis* 1978, 927–946.
A. Norodom, 'Les droits et obligations statutaires du membres, leur protection et leur sanction' in E. Langrange and J.-M. Sorel (eds.), *Droit des organisations internationales*, Issy-les-Moulineaux, LGDJ, 2013, 326–349.
A. Orakhelashvili, *Collective Security*, Oxford, Oxford University Press, 2011, 384 p.
A. Papaioannou, 'Strengthening EU-NATO relations', *NATO Review* 2019, 1–5.
A. Paulus 'Quo vadis Democratic Control? The Afghanistan Decision of the Bundestag and the Decision of the Federal Constitutional Court in the NATO Strategic Concept Case', *German Law Journal* 2002, 1–10.
A. Payton, 'Consensus Procedures in International Organizations', *European University Institute Working Paper* 2010, 1–24.
A. Peters, 'International Organizations and International Law' in J. Cogan, I. Hurd and I. Johnstone (eds.), *The Oxford Handbook of International Organizations*, Oxford, Oxford University Press, 2016, 33–59.
A. Peters, 'L'acte constitutif de l'organisation internationale', in E. Lagrange and J.-M. Sorel (eds.), *Droit des organisations internationales*, Issy-les-Moulineaux, LGDJ, 2013, 201–246.
A. Peters, 'Dual Democracy' in J. Klabbers, A. Peters and G. Ulfstein (eds.), *The Constitutionalization of International Law*, Oxford, Oxford University Press, 2009, 263–341.
A. Peters, 'A Plea for a European Semi-Parliamentary and Semi-Consociational Democracy', *European Integration Online Papers* 2003, 1–36.
A. Reinisch, 'Rationales for judicial abstention' in A. Reinisch (ed.), *International Organizations Before National Courts*, Cambridge, Cambridge University Press, 2000, 233–238.
A. Sari, 'Can Turkey be Expelled from NATO? It's Legally Possible, Whether or Not Politically Prudent', *Just Security* 2019, 1–8.
A. Sari, 'The Mutual Assistance Clauses of the North Atlantic and EU Treaties: The Challenge of Hybrid Threats', *Harvard National Security Journal* 2019, 405–460.
A. Tammes, *Hoofdstukken van Internationale Organisatie*, s'-Gravenhage, Nijhoff, 1951, 284 p.
A. Verdross and B. Simma, *Universelles Völkerrecht: Theorie und Praxis*, Berlin, Duncker & Humblot, 1984, 956 p.

A. Verhelst and S. Trifunovksa, *NATO: The North Atlantic Treaty Organization,* Alpen-aan-den-Rhijn, Wolters Kluwer, 2022, 178 p.
A. Verhelst and J. Wouters, 'Zeventig jaar NAVO: juridische kanttekeningen bij een bijzondere internationale organisatie', *Rechtskundig Weekblad* 2020, 1202–1215.
A. Vîlcan, *An assessment of the successive European Union treaty amendments from a federalist perspective,* thesis, Leuven, KU Leuven, Faculty of Social Sciences, 2011, 73 p.
B. Buzan, 'Negotiating by Consensus: Developments in Technique at the United Nations Conference on the Law of the Sea', *American Journal of International Law* 1981, 324–348.
B. Conforti, 'Le role de l'accord dans le système des Nations Unies', *Recueil des Cours de l'Académie de Droit International de La Haye* 1969-II, 203–288.
B. Deen, D. Zandee and A. Stoetman, 'Uncharted and uncomfortable in European defence', *Clingendael Report* 2022, 80 p.
B. Eriksen, *The Committee System of the NATO Council,* New York, Humanities Press, 1967, 101 p.
B. Grady, 'Article 5 of the North Atlantic Treaty: Past, Present, and Uncertain Future', *Georgia Journal of International and Comparative Law* 2002, 167–198.
B. Habegger, 'Democratic accountability of international organizations: Parliamentary Control within the Council of Europe and the OSCE and the prospects for the United Nations', *Cooperation and Conflict* 2010, 186–204.
B. Habegger, *Parlamentarismus in der internationalen Politik: Europarat, OSZE und Interparlamentarische Union*, Baden-Baden, Nomos, 2005, 270 p.
B. Haller, *An Assembly for Europe: The Council of Europe's Parliamentary Assembly 1949–1989,* Strasbourg, Council of Europe Publishing, 2007, 84 p.
B. Nemeth, 'Ukraine invasion: why eight NATO members triggered article 4 of the North Atlantic Treaty', *The Conversation* 1 March 2022, 1–2.
B. Rouyer-Hameray, *Les Compétences implicites des organisations internationales*, Paris, Librairie Générale de Droit et de Jurisprudence, 1962, 23–27.
B. Simma, 'NATO, the UN and the Use of Force: Legal Aspects', *European Journal of Law* 1999, 1–22.
B. Simma, 'Reflections on Article 60 of the Vienna Convention on the Law of Treaties and its Background in General International Law', *Austrian Journal of Public and International Law* 1970, 5–83.
B. Slay, 'Environment, Security and Development Challenges in the 21st Century' in S. Stec and B. Baraj (eds.), *Energy and Environmental Challenges to Security,* Dordrecht, Springer, 2009, 33–37 (part of the NATO Science for Peace and Security Series C: Environmental Security book series).
C. Amerasignhe, *Principles of the Institutional Law of International Organizations,* Cambridge, Cambridge University Press, 2005, 538 p.
C. Amerasinghe, *The Law of the International Civil Service*, Oxford, Oxford University Press, 1994, 712 p.
C. Bickerton, 'From Nation States to Member States in European Union Foreign Policy' in C. Bickerton (ed.), *European Integration: From Nation-States to Member States,* Oxford, Oxford University Press, 2012, 151–158.

C. Brölmann, 'Member States and International Legal Responsibility: Developments of the Institutional Veil', *International Organizations Law Review* 2015, 358–381.

C. Brölmann, 'Specialized Rules of Treaty Interpretation: International Organizations', in D. Hollis (ed.), *The Oxford Guide to Treaties*, Oxford, Oxford University Press, 2012, 507–524.

C. Brölmann, 'Introduction' in C. Brölmann (ed.), *The Institutional Veil in Public International Law: International Organizations and the Law of Treaties*, London, Hart Publishing, 2007, 330 p.

C. Brumter, *The North Atlantic Assembly*, Berlin, Springer, 1986, 223 p.

C. Colliard, *Institutions des relations internationales*, Paris, Dalloz, 1978, 964 p.

C. Cramer and U. Franke, 'Ambiguous alliance: Neutrality, opt-outs and European defence', *European Council on Foreign Relations* 2021, 1–8.

C. Dominicé, 'La personnalité juridique international du CICR', in C. Swinariski (ed.), *Studies and essays on international humanitarian law and Red Cross principles in honour of Jean Pictet*, Leiden, Brill Nijhoff, 1984, 81–91.

C. Jenks, 'Expulsion from the League of Nations', *British Yearbook of International Law* 1935, 79–83.

C. Kissling, *The Legal and Political Status of International Parliamentary Institutions*, Berlin, Committee for a Democratic UN Background Paper, 2011, 92 p.

C. Kraft-Kasack, 'Transnational Parliamentary Assmeblies: A Remedy for the Democratic Deficit of International Governance?', *West European Politics* 2008, 534–557.

C. Migdalovitz, 'Greece' in K. Donfried (ed.), *Kosovo: International Reactions to NATO Air Strikes*, CRS Report for Congress, Washington D.C., Congressional Research Service, 1999, 1-6

C. Moser and S. Blockmans, *The extent of the European Parliament's competence in Common Security and Defence Policy*, Brussels, Directorate General for External Policies In-Depth Analysis, European Parliament, 2022.

C. Navarra, L. Jančová and I. Ioannides, 'Qualified majority voting in common foreign and security policy A cost of non-Europe report', *European Parliament Research Service Study* 2023, 255 p., available online at www.europarl.europa.eu/thinktank/en/document/EPRS_STU(2023)740243 (last accessed January 2025).

C. Peters, 'Subsequent Practice and Established Practice of International Organizations: Two Sides of the Same Coin?', *Goettingen Journal of International Law* 2011, 617–642.

C. Riotta, 'Lindsey Graham turns on Trump over disaster Syria move', *Independent* 7 October 2019, available online at www.independent.co.uk/news/world/americas/us-politics/trump-syria-turkey-lindsey-graham-twitter-pomepo-isis-assad-iran-middle-east-a9146161.html (last accessed January 2025).

C. Ryngaert, 'The European Court of Human Rights' Approach to the Responsibility of Member States in connection with Acts of International Organizations', *International and Comparative Law Quarterly* 2011, 997–1016.

C. Ryngaert and H. Buchanan, 'Member State Responsibility for the Acts of International Organizations', *Utrecht Law Review* 2011, 131–146.

C. Stahn, 'International Law at Crossroads? The Impact of September 11', *Zeitschrift für ausländisches öffentliches Recht und Völkerrecht* 2002, 213–220.

C. Stavropoulos, 'The Practice of Voluntary Abstentions by Permanent Members of the Security Council under Article 27, Paragraph 3 of the Charter of the United Nations', *American Journal of International Law* 1967, 315–334.
D. Acheson, *Broadcast on Atlantic Accord*, Radio Address to the Nation, 18 March 1949, *The New York Times* 19 March 1949, available online at https://archive.nytimes.com/www.nytimes.com/library/world/global/031949nato-acheson-text.html (last accessed January 2025).
D. Acheson, 'The Meaning of the North Atlantic Pact', *U.S. Department of State Bulletin* 1949, 384–388.
D. Akande, 'What is the Meaning of Consensus in International Decision Making', *European Journal of International Law Talk* 2013, 1–2.
D. Andrews, *The Atlantic Alliance under Stress: US-European Relations after Iraq*, Cambridge, Cambridge University Press, 2005, 293 p.
D. Auerswald and P. Saideman, *NATO in Afghanistan: Fighting Together, Fighting Alone*, New Jersey, Princeton University Press, 2014, 280 p.
D. Bereuter, 'NATO Parliamentary Assembly – Three Priorities', *Hampton Roads International Security Quarterly* 2002, 50–54.
D. Bodansky and J. Watson, 'State Consent and the Sources of International Obligation', *Proceedings of the Annual Meeting of the American Society of International Law* 1992, 108–113.
D. Bowett, *United Nations Forces: a Legal Study of United Nations Practice*, London, Stevens, 1964, 579 p.
D. Fleck, *The Handbook of the Law of Visiting Forces*, Oxford, Oxford University Press, 2018, 790 p.
D. Grütters, 'NATO, International Organizations and Functional Immunity', *International Organizations Law Review* 2016, 211–254.
D. Hollis and J. Newcomer, 'Political Commitments and the Constitution', *Virginia Journal of International Law* 2009, 507–584.
D. Murswiek, 'Die Fortentwicklung völkerrechtlicher Verträge: verfassungsrechtliche Grenzen und Kontrolle im Organstreit', *Neue Zeitschrift für Verwaltungsrecht* 2007, 1130–1134.
D. Nauta, *The International Responsibility of NATO and its Personnel during Military Operations*, Leiden, Brill Nijhoff, 2017, 180 p.
D. Sarooshi, 'Delegation to UN Subsidiary Organs', *British Yournal of International Law* 2000, 413–478.
D. Sidjanski, *Political Decision-Making Processes: Studies in national, comparative and international politics*, Amsterdam, Elsevier, 1973, 237 p.
D. Simon, *L'interprétation judiciaire des traités d'organisations internationales*, Paris, A. Pedone, 1981, 936 p.
D. Tladi, 'Is the International Law Commission Elevating Subsequent Agreements and Subsequent Practice?', *European Journal of International Law Talk* 2018, 1–3.
D. Yost, *NATO's Balancing Act*, Washington DC, US Institute of Peace, 2014, 480 p.
D. Yost, 'NATO's evolving purposes and the next Strategic Concept', *International Affairs* 2010, 489–522.
D. Yost, *NATO Transformed: the Alliance's New Roles in International Security*, Washington DC, US Institute of Peace Press, 1998, 450 p.

D. Watkins and M. Burton, *Research Methods in Law,* London, Routledge, 2013, 260 p.
E. Bartolini, 'Simple Abstention and Constructive Abstention in the Context of International Economic Sanctions: Two Too Similar SIdes o the Same Coin?', *European Papers* 2023, 1121–1130.
E. Beckett, *The North Atlantic Treaty, the Brussels Treaty and the Charter of the United Nations,* London, Stevens, 1950, 75 p.
E. Bjorge, *Domestic Application of the ECHR: Courts as Faithful Trustees,* Oxford, Oxford University Press, 2015, 264 p.
E. Brüel, 'Die juristische Bedeutung des Atlantikpaktes', *Archiv des Völkerrechts* 1954, 288–300.
E. David, *Droit des organisations internationales*, Brussels, Bruylant, 2016, 832 p.
E. De Brabandere, 'Belgian Courts and the Immunity of International Organizations', *International Organizations Law Review* 2013, 464–504.
E. Debuf, 'Tools to do the job: the ICRC's legal status, privileges and immunities', *International Review of the Red Cross* 2016, 319–344.
E. De Wet, 'The Relationship between the Security Council and Regional Organizations during Enforcement Action under Chapter VII of the United Nations Charter', *Nordic Journal of International Law* 2002, 1–37.
E. Furniss, 'De Gaulle's France and NATO: An Interpretation', *International Organization* 1961, 349–365.
E. Hallams, *The US and NATO Since 9/11: The Transatlantic Alliance Renewed*, London, Taylor & Francis, 2013, 176 p.
E. Hallams, *NATO Beyond 9/11*, London, Palgrave MacMillan, 2013, 374 p.
E. Herold, O. Schmitt and S. Sloan, 'NATO's Strategic Concept: responding to Russia and China', *Defence Studies* 2022, 558–563.
E. Klein and S. Schmahl, 'Die neue NATO-Strategie und ihre völkerrechtlichen Implikationen', *Recht und Politik* 1999, 198–209.
E. Lagrange, 'La catégorie organisation internationale' in E. Lagrange and J.-M. Sorel (eds.), *Droit des organisations internationales*, Issy-les-Moulineaux, LGDJ, 2013, 1248 p.
E. Lazarou and L. Tothova, 'Climate change considerations for EU security and defence policy', *European Parliamentary Research Service Briefing* 2022, 1–8.
E. Lazarou, L. Tothova, 'Implementation of the common foreign and security policy (CFSP)', *European Parliament Research Service At-A-Glance-Note* 2022, 1–2.
E. Lübkemeier, 'NATO's Identity Crisis', *Bulletin of the Atomic Scientists* 1990, 30–33.
E. McIntyre, 'Weighted Voting in International Organizations', *International Organization* 1954, 484–497.
E. Perot, 'The art of commitments: NATO, the EU and the interplay between law and politics within Europe's collective defence architecture', *European Security* 2019, 40–65.
E. Posner and A. Sykes, 'Voting Rules in International Organizations', *Chicago Journal of International Law* 2014, 195–228.
E. Ramirez, 'The New NATO Strategic Concept: A Vision From Spain', *Revista Unisci* 2010, 22–32.
E. Reid, *Time of Fear and Hope: the Making of the North Atlantic Treaty,* Toronto, McClelland and Steward, 1977, 315 p.

E. Roucounas, 'Practice as a relevant factor for the responsibility of international organizations' in M. Ragazzi (ed.), *Responsibility of International Organizations: Essays in Memory of Sir Ian Brownlie,* Boston, Nijhoff, 2013, 159–171.
E. Shuckburgh, 'Political Consultation' in X. (ed.), *NATO Letter: Ten Years of Atlantic Cooperation,* 1959, 10–12.
E. Stein and D. Carreau, 'Law and Peaceful Change in a Subsystem: Withdrawal of France from the North Atlantic Treaty Organization', *The American Journal of International Law* 1986, 577–640.
E. Sullivan, 'Trump Questions the Core of NATO: Mutual Defense, Including Montenegro', *New York Times* 18 July 2018.
E. Suy, 'Rôle et signification du consensus dans le processes législatif des Nations Unies' in M. Boisard and E. Chossudovsky (eds.), *Multilateral Diplomacy,* Alphen aan den Rijn, Kluwer Law International, 1998, 490 p.
E. Suy, *Les actes juridiques unilatéraux en droit international public,* Paris, Pedone, 1962, 290 p.
E. Terzuolo, *NATO and Weapons of Mass Destruction: Regional Alliance, Global Threats,* Abingdon, Routledge, 2005, 264 p.
E. Ustor, *Decision-making in the Council for Mutual Economic Assistance,* Leiden, Martinus Nijhoff Publishers, 1971, 163–295.
E. Zoller, *Bonne Foi en Droit International Public,* Paris, Pedone, 1977, 392 p.
F. Beer, *Integration and Disintegration in NATO: Processes of Alliance Cohesion and Prospects for Atlantic Community,* Ohio, Ohio State University Press, 1969, 330 p.
F. Carr and K. Ifantis, *NATO in the New European Order,* London, Palgrave MacMillan, 1996, 178 p.
F. Delon, 'La concertation entre les membres permanents du Conseil de sécurité', *Annuaire français de droit international* 1993, 53–64.
F. Dopagne, 'Bruxelles et ses organisations internationales. Notes sur la politique de siège de la Belgique', *Journal des Tribunaux* 2012, 185–192.
F. Fabbrini, 'Do NATO Obligations Trump European Budgetary Constraints?', *Harvard National Security Journal* 2018, 121–129.
F. Hamzeh, 'Agreements in Simplified Form – Modern Perspective', *British Yearbook of International Law* 1968, 179–189.
F. Kirgis, 'NATO Consultations as a Component of National Decisionmaking', *The American Journal of International Law* 1979, 372–406.
F. Morgenstern, *Legal Problems of International Organizations,* Cambridge, Grotius, 1986, 147 p.
F. Scharpf, *Governing in Europe: Effective and Democratic?* Oxford, Oxford Univeristy Press, 1999, 252 p.
F. Scharpf, 'Interdepence and democratic legitimation', *Max Planck Institute for the Study of Societies Working Paper* 1998, 1–19.
F. Seyersted, *Objective International Personality of Intergovernmental Organizations,* Copenhagen, Krohns Bogtrykkeri, 1964, 112 p.
F. Wilcox and T. Kalijarvi, 'The Organizational Framework of the North Atlantic Treaty', *American Journal of International Law* 1949, 155–161.
F. Zeidler, *Der Austritt und Ausschluß von Mitgliedern aus den Sonderorganisationen der Vereinten Nationen,* Berlin, Peter Lang Publishing, 1990, 318 p.

G. Danneman, 'Comparative Law: Study of Similarities or Differences?' in M. Reimann and R. Zimmermann (eds.), *The Oxford Handbook of Comparative Law*, Oxford, Oxford University Press, 2006, 391–421.

G. De Freitas, *The North Atlantic Treaty Organization Parliamentarians' Conference 1955–1959*, London, The Hansard Society for Parliamentary Government, 1960, 3–7.

G. Fox and B. Roth, *Democracy and International Law*, Cheltenham, Edward Elgar, 2020, 327–352.

G. Gilbert, 'La jurisprudence de la Commission de recours de l'Organisation du Traité de l'Atlantique Nord de 1968 à 1972', *Annuaire français de droit international* 1968, 392–412.

G. Guest, E. Namey and K. McKenna, 'How Many Focus Group Are Enough? Building an Evidence Base for Nonprobability Sample Sizes', *Field Methods* 2016, 1–22.

G. Hernández, *International Law*, Oxford, Oxford University Press, 2019, 720 p.

G. Kostakos, 'The Southern Flank: Italy, Greece, Turkey' in A. Schnabel and R. Thakur (eds.), *Kosovo and the challenge of humanitarian intervention*, New York, UN University Press, 2000, 536 p.

G. Martin, 'The 1967 withdrawal from NATO – a cornerstone of de Gaulle's grand strategy?', *Journal of Tansatlantic Studies* 2011, 232–243.

G. Meier, 'Das Recht der Internationaler Organisationen zur Schaffung unf Bevollmachtigung einiger Organe', *Archiv des Völkerrechts* 1964/65, 14–33.

G. Rosen and K. Raube, 'Influence beyond formal powers: the parliamentarisation of European Union security policy', *The British Journal of Politics and International Relations* 2018, 69–83.

G. Schwarzenberger, 'The North Atlantic Pact', *Western Political Quarterly* 1949, 309–317.

G. Tunkin, 'The Role and resolutions of international organisations in creating norms of international law' in W. Butler (ed.), *International law and the international system*, Dordrecht, Nijhoff, 1987, 5–19.

G. Ulfstein and H. Christiansen, 'The Legality of the NATO bombing in Libya', *International and Comparative Law Quarterly* 2013, 159–171.

G. Ulfstein, 'Les activités normatives de l'organisation internationale', in E. Lagrange and J.-M. Sorel (eds.), *Droit des organisations internationales*, Issy-les-Moulineaux, LGDJ, 2013, 737–755.

G. Vandersanden, 'La Commission de Recours de l'Organisation du Traité de l'Atlantique Nord: son fonctionnement à la lumière de sa jurisprudence', *Revue Belge de Droit Internationale* 1974, 322–332.

G. von Molkte, 'Accession of new members to the Alliance: What are the next steps?', *NATO Review* 1997, 4–9.

G. Warg, 'Von Verteidigung zu kollektiver Sicherheit. Der NATO-Vertrag auf Rädern' in H. Schiedermair and B. Kempen (eds.), *Kölner Schriften zu Recht und Staat*, Frankfurt am Main, 2004, 324 p.

H. Adam, *Les organismes internationaux spécialisés*, Paris, L.D.G.J., 1992, 907 p.

H. Aust, 'Analysis of Parliamentary Group of the PDS/Die Linke in the German Federal Parliament v Federal Government, 2 Be 2/07', *ILDC* 20070, A1-A6.

H. Aust, *Modern Treaty Law and Practice*, Cambridge, Cambridge University Press, 2000, 520 p.

H. Ballreich, 'Wesen und Wirkung des Konsens im Völkerrecht' in R. Bernard, W. Geck, G. Jaenicke et al. (eds.), *Völkerrecht als Rechtsordnung, Internationale Gerichtsbarkeit, Menschenrechte, Festschrift für Hermann Mosler*, Berlin, Heidelberg, Springer, 1983, 1060 p.

H. Blatt, 'Rechtsschütz gegen die Vereinten Nationen. Internationale Immunitäten und die Streitbeilegung nach Section 29 des Übereinkommens über die Vorrechte und Immunitäten der Vereinten Nationen', *Archiv des Völkerrechts* 2007, 84–114.

H. Cassan, 'Le consensus dans la pratique des Nations Unies', *Annuaire français de droit international* 1974, 456–485.

H. Dellios, 'While government backs NATO, Greek hearts go with Serbs', *Chicago Tribune* 1999, 1–2.

H. Kötz and K. Zweigert, *Introduction to Comparative Law*, Oxford, Clarendon, 1998, 744 p.

H. Moinuddin, *Die Organisation der Islamischen Konferenz als Forum politischer und wirtschaftlicher Kooperation*, Bochum, Studienverlag Brookmeyer, 1984, 214 p.

H. Sauer, 'Die NATO und das Verfassungsrecht: neues Konzept – alte Fragen', *Zeitschrift für ausländisches öffentliches Recht und Völkerrecht* 2002, 317–336.

H. Schermers, 'Les bases juridiques de l'action des organisations internationales' in R. Dupuy (ed.), *Manuel sur les organisations internationales*, Dordrecht, Boston, London, Martinus Nijhoff, 1998, 967 p.

H. Schermers, 'Internationaal institutioneel recht', *Internationale Spectator* 1963, 292–304.

H. Wegener, 'The Transformed Alliance', *NATO Review* 1990, 1–2.

I. Atanassova, *The impact of ethnic issues on the security of South Eastern Europe*, Brussels, Report Commissioned by the NATO Office of Information and Press, 1999, 68 p.

I. Black, 'NATO crisis over veto on plans to defend Turkey', *The Guardian* 11 February 2003, 1–2.

I. Brownlie and G. Goodwin, 'Opinion on the Inter-Parliamentary Union', *IPU Archives* 31 May 1999, 27 p.

I. Dekker and R. Wessel, 'Identities of States in International Organizations', *International Organizations Law Review* 2015, 293–318.

I. Dekker and R. Wessel, 'Governance by International Organizations: Rethinking the Normative Force of International Decisions' in I. Dekker and W. Werner (eds.), *Governance and International Legal Theory*, Leiden, Nijhoff, 2004, 215–236.

I. Dekker and E. Myjer, 'Air Strikes on Bosnian Positions: Is NATO Also Legally the Proper Instrument of the UN?', *Leiden Journal of International Law* 1996, 411–416.

I. Detter, 'The effect of resolutions of international organisations' in J. Makarczyk (ed.), *Theory of international law at the threshold of the 21st century: essays in honour of K. Skubiszewski*, The Hague, Kluwer, 1996, 107–134.

I. Novotny and A. Boeva, 'Scope and Historical Developments of Article 6', *Emory International Law Review* 2019, 121–134.

I. Rossi, *Legal Status of Non-governmental Organizations in International Law*, doctoral dissertation, Leuven, KU Leuven, Faculty of Law, 2009, 427 p.

I. Seidl-Hohenveldern and G. Loibl, *Das Recht der Internationalen Organisationen, einschiesslich der Supranationalen Gemeinschaften*, Keulen, Heymann, 2000, 324 p.

I. Seidl-Hohenveldern, 'Gemeinsame zwischenstatliche Unternehmen' in F. Baer-Kaupert, G. Leistner and H. Schwaiger (eds.), *Liber Amicorum Bernhardt C.H. Aubin*, Kehl am Rhein, Engel, 1979, 193–203.

I. Sinclair, 'Estoppel and Acquiescence' in V. Lowe and M. Fitzmaurice (eds.), *Fifty Years of the International Court of Justice: Essays in Honour of Sir Robert Jennings*, Cambridge, Cambridge University Press, 1996, 104–120.

J. Barale, 'L'acquiescement dans la jurisprudence internationale', *Annuaire français de droit international* 1965, 389–427.

J. Becker, M. Duda and D. Lute, 'From context to concept: history and strategic environment for NATO's 2022 strategic concept', *Defence Studies* 2022, 489–496.

J. Becker, *Die Anwendbarkeit der Theorie von den implied power sim Recht der Europäischen Gemeinschaften*, doctoral dissertation, Münster, University of Münster, Faculty of Law, 1976, 129 p.

J. Bolton, 'Is There Really Law in International Affairs', *Transnational Law and Contemporary Problems* 2000, 2–48.

J. Burton, 'NATO's cyber defence: strategic challenges and institutional adaptation', *Defence Studies* 2015, 297–319.

J. de Scheffer, speech by NATO Secretary General Jaap Hoop de Scheffer at the Albanian parliament, available online at www.nato.int/cps/fr/natohq/opinions_22479.htm (last accessed January 2025).

J. Duffar, *Contribution à l'étude des privilèges et immunités des organisations internationales*, Paris, L.G.D.J., 1982, 391 p.

J.C.S., 'Problèmes juridiques de l'Organisation du Traité de l'Atlantique Nord', *Politique Étrangère* 1955, 689–706.

J. Crawford, *Brownlie's Principles of Public International Law*, Oxford, Oxford University Press, 2012, 888 p.

J. D'Aspremont and D. Ventura, 'La composition des organes et le processus décisionnel' in E. Lagrange and J.-M. Sorel (eds.), *Droit des organisations internationales*, Issy-les-Moulineaux, LGDJ, 2013, 425–436.

J. Castañeda, 'Valeur juridique des resolutions des Nations Unies', *Recueil des Cours de l'Académie de Droit International de La Haye* 1970, 205–216.

J. De Conick, 'The Functional Method of Comparative Law: Quo Vadis?', *Rabels Zeitschrift für ausländisches und internationales Privatrecht* 2010, 318–350.

J. Dempsey, 'Allies' Broken Silence over Turkey Brings Crisis of Credibility for NATO', *Financial Times* 11 February 2003, 1–6.

J. Dryzek, *Discursive Democracy: Politics, Policy, and Political Science*, Cambridge, Cambridge University Press, 1990, 242 p.

J. Dutheil de la Rochere, 'Article 7' in J. Cot and A. Pellet (eds.), *La Charte des Nations Unies*, Paris, Economica, 1991, 1571 p.

J. Eichler, *NATO's Expansion after the Cold War: Geopolitics and Impacts for International Security*, Cham, Springer International, 2021, 188 p.

J.-L. Fagnart, 'L'Immunité de juridiction des organisations internationales' in X. (eds.), *Mélanges Jacques van Compernolle*, Brussels, Bruylant, 2004, 900 p.

J. Gaddis, 'History, grand strategy and NATO enlargement', *Global Politics and Strategy* 1998, 145–151.
J. Gomula, 'The International Court of Justice and Administrative Tribunals of International Organizations', *Michigan Journal of International Law* 1991, 83–121.
J. Goldgeier and J. Shifrinson, 'Evaluating NATO enlargement: scholarly debates, policy implications and roads not taken', *International Politics* 2020, 291–321.
J. Habermas, *Between Facts and Norms: Contributions to a Discourse Theory*, London, Polity, 1996, 631 p.
J. Harned, 'Atlantic Assembly – a Genesis', *Journal of Common Market Studies* 1964, 183–189.
J. Hovey, *The Superparliaments: Interparliamentary Consultation and Atlantic Cooperation*, New York, Washington, London, Frederick A. Praeger Publishers, 1967, 202 p.
J. Husa, 'Research Designs of Comparative Law – Methodology or Heuristics' in M. Adams and D. Heirbaut (eds.), *The Method and Culture of Comparative Law*, Oxford, Hart Publishing, 2014, 328 p.
J. Jeffrey, 'Turkey: NATO's Odd Man Out', *Just Security* 9 July 2018, 1–2.
J. Klabbers, *An Introduction to International Institutional Law*, Cambridge, Cambridge University Press, 2020, 438 p.
J. Klabbers, *The Concept of Treaty in International Law*, The Hague, Kluwer Law International, 1996, 307 p.
J. Kriendler, 'NATO's changing role – opportunities and constraints for peacekeeping', *NATO Review* 1993, 16–23.
J. Liu, 'Accession Protocols: Legal Status in the WTO Legal System', *Journal of World Trade* 2014, 751–772.
J. Luns, 'Introduction' in J. Godson (ed.), *Transatlantic crisis: Europe and America in the 70s*, London, Alcove Press, 1974, 148 p.
J. Makarczyk, 'The International Court of Justice on the Implied Powers of International Organizations', in J. Makarczyk (ed.), *Essays in International Law in Honour of Judge Manfred Lachs*, The Hague, Brill Nijhoff, 1984, 760 p.
J. Makarczyk, 'Legal Basis for Suspension and Expulsion of a State from an International Organization', *German Yearbook of International Law* 1982, 476–489.
J. Makarczyk, 'La creation des organes subsidiaires et les statuts des organisations internationales', *Polish Yearbook of International Law* 1972–1973, 183–198.
J. Pauwelyn, 'Is it International Law or Not and Does it Even Matter?' in J. Pauwelyn, R. Wessel and J. Wouters (eds.), *Informal International Lawmaking*, Oxford, Oxford University Press, 2012, 580 p.
J. Marcus, 'Turkey signs deal to get Russian S-400 air defence missiles', *BBC News* 12 September 2017, available online at www.bbc.com/news/world-europe-41237812 (last accessed January 2025).
J. Maxwell, *Qualitative Research Design: an Interactive Approach*, London, SAGE, 2013, 232 p.
J. Olsen, 'Understanding NATO', *The RUSI Journal* 2020, 60–72.
J. Rosa and C. Johnson, 'Contextualizing reliability and validity in qualitative research: toward more rigorous and trustworthy qualitative social science in leisure research', *Journal of Leisure Research* 2020, 432–451.

J. Rehrl, 'Invoking the EU's Mutual Assistance Clause. What it says, what it means', *Egmont Paper* 2015, 1–3.

J. Ringsmose and S. Rynning, *NATO's New Strategic Concept: A Comprehensive Assessment,* Copenhagen, DIIS Report, 2011, 196 p.

J. Roper, 'NATO's new role in crisis management', *The International Spectator* 1999, 51–61.

J. Salmon, *Dictionnaire de droit international public,* Brussels, Bruylant, 2001, 1200 p.

J. Salmon, 'Les accords non formalisés ou 'solo consensu'', *Annuaire français de droit international* 1999, 1–28.

J. Seroka, 'Security Considerations in the Western Balkans: NATO's evolution and expansion', *East European Quarterly* 2007, 25–38.

J. Shea, 'NATO at full stretch', *International Politics Reviews* 2016, 36–43.

J. Simon, 'The next round of NATO Enlargement', *Strategic Forum* 2000, 1–4.

J. Smith, *Defence Logistics: Enabling and Sustaining Successful Military Operations,* London, Kogan Page Limited, 2018, 384 p.

J. Steffek, 'The Legitimation of International Governance: A Discourse Approach', *European Journal of International Relations* 2003, 249–275.

J. Stoltenberg, Speech by NATO Secretary General Jens Stoltenberg at the online Summit of the International Crimea Platform, 23 August 2022, text available at www.nato.int/cps/en/natohq/opinions_198268.htm (last accessed January 2025).

J. Stoltenberg, Remarks by NATO Secretary General Jens Stoltenberg on launching #NATO2030 – Strengthening the Alliance in an increasingly competitive world, 8 June 2020, available online at www.nato.int/cps/fr/natohq/opinions_176197.htm (last accessed January 2025).

J. Tallberg and M. Zürn, 'The legitimacy and legitimation of international organizations: introduction and framework', *The Review of International Organizations* 2019, 581–606.

J. Varwick and W. Woyke, 'NATO 2000, Transatlantische Sicherheit im Wandel' in K. Schubert and G. Wewer (eds.), *Analysen, Politik – Geselschaft, Wirtschaft*, Opladen, 1999, 262 p.

J. Velu, 'Les effets directs des instruments internationaux en matière de droits de l'homme', *BTIR* 1980, 293–316.

J. Verhoeven, 'Traités mixtes, assentiments partiels ou rétroactifs et règles non écrites', *RCJB* 2002, 396–397.

J. Vranken, 'Algemeen Deel. Een synthese' in Mr. C. Assers (ed.), *Handleiding tot de beoefening van het Nederlands Burgerlijk Recht,* Deventer, Kluwer, 2014, 840.

J. Wouters, C. Ryngaert, T. Ruys and G. De Baere, *International Law from a European Perspective,* Oxford, Oxford University Press, 2018, 1136 p.

J. Wouters, *Internationaal Recht in Kort Bestek*, Antwerpen, Intersentia, 2018, 490 p.

K. Honkanen, 'The Influence of Small States on NATO Decision-Making: the Membership Experiences of Denmark, Norway, Hungary and the Czech Republic', *Swedish Defence Research Agency Paper* 2002, 141 p.

K. Ifantis, 'NATO's Strategic Direction after Riga: NATO's Post-Cold War Adaption', *International Law Journal* 2007, 577–588.

K. Ipsen, *Völkerrecht,* München, Verlag C.H. Beck, 2004, 1404 p.

K. Kamp, 'Das neue Strategische Konzept der NATO. Entwicklung und Perspektiven', *Aus Politik und Zeitgeschichte* 1999.

K. Klaiber, 'The Membership Action Plan: Keeping NATO's door open', *NATO Review* 1999, 23–25.

K. Lemmens, 'Comparative Law as an act of modesty: a pragmatic and realistic approach to comparative legal scholarship' in M. Adams and J. Bomhoff (eds.), *Practice and Theory in Comparative Law*, Cambridge, Cambridge University Press, 2012, 302–326.

K. Lindsay, *Towards a European Parliament*, Strasbourg, Council of Europe Publishing, 1958, 164 p.

K. Magliveras, *Exclusion from Participation in International Organisations*, The Hague, Kluwer Law International, 1999, 298 p.

K. Pomorska and R. Wessel, 'Qualified Majority Voting in CFSP: A Solution to the Wrong Problem?', *European Foreign Affairs Review* 2021, 351–358.

K. Skubiszewski, 'Remarks on the Interpretation of the United Nations Charter', in R. Bernhardt et al. (eds.), *Völkerrecht als Rechtsordung, Internationale Gerichtsbarkeit, Mensenrechte, Festschrift für Hermann Mosler*, Berlin, Heidelberg, Springer-Verlag, 1983, 1057 p.

K. Skubiszewski, 'International Legislation' in R. Bindschedler, T. Buergenthal, H. Strebel et al. (eds.), *International Organizations in General Universal International Organizations and Cooperation*, Encyclopedia of Public International Law, Amsterdam, Elsevier, 1983, 494 p.

K. Vegh, 'The North Atlantic Treaty and its Relationship to Other Engagements of Its Parties: A Commentary on Article 8', *Emory International Law Review* 2019, 135–148.

K. Widdows, 'What is an Agreement in International Law?', *British Yearbook of International Law* 1979, 117–149.

L. Arditi, 'The Role of Practice in International Organizations: the Case of Government Recognition by the International Monetary Fund', *International Organizations Law Review* 2020, 531–585.

L. Burgorgue-Larsen, 'La structure institutionelle de l'organisation internationale' in E. Langrange and J.-M. Sorel (eds.), *Droit des organisations internationales*, Issy-les-Moulineaux, LGDJ, 2013, 375–401.

L. De Brabander and G. Spriet, *Als de NAVO de passie preekt*, Berchem, EPO, 2009, 344 p.

L. Diaz Gonzáles (Special Rapporteur), Second Report by the Special Rapporteur on the relations between states and international organizations, *Yearbook of the ILC*, vol. II, Part I, 1985, 7 p.

L. Fierens, *Grenzen aan de toepassing van de implied powers doctrine in het recht van de internationale organisaties: tussen autonomie en accountability van de internationale organisatie*, thesis, Leuven, KU Leuven, Faculty of Law, 2012, 114 p.

L. Hartley, 'The North Atlantic Assembly', *Atlantic Community Quarterly* 1975–1976, 486–491.

L. Ismay, NATO: *The first five years 1949–1954*, Brussels, 1955, 283 p.

L. Kaplan, *NATO before the Korean War: April 1949-June 1950*, Kent, Kent University State Press, 2013, 232 p.

L. Kaplan, *The Long Entanglement: NATO's First Fifty Years*, Santa Barbara, Praeger Security International, 1999, 280 p.
L. Kaplan, *The United States and NATO, The Formative Years*, Lexington, The University Press of Kentucky, 1984, 288 p.
L. Kestemont, *Handbook on Legal Methodology: From Objective to Method*, Cambridge, Intersentia, 2018, 98 p.
L. Martinez Sanseroni, 'Consentiemento del Estado y Organizaciones Internacionales', *Revista Española de Derecho Internacional* 1985, 41–65.
L. Michel, 'NATO Decisionmaking: Au Revoir to the Consensus Rule', *Strategic Forum* 2013, 1–8.
L. Michel, 'NATO Decisionmaking: How the "Consensus Rule" Works', *Croatian International Relations Review* 2006, 7–14.
L. Philips, 'Constitutional Revision in the Specialized Agencies', *American Journal of International Law* 1968, 654–678.
L. Risso, 'I am the Servant of the Council: Lord Ismay and the Making of the NATO International Staff', *Contemporary European History* 2019, 342–357.
L. Schaus, 'Le Conseil de l'Atlantique Nord, son fondement et ses structures, ses compétences et ses missions', *Chronique De Politique Etrangère* 1974, 337–386.
L. Tinel, *Should I stay or should I go? An analysis of the NATO decision to withdraw from Afghanistan based on the theoretical framework of international responsibility of international organizations*, thesis, Leuven, KU Leuven, Faculty of Law, 2023, 75 p.
L. Traugutt, 'Is Consensus Still Necessary Within NATO?', *NATO Defense College Research Paper* 2016, 1–16.
M. Adams, 'Wat de rechtsvergelijking vermag', *Ars Aequi* 2011, 252–256.
M. Bettati and P.M Dupuy, *Les ONG et le Droit International,* Paris, Economica, 1986, 318 p.
M. Brenner, *NATO and Collective Security*, London, Palgrave MacMillan, 1998, 317 p.
M. Brinkmann, 'Einstimmigkeit und Konsensverfahren: Zur Notwendigkeit und Entwicklung des konsensualen Abstimmungsverfahrens in der Generalversammlung', *Vereinte Nationen: German Review of the United Nations* 1979, 201–205.
M. DeJonckheere and L. Vaughn, 'Semistructured interviewing in primary care research: a balance of relationship and rigour', *BMJ Journal* 2019, 1–8.
M. Fierke and A. Wiener, 'Constructing Institional Interests: EU and NATO enlargement', *Journal of European Public Policy* 1999, 721–742.
M. Goldberg, 'Mirage of Defense: Reexamining Article Five of the North Atlantic Treaty After the Terrorist Attacks on the United States', *Boston College International and Comparative Law Review* 2003, 77–93.
M. Hodun, *Doctrine of Implied Powers as a Judicial Tool to Build Federal Polities: Comparative Study on the Doctrine of Implied powers in the EU and the United States of America*, doctoral dissertation, Reykjavik, Reykjavik University, Faculty of Law, 2015, 320 p.
M. Kacic, 'Commentary on Articles 2 and 3 of the Washington Treaty', *Emory International Law Review* 2019, 53–70.
M. Krajewski, 'Democratic Governance as an Emerging Principle of International Economic Law', *Society of International Economic law Inaugural Conference Paper* 2008, 1–17.

M. Lee, 'US Sanctions NATO ally Turkey over purchase of Russian missile defense system', *Defense News* 14 December 2020, available online at www.defensenews.com/pentagon/2020/12/14/us-sanctions-nato-ally-turkey-over-purchase-of-russian-missile-defense-system/ (last accessed January 2025).

M. Legge, 'The Making of NATO's New Strategy', *NATO Review* 1991, 9–14.

M. Naderifar, H. Holi and F. Ghaljaie, 'Snowball Sampling: A Purposeful Method of Sampling in Qualitative Research', *Strides in Development of Medical Education* 2017, 1–7.

M. Paris, 'The Comparative Method in Legal Research: the Art of Justifying Choices' in L. Cahillane and J. Schweppe (eds.), *Legal Research Methods: Principles and Practicalities*, London, Clarus Press, 2016, 226 p.

M. Ruffert and C. Walter, *Institutionalisiertes Völkerrecht*, München, C.H. Beck, 2009, 276 p.

M. Rühle, 'Crisis management in NATO', *European Security* 1993, 491–501.

M. Salvin, 'The North Atlantic Pact: International Conciliation', Whitefish, Literary Licensing, 2013, 90 p.

M. Shaw, *International Law*, Cambridge, Cambridge University Press, 2017, 1118 p.

M. Schmitt, 'The North Atlantic Alliance and Collective Defense at 70: Confession and Response Revisited', *Emory International Law Review* 2019, 85–120.

M. Smith, *NATO in the First Decade after the Cold War*, Dordrecht, Kluwer, 2000, 192 p.

M. Suchman, 'Managing Legitimacy: Strategic and Institutional Approached', *The Academy of Management Review* 1995, 571–610.

M. Taddeo and L. Glorioso, *Ethics and Policies for Cyber Operations: a NATO Cooperative Cyber Defence Centre of Excellence Initiative*, Berlin, Springer, 2017, 269 p.

M. Virally, 'Sources of International Law: Unilateral Acts of International Organisations' in M. Bedjaoui (ed.), *International Law: Achievements and Prospects*, Dordrecht, Nijhoff, 1991, 243–251.

M. Virally, 'La valeur juridique des recommandations des organisations internationales', *Annuaire français de droit international* 1956, 66–96.

M. Webber and A. Hyde-Price, *Theorising NATO: new perspectives on the Atlantic Alliance*, Abingdon, Routledge, 2016, 208 p.

M. Wiegandt, 'Germany's International Integration: The Rulings of the German Federal Constitutional Court on the Maastricht Treaty and the Out-of-Area Deployment of German Troops', *American University Journal of International Law and Policy* 1995, 889–916.

M. Yasseen, 'L'interprétation des traités d'après la Convention de Vienne sur le droit des traités', *Recueil des Cours de l'Académie de Droit International de La Haye* 1976-III, 1–114.

M. Zapolskis, '1999 and 2010 NATO Strategic Concepts: A Comparative Analysis', *Lithuanian Annual Strategic Review* 2012, 35–56.

N. Blokker, 'Constituent Instruments' in J. Cogan, I. Hurd and I. Johnstone (eds.), *The Oxford Handbook of International Organizations*, Oxford, Oxford University Press, 2016, 1192 p.

N. Blokker, 'International Organizations and their Members', *International Organizations Law Review* 2004, 139–161.

N. Blokker and H. Schermers, *International Institutional Law*, Leiden, Boston, Brill Nijhoff, 2018, 1366 p.
N. Blokker, 'Beyond Dili: on the Powers and Practice of International Organizations' in G. Kreijen et al. (eds.), *State, Sovereignty and International Governance*' Oxford, Oxford University Press, 2018, 298–322.
N. Novaky, 'Qualified Majority Voting in EU Foreign Policy: Make It So', *Wilfried Martens Centre Paper* 2021, 1–26.
N. Singh, *Termination of Membership*, London, Stevens & Sons, 1958, 209 p.
N. White, 'Decision-making' in J. Klabbers and A. Wallendahl (eds.), *Research Handbook on the Law of International Organizations*, Cheltenham, Edward Elgar, 2011, 544 p.
O. Costa, C. Dri and S. Stavridis, *Parliamentary dimensions of regionalization and globalization: the role of interparliamentary institutions*, Basingstoke, Palgrave Macmillan, 2013, 286 p.
O. Dursun-Özkanca, 'The Turkish Veto over the EU–NATO Security Exchange' in O. Dursun-Özkanca (ed.), *Turkey- West Relations: The Politics of Intra-alliance Opposition*, Cambridge, Cambridge University Press, 2019, 214 p.
O. Nikolov and S. Veeravalli, 'Implications of Climate Change and Disasters on Military Activities' in X. (ed), *Building Resiliency and Mitigating Vulnerability in the Balkan Region*, Conference proceedings, 2017 (part of the NATO Science for Peace and Security Series C), 185 p.
O. Schachter, 'The Twilight Existence of Nonbinding International Agreements', *American Journal of International Law* 1977, 296–304.
P. Bekker, *The Legal Position of Intergovernmental Organizations – A Functional Necessity Analysis of Their Legal Status and Immunities*, 's-Gravenhage, Nijhoff, 1994, 265 p.
P. Borcier, *The Assembly of the Western European Union – Its contribution to the defence and building of Europe since 1955*, Paris, Office of the Clerk of the Assembly of the WEU, 1975, 38 p.
P. Buteux, *The Politics of Nuclear Consultation in NATO 1965–1980*, Cambridge, Cambridge University Press, 1983, 308 p.
P. Cahier, *Le droit diplomatique contemporain*, Geneva, Droz, 1962, 544 p.
P. Cornish, 'A Strategic Concept for the Twenty-first Century', *Defense Analysis* 1999, 241–260.
P. Cot and A. Pellet, *La Charte des Nations Unies*, Paris, Economica, 1985, 1553 p.
P. Gallis, *NATO's Decision-Making Procedure – CRS Report to Congress*, Washington D.C., Congressional Research Service, 2003, 1–6.
P. Gautier, *Essai sur la definition des traités entres Etats. La pratique de la Belgique aux confins du droit des traités*, Brussels, Bruylant, 1993, 619 p.
P. Gordon, 'The Crisis in the Alliance', *Brookings Institution Report* 2003, 1–4.
P. Klein, 'Les compétences et pouvoirs de l'organisation international' in E. Lagrange and J.-M. Sorel (eds.), *Droit des organisations internationales*, Issy-les-Moulineaux, LGDJ, 2013, 714–734.
P. Klein, *La responsabilité des organisations internationales dans les ordres juridiques internes et en droit des gens*, Brussel, Bruylant, 1998, 673 p.
P. Lellouche, 'Foreword' in X. (ed.), *NATO Parliamentary Assembly 1955–2005,* NATO Press, Brussels, 10–16.

P. Necas, P. Terem and M. Keleman, 'From Washington to Lisbon: A new NATO strategic concept', *Obrana a strategie* 2009, 49–60.

P. Ochmannova, 'NATO: Evolution and Legal Framework for the Conduct of Operations', *NATO Legal Gazette* 2016, 31–38.

P. Potter, 'The Proposed North Atlantic Pact', *World Affairs* 1949, 5–6.

P. Reuter, *Droit international public*, Paris, P.U.F., 1993, 595 p.

P. Reuter, 'Quelques réflexions sur la notion de "pratique internationale" spécialement en matière d'organisations internationales', *Studi in Onore di Giuseppe Sperduti* 1984, 189–207.

P. Sands, 'Article 39 – Convention de Vienne de 1969' in O. Corten and P. Klein (eds.), *Commentaire article par article des Conventions de Vienne de 1969 et 1986 sur le droit des traités*, Brussels, Bruylant, 2006, 3024.

P. Sands and P. Klein, *Bowett's Law of International Institutions*, London, Sweet & Maxwell, 2009, 610 p.

P. Shishkin, 'Head of NATO admits standoff has hurt Alliance', *Wall Street Journal* 2003.

P. Spaak, *Why NATO?*, Middlesex, Penguin Books, 1959, 62 p.

R. Asmus, *Opening NATO's Door: how the Alliance remade itself for a New Era*, New York, Columbia University Press, 2004, 415 p.

R. Bernhardt, 'Ultra Vires activities of International Organisations' in J. Makarczyck (ed.), *Theory of International Law at the Threshold of the 21st Century: Essays in Honour of Krzysztof Skubiszewski*, The Hague, Kluwer, 1996, 1008 p.

R. Bernhardt, *Encyclopedia of Public International Law*, Amsterdam, New York, Oxford, Elsevier, 1983, 559 p.

R. Czulda, 'NATO Towards the Challenges of A Contemporary World', *International Relations Research Institute Paper* 2013, 39–45.

R. Dahl, 'What Political Institutions Does Large-Scale Democracy Require', *Political Science Quarterly* 2005, 187–197.

R. Dahl, 'Can International Organizations be Democratic? A Skeptic's View' in I. Shapiro and C. Hacker-Cordon (eds.), *Democracy's Edges*, Cambridge, Cambridge University Press, 1999, 19–36.

R. Gardiner, *Treaty Interpretation*, Oxford, Oxford University Press, 2008, 400 p.

R. Higgins, *Problems and Process – International Law and How we Use It*, Oxford, Oxford University Press, 1994.

R. Jordan, *The NATO international staff/secretariat 1952–1957: a study in international administration*, London, Oxford University Press, 1967, 304 p.

R. Hunter, 'Enlargement: part of a strategy for projecting stability into Central Europe', *NATO Review* 1995, 3–8.

R. Kolb, *The Law of Treaties*, Cheltenham, Edward Elgar, 2016, 296 p.

R. McCalla, 'NATO's persistence after the Cold War', *International Organization* 1996, 445–475.

R. Menotti, 'US Policy and NATO enlargement: Clinton's unspoken agenda', *International Politics* 1999, 235–271.

R. Moore, *NATO's new mission: projecting stability in a post-Cold War world*, London, Praeger Security International, 2007, 224 p.

R. Van Gestel and J. Vranken, 'Rechtswetenschappelijke artikelen', *Nederlands Juristenblad* 2007, 1448–1461.

R. Wilde, 'Enhancing Accountability at the International Level: The Tension Between International Organization and Member State Responsibility and the Underlying Issues at Stake', *ILSA Journal of International and Comparative Law* 2006, 395–415.

R. Wessel and V. Szep, 'The implementation of Article 31 of the Treaty on European Union and the use of Qualified Majority Voting: Towards a more effective Common Foreign and Security Policy?', Brussels, Policy Department for Citizens' Rights and Constitutional Affairs, Directorate-General for Internal Policies, European Parliament, 2022.

R. Wessel et. al., 'The future of EU Foreign, Security and Defence Policy: Assessing legal options for improvement', *European Law Journal* 2021, 371–390.

R. Wessel, 'Lex Imperfecta: Law and Integration in European Foreign and Security Policy', *European Papers* 2016, 439–468.

R. Wessel, 'Reparation for Injuries Suffered in the Service of the United Nations' in C. Ryngaert, I. Dekker, R. Wessel and J. Wouters (eds.), *Judicial decisions on the law of international organizations*, 2016, 11–18.

R. Wessel and I. Dekker, 'Identities of States in International Organizations', *International Organizations Law Review* 2015, 293–318.

R. Zacklin, *The Amendment of the Constitutive Instruments of the UN and Specialized Agencies*, Leiden, A. W. Sijthoff, 1968, 216 p.

R. Ziegler and J. Baumgartner, 'Good Faith as a General Principle of (International) Law' in A. Mitchell, M. Sornarajah and T. Voon (eds.), *Good Faith and International Economic Law,* Oxford, Oxford University Press, 2015, 220 p.

S. Anghel and C. Cirlig, 'Activation of Article 42(7) TEU?', *European Parliament Research Service Briefing* 2016, 1–11.

S. Babst, 'Startschuss für die Diskussion über das neue Strategische Konzept. Ein Bericht über die Konferenz NATO's New Strategic Concept: Launching the Process', *Zeitschrift für Aussen- und Sicherheitspolitik* 2009, 501–504.

S. Bölingen, *Die Transformation der NATO im Spiegel der Vertragsentwicklung*, Saarbrücken, Akademiker Verlag, 2012, 116 p.

S. Bumgardner, 'Article 4 of the North Atlantic Treaty', *Emory International Law Review* 2019, 71–83.

S. Carney, *Allied Participation in Operation Iraqi Freedom*, Washington DC, Center of Military History, 2011, 139 p.

S. Charman and K. Williams, *The Parliamentarians' Role in the Alliance: The North Atlantic Assembly 1955–1980*, Suffolk, published by the North Atlantic Assembly, 1981, 226 p.

S. Schmahl and M. Breuer, *The Council of Europe: Its Law and Policies*, Oxford, Oxford University Press, 2017, 1080 p.

S. Clapp and A. Verhelst, 'A comparative analysis of Article 5 Washington Treaty (NATO) and Article 42(7) TEU (EU)', *European Parliament Research Service At-a-Glance Note* 2023, 1–2.

S. Clapp, 'Outcome of the Madrid NATO Summit', *European Parliament Research Service Briefing* 2022, 1–2.

S. Clapp, 'Russia's war on Ukraine: NATO response', *European Parliament Research Service Briefing* 2023, 1–2.

S. Fournier and S. Bumgardner, 'Article 5 of the North Atlantic Treaty: The Cornerstone of the Alliance', *NATO Legal Gazette* 2014, 17–30.

S. Freeman, 'Deliberative Democracy: A Sympathetic Comment', *Philosophy and Public Affairs* 2000, 371–418.

S. Gareis, G. Hauser and F. Kerni, *The European Union – A Global Actor?*, Opladen, Berlin, Toronto, Barbara Budrich Publishers, 2013, 450 p.

S. Hartin and A. Hoehn, *Risking NATO: testing the limits of the Alliance in Afghanistan*, Santa Monica, Rand Publishing, 2010, 108 p.

S. Hill, 'The Role of NATO's Legal Adviser' in A. Zidar and J.-P. Gauci (eds.), *The Role of Legal Advisers in International Law*, Leiden, Boston, Brill Nijhoff, 2016, 213–236.

S. Kaufman, 'Ethnic conflict and Eurasian security' in J. Sperling, S. Kay and S. Papacosma (eds.), *Limiting institutions? The challenge of Eurasian security governance*, Manchester, Manchester University Press, 306 p.

S. Kay, *NATO and the Future of European Security*, Maryland, Rowman & Littlefield, 1998.

S. Lunn, 'The Evolving Role of the NATO Parliamentary Assembly' in X. (ed.), *The NATO Parliamentary Assembly 1955-2005*, 210 p.

S. Lunn, 'The NATO Parliamentary Assembly', paper presented at the Seminar on the 'Parliamentary Dimension of the European Security and Defence Policy', The Hague, 14 May 2001.

S. Marschall, 'European parliaments in transnational organisations: Parliamentary cooperation beyond the European Union', *Stifting Politik und Wissenschaft Conference Paper* 2007.

S. Marks, 'What has Become of the Emerging Right to Democratic Governance?', *European Journal of International Law* 2011, 507–524.

S. Mayer, *NATO's Post-Cold War Politics: the Changing Provision of Security*, London, Palgrave Macmillan, 2014, 334 p.

S. Sloan, *Permanent Alliance? NATO and the Transatlantic Bargain from Truman to Obama*, London, Continuum, 2010, 208 p.

S. Sloan, 'Negotiating Article 5', *NATO Review* 2006, 1–3.

S. Torres Bernárdez, 'Interpretation of Treaties by the International Court of Justice Following the Adoption of the 1969 Vienna Convention on the Law of Treaties' in G. Hafner and others (eds.), *Liber Amicorum Professor Seidl-Hohenveldern*, Leiden, Martinus Nijhoff, 1998, 105–122.

S. Rocchi, 'Questions on the NATO Communications and Information Agency', *NATO Legal Gazette* 2014, 7–11.

S. Rosenne, *Developments in the Law of Treaties 1945–1986*, Cambridge, Cambridge University Press, 1989, 535 p.

S. Rynning, *Come Home NATO: the Atlantic Alliance's New Strategic Concept*, Copenhagen, Danish Institute for International Relations, 2009, 30 p.

T. Achilles, 'The Omaha Milkman: The role of the United States' in A. de Staercke et al. (eds.), *NATO's Anxious Birth: The Prophetic Vision of the 1940's*, London, C. Hurst & Company, 1985, 181 p.

T. Bauer-Savage, 'Die völkerrechtliche Verwandlung der NATO aus Sicht der U.S. Constitution und des deutschen Grundgesetzes' in X. (ed.), *Europäische Hochschulschriften*, Reihe II, Rechtswissenschaft, Frankfurt am Main, 2005, 220 p.

T. Bouachba, 'L'Organisation de la Conférence Islamique', *Annuaire Français de Droit International* 1982, 265–291.

T. Christiano, 'Democratic Legitimacy and International Institutions' in S. Besson and J. Tasioulas (eds.), *The Philosophy of International Law*, Oxford, Oxford University Press, 2010, 624 p.
T. Dannenbaum, Dual Attribution in the context of military operations', *International Organizations Law Review* 2015, 401–426.
T. Flockhart, *Cooperative Security: NATO's Partnership Policy in a Changing World*, Copenhagen, DIIS Report, 2014, 154 p.
T. Flockhart, 'Masters and Novices: Socialization and Social Learning through the NATO Parliamentary Assembly', *International Relations* 2004, 361–380.
T. Franck, 'The Emerging Right to Democratic Governance', *American Journal of International Law* 1992, 46–91.
T. Frank, 'Legitimacy in the International System', *American Journal of International Law* 1988, 705–759.
T. Gazzini, 'NATO's Role in the Collective Security System', *Journal of Conflict and Security Law* 2003, 231–263.
T. Gazzini, 'NATO Coercive Military Activities in the Yugoslav Crisis (1992–1999)', *European Journal of International Law* 2001, 391–436.
T. German, 'NATO and the enlargement debate: enhancing Euro-Atlantic security or inciting confrontation?', *International Affairs* 2017, 291–308.
T. Ireland, *Creating the Entangling Alliance: The Origins of the North Atlantic Treaty Organization*, Santa Barbara, Praeger Security International, 1981, 245 p.
T. Ruys, 'The armed attack requirement ratione materiae' in T. Ruys (ed.), *Armed Attack and Article 51 of the UN Charter: Evolutions in Customary Law and Practice*, Cambridge, Cambridge University Press, 2011, 585 p.
T. Sayle, 'Canada, NATO, and the Berlin Crisis, 1961–1962: "Slow-boil" or "pressure cooker?"', *International Journal* 2013, 255–268.
T. Stein, 'Kosovo and the International Community. The Attribution of Possible Internationally Wrongful Acts: Responsibility of NATO or of its Member States' in C. Tomuschat (ed.), *Kosovo and the International Community: A Legal Assessment*, Leiden, Brill Nijhoff, 2002, 181–192.
U. Benecke, *Reconsidering NATO's Decision Making Process*, Philadelphia, U.S. Army War College, 2007, 24 p.
U. Fastenrath, 'Inhaltsänderung völkerrechtlicher Verträge ohne Beteiligung des Gesetzgebers – Verfassungsrechtliche Zulässigkeit und innerstaatliche Wirkung' in R. Geiger (ed.), *Völkerrechtlicher Vertrag und staatliches Recht vor dem Hintergrund zunehmender Verdichtung der internationalen Beziehungen*, Leipzig, Nomos, 2000.
V. De Graaf, 'Between dream and deed: review of international law by the Dutch courts' in J. Wouters and D. Van Eeckhoutte (eds.), *Doorwerking van internationaal recht in de Belgische rechtsorde*, Antwerp/Oxford, Intersentia, 2006, 654 p.
V. Engström, *Constructing the Powers of International Institutions*, Leiden, Brill Nijhoff, 2012, 226.
V. Engström, 'Implied Powers of International Organizations: On the Character of a Legal Doctrine', *Finnish Yearbook of International Law* 2003, 129–157.
V. Morelli, *NATO in Afghanistan: A Test of the Transatlantic Alliance*, Philadelphia, Diane Publishing, 2009, 40 p.

V. Rühe, 'Shaping Euro-Atlantic Policies: A Grand Strategy for a New Era', *Survival* 1993, 129–137.

V. Schmidt, 'Discourse as Framework for Analysis: Policy Construction and Legitimization for Changing Policies and Practices' in V. Schmidt (ed.), *The future of European capitalism*, Oxford, Oxford University Press, 2002, 209–256.

V. Schmidt, 'Discursive Institutionalism: The Explanatory Power of Ideas and Discourse', *Annual Review of Political Sciences* 2008, 303–326.

V. Szep, 'Making EU Foreign Policy More Effective: Qualified Majority Voting on the Horizon?', *Carnegie Europe Article* 2023, 1–3.

W. Alberque, 'The new NATO Strategic Concept and the end of arms control', *IISS Analysis* 2022, available online at www.iiss.org/blogs/analysis/2022/06/the-new-nato-strategic-concept-and-the-end-of-arms-control?_cldee=ilznOqPtloUz8hwGuLBVTacG_NuQwIDCJnHEzW5nd-fBmJv4YxOIGlds1mR23HYB&recipientid=contact-9fa954a76980de11b23000237dde6e5cb22028655db40999f434256035166f7&esid=3b4fcf4b-20f9-ec11-82e7-6045bd0e77d7 (last accessed January 2025).

W. Chen, 'Issues on Consensus and Quorum at International Conferences', *Chinese Journal of International Law* 2010, 717–739.

W. Churchill, *Triumph and Tragedy*, New York, Houghton-Mifflin Books, 1953, 800 p.

W. Devroe, *Rechtsvergelijking in een context van europeanisering en globalisering*, Leuven, Acco, 2010.

W. Friede, 'Das Estoppel-Prinzip im Völkerrecht', *Zeitschrift für ausländisches öffentliches Recht und Völkerrecht* 1935, 518–545.

W. Jenks, 'Unanimity, The Veto, Weighted Voting, Special and Simple Majorities and Consensus as Modes of Decisions in International Organizations' in A. McNair (ed.), *Cambridge Essays in International Law: Essays in Honour of Lord McNair*, Cambridge, Cambridge University Press, 1965, 186 p.

W. Karl, 'Die spätere Praxis im Rahmen eines dynamischen Vertragsbegriffs', in R. Bieber and G. Ress (eds.), *Die Dynamik des europäischen Gemeinschaftsrechts*, Baden-Baden, Nomos, 1987.

W. Karl, 'Vertragsauslegung – Vertragsänderung' in C. Schreuer (ed.), *Autorität und internationale Ordnung*, Berlin, Aufsätze zum Völkerrecht, 1979, 63–85.

W. Lafeber, 'NATO and the Korean War: A Context', *Diplomatic History* 1989, 461–478.

X, 'Een slag tegen de NAVO verloren, maar niet de oorlog', *De Morgen* 26 January 2013, available online at www.demorgen.be/nieuws/een-slag-tegen-de-navo-verloren-maar-niet-de-oorlog~bfd86559/?referrer=https%3A%2F%2Fwww.google.com%2F (last accessed January 2025).

X (Specialist in Middle Eastern Affairs, Foreign Affairs, Defense and Trade Division) (ed.), *Kosovo: Greek and Turkish Perspectives – CRS Report for Congress*, Washington D.C., Congressional Research Service, 1999, 1–7.

Y. Liang, 'Conditions of Admission of a State to the Membership in the United Nations', *American Journal of International Law* 1949, 288–303.

Y. Nahlawi, 'The legality of NATO's pursuit in regime change in Libya', *Journal on the Use of Force and International Law* 2018, 295–323.

Z. Barany, 'NATO at Sixty', *Journal of Democracy* 2009, 108–122.

Z. Sabic, 'Parliamentary Diplomacy and the US Congress: The Case of the NATO Parliamentary Assembly', *The Hague Journal of Diplomacy* 2016, 235–252.

Z. Selden and L. Oehman, 'The NATO Parliamentary Assembly in parliamentary diplomacy', in K. Raube, M. Müftüler-Baç and J. Wouters (eds.), *Parliamentary Cooperation and Diplomacy in EU External Relations*, Cheltenham, Edward Elgar, 2019, 544 p.

ANNEX
NORTH ATLANTIC TREATY

The Parties to this Treaty reaffirm their faith in the purposes and principles of the Charter of the United Nations and their desire to live in peace with all peoples and all governments.

They are determined to safeguard the freedom, common heritage and civilisation of their peoples, founded on the principles of democracy, individual liberty and the rule of law. They seek to promote stability and well-being in the North Atlantic area.

They are resolved to unite their efforts for collective defence and for the preservation of peace and security. They therefore agree to this North Atlantic Treaty:

Article 1

The Parties undertake, as set forth in the Charter of the United Nations, to settle any international dispute in which they may be involved by peaceful means in such a manner that international peace and security and justice are not endangered, and to refrain in their international relations from the threat or use of force in any manner inconsistent with the purposes of the United Nations.

Article 2

The Parties will contribute toward the further development of peaceful and friendly international relations by strengthening their free institutions, by bringing about a better understanding of the principles upon which these institutions are founded, and by promoting conditions of stability and well-being. They will seek to eliminate conflict in their international economic policies and will encourage economic collaboration between any or all of them.

Article 3

In order more effectively to achieve the objectives of this Treaty, the Parties, separately and jointly, by means of continuous and effective self-help and mutual aid, will maintain and develop their individual and collective capacity to resist armed attack.

Article 4

The Parties will consult together whenever, in the opinion of any of them, the territorial integrity, political independence or security of any of the Parties is threatened.

Article 5

The Parties agree that an armed attack against one or more of them in Europe or North America shall be considered an attack against them all and consequently they agree that, if such an armed attack occurs, each of them, in exercise of the right of individual or collective self-defence recognised by Article 51 of the Charter of the United Nations, will assist the Party or Parties so attacked by taking forthwith, individually and in concert with the other Parties, such action as it deems necessary, including the use of armed force, to restore and maintain the security of the North Atlantic area.

Any such armed attack and all measures taken as a result thereof shall immediately be reported to the Security Council. Such measures shall be terminated when the Security Council has taken the measures necessary to restore and maintain international peace and security.

Article 6

For the purpose of Article 5, an armed attack on one or more of the Parties is deemed to include an armed attack:

- on the territory of any of the Parties in Europe or North America, on the Algerian Departments of France, on the territory of Turkey or on the Islands under the jurisdiction of any of the Parties in the North Atlantic area north of the Tropic of Cancer;
- on the forces, vessels, or aircraft of any of the Parties, when in or over these territories or any other area in Europe in which occupation forces of any of the Parties were stationed on the date when the Treaty entered into force or the Mediterranean Sea or the North Atlantic area north of the Tropic of Cancer.

Article 7

This Treaty does not affect, and shall not be interpreted as affecting in any way the rights and obligations under the Charter of the Parties which are members of the United Nations, or the primary responsibility of the Security Council for the maintenance of international peace and security.

Article 8

Each Party declares that none of the international engagements now in force between it and any other of the Parties or any third State is in conflict with the provisions of this

Treaty, and undertakes not to enter into any international engagement in conflict with this Treaty.

Article 9

The Parties hereby establish a Council, on which each of them shall be represented, to consider matters concerning the implementation of this Treaty. The Council shall be so organised as to be able to meet promptly at any time. The Council shall set up such subsidiary bodies as may be necessary; in particular it shall establish immediately a defence committee which shall recommend measures for the implementation of Articles 3 and 5.

Article 10

The Parties may, by unanimous agreement, invite any other European State in a position to further the principles of this Treaty and to contribute to the security of the North Atlantic area to accede to this Treaty. Any State so invited may become a Party to the Treaty by depositing its instrument of accession with the Government of the United States of America. The Government of the United States of America will inform each of the Parties of the deposit of each such instrument of accession.

Article 11

This Treaty shall be ratified and its provisions carried out by the Parties in accordance with their respective constitutional processes. The instruments of ratification shall be deposited as soon as possible with the Government of the United States of America, which will notify all the other signatories of each deposit. The Treaty shall enter into force between the States which have ratified it as soon as the ratifications of the majority of the signatories, including the ratifications of Belgium, Canada, France, Luxembourg, the Netherlands, the United Kingdom and the United States, have been deposited and shall come into effect with respect to other States on the date of the deposit of their ratifications.

Article 12

After the Treaty has been in force for ten years, or at any time thereafter, the Parties shall, if any of them so requests, consult together for the purpose of reviewing the Treaty, having regard for the factors then affecting peace and security in the North Atlantic area, including the development of universal as well as regional arrangements under the Charter of the United Nations for the maintenance of international peace and security.

Article 13

After the Treaty has been in force for twenty years, any Party may cease to be a Party one year after its notice of denunciation has been given to the Government of the United

States of America, which will inform the Governments of the other Parties of the deposit of each notice of denunciation.

Article 14

This Treaty, of which the English and French texts are equally authentic, shall be deposited in the archives of the Government of the United States of America. Duly certified copies will be transmitted by that Government to the Governments of other signatories.

1. The definition of the territories to which Article 5 applies was revised by Article 2 of the Protocol to the North Atlantic Treaty on the accession of Greece and Turkey signed on 22 October 1951.
2. On January 16, 1963, the North Atlantic Council noted that insofar as the former Algerian Departments of France were concerned, the relevant clauses of this Treaty had become inapplicable as from July 3, 1962.
3. The Treaty came into force on 24 August 1949, after the deposition of the ratifications of all signatory states.

www.ingramcontent.com/pod-product-compliance
Ingram Content Group UK Ltd.
Pitfield, Milton Keynes, MK11 3LW, UK
UKHW051430041026
8980IPUK00027B/921

9 781839 705502